NFA

NO FIXED ABODE

Published
by
Colby Press
39 Madeira Avenue
Bromley   Kent   BR1 4AP

Copyright
©
and all rights reserved by
Douglas Legg
2002

Imprint
of
Bath Press Ltd
Midsomer Norton
UK

ISBN
0-9542051-0-3

Contents

Foreword

Introduction

Maps

Photographs

Chapters   Stages and Interludes

  1. **The Learning Curve:**   Days 1 to 95
    First Stage: Bromley - Maldon
    Second Stage: Maldon - Yarmouth
    Third Stage: Yarmouth - King's Lynn
    Interlude Three: Wasting six days in Norfolk
    Fourth Stage: King's Lynn - Bridlington
    Fifth Stage: Bridlington - Middlesborough
    Sixth Stage: Middlesborough

  2. **An Early Winter Attack on Scotland:**   Days 96 to 150
    Sixth Stage: Dundee
    Seventh Stage: Dundee - Aberdeen
    Eighth Stage: Aberdeen - Inverness
    Tenth Stage: Inverness - Cromarty
    Interlude Ten: The grand retreat

  3. **Scotland in the Spring:**   Days 251 to 301
    Eleventh Stage: Cromarty - Fort William

  4. **Summer in the West of Scotland:**   Days 309 to 347
    Twelfth Stage: Corran Ferry - Largs
    Interlude Thirteen: Glasgow
    Thirteenth Stage: Largs

5. 'Car Walking' in Cumbria and Lancashire:
Days 348 to 374

Thirteenth Stage: Carlisle
Fourteenth Stage: Kirkbride - Knot-End-on-Sea
Fifteenth Stage: Fleetwood - Preston
Sixteenth Stage: Preston - Rhyll

6. Free fall around Wales:
Days 378 to 416

Seventeen Stage: Llanymynech - Rhyll
 Including: -   Detour around Anglesey

7. The Bristol Complex:
Days 417 to 426

Seventeenth Stage: Bristol
Eighteenth Stage: Shirehampton

8. Follow the Acorn
Free Fall round the South West:
Days 427 to 467

Eighteenth Stage: Lyme Regis
Nineteenth Stage: Lyme - Weymouth

9. Detour to the Isle of Wight:
Days 468 to 475

Twentieth Stage: Ringstead - Portsmouth

10. Southern Seashore Suburbia:
Days 479 to 486

Twenty first Stage: Portsmouth (Hastings)

11. Around the Heel of England - the last leg:
Days 487 to 500

Twenty first Stage: Gillingham
Twenty second Stage: Gillingham - Greenwich

Appendix

List of Useful Dates

Index

Foreword

Not so long ago, there was an eye-catching advertising slogan for one or another software package which asked the question: Where would you like to go today? The unspoken proposition was that never again would you need to leave the soothing cocoon of your room, your chair and your PC. You could fly a plane, create a song, scale the Andes, swim the Pacific, exchange pleasantries with someone in the Aleutians, with just the click of a mouse. No exertion, no bother. No rain, no heat, no cold, no blisters. No contact with any living creature. Travel by proxy, and no risk of broadening the mind.

Douglas Legg sets out, in the following pages, the converse scenario of 'Where would you like to go today?' It's one that to many, certainly young people, will seem strange and foreign. To anyone who had not reached the age of thirty when the year Two Thousand began, and when Douglas' odyssey ended, it may seem unappealing. For it prescribes maximum exertion, frequent hardship and little, if any, discernible reward or acknowledgement.

The difference is, of course, literally all the difference in the world, the difference between being, on the one hand exultantly alive and, on the other, of existing, as most of us in the western modern world habitually do, most of the time, in a sort of misty vacuum in which hastening to and from the workplace are our daily accomplishments.

So. Where would *you* like to go today? Can you imagine it? Stepping out of your home, closing your front door, with a few pounds in your pocket, a few meagre possessions in a patched-up rucksack, a pair of cast-off boots, to walk around the coast of Britain? People would think you were mad, wouldn't they?

Very likely some of them would. For them, the unknown and the difficult are perils to be avoided. Foreign places are best viewed through a glass screen, strange folk who speak in a different way are not to be trusted, a strange bed - or, horror! no bed - is an affliction.

Fortunately, however, as Douglas demonstrates, it is, even now, in Britain, possible to be a quirky individualist, to be the beneficiary of innumerable little acts of kindness and generosity, and to walk unpersecuted among your fellows in strange places. (Although bureaucracy, officialdom and the strange land-hunger of Ministry of Defence are, as always, something else.)

There are many things in this book to value: a slow-motion panorama of the geography, heritage and culture of our islands; a do-it-yourself kit for those who, like Douglas, dream that they too might be free; a kindly hopefulness, usually fulfilled, towards human nature; and a wry dry and sly sense of humour at his and all our failings.

Rick Fountain   October 2001
(Former senior news editor and BBC foreign correspondent)

Dedicated to my Father
F G C Legg

who said
of travelling
all you needed was

a penknife,
a piece of string
a shilling
and
a handkerchief

Introduction

The difference between dreams and reality is a thin, narrow and precipitous strand. How often have I sat in a chair, or lain in bed, dreaming? Conjuring up exploits, expeditions and amours - with planning and logistics, routes and maps, imaginary encounters, mishaps, achievements and acclaim. All laid out in minutes. Or, perhaps, stretched them out all night, using half-dream-time to extend the saga. Expanding and contracting, elaborating and revising, enriching and embellishing: extending the ephemeral perception towards the watery margins of the memory banks which are themselves the receptors of real life experiences. But then I always was a dreamy sort of person. The reason why I never achieved much in any of my professions. It was easier to dream of success: of some startling discovery, of pupils fascinated by my erudite classes, of a well written illuminating scientific paper. That was easier and preferable to the hard grunt work required to achieve real results, the normal arduous and slow route to success. Though of course, when one is in the realm of reality - a trap is always ready to be sprung. Sometimes, the plodding donkey work can lead hypnotically to a dream state. The pure routine mechanics, used to attain something useful or interesting, simply become automatic and boring. Walking along a track, mile after mile with little to relieve the tedium, with no great changes of scene. The same sort of grasses. The same trees and the same stiles. The same grey sky. The same birds - or lack of birds. The same pain in the back. Mind fantasy worlds take over and make the time go faster. Then there is that sudden change in the real world. The scampering of a hare, the wet lash of rain or the sparkle of a sunset. Instantly the senses are twitching, reality has returned and a true vital perception becomes activated. Life has been restored and action is demanded. Dreams evaporate, like vanishing high cirrus clouds. Freedom is restored and removes one from the normal humdrum of earning a living. The essence of nature returns and its nearness is breathed in every pore.

Every achievement, every success, every intention has to start with a dream, a vision, an idea. The rate of development of that germ of thought into actual action or possible reality is a measure of the dream nature of the person involved. It is a measure of the quotient related to the ambition involved in any hunting chase intended to bring home the best meat or the best produce from market. Considering my own gravitation towards prevarication and my deep reliance on the dream world, it is surprising that a long cherished idea of mine should actually be started and that I should set forth in real boots, baggage, belt and braces. The nub of thought came to me while driving across the Sahara, on the way back to Europe, in 1978. Or at least that is the way it appears now. In truth it may have been earlier or later. But the dream part of my brain extrapolates a strong link with the experiences of that event. Perhaps the delirium of a heat stroke allowed the hatching of such an idea. Travel certainly does seem to spawn spasms of new adventures. Or maybe it was JM on another part of the planet, actually doing the walk that created ripples in the ethereal layer of thought patterns that surround the earth. Those waves may have activated a niche in my brain, a niche already primed by past experiences. The idea nestled into place and wrestled with others, grew a smidgen, festered, fought against work ethics and finally expanded like bubbling volcanic lava, beyond containment. This process took twenty years: the gestation period for a full blown adult! The final broach of the outer rim took a quivering eighteen months, before I could break free.

Simply - the plan was to walk around the coast of Britain. Not a new idea. In fact now rather passé, as four or five do it every year. (With the number increasing, perhaps an association should be formed. with the acronym ABWA and with JM as chairperson.) But it is still an undertaking requiring endurance, determination and time. It was the latter that I had most of. Initially my start date was to have been 1st January 1997. I contacted Save the Children, had a meeting with Nikki Skipper, the SE area organiser, who supplied sponsor forms, literature, collection box and a letter of authority. Letters to companies for assistance yielded little success. Clark's supplied walking shoes, Ladbrokes tokens and Mornflakes gave a heap of oat products together with bright yellow tea shirt and cap. I held back the letters that I wished to send to my proposed personal sponsors, as I strained at the bit. I wanted to tell them that I was off and out of their hair for a while. I hoped that these hundred people would, if I completed the walk make a valuable contribution to my collection for StC. I still await their reply.

I did not need much to start. Just the cancellation of my debts, a thousand pounds in my pocket, a mobile phone and a few other luxuries. But postponement followed postponement. I had some work in that period, part time supply teaching and part time gardening being the main activities while in addition I was being looked after by my brother in Bromley. There seemed to be no problem to the achievement and solution of my simple financial requirements. Indeed there was basically no reason why I should not, within a few weeks, surmount the small hurdles that lay before me and set out at last on the long awaited adventure. Unfortunately there were too many spare hours and too many spare days. Too much time not used for anything creative. There was spare time for a demon to creep back into the equation. A demon sent to spoil the financial daydreams associated with the start of my venture. The lure was too strong. Every cash step I made forward was cancelled out by losses made on the gambling train. There were days when the gambling paid off: money was made. But these were counteracted by those days that sucked the juices dry. The days that threw you on the pavement with only half a cigarette and two shillings worth of loose change. The treadmill started again - more work, more money and the next gamble. The whirlpool of this existence continued for twenty months. An ever circuitous spiral: money in and money out. Never ahead by an overwhelming margin and always hitting a black-spot which cancelled out the advances. The terrible backdrop of blood, sweat and tears, of wagers and defeats, sprinkled with bright minute pin pricks of successful bets. The acclaim of success pulled the tapestry forward only to lose its supporting rail. One day I might make a hundred pounds and the next lose two hundred. Crazy, crazy, Crazy!

In this period of stagnation, I had to act out an air of normality. Not only was money slipping away, but other fibres of my life were unravelling. In '97 my sister, aged 67, died of lung cancer, after a healthy, cigarette free, life. Then my father, who had always been so active, died in his 93rd year. My wife was slipping away, my feeble attempts at reconciliation rebuffed. My mother began a slow deterioration and, with her mind still alert, had to move to a retirement home. My elder brother was quietly suffering mental problems. It was a period of sad dark days. A door seemed to be closing squarely and firmly. By mid summer of 1998 it finally became clear that my steps to proceed were doomed to failure as my overdraft was up to a maximum of £1700 with no chance of any more credit. Then like a bolt from the blue, my brother asked me what my plans were. Stuck against the ropes, I leaked out some feeble analogue of my intentions, inwardly I still dreamt of a strike that would release me for my challenge on life. In August he left for a conference in Blackpool and to visit friends. These two things triggered the notion that I must do something. As if needing further emphasis I accidentally found an abandoned rucksack in the garbage near where I was gardening and, after being told its destination was the tip, it became mine, only needing a few stitches for its redemption. While for footwear - a pair of boots recently rescued from my mother's house sufficed. Together with a sleeping bag, a community waste throw away of a year before, my 'equipment' had shaped up. What was there to stop me? After squeezing out a last effort on a garden job to provide a 'pony' for my pocket finances and with oats, sugar and biscuits from my brothers cupboard complemented with borrowed maps I had little to lose.

Three days later, at 9.45 on 19th August I closed the front door, lifted my newly acquired rucksack and its miscellaneous collection of sundries, fastened my laces and set off into a bright warm day through the streets of Bromley and Lewisham towards Greenwich, the Thames and all those towns and places that were strung out, like a pearl necklace, around the coastline of Britain. Little did I realise my true naivety, my singular urbanity and my deplorable lack of knowledge of my own island home.

Douglas Legg

JM: John Merrill 'Turn right at Lands End'   StC: Save the Children Charity
ABWA: Around Britain Walkers Association!

Acknowledgements

Though many are mentioned in the text I cannot name here all those who lent a hand of hope and help along the way, but I must extend my heart-felt thanks to all those kind people who generously assisted me on my way and proved that the materialistic world has not completely hidden the spirit of charity. In particular I have to thank my long suffering brother, Roger, for holding the base in Bromley and my son Patrick for the help he and his family gave in Yorkshire.

Thanks to Paul Ceivers for backcover drawing and poem

Maps

Map Lay Out   Overleaf

Map 1: English Eastern Coast   p 16

Map 2: East Coast   p 54

Map 3: Scotland North & East   p 77

Map 4: Ullapool to the Crinan Canal   p 113

Map 5: Scotland South West   p 145

Map 6: Mid West Coast   p 188

Map 7: The South West   p 214

Map 8: The Heel of England   p 273

MAP LAY OUT

Map 3 – Northern Scotland
Map 4 – Scotland West Coast
Map 5 – Scotland South-East
Map 2 – East Coast
Map 1 – Eastern English Coast
Map 6 – Mid West Coast
Map 7 – The South West
Map 8 – The Heel of England

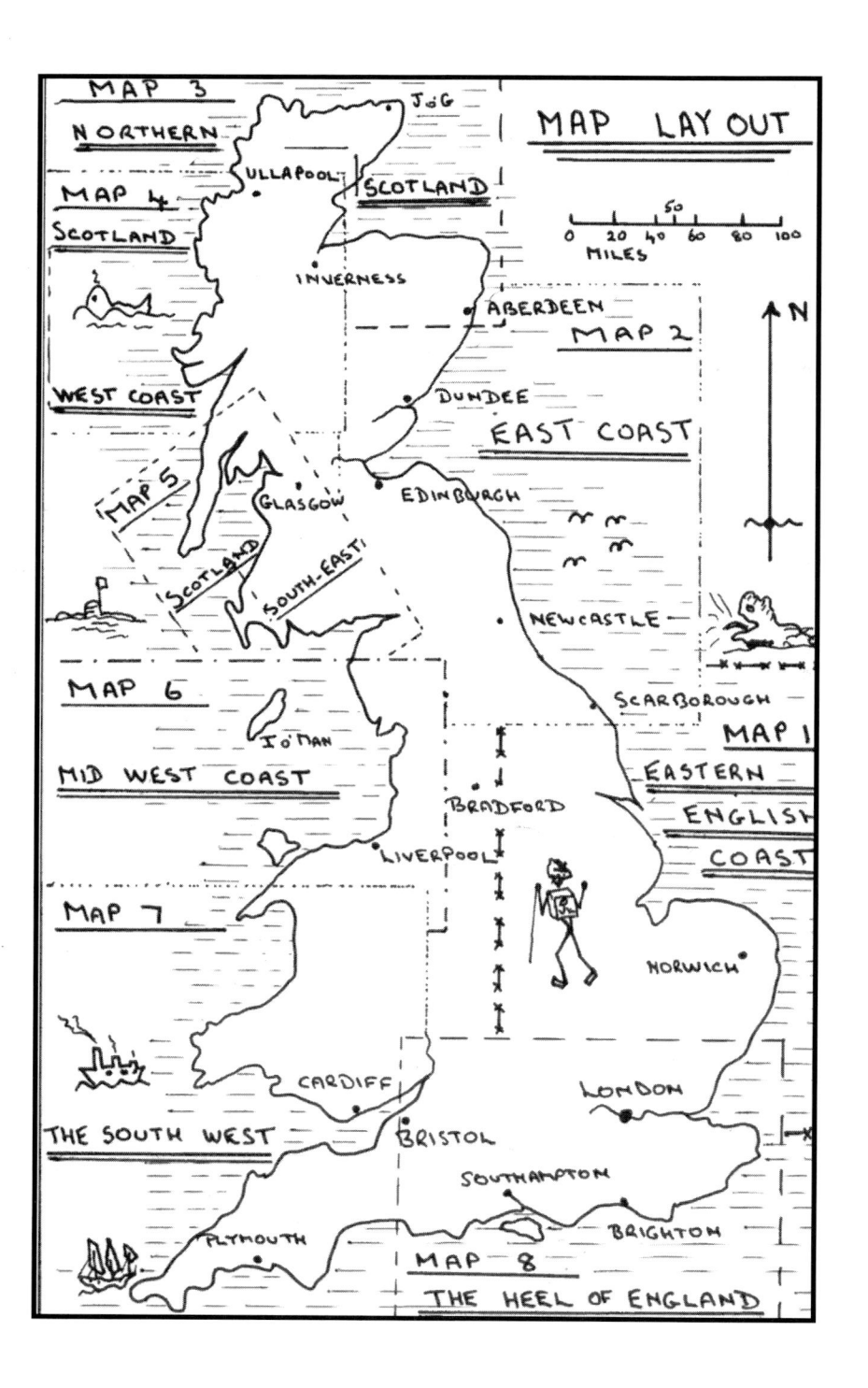

Scale: 0, 20, 40, 50, 60, 80, 100 MILES

N

Locations marked: J o G, Ullapool, Inverness, Aberdeen, Dundee, Edinburgh, Glasgow, Newcastle, Scarborough, I o' Man, Bradford, Liverpool, Norwich, Cardiff, London, Bristol, Southampton, Plymouth, Brighton

List of Photographs

Introduction p2: Total eclipse on Piel Island
- p 24.   Day 13 Essex man near Walton-on-the-Naze
- p 102. Day 260 War memorial at Latheronwheel
- p 122. Day 286 Hospitality at Strome Ferry with Helen (& Alan)
- p 129. Day 292 Loch Nevis and Sourlie
- p 131. Day 294 Tioram Castle in Loch Moidart
- p 144. Day 313 Chain saw Art at Ardfern, Loch Craignish
- p 148. Day 315 The last of the Normans at Kilmory
- p 157. Day 324 Loch Striven, an idyllic camp site
- p 161. Day 333 The sea, Irvine Bay
- p 162. Day 333 Robbie Burns watches the sea in Irvine Bay
- p 172. Day 343 Wallace the warrior, Kirkcudbright
- p 173. Day 343 Dundrennan Abbey, Solway Firth
- p 175. Day 344 An estate guardian, the unicorn in Dumfrieshire
- p 185   Day 354 Fishermen Sculpture, Maryport
- p 198. Day 373 A sailing lesson in West Kirby
- p 202. Day 379 Walk the plank, across the heather to Llandegla
- p 206. Day 382 Lugwormer in North Wales
- p 212. Day 390 Coastal golf: Dinllaen, Llewyn Peninsular
- p 226. Day 403 St Non's holy well, St David's
- p 254. Day 431 Appledore, wall mural, North Devon
- p 261. Day 440 Farewell at St Just's YH
- p 265. Day 441 St Winaloe cares for me after Penzance
- p 264. Day 442 The Lizard
- p 271   Day 448 Australian Veteran in Looe
- p 278. Day 455 Busker in Dartmouth
- p 280. Day 459 Paignton welcome/farewell: Jack & Joan Quarendon
- p 288. Day 471 Swanage remembers
- p 298. Day 487 Net huts at Hastings

Miscellaneous

p 199 Postcard   ::   p 308   Uncle Doug?   ::   p 320   Form

- p 46   Day 57   King Edward in Conway
- p 64   Day 279 Toilet Port Henderson
- p 95   Day 251 Sally Departure
- p 246   Day 430 Ilfracombe beach
- p296   Day 448 Path to Perranporth

Map 1

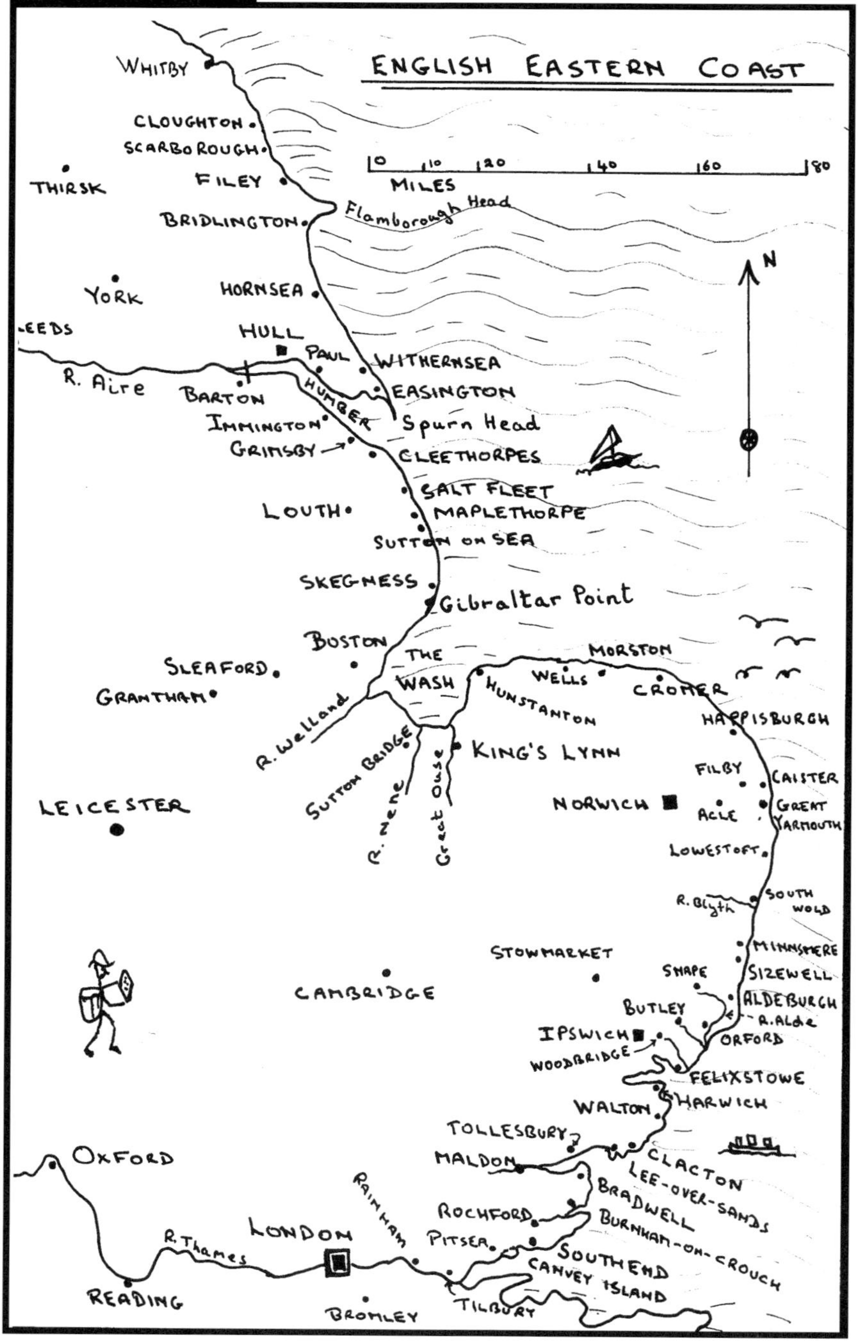
ENGLISH EASTERN COAST
0 10 20 40 60 80
MILES
N
WHITBY
CLOUGHTON
SCARBOROUGH
FILEY
THIRSK
BRIDLINGTON
Flamborough Head
YORK
HORNSEA
LEEDS
HULL
PAUL
WITHERNSEA
R. Aire
BARTON
HUMBER
EASINGTON
IMMINGTON
Spurn Head
GRIMSBY
CLEETHORPES
SALT FLEET
LOUTH
MAPLETHORPE
SUTTON ON SEA
SKEGNESS
Gibraltar Point
BOSTON
SLEAFORD
GRANTHAM
THE WASH
MORSTON
WELLS
CROMER
HUNSTANTON
R. Welland
SUTTON BRIDGE
R. Nene
Great Ouse
KING'S LYNN
HAPPISBURGH
FILBY
CAISTER
NORWICH
ACLE
GREAT YARMOUTH
LEICESTER
LOWESTOFT
R. Blyth
SOUTH WOLD
STOWMARKET
MINNSMERE
SNAPE
SIZEWELL
CAMBRIDGE
BUTLEY
ALDEBURGH
R. Alde
IPSWICH
ORFORD
WOODBRIDGE
FELIXSTOWE
WALTON
HARWICH
TOLLESBURY
OXFORD
MALDON
CLACTON
LEE-OVER-SANDS
RAINHAM
BRADWELL
ROCHFORD
BURNHAM-ON-CROUCH
LONDON
R. Thames
PITSEA
SOUTHEND
CANVEY ISLAND
READING
BROMLEY
TILBURY

Chapter 1
The Learning Curve

First Stage
Bromley to Maldon
Day 1
Wednesday

The preparations of the previous night had been distilled from eighteen months of thought mixed with prevarication and condensed into a few hours of sewing, sorting and packing before bed was finally found at 3.15 am. I was up at nine o'clock, ate breakfast, tightened the straps on my rucksack, tucked the two tens and a five in my pocket, closed the front door and, full of hope and optimism, was ready for the new adventure with all its uncertainties. At long last on the move and onto the first leg of the long long walk.

In hot, bright sunshine, I skimmed London's Green Chain Walk and strolled down that splendidly named conjunction of Burnt Ash Lane and Blackheath. On the rolling arid-green open space a park bench provided the first of a multitude of resting places which would be found in the weeks ahead and I briefly contemplated what I was about to attempt. But as the enormity of it was beyond me I thought of my GA* days - 'one day at a time'. An hour's walking and already I was tired and resting. But I knew that I had to recondition my body and limbs for this new way of life. After all my only recent training had been that of walking behind a lawn mower. Little did I know how long it would take to gain reasonable walking legs, a period matched only by a slow tedious story of slow tiresome miles over the first fifty days. But I was not out to break records and no target dates had been set. Nor had schedules been cast in hoops of iron. I wanted to be my own agent as well as accepting the unexpected.

At midday, the bare heath, stripped of trees, was nearly devoid of humanity on that warm summer's day. The splendid pale-grey modern Anglican Church stood prominent and I was moved to sketch. The first and nearly the last artistic endeavour of the trip. The best of intentions slipped away under the stronger flow of other efforts and ideas. On the far side of this dry grass space I passed a string of tired looking donkeys, giving rides to another descended generation of children. In Greenwich Park a multi-ethnic crowd of tourists, cut off from the heath by an undefined barrier, thronged to this special part of London where history, buildings, space and shade intermingle so attractively. At the museum, with my first view of the Thames, I thought grandly that this must lead somewhere!

By the riverside lay a copper clad tea clipper, The Cutty Sark, dwarfing the nearby Gypsy Moth V of Sir Francis Chichester. Within this historic nautical panorama stood a tower. A sentinel, like a doom watch turret in a computer game. The basement doorway was a yawning mouth beckoning one on into the unknown. I spurned the lift, descended the spiral stairs and walked beneath the Thames. This was the true start of the road leading to the Isles. For months I had asked myself which of the routes to take across the Thames. This was the premier river, which I had crossed many times since our father used to take us on holiday trips in punts, skiffs and canoes. and it never fails to give me a warm feeling when I see its murky waters. My first idea had been a publicity stunt of abseiling from the M25 Queen Elizabeth Bridge, but this was abandoned due to lack of rope! The last Thames ferry at Gravesend entailed too much dismal walking and I ruled out the free Woolwich Ferry, as I had used it frequently 40 years before when I worked in East Ham. Tower Bridge, I felt, was too close to central London. Thus my crossing place was chosen almost by elimination.

After emerging onto the north bank I started along the Thameside path, in the now fashionable Isle of Dogs, winding through modern housing complexes as my first view of the growing Millennium Dome appeared. Later I was to note the frequent use of that word in the names of bygone traders, viz Millennium Wharf, Millennium Engineers etc. - the word was overused then and now! Near the Thames Barrier, (imported after fabrication in Merseyside), I had a lunch of MacVities biscuits, which would become familiar fare. Nearby the theme shape of the barrier had been replicated inland - a wine store occupying one third of a huge barrel cut into three separated sections.

My assault on the escape from London now began. I tried some minor turnoffs to gain proximity to the Thames. But this was mostly a waste of effort as unexpected fences blocked the way. Consequently I was forced to use the main roads past Tate & Lyle, the huge Royal Docks and then onto the A13 over Barking Creek. A diversion through Creekmouth was hardly edifying and only slightly less arduous than the thundering dual highway to Rainham, where a southerly route on a minor road lay across the marshes. But as darkness fell I found some clean grass by the gates of the local landfill site and set up my very first camp opposite the dismal MOD marshlands which were seriously demarcated by fences bearing notices concerning dangerous entrapments filled with deep mud. But it was also a joyous habitat for many wide winged, wordless and unmolested herons. Eating a simple supper I crashed out in my sleeping bag for the first time, trusting in the utility of my flimsy ground sheet - made of four black refuse bags! and an accolade to my camping spot.
24 miles

Day 2
Thursday
I awoke from the sleep of an exhausted dog, packed my bag and tried to continue across the marshes between the danger area opposite the huge waste tip, but after a mile was turned back and had to retreat almost to Rainham, where I climbed up to the brand new - and unused - A13 which took me to Wennington and onto Purfleet. Alas, mesmerised by Betty's Bridge, which loomed in sight at the Dartford crossing, I missed the only connection to the riverside path and consequently it was hard road through Grays, where some interesting old cottages had frontal fasciae depicting their connections with Darwin and other notable maritime characters, and then finally to Tilbury. This area, together with that south of the river, teems with historical connections interspersed with modern developments. All it needs is the time for study, analysis and interpretation.

On a proper coastal path, at last, I walked round Tilbury river fort, infamous for an 18th century cricketing debacle, involving Kent and Essex, during which several people died - it seems sports hooliganism was as rife then as it is today. Next came the seemingly huge Tilbury power station on the way to Coalhouse Fort which was built by General Gordon in 1869 and is now a wonderful place for children to play. At Mucking Marshes I had more problems with a vast land-fill operation and only narrowly made it to the other side. From here the path led to Stanford-le-Hope nature reserve, which is full of ponds and phragmites. It was a hot day and a foot in front of me an adder slithered across the path. In Africa I have seen cobras and boomslangs but this was the first adder I had ever seen. After Corringham and Fobbing I struggled on some terrible paths across the Vange Marshes to a multi-churched, suburban Pitsea where I camped on the lawn at St Basil's catholic church: the visiting foreign priest was quite happy for me to be an overnight guard(!) and I had the church porch, with its hard stone floor, for shelter against the threatened rain. 24 miles

Day 3
Friday
A path beside the railway took me to South Benfleet and at last I felt I was escaping the sprawl of the metropolitan suburbs. Across the Creek lay the first of my 'islands' which I intended to walk. My guideline rule being that if a peninsular or island had two distinct marked routes on and off, then I would walk its coast. In fact I didn't use the first road, the A1301, for access, realising that in the future I would not be averse to altering my route from the main coastline objective. Practicability would be more important than the coast line rule, while places of interest and accommodation might well have priority over boring seaside promenades. But the main principle would have to remain intact, i.e. that my journey would be a continuing line of walk close to the coast

around Britain, albeit with nightly, weekly and sometimes even monthly interruptions, through health and social commitments, provided the thread of the tour was picked up again at the very last place that I paused.

I tried to leave my bag at the railway station. But the staff were heavily ensconced in the popular TV view that everybody is a potential bomber. Lateral thinking had been leached from their minds. In the months ahead, I was to find that this was a frequent trend in middle management. I had better luck at a local taxi firm and thanks to Catherine, the receptionist; I was able make the five hour walk around Canvey without my rucksack. It was dreary walking, dominated by the adjacent oil refinery, oil storage tanks, sea wall, fresh wind and miles of holiday chalets and retirement homes. Though why anybody would want to retire here, I cannot imagine, especially after the disastrous floods of 1953 (Feb 1st -my birthday) when fifty eight people died through cold and wetness. One couple who had decided to stay and who were busy gardening gave me my first taste of British charity. When I asked for refreshment, they gave me, no, not a flea in the ear, but a carton of fruit juice as well as water.

After retrieving my pack in Benfleet I found a downland path to Hadleigh Castle. This, my first splendid ruin, stood high on the escarpment and overlooked both Canvey and the scruffy scrubby Two Tree Island. The castle's origins lie in the 11th century, with latter day improvements, but a substantial amount was lost in a land-slip of the 19th century. I sat and sheltered by an ancient watch tower while I wrote a post card to my doctor brother, seeking assurance that my leg pains, incurred in stopping and starting, would decline. Why was I expecting my proper walking leg(g)s to develop so quickly?

Towards evening I walked through Leigh and approached Southend. I scrounged a free meal at the Westcliffe Club which has Turneristic panoramic views of the broad Thames,which are often illuminated by the setting sun, and enlivened by shipping and nautical lights. Several hours later I slept, undisturbed, beneath a handy tree in the sloping frontal park across the road.
23 miles

Day 4
Saturday
On the walk along the gaudily touristic front of Southend I passed eighteen hundred concrete pillars, built by a Mr Mannering in 1904 as a protective sea defence against invaders! Stretching out into the Thames lay the remains of a long anti-submarine fence. All part of a continuing theme; there would be many more solid reminders of the prolific efforts and wondrous schemes which have been built to protect our shores both in war and peacetime.

Near Shoesbury I had breakfast in Gunners Park, a haven for dogs and their walkers. In the nearby ranges a uniformed guard with his Alsatians told me of the public path through the military land to Wakering Sands where I saw the Broom Way, my intended route onto Foulness, disappearing into the sea. Years ago this used to be the only way to the island, but now it is in disrepair and only available to the most intrepid and foolhardy traveller even at low tide. I was forced to take the sea wall to the Swing Bridge, which I crossed unchallenged, and made my way to Churchend, across my first taste of flat farmlands. Under a huge sky, they struck me as a charged landscape - rich fertile fields under busy agricultural activity lay beneath a backdrop of scudding clouds and etched by bright flint-sharp sunlight. This place had its own beauty.

After visiting the ancient tomb-stoned church yard, I contemplated my next move over a quiet and thirst quenching half of bitter in the adjacent pub. Suddenly a posse of two policemen arrived. One of them was the same guard I had spoken to at Shoesbury ranges. They told me that this was a military area and non-residents were banned. My objections were overruled and I was escorted, by Land rover, back to the Bridge. The MOD had struck and shown me my first taste of officialdom.

Continuation was along the sea wall around Barling Marsh then westward to Rochford into the setting sun until I made camp for the night by a tree in a school playing field near Sutton Bridge Farm. It was still and surprisingly quiet - had I at last left the throb of London behind?
23 miles.

Day 5
Sunday
The English countryside appeared to start at Rochford. That strange mix of trees, small fields, churches and ambling by-ways. But this was an illusion that didn't last long and I was soon back in the scenery more typical of this area. Past the boat yard at Eastend I collapsed on a bank for a bite to eat as a man slithered ashore in an inflatable dinghy. He told me that the ex-arctic supply ship, tied to the dyke, was his. He had been forced to carry out his repairs here, because the local harbour master would not allow them in his boatyard, and was singularly optimistic about refitting his battered hulk before sailing off for Antarctic waters. Parting with the epithet that 'God would provide' he trundled his wheel barrow off along the dyke to collect supplies.

I continued along the sea wall to Lion Wharf and Wallasea Island where by courtesy of the boatman, Trevor Taylor, the Lady Essex II took me to Burnham. Before setting out on this walk I had decided that if a ferry was a suitable method of crossing water then I would use it, but only with a free passage. I reasoned that these boats were an integral and active part of the coast and therefore should not be lightly missed - as they are a kind of bridge.

In Burnham-on-Crouch it rained for two hours and I sheltered under the tower of St Mary's, which is now a hostel for homeless girls. At that stage my only foul weather gear was my Falkland's Barbour Jacket and I had noticed there was little protection on the sea walls of this low level exposed area. In the evening it stopped raining and I set off into a stiff breeze under a threatening sky. It was very cool and I was glad, even in August, to be wearing my bright wool-knit mittens - the last present from my departed sister.

The land was rich and fertile, the fields flat and big, many coloured pale blue with burgeoning lucerne. On the seaward side the low tide exposed expansive reaches of sand and provided a panorama of emptiness. A scattering of pill boxes, along the wall, peered eyelessly out to sea, but none were inviting. Just in time, as darkness rapidly approached, I found an empty weather beaten corrugated iron shed. Inside was a single 8x4 sheet of ply and with the addition of bank side hay I had a good bed, comfortably dry and sheltered from the wind and rain.
17 miles

Day 6
Monday 24th August
It was clear and sharp as I walked northwards along the large sea defences. The path was green grassed but the view was practically featureless. The monotony was broken by the Saxon church of St Peter's, where the local Othona Community, arriving by a 'pilgrimage' around the adjacent, flat, stone marked square outside, were about to have a service. The old one roomed church, simplistically beautiful, was built in 654 AD with stone taken from the adjacent broken down Roman fort. I would often marvel at the fortitude of old-time travelling clerics, who without roads, maps or Doc Martins(!) were so mobile and dedicated to church building. But on this occasion I was not in a mood to loiter and pressed on along St Peter's Way to the Bradwell nuclear power station with warm sunshine, dancing blue Essex butterflies, grazing sheep and the occasional hare adding enchantment to my walk. The dyked path began to meander wildly up the River Blackwater through the villages of Ramsey Island and Maryland. At Brick House farm I failed to secure a barn for the night and instead found a grassy furrow on the dyke some four miles short of Maldon and slept under a bright starry sky.
24 miles

Day 7
Tuesday
I lazed in my sleeping bag till 7.15 then ambled into Maldon with its picturesque frontage, an anchored line of big business-like barges, each full of hoist-

ed and stored sails. But the rest of the town was something of a disappointment with its standard moratorium of modern shops and precincts set around the old church on the hill.

After making arrangements at the local Tescos concerning supplies and parking for my return, I hitch-hiked to Southend. Eventually walking out of that place in the dead of night and lucking out with a lift from a lone lady driver, Ria, who said she was an ex-taxi girl and could take care of herself. She was on her way to start a shift at Hackney bus depot where I waited for her to clock on, and was then taken via her route to the Isle of Dogs but sadly I left my father's old watch on her bus.

Once again I walked under the Thames and then in the early morning before the traffic had fully developed, marched the hard streets back to Bromley.
6 miles

Interlude One
Days 8 - 10
Wednesday - Friday
The house was empty and I spent the next three days sleeping, eating and tending the gardens of clients gathered over the previous three years, telling them of my departure and immediate intentions. Having gained confidence and a little walking ability, I now intended to do the next section with the aid of my car as a mobile base. The idea was to park at the last point reached on the tour, walk for one or several days and then move the car to the next place on my route. In this way I could carry supplies which might otherwise weigh me down; the car could be used as cheap accommodation and would also provide the facility to travel home quickly if necessary. I called this leap frog walking. To the purist it might seem like cheating. But I rationalised that my sense of continuity was as good as anybody else's and my adjustments would not alter the spirit of the event. It would also often entail seeing the countryside thrice, once walking; secondly while journeying back to the car and thirdly driving a similar route on a parallel system of roads. I would see more, meet more and perhaps pay less. But like all ideas, the method had to be tested.

Second Stage
Maldon to Yarmouth
Day 11
Saturday
The previous evening I had set out at eleven to avoid the London traffic and after unravelling the new roads of the northern suburbs arrived in Maldon at 2.00 am and parked in the Tescos car park for sleep. I had practised kipping in

Day 13 Essex Man near Walton on the Naze. one of the wealth of sculptures in gardens, paths and towns

the back of the Ford Escort on several occasions over the previous 18 months and found it practicable if not entirely comfortable. Refinements needed to be made!

After the store opened, a series of requests eventually led me to a manager who had the authority to help with my previous arrangement. They were suitably generous in providing stores for the coming week and allowing me to park the car. This benevolence was extended in the town's high street, where a bookshop gave me the next appropriate OS. I was continuously astonished by similar spasmodic generosity in the days ahead. At that early hour the town was nearly deserted and the slow awakening of this and similar small conurbations often surprised me, being used to the continual business of London.

9.30 saw me walking out of Maldon. I had been excessively ambitious when packing my rucksack for this stage and soon found out the hard way that I was carrying too much. After the intricacies of the industrial parts of the town I was soon on the sea wall, winding down the northern side of the Blackwater. My legs were still not in shape and I had to make frequent stops, gradually extending the time between halts. But each day it became a trifle easier, especially as my supplies decreased and the exercise improved my muscles. One rest stop was by the causeway to Osea Island. Local rumour has it that this is used by a brewery to dry out alcoholic staff. But, I do know that my father and uncle camped here as boys and it is where the latter gained his love for the sea and then joined the navy. I edged on towards Tollsbury, picking up ripe windfall plums as I passed through a scattering of local orchards. After lunch beside St Mary's, a Norman church built in 1090, I left my bag in the pub opposite and then walked around the Tollesbury Wick marshes unimpeded. As it was early, I continued to Salcott but cheated a little, missing out the circumnavigation of Pennyhole Fleet. It looked featureless, dull, had no named map points and the dull weather was doing nothing to commend it either. The only thing that intrigued me was the common use of the word 'fleet' hereabouts, which means flowing water and is not necessarily associated with a group of boats.

Attempts to hitch back to Maldon met without success and so instead I walked back to the pub for my pack and over a drink chatted to the locals, who were all dressed up for a fancy dress party. They said it was possible to get a lift in the dark, but in the end I bedded down in the local cemetery. When the gate man came round later, to lock up, I explained my predicament and he gave me his blessing for sleeping there but my plans to use the car that night had been thwarted.
19 miles.

Day 12
Sunday

I retraced my steps and went to Salcott by yet another route and after breakfast there continued on the sea wall towards Mersea Island. On the other side of the Strood Bridge, a police-lady was controlling traffic for a fun run. She signed and authenticated my 'form' of the trip. During 'interlude one' I had printed up a 'form' with headline banners about the walk and its benefits to Save the Children (StC), intending to use these each day, collecting signatures of people who helped me or showed interest and also as a record of places visited. Extrapolation of my first week's effort had prompted me to insert on the 'form' a finishing date: 31st December 1999!, and marching away from the entrance to Mersea I could almost hear Gould's 'Onward Christian Soldiers' ringing in the church bells, driving me forward to that time and finish.

After more sea wall, I headed towards Colchester across military ranges, where the red flag had just been lowered, through increasingly wooded and undulating country and past a growing profusion of gravel pits. At Rowhedge spotting 'Ferry Lane' I questioned a lady posting a letter who informed me that it ran on Sundays. But at the end of the lane, by the ferry, which was unmarked on my map, a notice declared that this was the one Sunday it didn't run! I hailed a passing canoe for verification of the facts, but, without hesitation, the two paddlers kindly offered to take me over to Wivenhoe as part of the local service. Thus I never saw Colchester.

Orange juice was sipped in the bustling waterfront pub, which was just closing, before I hot footed it to Alresford, hoping to cross the creek if the tide was still out. At least I found that speed walking, if necessary, was not beyond me, though it is usually a mistake to be in a hurry to arrive - time usually takes care of all things. Indeed on arrival at this crossing point a sailor told me that the water was 20 ft deep with a very muddy bottom and so he rowed me across, also as part of the extended local facilities.

At Brightlingsea, a lady gave the very first contribution to StC and the harbour taxi gave me a free ride across to Stone Point which allowed me, as darkness approached, to reach Lee-over-Sands where I asked a man, who was painting his boat, about local barns. We chatted for a while and then he decided I could sleep on a mattress in his camp-a-van. He was into a number of projects including renovating cheap houses and selling them on. His yard had a mixed collection of useful things from a host of different jobs, while in his house he had a collection of old motor bikes including an old hybrid Norton reminding me of my own past motorcycling days.
21 miles

Day 13
Monday 31st August.
After the first few miles, the morning was spent on concrete promenades, passing Clacton, which remained hidden behind an enormous earth bank. I only remember the pier and that was worth forgetting, and then on past Frinton, stopping in Walton-on-the-Naze at the helpful tourist information office (which I always refer to as the big 'I', and they're watching out for you too!). Beyond this busy little town, while resting on a bench, a cyclist stopped and told me the way to Kirby-le-Soken and beyond, while a curious young boy also asked me a string of questions before he left with his 10-year old girl friend.

 I followed my gleaned instructions and went along Quay Lane. In Kirby Cross, luckily asking for further direction, two hikers put me on the correct left fork to the sea wall. Lacking the relevant OS map I was having problems.

 The path was not good and deteriorated so much that it was necessary to use the fields for progress. Finally at Beaumont Quay the sea wall was blocked and further directions required. A caravan family in a field, relaxing in the sun, gave me a local, hand-drawn, map which provided adequate directions through this wooded area. At Great Oaksey, I spoke to the gate guard of Exchem Organics, forced out a smile and gained a cup of coffee. More directions were given at Oakley Hill Farm and these finally led me to the sea wall and, through the darkness, into Harwich.

 During the last few miles I'd had a fixation and to satisfy my dream, I splashed out on fish and chips, which, after wrangling with the Chinese proprietrix, I ate 'in shop' at the take-away price, before crashing out, behind a scout hut, in the grounds of the nearby Cliff Park Gardens. I fell asleep looking at a surrealistic view of dark tree shapes silhouetted by a glitter of pinprick street lights just as a few spots of rain began to fall, and then dreamt of nightlight photography.
26 miles

Day 14
Tuesday
Luckily the rain came to nothing and I woke up dry and refreshed for an early start. After initiating attempts to gain publicity for my charity walk, I made several calls to Talk Radio, but they seemed only to be interested if I was carrying a radio. However the local paper - the East Anglia Times - interviewed me and I made contact with BBC local radio -Essex. This exercise took me on a meandering walk around Harwich, parts of which were surprisingly attractive. In 1566 Elizabeth visited the port and said 'it lacked for nothing' but now it has been decimated by the decline of shipping and definitely now needs something. For me it was a pub in West Street - the Haywain - where I treated

myself to early morning tea.

At 10.30 ferry man, Mr C Spragton, gave me a free passage on the crossing to Felixstowe Jetty and after a walk through the old town there was another free ferry across the River Deben to Bawdsey Quayside with its school of water sports. Somehow, while having my travelling lunch on the waterfront, I managed to lose my bright yellow Mornflake cap. A sad loss as my hair now began to get in my eyes! In Bawdsey, the church had quaint iron torch-holders for lamplit services while at Alderton I had to buy a local hand-drawn map to find my way. A welcome change in the last two days had been the increasing amount of woodland, and I was now on the defined Suffolk Coastal Path (SCP). Across the marshes and by the sea wall I came to Shingle Street, by-passed the Hollesley Bay Colony for young offenders and, in the evening, reached Butley Hard only to find the ferry deserted. Making enquiries at a local farm, the lady resident told me that the boatman, Brian Rogers, was away until the next day and then very kindly allowed me to row over. And then she took the boat back as I waved farewell before marching off into the deepening twilight to find shelter in a lonely hay-packed barn.
16m

Day 15
Wednesday
Setting off my mind was bent on early tea in Orford and I was sorely disappointed on finding nowhere open and so quickly started out on the sea wall around the Sudbourne Marshes. I was frequently amazed at the vast expense that these sea defences must have incurred, by the forethought that had been engendered and the audacity of construction of those who had first proposed them. The country here is populated with cattle and sheep and the farming is a mix of good and poor husbandry. Today the landscape was veiled in a thin still mist; a quiet somnolent scene, which was suddenly perforated by the phut-phut of a green four wheel motorised bike. With two alert black and white sheep dogs on the back, a shepherd was checking the ditches for strays. In the mid-distance a herd of horses grazed. One was down, inert on the ground. Was it resting or in trouble? But I could only watch, as intervening ditches blocked the way.

There was no ferry to Aldeburgh and I walked beside the lower reaches of the Alde to The Maltings of Snape, had tea in this modernised tourist spot and took a further step forward in the StC stakes by flashing my collection tin around the assembled snacking tourists. Down river I went through woodland and along the wet grass-lined paths across the bog-lands of Hazlewood Common. My trousers became saturated, wetter than when rain falls. However walking and fresh air soon dried them out again as I continued through Aldeburgh, passing the house where Millicent Garrett-Fawcett once lived

(1847-1929). A remarkable person, a well educated and connected woman, seventh of ten siblings, who founded Newham College of Cambridge and was for many years leader of the Suffragette movement, but didn't agree with the more violent actions of Ms Pankhurst. Amongst her publications she wrote 'A different world for women'. It is difficult, now, to think that universal voting in this country arrived such a short time ago. Her father was also a forceful man and a radical who encouraged Millicent's efforts and helped his eldest daughter to become the first woman doctor.

The path went northward up the coast and later in the darkening wet evening; I passed the quiet monolith of Sizewell power station before finally finding refuge in a bird hide at Minnsmere RSPB reserve. The boards were hard, but at least it was dry and sheltered.
22 m

Day 16
Thursday
This was better than watching breakfast TV; instead a host of wonderful birds performed for me as I watched from my eyrie and ate an early morning meal. My usual waking food was a mix of porridge and sugar with milk or warm water, saved from the previous evening and this was the main source of my daily nutrition, sugar the main energy supply. My entertainment continued in the nearby conveniences, where a cheerful toilet cleaner whistled happily and without cooncern while he beavered away. He had been an accountant and a park warden, but now had a more relaxed view on life.

The morning was wet, brightened by colourful splashes of red heather and yellow gorse. Nearing Dunwich, I went through woodland - a collection of strange oaks. A small concrete bridge crossed my path and I knew immediately of my visit to this spot, two years before when I had come for a 'look see' with Jeff Redgrave, husband of my niece Ruth. He was at that time a keeper of this Suffolk Coastal path (SCP).

After a chat with the custodian of the adjacent ruined abbey, I walked to Dunwich beach and I heard a familiar whistle and again met the itinerant cleaner of Minnsmere continuing his rounds. In the cafe, I sat over tea and wrote cards. Dunnet used to be a large and important town since Roman times, but in the second millennium the sea took its toll and most of it slipped into the water and hence the place lost most of its previous eminence.

The path led north, past the marshes and Walberswick to a little ferry over the river Blyth. In Southwold I visited a poor 'I', obtained food at Gateways and left by the Might Bridge. The SCP continued as a blur of sea wall and heavy beaches punctuated by flocks of geese flying overhead or grazing on the cliffs above. Eventually I ascended the cliffs to gain the fine views up and down the coast. Along the way a couple from Kent stood on the edge, catching the impressive scenery in watercolours. I passed Benacre Broad that was only half full and several pill boxes that had nearly fallen into the sea, which tugged and clawed at the soft cliff faces. Dramatically, some small roads just finished at the cliff edge, while sections of fields had been completely washed away.

Kessingland Beach is a holiday village, while the adjacent 'one street' Kessingland is a 'dorp' village, although I did find some shops and at last a telephone kiosk to put a call through to Suffolk Radio for a broadcast. Back on the tops I could see Lowestoft, while below lay acres and acres of clean beach sand. Had I left the mud flats behind? The path petered out through old MOD ranges and crumbling cliffs, but I managed to forge a way through, passing hordes of caravans and holiday homes on my way to Pakefield with its prominent church and wonderful coastal seascapes southwards. After walking along Britain's most easterly sea front, that of Lowestoft, I bought milk in the city centre before marching to the other side. At a campsite the warden told that it was £5.80 per night with or without tent so I pushed on to find a clean dry pill box in the sandy marram dunes. This was an ideal bivouac against the promised rain which nevertheless stayed resolutely away.
22 m

Day 17
Friday
Today I really struggled and my left foot was sore - giving me gyp - and it was a good job that there was only some ten miles to cover that day. My route lay on the cliffs, the beach, a nine inch wide wall, by a golf course, on a promenade and finally by a long dragging road to Gorleston and Great Yarmouth, which I reached just before noon.

When I rested by the main waterway a 75 year old said that the town was now like Las Vegas, there was nothing substantial left, all the industry had gone and there was little shipping to count. But as he spoke, there, on the other bank, lay a huge barge being prepared for somewhere in Africa. The town hall 'I' and library were both helpful, the local paper was busy with a road accident, but at a Radio Norfolk studio I prepared a piece for broadcasting while Imperial Locks gratuitously sewed up a loose seam in my pack. In the central market area a huge crowd of holiday makers were on parade. Many were sampling the town's speciality: chips. I declined but did have a mug of tea from Mr Chips, before setting off back to Maldon. After taking a bus to Gorleston and then a longish walk to the A12 a young and helpful lorry driver, Paul, took me all the way to Maldon via his video drop-offs in Lowestoft and Stowmarket, but unfortunately I left my light summer jacket on his truck.

After retrieving the car from Tesco's I drove to Southend, eventually pulling into a sea front parking bay to sleep. When I awoke the next morning a ticket had been stuck on the windscreen and it was six months of negotiation and letters before the fine was waived!
10m

Interlude two
Days 18-19
Sunday
Back in Bromley in the wee small hours, I slept and then went to do some long promised gardening for a client who was about to have one of her family parties and wanted some instant neatness and colour.

Days 20-34
Monday 7th September to Monday 21st September
Gardening, computing and time wasting, what else can one say of a static period.

Day 35
Tuesday
On any one day, one never knows what bolt will hurl itself out of the heavens. Today's catastrophe was farcical. Leaving Bromley, full of high hopes for continuing the walk, carrying five ten pound notes to support me I rushed off to Southend, land of sunshine, water, low tide mud flats and a crowd of the rough, the rich and the retired. Knowing that free parking was difficult, I parked at Westcliffe and walked through the town's well formed and attractive gardens to the Civic Centre, where I hoped to negate my previous parking ticket. I waited for ages to see an official, who then passed me to a second, who told me to write to the retrieval officer. Two hours after parking I walked back to the car. Surprise! Surprise! It had been clamped. I did not believe it and had to look twice. The fee £60. I spent a long time thinking about a solution, free loaded on tea and sandwiches and then slept in the car bedecked with Save the Children stickers and ribbons, hoping to gain local sympathy.

Day 36
Wednesday
After splashing out on biscuits I wasted more time in the car. Could I out-wait the clamping man's patience?

The first lot of police arrived and checked me out and left satisfied. At noon the burly parking Fuehrer arrived and demanded payment. My fabricated story of arriving funds dispatched him. In mid-afternoon the police arrived in force and questioned me severely about the car stickers and my possible bogus charity collecting status. A phone call to Nikki together with a display of diaries, signatures and letters sent them away. But they left a warning behind; after all they had to appear officious. Around five o'clock the heavy-handed clamper swung into action and demanded payment. I refused, but after verbal and physical threats, finally escaped on paying £20. The clamp was removed at last, releasing me and enabling my drive towards Great Yarmouth, and. moreover there was still a pony in my pocket.

Once on the road I changed my plan and drove to Easton near Woodbridge and sought shelter for one night at the home of my niece Ruth. It was a nice return to normality and besides she's also a good cook and her children are courteous and brightly entertaining.

Day 37
Thursday
The morning was spent word processing letters and restoring my humour. After Ruth gave me a vital bright orange survival bag (my new ground sheet) and some sandwiches, I said my farewells, drove to Gorleston and slept undisturbed in the shopping precinct car park.

Third Stage
Yarmouth to Kings Lynn
Day 38
Friday
In Yarmouth I located Sainsbury's, arranged parking for a few days but received no grocery handouts and left at ten o'clock. Now more confident of walking and having cut my pack load down I felt positive about continuing - but who knows what fates lie around the corner and how they may twist their barbs. In Caister a manageress of the All Day store heard my story and kindly supplied some basic groceries. Cliff tops took me to California, Scratby and the yucky archetypical music town of Newport, with its last remnants of holiday crowds.

A straight path burrowed through dune country. Rich ochre, orange and brown bracken on my left opposing the white streaked marram locked sandhills on my right. Near Winterton the sandy path began to meander over larger dunes with good views springing into sight, while keen eyed kestrels hovered above me. The day continued with a good path, road and sea wall to Waxham, Sea Palling and a final half mile of beach, past sand and clay cliff exposures, to Happisburg. I believe this should really be called Sadisburg, since in 1801 the HMS Invincible sank off here with the loss of 400 lives. A commemorative stone in the church yard recalls this dismal event. This major tragedy was preceded by a vicious storm in 1789 when seventy ships were lost with over 600 men. It was hard to imagine such devastation on such a balmy evening but this was my prelude to the stream of stories about distressed shipping that has found its fate on our shores.

A mile further on lay the shuttered shack of the Coast Watch and two adjacent stone brick shelters, which had been cleaned up - volunteer recruits had obviously recently been in action. This was shelter in case of rain, but I camped alongside on the soft green grass. My supper of bread, cheese and oats was eaten under the last remnants of a blistering sunset which drenched the undulating country in warmth and silhouetted the hillside church while a hypnotic flashing lighthouse in the south eventually sent me to sleep.
19m

Day 39
Saturday
Early road walking today was compensated by my breakfast beside the windmill at Stow although it had a disappointing lack of internal workings. At Mundsley I was forced to the beach, which is often tough walking and therefore to be avoided, unless the sands are firm. On this stretch, good cliff exposures of lime and flint were compensation for the extra effort involved. But I decided to exit the beach and took a stiff climb up the cliffs to Trimmington and at the top found an old fashioned joiner's shop in which craftsmen were making window frames. They surely had a wonderful view at tea break times.

A road took me to Sidestrand, where I rested in the church yard, and then at Overstrand I cadged some milk from the village store. A cliff path led past a golf course bristling with players and onto the unspoilt town of Cromer, nestling on the cliffs overlooking the harbour - a town worth visiting. Therein lies a bronze bust to Mr Henry Blogg, a prominent coxswain, the archetypical lifeboatsman, who died in 1954 after fifty three years service, thirty eight as coxswain, having helped to save over eight hundred lives from the savage seas of this dangerous coast. A modest man reluctant to talk about his work but awarded a raft of gold and silver medals by the RNLI. The Red Lion provides more mementos of these tussles against the elements but I was not that thirsty. Instead, I lunched, just west of the town in a big grassy car park with plenty of inviting benches, and contemplated the start of the Norfolk Coast LDP, which begins here and runs to Hunstanton.

After East Runton the cliff path trailed up a hill which overlooked Sherringham, a sprawling town of brown roof tops and further spoilt by its touristy main street. Beyond the town, at the Coast Watch station they told me that this was presently the last in the chain of lookouts on the Norfolk coast, though there would soon be one at Wells. It is an entirely voluntary organisation and was started in Cornwall by Capt. Starling Lark, an ex Trinity Light

House man, who probably had time on his hands after so much automation of lighthouses. They were hopeful that it will be extended round the entire coastline. But it would be many miles and months before I saw the next lookout.

This very attractive coast has steep cliffs and excellent views, but, as all good things end, the sea defence path deteriorated and the last two miles, between Fresh Marshes and the sea, went along a huge gravel bank of very hard walking, especially at the end of the day, towards Cley Eye. There were scores of bird watchers in this area and a fortune in binoculars and telescopes, but the number of birds was scant. I heard reports of exotic sightings and was even given a view of a gannet! Unfortunately my enthusiasm for such glimpses had been ruined by my time in the Falklands where one could practically sit on an albatross or dance with a rock hopper penguin. Next came Blakney and then Morston with its church poised on a hill. I passed a closed inn and the hall before taking a path back to semi-marsh land, finding a place to camp in an unfenced boat yard, amongst a mess of sailing boats with the deck of a catamaran lay close by for emergency cover against rain.
27m

Day 40
Sunday
On waking to the damp misty morning, a solitary lug worm digger passed me heading to the beach for his day's work and I set off past Stiffkey to Wells Marsh where another lone man was picking up litter. What a life of contrasts he'd had. After twenty years in financial Zurich he was now happy being an international volunteer working on nature projects including Montana bears and Namibian lions. Now while waiting for a placement in another overseas project he was simply content with keeping the path tidy and communing with the fauna of the local marshes. In the sleepy water-front village of Wells, preparing for a race was a small flotilla of sleek Sharps, attractive wooden sailing craft - looking capable of cutting through the water with panache and speed. The one that took most of my attention was built nearly seventy years ago. Further connections to the sea were shown by plaques on the quay. One commemorated the disaster that beset the local lifeboat and another the wanderings of the working trader' the Albatross, while the maritime picture was completed with a flight of swans flapping off across the water.

On the B1105 to Holkam, the boundary for the estate of Holkam Hall, the ancestral home of the Earls of Leicester, was a five foot brick wall that stretched the two miles to the Dale Hotel. What a lot of bricks and labour! Justifiably, in the enclosed park woodland, scattered deer enjoyed the shade and solitude. At Burnham Overy I regained the LDP which led me to the sea wall and a good grass path to Burnham Deepdale and then beside the creek the route was thoughtfully laid with sleepers covered in boot gripping wire mesh.

The Roman Fort at Brancaster was a big disappointment, an apparently empty field and only a notice proclaimed its past significance. Like an addict I then followed the path that led to the sea wall and back to Titchwell, an uninteresting detour of two unnecessary miles. In Thornham, the vicar told me that Hunstanton Baptist church was closed but the Methodist one was open. Once more the track led out to the large sea dunes, thick with bird watchers. The Peddars Way disappeared south as my plank path led to the sea wall and onto the glorious but empty golf course at Hunstanton. From here it was but a short distance to the light house and the remains of an old chapel standing on the public greens at the edge of the town. At the Methodist church I met a sad group of a dozen oldies having their harvest festival, with one fatigued and bedraggled loaf adorning the communion table.

Outside the rain was falling heavily and as it was Sunday the Youth Hostel was closed. Consequently I had to sleep on the hard concrete floor of the only shelter available which was in an archway of the deserted water-front fun fair. It was at least dry but extremely hard despite making a mattress out of all my clothes.
27 m

Day 41
Monday 28th September
It had been a poor night on the concrete and I set off at 6.30 along the coast path to Shepherds Port. It was a comparatively fast walk on a grassy sea wall beside wet, green, cattle grazed, higgledy-piggledy fields. At the caravan site shop, the lady owner kindly supplied me with a cup of tea, a packet of biscuits and an orange. I had only gone in for cigarette papers and to ask where I might get refreshment. Generosity had struck again. Then passing the last chalet in a street of ancient holiday homes I was back onto the sea wall and into the marshes, alive with birds and one of the RSPB hides made a suitable resting place for breakfast. It was at this point that I should have taken a path to cross the lagoons, but instead carried on coast wise. My track quickly petered out and I had to struggle over marshland, leap muddy water courses and push through soggy wet grass until re-finding the dyke. Gratefully I took the good track beside this wall and crossed a vast open space of flat, fen-soil farmlands to Vineye Middle. This area had a certain strangeness - appearing to hang suspended from the heavens over a bowl of water. It was private land (with its own shooting rights) but nobody seemed to mind my trespass. The track was a curiosity; mostly composed of white beach shingle - rich in sea shells, many of which were still whole. Isolated groups of huge modern farm buildings indicated the large scale farming operations in progress, while enormous ricks of big straw bales showed the extensive production of wheat. With the aid of map and compass I found the path that went beside the Great Ouse and into the port of Kings Lynn. But as I'd come in the back way I could not get out of the docks

and had to ask the gate-man to unlock the electronically operated gate. Kings Lynn is a rather splendid town. There are the usual modern shops, but they somehow nestle contentedly in the town centre and do not dwarf its character. The central piece is the striking cathedral with its copper plate clad spire. The local paper took my details and was glad to have my story. At the end of Ferry lane I made arrangements for my eventual transfer to West Lynn. There was a bus to Great Yarmouth, but in order to save time and money I decided to hitch. In truth, I was down to £3 and could not afford the bus anyway. A student of sports studies took me, in his mini, to Narborough where I stood for hours while hordes of traffic passed, especially army convoys, but none were giving lifts. Eventually, towards evening, I persuaded a driver coming from the side road to pick me up and take me to East Dereham where I spent another hour on the slip road, in the dark but to no avail. A nearby chip shop consoled my disappointment with chips and tea while, the weather being dry, I found a sleeping place under a yew tree near the main interchange.
17 m

Day 42
Tuesday
In the morning I continued hitching and finally arrived in Yarmouth at eleven. The car was still in the Sainsbury car park for breakfast and a change of clothes. I spent rest of the day in the town and called at the radio station to tell them I'd reached Lynn while in the library I checked maps and routes - before sleeping again in the same Yarmouth supermarket car park.

Wasting Six Days around Kilby
Days 43-48 (Early October)
I expect, if you were asked to fritter away six days, that you would readily declare the easiness of such a trivial activity. A week's holiday is often spent in such frivolity and passes all too quickly. Or you might potter around your garden for a week doing all those little jobs that have been put off. Maybe spend a week visiting relatives otherwise not often seen. No problem. I hear you say. After all, you do a week's work and you don't know where the time has gone. But wait. Put a few restrictions on your attempt. Move yourself 120 miles away from home. Where do you stay? An hotel, in a B&B, at a YH, in a tent or a caravan. No problem is the usual response. But now extend the problem to include a reduction in funds and then the list gets shorter. Put in the additional factor that Autumn is here, the weather is damp, if not wet and the nights are colder. Still no problem, I hear you exhort. Your plastic emergency credit card will buy you accommodation, fuel to drive home or the fares on trains if not buses. But suddenly you find that you have lost your celluloid safety net or that it is up to its limit. There is no immediate access to replacement of card or money stocks and you further discover the petrol level in you

tank has sunk below the red mark. The list of possible actions has now radically decreased. Take away your bank account and any means of identification and reduce the change in your pocket to less than a couple of quid. Is there now a problem? If not, then your lateral thinking is way above mine.

   I now faced this very situation and I was in the middle of Norfolk. Amongst many mental compensations was the adage that every problem has a solution. My only real asset was my car, an ancient Ford Escort but this was extremely low on petrol with less than 25 miles left in the tank. Nor did I have any prospect of any more money for a further week. In reality it was a bit like being in a open prison - except that in prison your bodily requirements are catered for - and in both the time can go awfully slowly. What do you eat? What do you do to fill in the time? The situation brought forth a plethora of laterally stimulated ideas - most of which had to be rejected. Break a window and get arrested! Go into a super market - put food in a basket and walk out, if caught - tough, if not - okay. You might get away with it after all. You could prepare by stripping away all your identification so that a fictitious name could be given if stopped. Get petrol at a service station and drive off without paying? In the end I was too tired for all these fantasies and opted for sleeping in the car and sinking into a state of low energy output - almost hibernating! Having discovered my plight and settled my plan I fell asleep in the Sainsbury car park.

   At first light I rummaged around the car for any spare change that might be found on the floor behind the seats or in the glove compartment. None. All I found was a bag of oats - three quarters full; something to eat at least. After driving the short distance out to Caister, and some prevarication I stopped in a deserted sea-side car park to formulate my survival plans which led me to the nearby, appropriately named, Rainbow supermarket. But my plans for charity handouts fell on deaf ears as such requests had to be channelled through head office in writing! After patrolling the aisles for low price products I eventually spent 47p on reduced priced rolls and milk and having established this first basic of sustenance drove out to the Filby area to check out suitable long term parking locations. My first stop was at a zoo and vintage car museum that had looked promising on the map but on the ground offered no privacy. Nursing my petrol and anguish I finally found the reasonably secluded car park at Filby Bridge and in this quiet spot started my week of waiting as the weather gathered dark and gloomy about me. To fill in time I began playing endless games of patience, scouted for blackberries from the woodland beside the planked walk to the bird hide on the broad and left my mind in neutral as there was no book to read. I did have my sleeping bag and a blanket and could therefore spread my six foot out in reasonable comfort for the night- although this was never entirely satisfactory because of the two inch step between the folded down seat and the rear baggage area. That small step was always bugging me

- niggling at my resolve.

On the Thursday, bored with my claustrophobic surroundings, I moved to Rollesby wild fowl sanctuary and on the way ran out of petrol. Fortune favoured me however as I still had a third of a gallon in a petrol can and, with this transferred to the tank, set the tripometer to zero, guessing that I then had some 15 miles of driving available to me. Having parked I walked through the village and bought bread in a very run down shop which had little on the shelves and a very bored shop assistant serving. I gained hot water at a local house and a short explanation of my predicament led to the further donation of milk, tea bags and sugar - a beneficial and unexpected bonus. At the sanctuary, the swan man came at six o'clock to release his load of recently treated rescued swans. He told me that the chief gates-man came at seven and the place would be locked. But after telling him that I didn't mind being locked in, and I duly was, as I was not going anywhere except to sit, watch and envy the ducks being fed with copious scraps scattered by a host of late autumn visitors, thinking of asking if I could be a surrogate duck needing to be fed.

The next day my car battery was flat, necessitating carrying it a mile to the garage in Rollesby and while being recharged I ventured out on an exploratory walk, found a wind farm to the north, picked blackberries and scrumped some apples. The weather remained dull and dismal as I recovered the battery and carried it back to the car. After cadging hot water at the adjacent cafe (free - just this once, they said) I moved, never feeling happy in one place for too long, to the more secluded car park beside Rollesby Church.

On the Saturday I moved again, this time to a grass verge on a very quiet road on the other side of the church, and then went for a four mile walk. At a place that bred carp I obtained warm water but got better boiling hot water from another more thoughtful farmer. On the Sunday I inspected the ground round a derelict church near Burgh St Margaret but soon found myself back again at the Filby Bridge car park I'd used before. I spent part of the day trying to walk around Filby Broad, but this was a failure, especially as I got rather damp. However it did inspire me to further activity, investigation and exploration. On the following day, at the local grocery shop I bought milk and chatted to the owner, David Thompson who had started the enterprise 30 years before in one small room. With the help of his family he had gradually expanded and turned it into a cornerstone of Filby community life.

On Monday I managed a good long walk around the Broad, finding a good range of activities ticking along;- the small village school, the remains of an original Unitarian Chapel, a zoo - the brain child of someone returning from the East twenty years before, Charity Farm (Manor Farm) where they were sorting potatoes, maize was growing and cattle munching, a talk to an ancient shepherd now confined to a three wheeled motor bike, the Bygone Village with its attractions for the day visitor - its fortunes being turned around after being bought from receivership and an excellent near empty caravan site which provided me with hot water and cakes. I found that the footpaths around here were mostly in a poor state, with many nearly ploughed up and a lack of sign posts - indications that most tourists are interested only in the more obvious attractions rather than the natural aspects of the area.

In the afternoon I talked to a class of first school children in the local primary and introduced to them my travelling companion - Jack Sprat, a three inch woollen penguin which my wife had knitted whilst in the Falklands, a map of the coast of Britain and told them what happened when teeth weren't cleaned, i.e. false teeth.

On the last part of the day I still had 79p left and made a dash for Yarmouth, but on the way ran out of petrol just short of Caister and had to walk to the nearest filling station, for a litre of petrol before making it back to Sainsbury's as the last whiff of fuel was used up. I spent 25p on a can of baked beans and slept once again in the car park - thankful that the week was over, but pleased that in the end it had been an eventful, enjoyable and recordable interlude.

Days 49-50
On the Tuesday night whilst asleep in the back of the car I woke up, disturbed by an unfamiliar noise, and twisted round in my nest to look. In the front was an unfamiliar shape, silhouetted by the town lighting. As I struggled to the surface of consciousness, this shape became a person who suddenly shot out of the car like ignited high powered octane fuel, never to be seen again, alarm signals ringing in his head as the situation behind him changed. I expect he was as shocked as much as me. Did he think a hungry guard dog was waking from its slumbers? But it made me realise, at least, that my situation was not so desperate as that of having to the scour the streets for a place to sleep and a morsel to eat.

After resuming sleep for a few more hours I spent the next three days in and around Gorleston and Yarmouth having my ancient car battery recharged, buying a little petrol, finding some food at Somerfield's and visiting the library.

The problem was that I was still broke but I did not wish to stay around here any longer. The only solution was to continue walking on the little change I did have. It was less than a pound and my food stock was only enough for a thin week. I was now really on the edge. But the main dilemma was petrol - I had enough in the tank for some ten miles. All I had to do was to find a garage which did not advertise its approbation to check one's ability to pay - and so taking the bull by the horns, set off towards Yarmouth in search of a petrol station. It was a wet and windy night and by chances of misread road signs and a loss of direction soon found myself on the A47 going across the Broads, heading for Norwich. Now this is a very straight and exposed road lined with frequent emergency telephones in case of problems and it was not a place to be in trouble. About two miles from Yarmouth I had my first hint of those impending trials and tribulations. The tripometer hovered on the ten mile mark as the engine stuttered, the fuel was very low and I was glad I wasn't flying. A petrol station was high on the agenda but Acle was eight long miles away. Meanwhile outside it was throwing it down and a mini-storm was blowing. Swinging the car from side to side sucked petrol into the carburettor and the engine kept on going. But finally with the mileage at 14, the inevitable happened, all the juice was gone. Just on the hard shoulder, by great good chance, I had stopped opposite to Mill House, the only residence for miles. A small break in the traffic allowed me to back peddle the car onto their gravel yard across the road - wet work in the wind-swept showers. I wandered around the house, looking for signs of life - but nobody stirred -and so I returned to the car to get some sleep and to see what the morrow would bring, Half an hour later I was rudely awakened by flashing blue lights because of an apparent report about erratic driving and a car in a ditch. Surrounded by three police vehicles, the rain blew into the car, wetting me and my papers as the questioning began. A breath test revealed abstention and eventually they were satisfied with my credentials and story, but were otherwise unhelpful, and departed, leaving me to resume my slumbers.

Day 51
Thursday
I awoke, ate and sat, watching the bad weather and the activities associated with the adjacent house and when my lethargy finally dissolved, asked for assistance which was given willingly. The owner and his son pushed my car to a better spot, found some petrol and jump-started the engine thus enabling me to drive another mile to the large empty car park of the nearby pub, which was closed at that time of year, where I sat for the rest of the day, watching the canal traffic, the rain and wasting yet more time.

Fourth Stage
Kings Lynn to Bridlington
Day 52
Friday
In the morning, a little more prevarication, before setting off for Acle, where at the Q8 service station, I slipped five gallons of lead free into the tank. Unable to pay, I had to leave my passport as a guarantee for future payment. My son Patrick sent a cheque ten days later but I'm still waiting for the passport. Almost free again, I drove to West Lynn and, after parking, did the busi-

ness with the ferry to cross the Great Ouse.

I was not particularly looking forward to the Wash walk, expecting it to be void of interest. The march down the west bank of the River Ouse was indeed much as I thought, a straight walk on grass between hawthorn trees and Wash Path (WP) markers were found every 150 metres, rather OTT on this undeviating way.

The path continued on big dykes past the sea washed marshes, the magic of big open spaces gradually beginning to assert itself, as the sun emerged and the fresh air cleared my senses. I met a bird watcher who showed me some Stints, but not much else moved to stir the imagination and this was surprising because the latter part of the WP is also known as the Peter Scott Walk. Out at sea two curious flat topped islands appeared, which were man-made and had been quickly colonised by sea birds, perhaps scared of coastal bird watchers. At the end of this walk, twin lighthouses appeared on either side of the straight ditch-like river Nene. They were built to commemorate the opening of this outfall in 1831 and were used, as an abode, by Peter Scott some hundred years later. From these it was a bee-line walk to Sutton swing-bridge, a workmanlike structure built in 1897 by Handiside and Armstrong while in the port, close by, big barges were unloading steel and timber.

After hitching back to West Lynn I had to walk the last mile back to the car. An obliging girl in a nearby house gave me hot water through her window before I drove back to Sutton Bridge, begged some milk and a Kit Kat from a mini super store and then, in the fading light, found a sheltered parking spot beside some aging agricultural machinery on a farm next to the port. I ate well enough but slept rather badly.
14m

Day 53
Saturday
My morning started at 7.45 and I was soon back at the twin lighthouses, but on the other side of the straight ditched Nene. The usual banks took me to RAF Holbeach, and its danger area with a line of prominent observation towers. Rather a dreary scene. But then, suddenly, for half an hour, the sun came out and lit up the whole area, the slanting autumnal light brought the coast alive, and me as well. At the control centre there was one man on guard. He was reading about submarines when I startled him by knocking on his window. However he recovered and after telling me of the security position he was gracious enough to make me some tea. A little later by the last MOD observation tower, having another break and writing up my diary, I noted that there was only ten miles more to do that day. How wrong this turned out to be.

I crossed the bridge over the River Welland where, in yet another port, ships were unloading vast amounts of fertiliser including ammonium nitrate from Russia. Then once on the road I tried but failed to get a lift and, for want of action, decided to take the Macmillan Way to Boston. The path was easy to follow but I was also guided by the silo-shaped local landmark, Boston's 'Stump' which turned out to be Boston's splendid cathedral tower. After ten miles, I wound up the haven and arrived in the town as darkness fell.

With rain threatening and no prospect of returning to the car, shelter was needed. A bright idea sprang to mind and after consulting my nationwide list of Scrabble Clubs, I phoned the local number. The wife of the organiser gave me some positive overtones and I said I would call round. However before setting out, whilst still in the middle of town, I virtuously called at the police station to tell them about my whereabouts in case there was a worry about my non-return to the car and the farmer began instigating search parties for my body. The constabulary were not at all concerned and I walked out the two miles to the Fishtoft suburbs to meet the local scrabblers. After knocking on my arrival, a truculent son asked me what I was doing speaking to his mother, who I now realised was in her seventies. Threats of imminent violence fell on my ears and I began to beat a hasty retreat towards Boston. Within 15 minutes the police were on my tail. Heavy questioning began and they soon whisked me off again to the police station, this time by the back door, where they arrested me on the basis of no ID, possible bogus charity status and the accusations of the son that I had just seen. Locked in a cell, my possessions and belt were removed. However they provided a welcome meal and a mug of tea. Some time later after finally relenting from my reluctance to give a home-based contact, they were able to reach my brother via a Bromley police patrol and when he vouched for me they were ready to release me at 2 am, out into the night. I thought 'great!', now I would have to sleep rough on the streets of Boston. Luckily the first sign of lateral thinking arose and a thoughtful inspector allowed me to hibernate in a ladies cell for the rest of the night. That cell was not locked on me and although the heated bed was excessively warm this did not prevent me from sleeping soundly.
29m

Day 54
Sunday
After waking me with a cup of tea, they provided a WPC with her car to drive me back to the main road where I hitched back to Sutton Bridge. A fisherman took me the first two mile. In this small world of ours, a man called Gillam Beck drove me to Long Sutton and it transpired that he is a pedigreee dog judge who knows Liz through the show ring and other canine interests and was today judging clumber spaniels. After this two painters lifted me to Sutton Bridge in their paint smeared van.

Walking through the Sunday-silent port, I found a thick teak plank. It was 6 ft x 1 ft, an ideal firm base for my foam mattress and which fitted the back of the car perfectly. This overcame the floor ridge that had bothered me before and also raised the bed from the sometimes damp floor.

The drive back to Boston was uneventful! This attractive town is full of associations to the Pilgrim Fathers with their tribulations in the early 17th century. I walked down river to the Pilgrim's memorial:-

> Near this place
> In 1607 those later known as the Pilgrim
> Fathers set sail on their first attempt to
> find religious freedom across the seas
> Erected 1957

But it would be many months before I saw their true departure spot.

The path drifted away from the sea passing through North Sea Camp Farm for young offenders - I just walked through. Though unchallenged a not-so-young inmate asked me what I had brought for them! It wasn't until much later that I realised they wanted tobacco or maybe a little pot. My route north was then divided between the inner and outer sea walls either side of the flat prison fields of cabbages, Brussels sprouts and potatoes. The good inner track was the more sheltered from the strong morning breeze. At one place on the wall a huge granite slab commemorated John Saul (1927-97), but without further explanation.

Near to the evening I staggered towards Gibraltar Point, missed the correct bridge and instead crossed a gated but unlocked footbridge into a pumping station yard with no exit, becoming trapped in this cul-de-sac as gloomy night rain threatened. Then, as I fumbled around looking for a way out, a car arrived on the other side of the fence and a voice broke the silence. 'We've just arrived back; you'd better come in for some tea.' A spontaneous and generous offer, quite out of the blue. Gratefully I climbed over the seven foot gate to meet Dawn Slater and her visiting friend. Tea turned into a roast lamb dinner, coffee, smokes, and lots of chat. Apparently quite a few long distance walkers and cyclists pass this way and the house needs to be renamed the ABWA hotel. Dawn provided wonderful hospitality and followed this up by keeping in touch. Around ten o'clock a move was made for drinks in town. I declined the offered lift and instead walked half a mile to a car park near Gibraltar Point and in the darkness found a suitable sleeping spot beneath a fir tree.
22m

Day 55
Monday 12th October
A noisy gaggle of low flying geese woke me, as they flew overhead while a man out for an early stroll with his dog passed by and peered at my camp and soon after beginning my walk into Skegness a police patrol arrived to stop and question me again. This time escaping detention, I noted in my diary: 'Police State!'

Skeggy was the usual collection of yucky tourism reminding me of other seaside towns. I walked past the station before hitch-hiking back to Boston and was picked up by an ex-RAF electronics man who now taught business studies. He'd had experience of of team walking events in Germany and was therefore sympathetic to my trip. He dropped me near Fishtoft and it was an easy walk back to the car. On the way a retired dock worker with his bicycle said he was now happy watching birds. His retort 'People didn't care anymore' rang, disconcertingly, in my ear; because some did.

After my usual breakfast of oats, I drove back to Skegness, checked maps and other data in the library, parked near a beach side hotel and then walked along the sea wall promenade, much of which was heavily drifted with washed in sand. After an austere but striking house devoted to Derbyshire Miners Convalescence I came to the mega-vast prison of Butlins Holiday Camp, guarded by a long run of protective fencing. Was this to contain the inmates? This was followed by spreading acres of caravans. With all these holiday makers, I decided that the air round here must be very bracing!

I finished the days walking in Sutton-on-Sea and then made my way back to Skeggy with a Grimsby fish merchant who was taking fish to Norfolk and bemoaning the inability of youth to do a full days work. He dropped me in the middle of the town and I walked to the hotel. The chef kindly filled my flask with hot water for my supper, which I had there and then, before driving back to Sutton. Once there, it was a little while before I selected the central restaurant car park, obtained the owners approval and was able to listen to the radio before falling asleep.
17m

Day 56
Tuesday
After breakfast I walked along the promenade, past run down beach huts, to characterless Maplethorpe, found the bank, library and Co-op and then hitched back to Sutton with a young fairground mechanic. After moving the car onto Maplethorpe, I banked and shopped but found the library devoid of OS maps for checking my route. The way north was heavy going in the thick cluster of dunes and was not well signposted. Trying to escape this maze I found myself

in a highly electrified fenced field and when I went over the barrier at the far end I didn't know whether it was switched on or off. But no shock came(!) unlike later farm fences. After struggling with more sand, the path dithered through scrubby undergrowth, which partially concealed rolled nets used for trapping birds. The grass footing improved but the peace was shattered by the sounds of heavy military demolition works in the north east.

A map would have been useful as I had to ask for directions three times. At the English Heritage workshops I asked again and thus took the road to Saltfleet, where I had tea and a Kit Kat in the village shop. They said parking was available in Sea Lane, but I made a better arrangement at the New Inn opposite. The landlord later saw me on the road south and gave me a lift most of the way back to Maplethorpe.

In the evening I drove to the ancient, forgotten, market town of Louth and looked for the local chess club. The information in Skegness library was that meetings took place in the Greyhound but on calling there at the appointed hour I raised blank stares, only relieved by a phone call which gave me the real date, place and time. I should have known! Always check and double check!

I struggled by the poorly signposted dark back roads to Saltfleet and parked in the works yard of the pub where in the bar I had a whisky, got hot water and had a chat with the friendly crowd. Over the bar there was a display of plaited dog leads at £10 each - a local industry,and also a bell for calling time, labelled:-

S S TITANIC 1912

A topical reminder of the £200m film of the year. The bar staff reckoned they had sent the landlord down to get it!
10m

Day 57
Wednesday
From the Inn's caravan site I forced my way, through a ditch and hedge, onto the path which ran on the seaward side of the sea wall. The carcass of a dead seal lay near the track, proof of their existence, but apparently they would be more prevalent in November when breeding started. This was at least a start in the right direction after I had started looking out for these animals after seeing a sactuary near King's Lynn. The route now went inland towards Somercotes and out again to Donna Nook and on the way, a kind old man captured me. He carried a milk crate and led his trailing dog as we walked back to his cottage for coffee and biscuits. He said he was a Murgatroyd from Bradford and Shipley, the ginger haired lot!

King Edward, a key player in English history: Conway, day 382

There were more firing ranges at Donna Nook and out at sea there was a striking bright fluorescent ship marker to be shot at. Noisy jet fighters practised dipping runs over the waste land disturbing the peace but it was fascinating to watch their swooping dives and climbs, while at the Grainthorpe outfall a car bristled with antennae and the owner was talking to his friends in Australia.

Despite all the technology, it was a lovely walking day. The rain had cleaned up the landscape and the sun, in sporadic bursts, chased my back all morning enhancing the wonderful views as I left the flat lands of the fens and their own charms behind. On my right was the outline of Spurn Head and vast stretches of sea wet sand. Near a crude oil pipeline the NW wind began to stiffen and slowed my progress along the sea wall to the Humber Mouth caravan and yacht club. - a good spot for sailing with bold brightly coloured Picos and fast moving wind surfers riding the waves. Then it was a good grassy walk to Cleethorpes, where I had solitary tea in the empty cafe of a cheerful Madeiran. At the leisure centre I arranged parking for Thursday then walked four miles back along the A1098 and A1031 before a lift materialised which unfortunately left me walking the last three miles from Somercotes back to Saltfleet, which was reached in the dark. In the bar, a team was preparing to play an away pool match and the barmaid had little to do. She was a midwife who had helped out at the bar for three months which turned into nine. Her husband repaired helicopters in the Middle East and she had travelled there, to Nigeria and also the USA but was now temporarily in sleepy Salt Fleet. I played pool with a young lad and was thoroughly thrashed, then, after making some fruitless phone calls to Scrabble clubs, slept in my car close by the Inn.
15 m

Day 58
Thursday
It had been a cold night and after waking to a red sky sunrise I drove to Cleethorpes, found the Meridian line and shyly parked beside the hall of leisure. The short walk to Grimsby was along promenade, waste ground and sea wall. Facing a dead end I dropped seven feet to reach the beach below and skirted round the port to the fish market.

The guiding landmark towards Grimsby had been a tall sentinel, an old red brick tower, standing in the port. But was, in fact, a high rise water reservoir that used to help operate the dock gates, but now only stood as a reminder of the past. There was also a bust to Prince Albert, who having done a similar thing in Liverpool in 1846, also opened the docks here in 1852:-

'We have been laying the foundation of a dock, not only as a place of refuge and refitment for our mercantile marine and calculated to receive the greatest steamers of Her Majesty's Navy, but I trust it will be the foundation of a great commercial port. This work in future eyes, when we shall have quit this scene, and when perhaps our names will be forgotten, will I hope, become a new centre of life, with the vast and ever increasing commerce of the world, and as a most important link in the connection of the East and the West.'

These were probably the best two things about Grimsby. The central town is a jewel of shopping brightness but in contrast it is surrounded by a dilapidated fishing industry and grimy, smoke belching factories. The offices of the Evening Telegraph sat below its roof which declared a temperature of 9.3 C and they interviewed me for my story before I collected mail at the PO and checked maps in the library.

The concrete sea wall path was not attractive, though it was easy walking to the petroleum works at Illingham, where I was forced inland through oak and ash to the village. A man on the path said that life was so ordinary that he was glad to meet me doing something totally way out. From the twin lighthouses beyond Immingham Dock I hitched back to Grimsby with an off duty taxi driver before walking the three miles to the car. Driving back to the light houses, in the dark and wet, I found someone repairing cars and he allowed me to park close by. His wife produced hot water and their little girl, thoroughly intrigued by my appearance and unusual arrival, kept bobbing up and down around my mobile home.
10 m

Day 59
Friday
The concrete sea defences petered out two miles further on, just as the Humber bridge came into view and began to dominate the skyline. The bank changed to grass while inshore the signs of past industrial activity appeared. Near Barton the rain started in earnest and I sought shelter at some nearby work sheds. There I met the last nine men who still made tiles; 150 years after the firm had started, though the Romans had also used the site. This is the final bastion of hand crafted tiles, each with a typical deep 'S' relief profile and their special red colour from the clay. I stood in the shed of Steven, a cool character who gave me tea, factory details and demonstrated his skill before reverting to the more interesting job of cleaning of his gas pistols. Eventually Clive,

a manager, gave me a lift up to slumbering Barton town, once a kick off point for a ferry across the river. He suggested I parked in the unlocked yard for the rest of the day. Then I took a lift with a driver, doing house maintenance work and who wanted to waste a little time before returning to his base. After retrieving the car from Immingham and parking at the allotted spot in the tile yard, I walked, during an evening pause in the rain, to the Proudfoot supermarket near the 'Bridge' and close to the long, long-shed of an extinct rope maker, now used for youth work. I got no free stores as the bachelor owner was absent but I arranged parking for the morrow and then walked back to the car, settling in for a wet and windy night.
14m

Day 60
Saturday
After moving the car to Proudfoots I was able to concentrate on the walk to Hull and it took half an hour to haul across the mighty bridge which when it opened in 1981 had the longest suspension span in the world at 4,626ft. The riverside path on the other side had a variable surface and had undergone recent improvements. But it was littered with fishermen catching cod and obstructing the path with their rods. On coming to the docks and its exit, the traffic and security controller told me that I was not on the right path. However he made me some tea and pointed the way to the eastern exit and into Hull, a big bustling town. After doing a few things in the centre and leaving some of my luggage at a charity shop I walked out along the straight A1033 where firemen were busy cleaning hydrants, while on my right lay some big docks with its shipping, including the Dunkirk ferry. By the BP oil refinery a right turn pointed to Paul with more road and yet more road. As I trudged along a lady stopped her car and waited for me, and expecting the offer of an unwanted lift I greeted her but instead, with me apparently looking a worthy cause, she gave £5 for StC and a few words of encouragement.

Spots of rain had dogged me all the way out of Hull and now the sky blackened and the wind increased. Suddenly a storm broke becoming increasingly cold, as I took shelter in a barn-garage for an hour until most of the rain had blown away. With the strong wind behind my back, I staggered onto the next farm but found no refuge there and instead was given directions to walk in the blustery conditions towards Spurn Point. With the gloom gathering I found a farm with big modern barns and a stern notice declaring 'Private Property'. Another barn, filled with straw, lay across a field but without immediate access. After debating what to do and knocking on the door of the farm house, not expecting any solution to my dilemma, I was surprised and immediately shown to the huge cavern of a near-empty barn. It had two or three large straw bales and most of the grain had recently been removed. Barry and Linda, with spontaneous hospitality, made me very welcome and gave me soup, bread, hot

water, tea, milk and sugar. With Hessian sacking as an extra blanket and a bale for a bed I was able to have a really warm, dry and sheltered night, as the storm outside gradually blew itself out. Barry was the main farm-hand and had been on this thousand acre farm for 30 years, as a part of the Caley & Leake agricultural empire.
22m

Day 61
Sunday
Barry and his family were exercising their dog in the fields and we exchanged greetings suitable for the bright frosty morning with the rising red rimmed sun suggesting a good day ahead. The slanting light lit up the drilled fields producing a striped corduroy effect like parallel wrought iron bars, straddling the tilled flat fertile earth. On the sea wall I marched forward and when the grass roughened and toughened I tried a short cut across the marsh, only just making it, getting wet and soggy feet in the process before coming to the packed pub at Kilnsea for warming tea. Down the sandy track of Spurn Path, I passed the Heligoland bird ringing nets while at the Head, the defunct lighthouse is now only a tourist decoration. The real job is done in a modern control centre and its door at the bottom was open. After climbing the stairs to the control room I met the assistant harbour master busy on his dials and switches, amidst an impressive range of screens, and the pilot master directing ships up and down the wide Humber. However they had enough time to give me a signature, some tea and a chat. Leaving them to it I found the sandy beach on the fringe of the head, and followed it faithfully and slavishly - round and back to the lighthouse so that I could say I'd walked around Spurn Point. While having my lunch here a Yorkshire lad from Malton and his Japanese girl friend stopped to take a picture and after cajoling them took one of me - but I'm still waiting for a print.

On the eastern side of the peninsular, I sat in a bird hide on foam pillowed seats while two specialists gave me reports of arctic terns and told me of another two hides further up the coast. So I walked on expecting the same luxuries in the huts beyond. The first was very sandy and wet while the second had disappeared. But in the dunes I did find a damp foam mattress which I carried all the way to the quiet hamlet of Easington. Arriving in late evening, I messed around for an hour, ate supper on a bench by the church, chatted to some local children, trying to whip up some home grown hospitality, and finally found sanctuary in a scruffy garage-barn at the adjacent Rectory Farm.
22m

Day 62
Monday 19th October
Having, yesterday, walked towards the beacon of Spurn Lighthouse, today I

headed for another distant finger in the sky believing it to be Withernsea church, a symbol of hope in otherwise rather boring country. Though on arrival it was another lighthouse! This eastern coast line differs greatly from the western side of the peninsular and undulating cliffs hugging the North Sea were suffering extensive erosion from the constant battering of waves. In the quiet town of Withernsea, relatively unspoilt by mainstream tourism, there was further erosion and the library was closed on Mondays. At Barry's cafe I treated myself to an excellent breakfast and as the only client I was served by the wife and daughter combination, Cheryl and Jolene. Afterwards the local paper took my story and I set off for Hornsea, reaching it just before five o'clock. On the other side, looking for barns, the first tractor driver said yes but on arriving at his buildings he changed his mind and said 'no, try up the road'. Luckily the very next farm took me in, offering me a straw bed beside the cattle, but then in the house produced a meal of beef, chips and the trimmings. A couple of hours slipped by in pleasant company, agricultural matters and family chat before I succumbed to a warm slumber in the byre.
23m

Day 63
Tuesday
My early morning surprise was a gift of hot tea and sandwiches to see me through the day. I walked to Bridlington without too much trouble, but afterwards remembered little about the country except the last three miles across the sands as the weather improved. Leaving the town to it, I had other pressing matters,but it was a two mile slog out of Brid before a scene-of-crime cartographer picked me up and took me all the way to Hull. I retrieved my spare clothes from the Sailors Charity shop and later, when dark, wet and threatening more, I set off for the ten mile walk back to Barton, across the Humber Bridge, arriving at Proudfoots by nine.

My next plan evolved around location, tiredness and finances becoming a decision to visit my son Patrick in, not too distant, Keighley. I had 69p in change, a gallon in my spare petrol can and some ten miles in the tank. Also one of the tyres was soft. The problem was how to stretch my resources the 70 - 80 miles to Bingley, the other side of Bradford, without pulling the Acle trick. My estimations made it seem possible especially after persuading a petrol station to inflate my tyre with their money, with.20p saved. On running out of petrol at exactly the ten mile distance, I emptied the spare petrol into the tank while further on my loose change bought a little more. By driving very carefully I was able to coax 53 miles out of the petrol. My senses and the fuel gauge told me I was not going to make it. But by swinging the car from side to side I made it to a garage on the outside of Bradford and managed to wangle another litre of fuel before setting off again for Bingley. Passing through, a parked patrol car stood waiting. 'Keep going' I cried, not wanting to be

stopped and questioned. A quarter mile short of target the petrol ran out again, though there was just enough in the can to fill the carburettor through a disconnected pipe. In the excitement the battery had been drained and was now too low to restart the engine so I sat, smoked a cigarette and waited, before retrying the ignition. Just enough life returned to start and I finally made it bar the last 30 yards, only having to push the car around the corner and park in the yard before falling asleep in the back some time after midnight.
13m

Interlude four
Sojourn in Crossflatts at the end of October.
Days 64 - 76
In the night, I'd arrived at the house of my eldest son, Patrick, his wife Diane and two of my grandchildren, Kyle and Nathan. It was there that I spent a few days recuperating health, weight, funds and clothing, and a considerable amount of time exercising their self willed golden retriever, Harry, while watching the rain fall out of the sky. The sun did come out and the clouds briefly dispersed, only for the rain to quickly return and dampen everything again. In between the showers I enjoyed the manual labour of cutting the hedge and yet more dog walking, ate well, did some child minding, restored my morale and finances managing to repay my loan for the petrol in Acle and other small debts before preparing for the next stage.

Day 77 Tuesday
After saying farewell at mid day I put ten pounds worth of petrol in the tank, kept a fiver for my trip and pottered around before sleeping somewhere near York.

Day 78 Wednesday
Having frittered time away in York, I drove, in the evening, to Bridlington to park on South Beach but had only been there an hour when the police arrived. They had spotted me on the overhead CCTV and suspected my presence next to the boatyard. Luckily they didn't question the validity of my out of date tax disc too much but I began to believe that Big Brother was watching me.

Fifth Stage
Bridlington to Middlesborough
Day 79
Thursday
In the morning more police arrived and took away my StC collection box - this was the aftermath of what had happened in Southend catching up with me - and now knew I had a marked car! In fact it was a relief to be shot of that dan-

gling noisy red box and I collected charity money quite easily without it. Only on a couple of further occasions was it suggested that an official collecting card was more in order, but I have never thought much of rules like that. You can either trust people or not!

Out of Bridlington, past Sewerby, where a huge bonfire was being built for the Saturday fireworks, the path continued, past the evocative Danes Dyke, to Flamborough Head, where the lighthouse was being cleaned by the local fire brigade, and then up the heritage coast to Reighton. Flocks of gulls squabbled over the sea's harvest while masses of pigeons roosted incongruously on the cliffs. Were these the progeny of failed racing pigeons? But where were the vaunted gannets, guillemots, kittiwakes and razorbills? Returning to Brid the car battery was low and needed a quick recharge in the town before I carried it back to South Beach. The evening was spent socially in the local scrabble club, which met in the hub of a B&B. I played and won three games before parking at the nearby supermarket for the night, veiled hints having fallen on deaf ears. Perhaps I should have lost!
15m

Day 80
Friday
After hitching to Reighton I walked to the front and along difficult beaches to Filey where Frederick Delius had once lived and you can imagine the scenery inspiring his music. On a sea-front plaque, an appropriate, timely motto said:-

Psalm 93.4:
'God is always greater than all our troubles'

And realisation began to dawn that something was looking after me despite my own efforts to self destruct. Fortune favours the brave and I was to have many favours heaped on my shoulders during the journey's diversions and perambulations.

The path sweeps out of Filey up towards the Brigg - the Devils embryonic bridge to Europe - a headland standing high on millstone grit and providing dramatic coastal views southwards and northwesterly to Scarborough, towards which I now walked along the start of the Cleveland Way (CW) as it lay perched on the cliff tops. By mid-afternoon I arrived in Scarborough, worked my way up the terraces to its well structured centre and wandered around for an hour before heading north. The spa waters here were supposed to work miracles but they didn't do Anne Bronte much good as she died here in 1849 soon after arriving. On the path near Cloughton I began looking for shelter for the night. The few possibilities did not appeal and as my vacuum flask was empty I stumbled across fields in the dark, lured by lights suggesting supplies and

Map 2

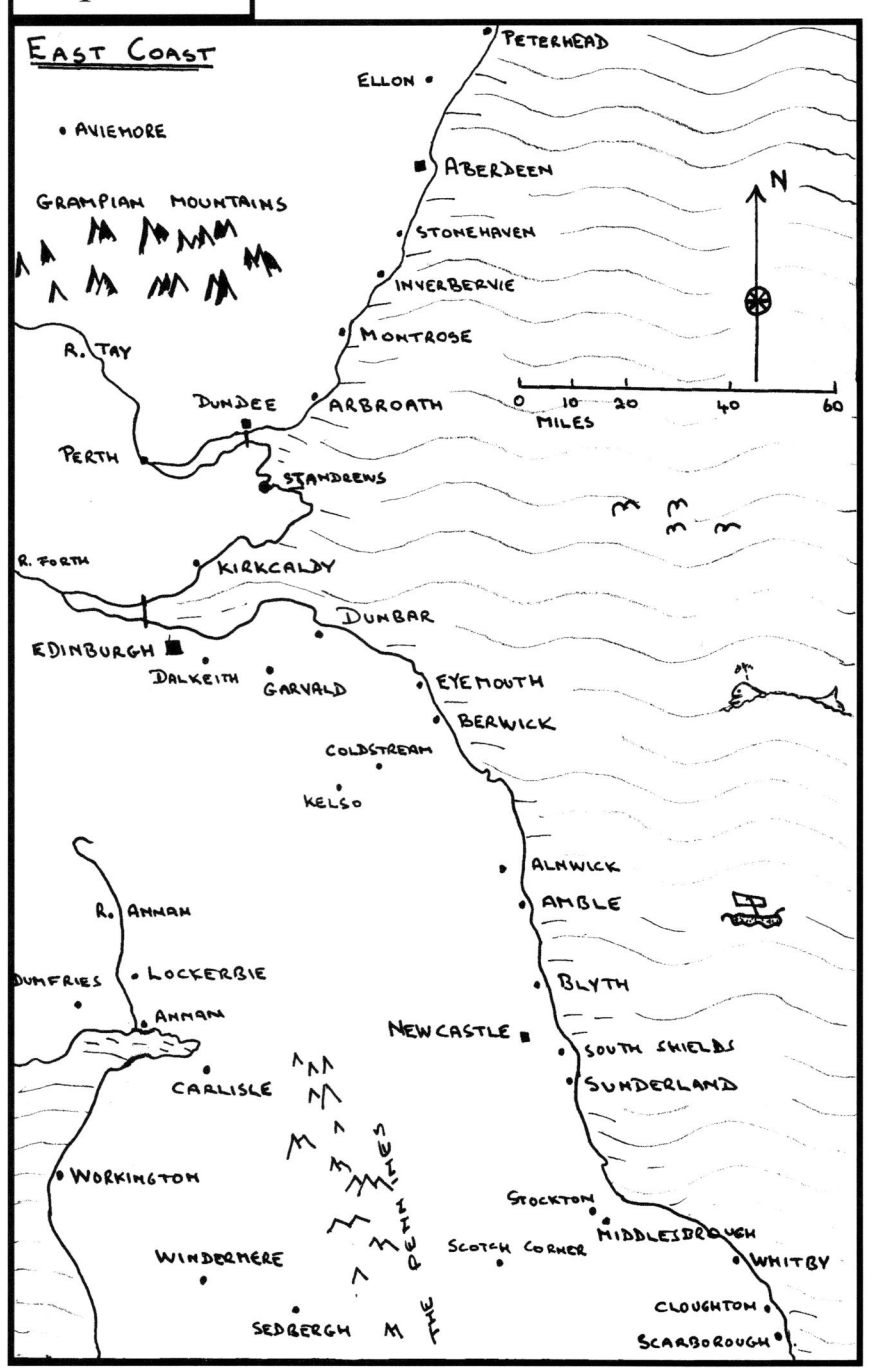

suddenly found myself on the footpath of an old rail track. Within minutes a shape appeared, barely perceptible in the darkness. The shape became a man on his bicycle with his black mongrel dog. On asking about barns, the man, without a flicker of apparent hesitation, suggested a stay in his caravan. He said 'You go up this track four miles, under a bridge, up a bank, over a fence, up a hill through some gorse and there it will be'. I said 'Thanks', my aching legs said 'Ouch' and we parted, me to the black north and he on his unlit way south. Just as I got to the bridge, he appeared again on his bike and still with his dog - Spike. 'I thought I'd better show you the way.' He was right as the caravan was well hidden. He got me installed, apologised for the chaos, the lack of lights and gas etc and then departed again. I managed some supper with the aid of the stub of a candle and made my bed, the clouds cleared and the bright sharp Plough filled the window view. As I drifted off, Phil Taylor unexpectedly arrived back, this time in his Land Rover, with hot stew, potatoes, candles, hot tea and gas. This rugged ex-steel erector was a real diamond and as he departed he said I could stay as long as necessary.
17 m

Day 81
Saturday
In the morning I was greeted by a dramatic view that was unimaginable the previous night. The North Yorkshire National Park lay beneath my feet and spread out across valleys and trees to the sea. The invitation to stay was almost too strong to resist. But on this damp and grey November day I left the caravan and its basic comforts behind, descended to the railway track of yesterday and continued heading north. I soon met up with a lady exercising her dog and as we ambled along, we talked of nothing in particular, just Saturday morning talk. At the next bridge she met her relations and after giving me a donation they left to do more 'weekend' things while I, myself, pursued the cinder path to Raven scar, which used to be a stop on the old line. The station had gone as had the shops, leaving behind a deserted square with the lonely Foxcliffe tea rooms, and even those were closed. More picturesque is the thought that the name of the place derives from the marauding Danes and their flaunted Standard bearing the Raven.

The Cleveland Way now left the mundane and clung more closely to the sea on its way, past itsy bitsy farms each with its quota of black faced horned sheep, to the wonderful, dark little town at Robins Hood Bay. A steep road led out on the other side and nearing the top a local chef, Mr Hudson, tried to enlist my support of the re-enactment of the rescue of the Visitor. The memorial stood close by:-

On the 18th January 1881 the Brig 'VISITER' [misspelt] ran ashore in Robin Hood Bay. No local boat could be launched on account of the violence of the storm, so the Whitby Life Boat was brought overland....... a distance of six miles, through snow drifts seven feet deep, on a road rising to 500 ft, with 200 men clearing the way ahead and with 18 horses heaving on two lines, whilst men worked uphill towards them from the bay. The life boat was launched 2 hrs after leaving Whitby and on the second attempt; the crew of the Visitor were saved.

So that future generations may remember the courage and dogged determination of the people of West Hawker and Whitby and Robin Hood Bay this memorial was erected in 1981

I also noted that St Bees in Cumbria was only 190 miles away on the Wainwright Coast to Coast path - a tempting short cut!

The way followed the old railway again and then the road to Whitby which was amusingly twinned with Whitby-Ontario, Anchorage and the Falkland Islands. There was a heaving crowd of tourists around the attractive harbour settlement and we all jostled for pavement space. While I watched the massive harbour gulls, a man told me he was about to embark on a marathon session of all the Gilbert and Sullivan pieces. It was to be at some other place in Yorkshire and I liked to think he was at that moment drawing his strength from the sea.

Tea was had in a water front cafe, which was being run by foreign students who were diplomatically struggling with the local accents and idioms. It overlooked the mediaeval heart of this fishing town and the fine ancient ruins of the abbey poised above. The Capt. Cook Museum also looked worthy of a visit had it been open.

Into a stiff breeze I left along the winding coastal path and towards evening was buzzed by a hovering helicopter practising cliff top rescues. As darkness began, I asked for barn space at Kettle Ness. Alas, stock took precedence over wayfarers and in the dark evening twilight I climbed down a steep bank and gully to the beach at Runswick Bay, the path continuing below the cliffs, and as high tide was due I was lucky to squeeze by. Two fishermen told me the next bit of path would be covered by the sea and the muddy cliff would be difficult to unravel in the dark so I was forced to stop and camp beside an old beach hut and its boat.

24m

Day 82
Sunday
After a bad night battling the sloping grassy ground and avoiding the intermittent rain, I was glad to be on my early way across the slippery twisty path to the village of Runswick. There was a steep road climb out of the village before the CW path continued again. Lots of walkers were out today. The first group was a cub pack being given the story of the old alum workings, which were connected to leather tanning using a recipe stolen from the Pope!, while the second was the gaggle of a large all female party.

Port Mulgrove hardly deserved the title. But at Staithes I had free coffee and breakfast at the Black Lion Inn, thanks to the publican Richard and a resident walker John Simpson who took my photo and actually sent me a copy! Unfortunately I missed the grocer's shop where (Captain) James Cook had his first work experience.

The path now began to rise and fall as it neared Boulby and its deep Cleveland salt mines. On the steep road away out of the village, I asked at a local house if they charged for the view, it was so stunning. The quiet B road climbed and climbed past scruffy little farms, several of which had flocks of magnificent peacocks. In bedraggled Skinning Grove a house full of kids gave me orange juice instead of water and I climbed out, past old mine workings, to the much used salt rail line. At the top there was an iron wheel sculpture and one seat. I sat down for lunch with three other walkers who, when we parted, insisted on giving me a mixed assortment of survival food and £10 for StC. I continued with Percy Marshall, the elder and unrelated member of the group until he branched off a mile later. It was wonderful walking up here, at 600ft - the highest cliffs on the English east coast. The path passed the site of an old Roman signal tower and then ran on to the modest Victorian town of Saltburn. The Cleveland way ended here but a straight walk across beach sands took me to bawdy Redcar. After eight dreary miles, past the giant steel works and other factories, I reached Middlesborough in the dark, the police sending me to the Wellington Street doss house. But this was a 'no go' for genuine vagrants. Back at the police station a kind police lady found me a bed in Stockton. Alas her directions sent me down a busy major road and it was only by some God-given navigational sense that I climbed down a bank to an under-road, enquired in a pub and then located the Bridge Street Hostel. They made me very welcome when I arrived at 9.30, very tired after a really good days walk. It was all bustle as they were about to have a meeting, but after a bath I was well fed and finally slept soundly in a bed.
26m

Interlude Five
Day 83
Monday 9th November

Did I look like a tramp? Whatever, the hostel staff gave me trousers and a thick shirt, a Littlewoods special, which lasted me the rest of my journey. After breakfast, I said goodbye to Derryck, Hazel and Peter and all my new found friends, who had introduced me into the world of the homeless, its jargon, its habits, its misfits, its benefits, its starkness and its carers. Was this experience a turning point towards which I seemed to have been spiralling in some unconscious haphazard way? What new ideas would evolve from it?

A dull cool morning saw me walking along the river banks of the Tees, past a selection of bridges to the Girder Bridge. After a diversion into the middle of Middlesborough I made my way to the Lift Bridge and talked to the maintenance crew, who conjured up some tea for me. The bridge, closed for necessary repairs, is kept open mainly for tourists; otherwise it is uneconomic as there are now too many other routes available and the port traffic has seriously declined.

Having established the impossibility of using this bridge in the near future and deciding it was time to retrieve my mobile base to keep a date in Sewerby, I retreated. Firstly by bussing to Redcar, having to pay £1.40 for the privilege which aggrieved me, especially as this town had not improved since Sunday. My valuation of the area decreased even further as I traipsed through towards Maske while trying to thumb a lift but without success. Reluctantly I caught another bus to windswept Lingdale up on the moors; and from there had to walk to the busy A171.

After fifteen minutes of heavy thumbing on the main road, despair started to creep in. I took off my hat, put on my lucky balaclava and was almost instantly rewarded when a Jack of all Trades, out with his wife and child, took me to Whitby. He explained that the brown pines I had seen locally were deciduous Japanese larch and not trees suffering from acid rain. Then a life saver, who was full of his plans for a hitch- hiking tour around Malaysia and Australia, took me to Scarborough. Hey Ho for the hitchhiker's association! Unfortunately it was now nearly dark and I had to part with another £2.50 to ride the bus to Bridlington. It was only a short walk back to the supermarket with the car still there, unticketed and moreover it actually started.

Out at Sewerby, I found the Methodist church hall with its distinctive blue neon cross and waited for my 7.15 appointment: to play Scrabble. The club made me really welcome. I made a small speech about my trip, won three games, had some food and was given a £20 cheque for StC. It was an enjoyable, interesting and intellectual interlude. It was also my last game for many months.

A deserted car park two miles north of Scarborough was my selected spot for the night. After an hour, the police, almost predictably, arrived, inquired about my intentions, spotted my non-tax status, but were otherwise helpful and friendly.

Days 84 - 88
An idea came to me and I drove to Cloughton where, after some hesitation, I parked in Phil's field. His presence was ascertained from a sighting of his old working bike and occasional hammering sounds but it was a while before he was tracked down in the bottom corner of the field, repairing fences. I soon became involved in this maintenance work which continued for a couple of days. It was necessary fencing prior to letting the grazing out to another fellow, a farm hand, with some sheep and also prior to Phil's departure on a cycle tour of New Zealand.

In fact I stayed for five nights, with a little light walking, some work, some cooking and eating, patience, reading and simple relaxation, enjoying the wonderful view. I was extremely grateful for the generosity which allowed me to establish the caravan as a base camp. On Friday I walked down to Hay Burn Wyke, National Trust land, past waterfalls and into the isolated stony bay. It was good enough but would be fabulous on a warm sunny day. On the clamber back up along excellent woodland paths I unwittingly dropped my gloves and had to go back half a mile to retrieve them from the trail. Saturday was a day of showers but I walked to Cloughton for supplies. They didn't have candles so, on the off chance, on the way back, I called in at Moor Lodge, which used to be part of the Estate of the Duchy of Lancaster. The residents, two old ladies were intrigued by my tale, bowed to my scrounging and gave me a handful of ancient candles. Phil also brought me some more food and a battery for the radio. So I ate well and had entertainment in my solitary eyrie.

Sixth Stage
Middlesborough to Dundee
Day 89
Sunday
With the car left in the field I set off for the north. It was damp, it was wet and it was raining, as Phil picked me up and set me down in Cloughton and left me with a vague invitation to lunch at Haigh Road and even vaguer directions: an invitation in case my attempted escape failed! Rainbows were throwing insults at my perfidy as I hitched to Whitby, where I was taken by a Sheffield man. After a short lift to Staithes, a man who had just bought his wife a crystal ball in Whitby took me all the way to the Middlesborough Girder Bridge, which

was perfect, apart from the weather.

Into the gloom of midday I set off for Port Clarence and the lift bridge and from there headed for Hartlepool - my objective for the day. It was all road walking. Luckily the weather did gradually improve and this mellowed the dreary scenery which was a flat plain landscape of yellow and brown grassy marshes, pocked with water pools, spiked with the necks of dragons: Shell's elevated pipes, valves and storage tanks standing unnaturally on the plain. They belched white spurts of Sunday steam....lazy sleepy breaths..... waiting for the week's work to start, for the cyclic tumbling production of goods for the urban sprawls which lay on the horizon, crouched and ready for succour. Nearby a landfill project rattled its presence and machines pounded down on the industrial artefacts and digested waste. A melange of smelly human junk, of fridges, cars and beds and jostled with the latest waste in rivulets of decay. A dreary pulp of cardboard and wind tossed plastic bags. But then a water space appeared. 'Brine Moor Pool'... reserved for the conservation and wild life and was remarkably inhabited by a respectable collection of water fowl. A token reminder of the past glories of the flocks which once filled these marshes, and once made this empty quarter wild and beautiful, with their cries and calls they brought natural magic here, and the birds lived well with only the occasional shot from a needy wildfowler or maybe the odd rustic country sporting gent. Beauty is often gone before we know it's there and now the bird numbers have been reduced simply by the pressures of modern urban communities which sprawl and spread their lusty demands for power, goods and materials.

At Seaton Carew I was back by the sea, but the roads continued. Not surprisingly, Hartlepool was reached in the dark and when I asked the police about accommodation they sent me on an unsuccessful chase around town. In addition the Methodists barred tramps and late comers from their services. So full of gloom I headed north, expecting an all night walk. Three miles out of the town I spotted a caravan, just off the road, in a field, and on trying the handle found it unlocked. It was one of those lucky coincidences that I should even bother to try the door. It was a bit of a wreck, but there were cushions on the seats, it was practically dry and with hot water for supper, cigarettes and my sleeping bag, I had an excellent night.
13m

Day 90
Monday 16th November
Emerging from my night's lodging, opposite a real caravan site, I found that fortune had really favoured me, as the morning was heavy with frost whilst all the walk-ways were icy and dangerous. More road led past a selection of viaducts to Blackhall Rock where a Chinaman's humour declared:-

'Blackhall Wok........Take Away'

In dreary but bustling Easington, there is still a working colliery with real workers and on diving into the nearest steamy cafe was given free tea and cigarettes - a pit stop welcome. While at Ryehope I sat opposite the old 'Rent Office' (1826-1873), an attractive grade II building, now used as a library, and thought what tales that building might tell of this industrial area, of the wealth and destitution of times gone by. Then via cliff tops, ports, mud, limestone and fishermen I arrived in Sunderland in daylight and sought shelter at the Salvation Army which gave me one free night in their clean, clinical and well run hostel. On a walkabout of the town, the Girder bridge had an epithet:-

'Nil Desparandum   Auspiles Deox'

Which I thought well written: as it had been rebuilt three times...1786, 1857 and 1927 and was also suited to my changing circumstances.

In the hostel, after my first bath in eight days, sleep somehow came reluctantly.
17m

Day 91
Tuesday
At nine o'clock I said goodbye to Les, the gatekeeper and set off, not looking forward to the walk to Newcastle and the possible industrial sprawl ahead. But with the sun on my back, cliffs of lime and sandstone stiff below autumnal oaky woods I was back in my element again. At Marsden, old lime kilns were dominant - a reminder of past industry, while at Souter the striped lighthouse stood tall - a reminder of my coastal route. The River Wear Walk led me to South Shields, 'Catherine Cookson Country'. The ferry took me to North Shields across the bustling Tyne, full of busy ships, cargoes, river scenes and smells. On the other side the 302 bus to Newcastle was waiting for me!

After visits to the police station, library information centre, bank etc, I went up the hill and found wonderful lodgings at the Cyrenian Project in the hidden Elliot House. It was 5.15 and Christine greeted me like a long lost soul. There was just one bed available!
10m

Day 92
Wednesday
Newcastle is packed full of sight seeing ideas. In the centre, a column to Charles Grey who introduced important Parliamentary reforms in 1832.The

castle started by William the Conqueror's eldest son and improved by Henry II(1168-78) and then partly rebuilt with some ornate stone work after a devastating explosion of turpentine in 1854.The Philosophical Institute associated with a demonstration of miners lamp in December 1815. The museum of Discovery with Mr Parson's record breaking boat (The Turbinia) and also highlighting the achievements of Swan and those of the Stevensons - George and Robert. But I was back in the hostel that night before the 12.00 curfew fell.

On Bentine Street
Out of the black
Newcastle grime
A door, a face
Georgian windows lit
A crowd locked in time

Day 93
Thursday
When I left Elliot House at 7.45, instead of my usual weekly fund of £5, two Giros had come through and I had £92 in my pocket, giving me a little more freedom and certainly more choice. I marched buoyantly downhill towards the middle of the city which lay shrouded in mist. A spire of a church thrust out through the veil and was caught by the early morning light as the sun rose through its cloud blanket into the clear blue sky above. A good start to the day and I was soon on the bus back to North Shields.

The smells of unloaded fish invaded my nostrils as I walked east, away from the ferry along the north bank of the Tyne, passing a grand statue to Cuthbert Collingwood (1826 - 1908). He was a Doctor who trained at Guy's and lectured in Botany at the Royal Infirmary in Liverpool. He was also the naturalist on the Rifleman and the Serpent in expeditions to China. Later he lived in Ladywell, Lewisham (my birth place) and was obviously a man of many talents. At Pen Bal Crag lies the Monastery of Tyne. This had been sacked by the Danes in 800, rebuilt in 1095 and used by three kings: Oswen Osred, Malcolm III and King Edward. It is an old strategic spot and from here the scenic coast turns north. Small attractive coves appeared, each bound by small rocky bluffs, filled with sand and cloaked by the Victorian homes of the Tyne's wealthy and successful. Notable was Longsands and Cullercoats where stands the intact remains of the Dove Marine Laboratory of 1908, the year Collingwood died. At St Mary's Island I stopped for a snack and a smoke. A classical white lighthouse has sat on this rocky island since its building in 1896-8 and at this point of coast the upper carboniferous begins its prominence as can clearly be seen further on. There are good exposures of folded strata, which would be ideal for school trips. The path became road as I passed Hartley and Seaton Sluice

Bridge. On the way into Blyth a group of police horses were being groomed after exercise and one policeman voiced his encouragement to me. Entering Blyth I passed a long line of wind powered generators and wondered how much they contributed to the grid. Soon, missing the possibilities of a ferry to the delights of Cambois power station, I crossed the river bridge for the road walk to the Seatons and Newbiggin, as night time came all too quickly. After the giant Lynemouth colliery, humming in the dark, I wound towards the shore and nearby found an encampment of gypsies who allowed me to make a bed amongst a pile of hay bales in a field. I soon fell asleep, only to be awakened and rehoused in a caravan where I was given some tea and soup. It was colder than the bales but certainly more comfortable.
20 m

Day 94
Friday
There was a lovely winter sunrise after a cold night. A minor road took me north past numerous outcrops of sea coal, which the locals glean into sacks and use as cheap fuel for their fires. Walking past unimposing Cresswell, it's Pond and around the broad sweep of Druridge Bay I came to Hauxley Nature Reserve with its well hidden hides, one of which made a useful stop. Then came humble Hauxley with its island lighthouse and smudgy Amble which had managed to retain some redeeming features while out at sea stood Coquet Island. I had a belated breakfast and phoned my mother and son Patrick before leaving just after three o'clock. That evening, upriver (The Coquet) I found a crossing and walked over the local darkened golf course, near Birling, to find the remnants of an abandoned and deserted holiday site. All that was left was some unlocked weekend sheds, each with its assortment of useful weekend things, which were too small for me - horizontally. However there was reasonable shelter in the clean, dry and abandoned toilet block and some discarded pallets to make a possible excellent bed in the 'convenient space' available.
14m

Day 95
Saturday
It wasn't that good a night or bed and I was away by 7.15. There was a mapped footpath across to wicked (according to John Wesley) Alnmouth. But I chickened out from wading the water and circled the estuary to the bridge, before getting back to the sleepy village. It was a dull but dry day as I passed more golf courses followed by a rusting rambling mixture of caravans and holiday huts on a site set higgledy piggledy amongst brown bracken and grassy hillocks. The coastal walking was excellent here and at Boulmer; looking south the painter's picture sprang to life: a host of worm diggers were busy on the shore beset with boats and fishing nets. At Craster I gained a free break-

fast in a cafe which had only been established for four years, though I didn't get a sniff of the town's famous kippers.

There was a good crowd of ramblers out today, but I found a less frequented route past the splendid remains of Dunstanburg Castle. This was started by the Earl of Lancaster in 1313, improved by Gaunt and destroyed by the Yorkists. It is now a wonderful attraction for weekend tourists. After this, there were more golf courses and even better examples of warped rock strata by the beach together with a respectable bird hide at Newton pond. Evening fell and it was then a long hard walk through Beadnell, Seahouses, Bamburgh (where I missed the castle and the epic of Grace Darling), Warren Mill, Easington and along the busy A1 to Beal and Holy Island. Before going out to the Island I stopped in the A1 West Mains Inn for a drink to slacken my thirst and then, in the dark, crossed the causeway on a falling tide, arriving at the abbey soon after nine o'clock to find that the monks had left 700 years before. The high hopes raised in Newcastle were suddenly dashed. I reverted to wandering the village streets, looking for comfort, and eventually found a kind lady in a retreat house who gave me food and water, before stumbling around to find a sheltered spot inside the abbey ruins, breaking a leg falling over walls and stones in the dark being a distinct possibility. Supper was by the light of a candle in a niche in the wall and then after my longest day's walk so far an excellent night's sleep took me into the land of dreams.
37m

A convenient use of a telephone box in Port Henderson: Day 279

- Chapter 2 -
An Early Winter Attack on Scotland

Day 96
Sunday
Holy Island is a delightful spot to visit. I walked down to the inhabited castle and then around the abbey ruins, which had, last night, almost been my downfall. Originally started in the 7th Century by St Aiden, it was then in Benedictine hands at the turn of the 1st millennium. But the mead took over and they went elsewhere, leaving the place to decay.

A van took me back to the A1 and the main road took me to Haggeton camp site. A mile beyond that I found a path across fields and the railway to the coast and Philadelphia with its lime kilns and the coast guard. Just before Berwick there was jumble of large logs on the beach and a man was busy getting free winter fuel. He was a physics teacher who had strong opinions about education, chain-saws and the coal outcrops which stopped here. Three bridges lead to Berwick. The oldest and most picturesque is a curious long non-symmetrical stone structure with indented parapets for counter-flow movement and dates back to the early 17th century - when they must have had cart congestion problems even then. There are salmon in the river and salmonaries on the banks. The much expected Salvation Army was found but it was non-residential and the police were no help either. At WH Smiths I cheekily exchange my used OS map for a new one and then bought stores of bread, beans, sugar and tobacco, before leaving for the A1 parallel to the sea. It started to rain and for the first time I put on my water proof trousers, those which Barry had given me on that farm between Hull and Spurn Head.

I crossed into Scotland at 3.00.

At Burnmouth a scrambling cliff coastline walk eventually lead me to Eyemouth which at 4.30 was already dark. I was exhausted, but enquiries in a water-side cafe led me to an excellent B&B run by Mrs McGovan. She cooked my beans and I had a very lazy evening in front of the TV. It was my very first bed and breakfast and indulgence was the order of the day since, notably, there were blisters on my blisters!
19m

Day 97
Monday 23rd November
After a very enjoyable and welcome breakfast I was away by 8.30. In the town there was a statue to Seaman Willy Sears concerning yet another sea disaster -

presumably the Great East Coast Fishing Disaster of 1881 when 189 souls were lost. But the shops had no useful maps. An attractive undulating path took me along this stunning coastline to St Abbs which has a life boat and a small PO where I got a signature and recorded that it's a new life in Scotland!! The sun was bright, lighting up the red sandstone cliffs; the sea was calm and lapped the dark Coldingham sands of this popular holiday area. I missed out the head and arrived in Coldingham village at 6.30!? This was a sad reflection on modern times. Although I was carrying my grandson's MacDonald's £1 watch - which kept going accurately for six months! - I don't usually carry a watch, believing that there is frequently an outside clock not too far away which will give me the hour. But alas nowadays a large number of public clocks are defunct or wrong. A litany recounted on several occasions. We should outlaw all incorrect outdoor time pieces and all inaccurate signs. The sign posts for closed 'I's and B&Bs ought to be covered up or a rider added: - 'temporarily closed'. The nearby 13th century priory had also been largely demolished by Cromwell in 1648!

On the map I saw the measured mile nearby and wondered how it was measured? And for what purpose? A poor track took me past waterfalls and Fast Castle, used by Margaret of England, 14, on her way to marry James IV, while huge flocks of geese grazed and flew aloft. After a short spell on the A1107 I unexpectedly found the LDP, the Southern Upland Way, crossing the road, pursued it to the coast and on the way passed a maintenance man busily strimming the path and whose signature I secured. After East Barns Quarry the road led to Dunbar which was the 19th century birth place of John Muir, the celebrated conservationist and was where Edward I beat the Scots in 1295 and Edward II fled from Bannockburn in 1314. The castle withstood a 6 week siege in 1339, was used by Mary Queen of Scots and her husbands in the 1560's before Cromwell tossed it into the sea in 1650 to improve the Harbour.

It was dark again and my visit to the police station produced only general directions for my intended destination. So through the evening, I walked to Garvald and finally down a wind blown avenue of tall dark trees to the stark outline of Nunraw Abbey. In the pitch night blackness of 9.30 I knocked on the darkened door of the unlit building. Footsteps were heard from the echoing uncarpeted hallway, bolts were shot and a light burst out. A visitor on retreat greeted me with surprised tones and took me around the corner to the rest room, a gloomy, faintly damp place, equipped to shelter weary wandering travellers like me - a very welcome stop - with myself as the only occupant. I had deliberately left the coast to get here - solely on a good tip-off in Newcastle - but it had been another long day.
32m

Day 98
Tuesday

A basic breakfast was served at 9.00 in the wood panelled Abbey foyer, presided over by Father Raymond. Restored from yesterday's trek, I went for a stroll through the rambling, poorly maintained grounds. It was a walk into the past through woods of gnarled oaks, lofty hornbeams and tall limes which edged up to the newer pine plantings of Douglas firs. My imagination saw monks with black cloaks shuffling through the trees along the paths beside the dark ravine with its strong gurgling brook, each figure on its way to prayers, vespers or work. Some knelt beside a tiny shrine in the bowls of an ancient oak, tending the saintly relics, bringing respite to dead souls and hope to wandering spirits. Others tended an old multi-nested dovecote and under the flapping of white wings, fetched a bird for the stew or barrowed dung away to the fields.

Beyond the woods I passed through a gate onto hilly pastures across to a farm yard with its assorted barns and pungent silos, the aroma of silage lay thick and sweet, a clawing tang ripening for the winter cattle. The on-going re-enactment of the age-old rituals of birth, feeding, fattening, selling and killing in the production of beef and lamb for the market. New machinery jostled with stocks of fodder, discarded waste, old broken rakes, rusty ploughs, tired tractors with corroded cutters and hay rakes. The relics of past use and management stretched out along the track away from the yard and lurked between the tall bare trees. Rusted and waiting for burial, they lay wasting and rotting alongside discarded carved sandstone masonry blocks, rejected in the final construction of the abbey. The track continued curving gently past the high dark line of trees and ran silently back to abbey, a tranquil quiet spot dedicated to meditation and harmony with nature, standing aloof from the discarded implements and debris lying beside the track. It stood quietly only a mile away from the busy noisy world of normal modern commerce and hectic living.

The adjacent book shop was open and in the hands of a resident monk in his flowing white habit. A store of religious texts, pictures and morals, far removed from the realities of the bustling world, graced the shelves. A quaintness hung suspended in time as two old ladies enquired about coming events.

In the afternoon I wandered back up the paths on the far side of the farm to the monastery, a fairly new building, only 40 years old, but retaining an air of timelessness, nestling in extended woodland and sited on a slight hill, graced with magnificent views of rolling farmlands into the far western distances. Inside was a simple church with rich wooden floors, pews and walls awaiting the warming rituals of prayers which began at 4.00 am each morning. Outside, the grounds were laid out for further contemplation in which a memorial garden had been added in simple taste to commemorate the work of six monks, associated with this monastery, who were killed in the Atlas mountains of Morocco, laying down the truth of religious sacrifice and martyrdom.

Day 99
Wednesday
A simple breakfast and I was on my way again, along hedge-lined rural lanes, heading for Edinburgh and at eleven was resting on a seat in the middle of neat Gifford, a purpose built 18th century village, watching the slow motion actions of rustic life, punctuated only occasionally by the intrusion of modern motoring movements. Then at the town of East Salton a wall plaque mentions this area's roots back to the 12th century. Lunch was at a peaceful spot overlooking the river at Winton House, an old Manor (1620), just off the road, and along my first track for the day. Afterwards I went through woodland and meadows that were filled with sheep and grassy water pools swollen by the recent rain. This led to the Pencaitland walk along the cycle track laid on an old railway which used to take the coal away from the, now long abandoned, 19th century pits. All that remains are named concrete slabs by each pit along the way and the black scars on the landscape, memories of the toils of black-faced men who had worked and survived in that stark reality and who had dug the coal to feed the industry which itself fed the might of the Empire.

My long drag that day took me past Dalkeith, the Palace and the park, and into Edinburgh, naturally, arriving in the dark. As I passed the University, active with students, one girl directed me to the Salvation Army. But, once again, it was not a hostel and I had to walk down to the more central parts of the city where the Greyfriars hostel near the Cowgate redirected me to the city's night shelter. As this didn't open until ten , I sat, nearby, on a cold granite seat for a smoke. A couple on the next bench were resting after shopping and took pity on my worn frame giving me packets of crisps together with my first basic tips on street survival in the Scottish Capital. The first item on the dosser's agenda was the 9.15 soup kitchen at the Waverley Bridge, where I met a youth full of rings in his pierced ears, nose and tongue. What other parts were adorned I daren't think about. He was sleeping out, a doorway traveller who used skips and doorways and I saw him several times again as an ad hoc advisor on tips for low cost living. It was not freezing, but cold enough to drive me to the warmth of the carpeted night shelter. Some twenty souls stayed there on the floor, drinking tea, talking, smoking, eating inexpensive meals or seeking advice from the night time helpers.
25m

Day 100
Thursday
After breakfast at the Convent, one of the spread of free eating places catering for the homeless of Scottish cities, I wandered around the main town, getting

my bearings.

Day 101
Friday
Very early in the morning I walked the seven miles out of town to the Forth Road Bridge. The lack of traffic made it bearable and this is probably the best time for leaving a town, when most people are asleep. On the long walk across the bridge, over the still calm waters below, just as the dawn was breaking, I had an excellent view of the much photographed rail bridge (1883-90) which bore a bright red sign saying 400 (....days left...to the millennium). On the far side I sat on the steps under the bridge for a smoke before wandering off by the river bank to the town of Inverkeithing where in a cafe, for a tea break, realisation dawned: I had mislaid my tobacco tin, my father's old Navy Cut - cum - nail tin. Leaving my bag at the cafe, I walked back to the bridge by the short cut along the main road. Luckily the tin was still where it had been left and the walk back to the cafe was more light footed - a little faster. Reunited with my pack I worked my way to Dalgerty Bay and the ruins of Braggers Church (1244) and at, Aberdour, sat watching the picturesque view of Edinburgh, cloaked in sunny southern clouds and a chain of hills while in the middle ground stood the strong features of the lighthouse and Abbey Island.

Leaving that harbour haven, I was now on the Fife Coastal Path (FCP). But within a mile it petered out at a rock face. Luckily the tide was out and I was able to clamber over the rocky headland to the car park beyond. The footpath which continued was marked in red 'CLOSED', but trusting to luck and intuition I followed it anyway. There was only a short stretch which was actively being repaired, by a small gang with their mechanical digger, and that was quite passable, before carrying on beside the Aluminium Works with its long lines of big bags containing white bauxite powder awaiting electrolysis, and into the appropriately named town of Burntisland.

A road led to Kinghorn and a slippery track to spread out Kirkcaldy. Here I found a £20 note lying in the street, an event which had an interesting follow-up a week later. But I had no luck with accommodation, despite police insistence that the Kings Hotel catered for NFAs* and at a supermarket a young Big Issue seller told me a similar story. Kirkcaldy closed against me as the local priest sent me packing with hot water and a few meat sandwiches. On tired blistered feet, I slowly crept out of the town, found a big park with its possibilities of a hidey hole and finally settled for a spot in the woods on the far side. After piling fallen leaves together for a warmer softer bed, I clambered into my sleeping bag, ate supper and had a really good nights sleep despite some rain during the night.
30m

Day 102
Saturday
It was a still, calm but damp day and my feet were a little better after the hell of yesterday, details which seem so important in a nomadic life, as I left Kirkcaldy on the main road, to Coaltown of Wemyss and East Wemyss before taking a path to Buckhaven, where I had breakfast in my third try cafe.

A sign on the other side of Leven proclaimed my entry to the:-

'East Neuk of Fife'

The Fife Coastal Path led to Lower Largo, the Crusoe Hotel and a statue:-

> In memory of Alexander Selkirk, mariner, the original Robinson Crusoe, who lived on the Island of Juan Fernandez in complete solitude for four years and four months, he died in 1723 as a Lieutenant of HMS Weymouth aged 47 years.
>
> (Erected by David Gilies, net manufacturer, on the site of the cottage where Selkirk was born)

The path drew ahead in a straight line, a state I thought would continue. But actually it veered off into sand dunes, to thread past WW2 shelters and defences, after which, it was easier to walk on the beach around Largo Bay. At the end of the beach, thinking of making it around the next headland, a stream intervened and I had to remove my boots and socks for the first time to wade across the icy water - my feet had needed the wash anyway. On the other side lay an unexpected caravan site, protected by a shield of strong conifers, and a weekend crowd of walkers. A surveyor was doing a Saturday shift with his theodolite, taking bearings and distances on a ship in the Forth. It was a good excuse for him to enjoy the views as well as me. Then the path snaked around the headland to Earlsferry, which is bigger than it looks on the map. At Elie the last house with lights beckoned as a welcome water hole and they also gave me bread and mince pies while telling me that the locals were hostile, a reference to the large local estates. But at a farm a mile further on I found a barn and was given a meat and chip tea.
17m

Day 103
Sunday
It was a good morning as I continued on the FCP. A seashell path took me to Pittenweem and past another of the ubiquitous golf courses to the quaint Anstruther Bridge, built in 1730 and rebuilt in 1795, and there were good sea

views eastward to the Isle of May which is a nature reserve. The path took me to Crail, Fife Ness, more golf courses and Cambo Farm where I sought water at a cottage. It was deserted but the owner suddenly arrived, worried that I might be an intruder. He was a youngish lad with a penchant for living in upheaval and from the chaos he conjured up tea and sandwiches as we had a chat about the world and the problems with the spread of golf blotting out the coast. On leaving he told me of his mate Chris Robinson, on the other side of the next town, and encouraged me to look him up.

After a path to Boarhills, I took the road, in the glorious prolonged winter sunset, to St Andrews. And as the last bit of daylight faded away a three quarter gibbous moon hung bewitchingly in the sky.

St Andrews is a solid university town, worth visiting, which even on a late Sunday afternoon had many shops open. The police were helpful and drew me a map for the Hungry Horse and Chris Robinson's hideaway on Kincaple Farm, some four miles along the main A91.When I arrived Chris was out, but Colin the farmer directed me to a loft he said would do for shelter. It was dirty and dusty as I stumbled around with a stuttering candle, despairing at the thought of sleeping on the hard dirty boards. Exploring my dismal refuge I found a door at the far end and, expecting more dust, tentatively opened it. Lo and behold a rainbow at the far end shouted a welcome. There were carpets on the floor, settees, electricity and a kettle. I had fallen into heaven and the farm children's Jesus project.

I left a succinct note at Chris' house, collected water, returned for a hot supper and a soft comfortable cushioned sleep on the floor after surveying the wall 'graffiti':-

> What the children of God want from this project
> prayer
> fun
> laughter
> growth
> tolerance
> sweets
> music
> God
> shakers
> improved worship
> light
> something to do on Friday nights ....Alex
> prayers
> love

> warmth in the shed
> peace in nations
> joy
> team effort

What, I wondered, is little pragmatic Alex like now, some seven years on?
24m

Day 104
Monday 30th November
After leaving the heavenly loft, my route by road went past RAF Leuchars. At St Michael's Inn the landlord gave me free coffee and biscuits before I took to the back roads. A few miles on, from a building site of a new hotel, joking construction workers suggested tea in their bothy, but on entering the foreman threw me out.

At Tayport I rested on a seat overlooking the harbour, with the view illuminated by a bright emerging rainbow. The path continued by the Firth, but gradually petered out on a rocky shoreline littered with the detritus of sewage waste and marine flotsam. I picked my way through the rocks, pebbles and garbage, while dreaming of diamond necklaces washed up on the beach. But alas no sparkling gems were found.

From the shore, a climb up through a field led to the approaches of the Tay Bridge which was closed to foot traffic due to road works and I was forced to take the free mini bus across. Dundee lay to the north, while to the west was a view of the old Tay railway bridge well known for its train disaster and hence promulgating a popular poster of a fallen train with the pithy epithet - 'Oh Shit'. Buried in my thoughts, a commuter traveller chatted to me on the bus and I lost my attention, my hat and my gloves.

Early in the afternoon, it was still daylight, I found the police station, gaining directions to the town's Sally and ambled there through the confusing curving Dundee streets, past the central high school, alive with busy bubbling children, a happy educational endeavour within the town community, so different to the standard English comprehensive stuck out on the edge of town. Accommodation was secured for two nights with the hostel dinner at 4.30 and in the evening a visit to the library, some TV viewing and a bed between clean sheets.
12m

Interlude Six

Day 105
Tuesday

After breakfast, I tried to see a doctor about my feet, but the earliest appointment was on Thursday. Even more annoying was the non-existence of a Midland Bank. All the others wanted to whack on a hefty charge for cashing a cheque. A phone call to my Branch decided my fate and the necessity of returning to Edinburgh to arrange a bank card for easier banking in the rest of Scotland.

Lunch was at the hostel and in the afternoon I looked for my missing gloves, used the phone and made enquiries about boot repairs. After dinner I chatted to other residents and finally wasted time in front of the television before sleep came after midnight.

Day 106
Wednesday

Away at 9.15, I happily recovered my gloves and balaclava at the Bridge offices and then caught the bus back across the Tay. The only other passenger was a male nurse returning after night duty.

It was a fine day with developing clouds as I hitched south but an hour passed before getting my first lift with a driver who had been a teacher in Ramotswa at the same time in '93 when I had also gone to Botswana to dispense facts about agricultural science in a Junior Community school. Short lifts and a little walking followed before a white four wheel drive vehicle suddenly stopped. Two lads, Michael and Robert, had just bought it to trade on - ostensibly. Very soon we were in Kirkcaldy and back in the street where I had found that £20 note some five days earlier. I was ushered into a terraced house by the back door and met uncle Tel, who had to be dragged out of his bed at one in the afternoon! After everybody was seated the pantomime started and the house rituals began. White powder was poured into a spoon, ammonia added, the mixture stirred, resin produced, twirled and extracted bit by bit before being mixed with cigarette ash for smoking in little pipes. This was their way of getting smacked up. Everything remained normal apart from the peculiar hiccups in speech and movement. A conversation continued, tea was made and food was produced. Other gang members came and went. Telephones rang and calls were made. Disjointed menaces threaded the wires and offers exchanged. The talk was of cash and holidays to pay for violence. There was talk of a job for the following Thursday and the vehicles needed - note the date!! A bizarre three hour insight into another world. What other revelations were coming? Finally Jason was summoned and told that I was Michael's uncle, needing urgent transportation. We were soon in a high speed truck to Edinburgh, where we arriving at the bank with five minutes to spare. It was a good night and later I retreated to the night shelter in the Cowgate for a few hours sleep.

Day 107 & 108
Thursday & Friday
The Ark and St Catherine's Convent provided breakfasts. Most of the day flashed past as I ordered a Bank card and arranged its dispatch to Aberdeen. For £10, a back packer's hostel allowed me to sleep until midday on Friday when I lashed out on proper OS maps, a real luxury after using 3m/inch road maps and library maps for so long.

The 4.30 bus to Dundee was another luxury and certainly worth the £6. The traffic was awful as we crawled out of Edinburgh very slowly. Graham sat next to me. He was a daily commuter from Perth, who worked in the tourist board as a trouble shooter, enjoyed hill walking and the chat certainly decreased the 'journey- time'.

Seventh Stage
Dundee to Aberdeen
Day 109
Saturday
My escape from Dundee started in the early hours, into a black night and two inches of snow on the ground. It was not particularly cold. Both the air and the sea were still and the traffic was zero. The only movement came from a few insomniacs and dog walkers. One elderly gent, in thick Scottish brogue, told me he was up at four every morning because that was when he used to tend the farm horses! I walked most of the morning by road, avoiding the danger area of Buddon Ness, firstly to Carnoustie, famous for hosting golf tournaments which I would hear about much later. Then back roads went to East Haven continuing past the old aerodrome to the A92. This was busy with traffic and the heavy lorries dragged along large buffeting pockets of air while I struggled along in the slow lane of the uneven grass verges. In Arbroath, at 10.30, I had breakfast at Scotties. The waitress took pity on me, gave me an almost free meal and told me of the town's fame in salmon fishing and 'Smokies'. Out of town, on the promenade, the kids were busy tobogganing down the slopes in bright sunshine and from here a cliff side path meandered to East Seaton Nature Reserve before rambling to Auchmithie. It was empty rolling countryside with red sandstone forming its seaside edge and the solitude only broken by a lone American walker going the other way.

The tracks continued, with wonderful views of snowy hills, to New Mills and a difficult path led to Lunan. From there I went back to the roads to find the bridge into Montrose, just as the light faded, and trawled the town for a B&B. But on Saturday night they were either closed, full or too expensive. Exhausted

I found myself in the Star Inn and asked about beds. 'All full' I was told at the bar. A cheer went up - a response to the notice on my back, which I had carried all those miles. Wow! Walking round Britain. Drinks were bought, thirsts quenched and questions asked and answered. I had stumbled into the the local's drinking headquarters. To the forefront came Derek, the local poet, full of booze and knowledge gleaned from his wayfaring and seafaring lives. Partial normality was restored on the appearance of his American wife, Liz. Then wonder of wonders they took me to their place across the road, where, after a hot bath, I was fed and given a bed for a solid ten hours sleep.
34m

Day 110
Sunday
A cooked breakfast, as promised, then Derek and Liz escorted me to the old rail track which would lead me north. They indicated points of interest: the statue of Robert Burns and other buildings. Wallace had sacked the town which had been later rebuilt under Dutch influence and the main street had been widened by combining two thoroughfares into one. This dinky historic town is certainly worth another visit. A good start to the day: still sunny weather and a good marching path. But gradually the rail-track path deteriorated which meant jumping over wire fences to enter forbidden woodlands and overgrown banks to make the road for the river Esk bridge, built in 1770 by public subscription. On the other side I lost the path and scrambled up to the A92 until able to descend across fields to a snow and ice bound road for St Cyrus Nature Reserve. The path twisted along beside the old railway, between small sand dunes and beneath cliffs enlarging menacingly above me. I escaped via an old donkey track to the top of the cliffs and then continued to Milton Ness. After some road I assayed a short cut to Milton of Mathers, which took me through a ravine, a stiff muddy climb out and past ramshackle farms. Directions for the coastal path were obtained and a sign indicated a B&B accommodation but on arrival the hostess was packing for their trip to the USA and they were therefore closed. These false signs should be covered up!

The path continued by the sea. At Johnshaven I considered that £17 was too much for B&B and then also turned down the little pig shelters lying in darkened fields further on: the sows were too active. At the busy Harbour Bar near Gourden, Scottish hospitality prevailed. My sponsor was a high speed car freak, and two hours later, light with whisky and Guinness and in a happy state, I walked a further mile through the cold dark night, seeking the Anchorage in Inverbrevie, missed it and found myself having tea with two oil workers cum trouble shooters. They gave me directions to the B&B which for a mere £15 gave a welcome night's rest.
15m

Day 111
Monday 7th December
After an 8.00am breakfast the day's walking started with a splendid twisty cliff path, but as it hovered on the edge I had to climb higher and there found the whisper of a faint grassy farm track which took me to Grange. Some of these tracks had disappeared under the plough. and on the red stony soil of these rolling fields, sleepy stockade farms stood waiting for winter, looking silently towards hibernation, as they thought of the first new shoots of spring to burst through the browns, greens and whites of their fields. Meanwhile two frisky farm dogs kept up the appearance of life. Thus I climbed the rural coast to Stonehaven, the birth place of R W Thompson of pneumatic tyre fame, and of the vast industrial repercussions of that invention. I had passed Catterline without seeing much and bypassed Dunnottar Castle, an excellent looking ruin which had lured one lone Australian from Melbourne for a visit on the local bus. The fields were guarded by electric fences, rows of black silage bags lined farm tracks, and a memorial stood on a hilltop as I dropped down to Stonehaven for tea in a sedate little coffee shop. Outside it was dull but warmer with the snow melting but it was a long hard walk into Aberdeen, mostly along the busy A92. At one stage, on some minor roads, I had to seek directions in the dark, and so knocked at the door of a house to ask for a light to read my map, only to be taken in, given a meal and afterwards offered a lift to Aberdeen. They were farmers and he was largely restricted to a wheel chair after the over-use of 'safe' OP sheep dips had got to his nervous system. They also told me that the escape route of the previous Thursday's £2m heist had come down these lanes and this conjured up more speculation in my mind about my Kirkaldy encounter. Eventually I set off again in the dark to the busy city to spend the night on the floor in the Oasis, night-stop for drop-outs, under the arches of Theatre Street near the docks.
26m

Interlude Seven
Days 112 - 119
Big burly Steve, warden, revived all the recumbent bodies with tea. Life returned with the first puffs on cigarettes and tobacco tabs. Everybody was cleared out by eight and the door beneath the arches closed until evening.

My first visit of the day was to the Cyrenian Day Centre in Summer Street. A kindly lass called Claire talked to me about the NFA situation in Aberdeen and the other facilities offered by the centre. After midday I was led to the Convent and, together with another dozen misfits, had a healthy lunch stew in the draughty converted garages. Replete again, I walked to the other side of town and found accommodation at Victoria House. This is a tough, rough, no frills, 28 day stop hostel. It caters for those coming out of prison, for recover-

Map 3

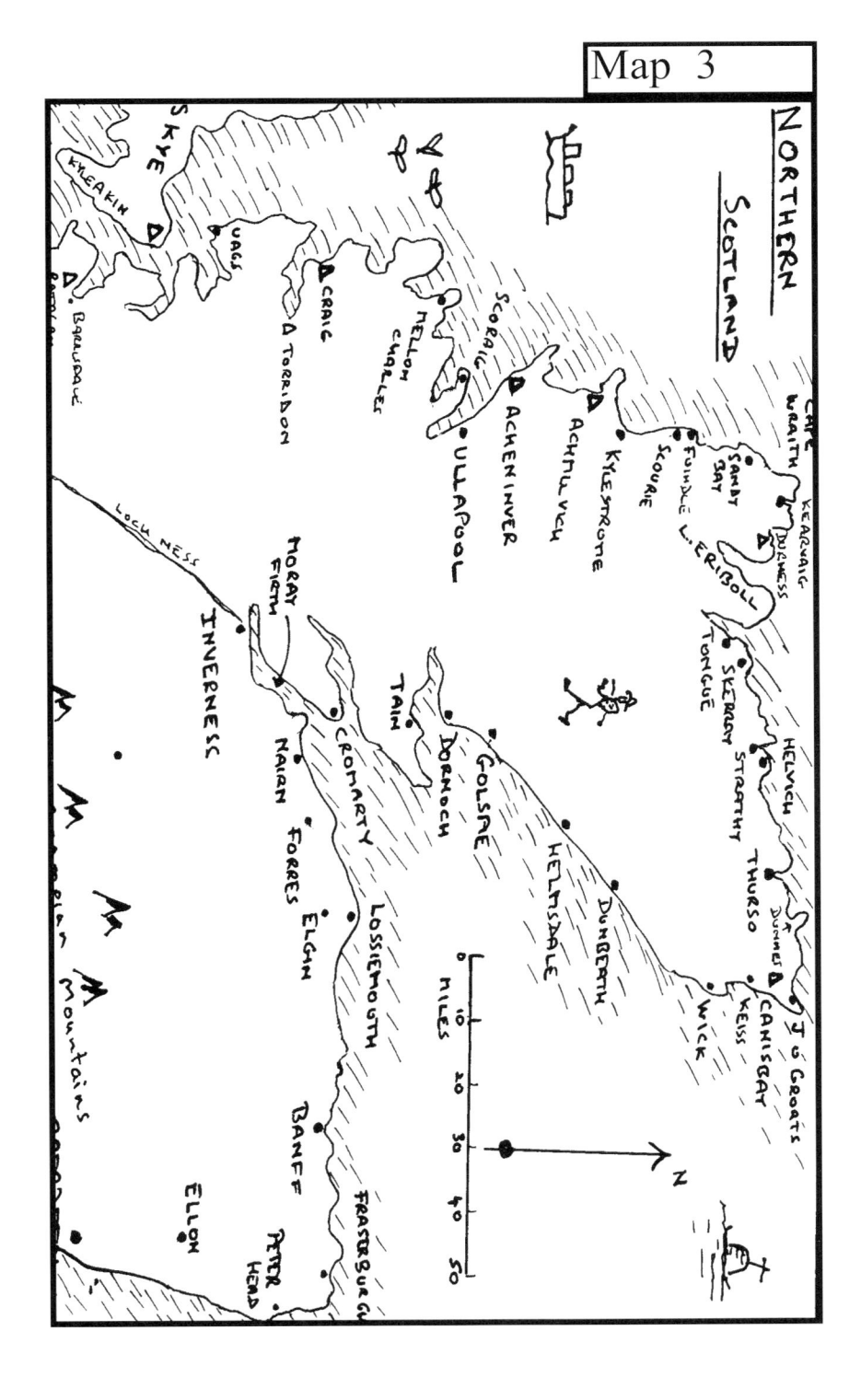

ing drug addicts and for wayfarers. My room was shared with Eammon, an Irishman married to an East European, a drinker, always short of money and forever forgetting what he had told me. He was a nice enough fellow, who just needed that extra edge to get control of his life. The food was excellent with three meals a day and an endless supply of tea or coffee in the snooker room, where an almost endless boisterous game continued until eleven in the evening.

Short of money again, Eammon instructed me in the art of tab making and sent me gathering spent butts from the rich pickings in the streets of this moderately attractive town with its large solid granite buildings but which always seemed a little drab and dark, especially I suppose in December. What a difference to when I had been here on interview ten years before.

The days passed as I picked up my very first brand new Bank Card, but had to wait for my pin number which had, rather stupidly been sent to Bromley, and hence prolonging my stay in Aberdeen.

Another visit to the Day Centre produced rapid assistance at the local medical centre, where a newly qualified chiropodist sliced, prodded, medicated and successfully sorted out my feet. She gave me a whole raft of bandages and sprays which had their best effect just by keeping them in my pack!

Eighth Stage
Aberdeen to Inverness
Day 120
Wednesday

The hour of 9.30 found me walking out of town but it was road walking again, firstly along the A92 and then the quieter B999, deliberately striking inland on the advice of Aberdeen's 'I'. On the way a dead badger lay beside the roadside verge - it was only my third time to see such an animal. At White Cairns (hence a dormitory so named at Wellington College!) I had a refreshing glass of water in a bar where the publican did not like my sitting on his steps before I set off even further inland along the B979, and near Newmachar found what I was looking for - the old railway track which had been turned into a good path - the Buchanan Walkway. This point on the line was infamous for its snow drifts: in 1960 the line was blocked for 2 days. The rail link itself finally closed in 1979 due to the proliferation of road traffic; in the tourist brochure it is called the old R&M line and for me made a pleasant walk for the rest of the day. Past Udny Station and onto Ellon where the converted toilets read:-

U R IN AL'S   Hairdressers

Soon the sun was setting and the prospect of sleeping in the now derelict rail huts was not appealing. At Gallow Hill I climbed out of the cutting and up to a farm, hoping to use a barn, but was told the only animals there were the cows painted on the walls and they were not theirs anyway - I was at another farmstead taken over by city commuters. However despondency was quickly dispelled by generosity and I was offered tea and soup. When the lady of the house returned an hour later she heard my tale and offered a bed without hesitation. Thanks to Phil and Christine Coplane I had wonderful night in civilised company, a bath, food and comfort. Their two boys Danny and Michael were rather puzzled by me and perhaps thought Father Christmas had arrived early. Phil was a civil servant scientist working in a fish laboratory on the sonic mapping of fish stocks and a common thread of technology provided an easy conduit for conversation. Similarly Chris was involved in school classroom work and of course with her two boys. They had a new word for me......an 'orra'...someone who does the dirty jobs around the house or farm. In my arriving state...it was very appropriate.
21m

Day 121
Thursday
Today the wind was behind me and the sun was shining, the sky was blue and the clouds were few - a contrast to yesterday. I continued along the railway line past green fields, where sheep grazed on well managed grass in scattered little farms, the scene enhanced by a bonny brae beside the path and patches of Douglas firs. Along the way there were more railwaymen's huts of wood or concrete and their condition improved northward. At Maud I stopped on the old station platform where workmen were busy pruning but ready to stop for a chat. An old sailor joined in and, from his house, brought coffee for the restoration of our morning spirits.

From here there were some difficulties with the path but otherwise it was easy walking to Strichen, where I took the road to New Aberdour, a clean town but lacking charm and with no B&Bs. Two miles later Towie Farm appeared in the gloom. Although the farmer was busy, he lent me a torch and sent me down the hill to an empty house which had seen better days and with the lamp and candles I made a bed amongst the broken glass littering the floor. Later Andy collected me and took me back to the farm to meet his wife Francis and to share a very enjoyable and welcome meal. They told me of a round Britain walker who last year had passed this way, hauling his supplies in a wheeled cart. But he was apparently in poor health, sweating badly on the uphill bits and may have given up.
24m

Day 122
Friday
Quitting my cottage I was given a quick breakfast and left the farm at 8.30, with the slow rising sun. After Pennan and Macduff came the typical Scottish coastal town of Banff where I met Ronnie selling the Big Issue. He was making a living out of it too, regularly driving to his pitches in Peterhead and Fraserburgh etc and chatting up his regular customers. Sadly, I had missed that corner of Scotland out, my excuse a lack of decent maps and the use of the railway path. Out of Banff, heading west along the A98, I found an another old railway converted to footpath, which did not last long before heading to Whitehills through Auds, where I had a sharp reminder that Christmas was close as a local man, on foot, delivered his seasonal greeting cards. Soon I turned left onto the B9139 and headed for Portsoy. On towards Cullen I passed some small farms and barns and at one isolated farm house, asked for a night's shelter, but it no longer belonged to a farm. A Sussex lass lived there all alone with her two boys. She gave me tea, mars bars and cigarettes and then directed me to Seafield Estates up the road where the foreman-manager in the huge farmhouse redirected me further along the road to Dydack. This was reached down a lane, in the dark of course. An elderly couple lived there and required a mite of persuasion to allow me to shelter in their wood store, filled with logs all chopped and sawn by the lady of the house. Later they had a touch of softness and provided sandwiches and a thermos of coffee. Though they worried about my comfort, the sawdust floor was soft enough for me.
23m

Day 123
Saturday
Coffee warmed me for the day's work and I was out of the woodshed just after eight, though it was still not properly light, and back on the A98 heading for Cullen, Portknockie and Findochty. At Connage Farm near Buckie I asked for hot water and was given a snack of milk and biscuits. On passing through Whiteash Hill Wood I stopped briefly at a Tyrolean styled house, which was empty and abandoned but locked, presumably for the winter lay up and soon afterwards came to Fochabers before crossing the River Spey.

It was a weary road all day to Elgin, arriving just after four. Three miles before the town I cadged free tea at a roadside snack bar from a young girl assistant who was taking pity on tramps especially as a blizzard of a snowstorm had just started, making me don my infrequently used leggings. Happily, a footpath appeared beside the road to provide safer walking and the white out lasted only for a short time. In Elgin, the police told me about the night shelter which opened at ten and I began a five hour wait at the railway station. After an hour I was joined by Michael, a fellow traveller who was well under the influence of the whisky bottle. He told me about his sojourn at an Abbey some six miles distant (probably Pluscarden at Barnhill), where he had slept in a cow shed shelter and had been awakened at dawn by a line of guns shooting grouse. It didn't sound attractive enough to walk the distance.

   In due course we set off for the night stop and on the way sought sustenance at MacDonalds, where we wasted a couple of hours, while entertained by the consumerism of the Big Mac eaters and the flood of children primed by big TV adverts. Across the main road, we prowled the industrial estate along its Perimeter Road, searching for our goal. At a pulsing night club we asked directions but instead were quickly ejected. However like moths to a candle we were drawn to the centre of this estate - a room in an extinct business site lying within the vortex of this drab industrial area. Joe took us in, to a warm dry cavern with mattresses on the floor and the obligatory TV. He provided tea and soup so that warmth could return. More travellers arrived, some of whom I had seen much earlier, drinking in a wayside bus shelter. For me, sleep that night came deep and strong.
27m

Day 124
Sunday
Ejection time was at 7.45. We all tramped off, in the damp early morning mist, towards the middle of town and I headed out to Lossiemouth and its airfield. An RAF contingent from here was bombing Iraq, but apparently they stopped the next day and on passing the airfield the internal activity was curiously muted. I was at last near the coast again and headed along the coastal road to Hopeman arriving at the Baptist church soon after eleven. Unfortunately the children's service had started much earlier, though I did catch the end of their nativity play. It was a real happy old fashioned family service and, moreover, afterwards there was tea, mince pies and shortbread in the vestry at the rear. I met and talked to a variety of people and then, soon after noon, went on my way, towards Burghead, loaded with a stash of mince pies and a carton of milk.

   Passing through Cummingstown there were wonderful views of the Moray Firth and snow covered hills stretching to the north whilst the flat pine forests of Charlestown reached towards Kinloss and past the dominant local distillery. It is all RAF at Kinloss and very boring. I hurried on towards Torres in the gathering gloom and then the main road towards Nairn. Soon after crossing the River Findhorn I took a minor road north and then gradually circled round to a farm, Mudhall, near Kintessack. Some chat produced a vast empty barn with some old sofa cushions to provide adequate comfort for fourteen hours sleep.
26m

Day 125
Monday 21st December
In the morning the farmer took pity on me and provided coffee and toast. He told me about the bad economics of farming and in particular of the perils of arable potatoes, lettuce etc, the fickleness of the supermarkets and how the system had its downs and occasional ups as affected by the weather, market forces and foreign imports. At Dyke I walked and talked with an elderly lady exercising her elderly spaniel, before taking the main road to Nairn. A little further on there was half an hour of snow, so at Petty I rested in the grounds of the locked Church of Scotland, which sat isolated beside the main road, and was amused by the ambiguous sign: 'Visitors Welcome'. In the graveyard a monument to Thomas Campbell, born in Newfoundland (1922) and died in Inverness (1992) was an indication of the scattering of Scottish clans. It was then eight miles to Inverness along the busy tarmac. Half way, on the left, a sign pointed to the Culloden battle ground, a poignant reminder of the history hereabouts, where Bonnie Charles, full of Gaulish bravado and wine lost to a better disciplined and provisioned Hanovarian army under Cumberland. Further on, I had my first view of the bridge across the Firth, the sprawling town and the background of hills.

Night time had come when I asked for provisions in the out-of-town Tescos, but on this occasion was unlucky as the manager had already given away a thousand pounds to charity. Into the town, past the signs extolling the use of 'park and ride' but without any visible buses, I sought the Salvation Army, found the temple and then headed for the hostel. On the way I was 'spotted' in Huntley Street and re-directed to the newly opened night shelter in Barmain Street, close to the Grey Street suspension footbridge.

The shelter was adequate for camping on the floor and had the the further benefits of food, TV and companionship. It was staffed by Dave and Heather, and a stream of volunteers including Isobel, Margaret, Tania and Helen, all of whom tended to the needs of the local homeless. In fact we were waited on hand and foot as insurance precluded our involvement in any operation. Thus it was a time for relaxation, the easing of tired limbs and the dispelling of exhaustion. I hadn't been there long when lo and behold Michael, of Elgin, arrived and we greeted like lost friends. Another interesting 'inmate' was Dutchman, Bertus Noot, who was 'touring' Britain and living by survival, poaching salmon, lifting vegetables and using a large knife for rabbits. He said we'd meet again in 2000.
25m

Interlude Nine
Days 126 & 127
I scanned the town, bought maps, visited the PO and collected mail, visited the DHSS for the correction of an out of date winter fuel payment, visited the library, posted cards, went to the bank with my brand new pin number and made phone calls. At four o'clock the night shelter life started again. More NFAs arrived and found space for survival. Swampy, a tall lanky potential guitarist, Steven, Willy, a Big Issue salesman with a drink problem, George, Scratcher, Howard of London, inseparable Herpes & Clap and a rich collection of others, sleepers, eaters and wanderers. At midnight we all claimed floor space and, like sardines in a tin, caught some sleep.

Tenth Stage
Inverness to Cromarty
Day 128
Thursday
The date seemed insignificant as I left at 9.30 for the Longman roundabout to cross the A9 bridge. Once over the Firth I hit some pleasant paths close to the sea with excellent views back to Inverness and at the deserted hamlet of Kilmuir found a seashore telephone to call Patrick and inform him of my location and intentions. Next my way wound along uncertain paths through mixed fir woodland and grazing lands to muddy Munlochy Bay and the nearby village. The main road took me east until I could make my way on some minor ones into Avoch, but then a trudge along the A832, by the sea, to Fortrose and Rosemarkie. From here there was a climb up through the Fairy Glen and onto the very quiet minor high road, past the radio mast at Craighead and over to Newton and Cromarty, the last few miles being in the dark. I found the town's lone policeman at his station and he directed me to the main town bar where a Mr Mcphee plied me with Christmas Eve drinks and we reminisced about shared African experiences. There was no B&B at that inn, but arrangements were made and I was driven a short distance into the village to meet Hugh McDonald who, by good fortune, took pity on me and fed me as we relaxed over bottles of wine in front of the wavering flames of his log fire. He told me of his troubles with wives, one a crazy white woman and one an asylum seeking 'black bitch', about his seven children and of his connections with law. We were waiting for a son (who didn't arrive until four in the morning by taxi from Inverness). Hugh went to bed while I mused by the hot embers until midnight and then went aloft for a deep sleep. It had been a wonderful ending to a tiring day.
24m

Interlude Ten
The Grand Retreat
Day 129
Friday: Christmas Day
When I arrived at Cromarty I had found that the ferry was closed until May and there were no other boats. The general consensus was that it would be impossible to cross the water in the holiday period. My impetus to move north had been blunted and reluctantly I decided to beat a retreat to Yorkshire for the New Year.

I said goodbye to the MacDonalds on a damp soggy morning and explored the lofty statue to the town's giant, Hugh Miller (1802 - 56), writer and geologist. In the 19th century he was considered one of the finest geological writers. His 'The Old Red Sandstone' (1841) had included fish fossils of the Devonian Period found in Cromarty. He reckoned that the perfection and intricacies of these 400m year old fossils disproved evolution. Beneath the statue was a dirty and despoiled room which might have to suffice for a future shelter and musing on that, I tried to hitch. Stuck on the horns of a dilemma, either to go west to Canonbridge or south to Inverness, I tried in both directions, letting the random throw of fate decide the destination and finally after a three hour vigil in the rain, got my first lift. It was going south and two ladies took me to Rosemarkie. Soon I was in Fortrose from where a small van, full of chickens, took me to Tore. The loose hens were on transportation as a Christmas gift to a daughter and the van was a veritable junk yard of a rambling rustic. It contained all the paraphernalia of a hundred ideas associated with the driver's country pursuit of making a living - a worse collection of crap, garbage and 'useful things' than I could have accumulated in a year of car sloth. He had a preoccupation with mushroom picking throughout his favourite spots in the local glens and woodlands but which he could sell at favourable prices to a local agent or direct to London.

I finally arrived back at the Inverness night shelter in mid afternoon and sank into a couple of days of laziness and eating. We had Christmas dinner and were allowed to watch Godfather II on the TV, being glued there until 2.00 in the morning.

Day 130
Saturday: Boxing Day
A walk around the town was my sole exercise, but, in the gloom of evening, I was rewarded by a sight of seals in the river. It was hard to believe - seals in the middle of town. At the night stop we were given presents and mine were useful soap and socks.

Day 131
Sunday
The High Provost gave us an early call as we struggled from sleep on the floor and ate breakfast. What an extraordinarily ordinary chap and he actually seemed to care about drop-outs, NFAs and the homeless.

At 9.30, again (!), I set off for the other side of town to hitch. A red car and a lady driver, doubly unusual, was my first lift. She was a Jill of all trades and loved to travel by land and sea. Her work was merely to pay off the last expedition expenses and prepare for the next. After she dropped me an engineer took me to Elgin and a Tesco man, brimming with ideas, to Fochabers But I was then forced to spend £6 on the bus to Aberdeen.

Day 132
Monday
28th December: Bank Holiday
After a night in the Oasis, I set out for the longish walk to the edge of town and, while waiting hours for my first lift, a man who saw me hitching suggested that I should get an old tachograph disc as a useful aid when lorries passed. But eventually I was given a good long lift to Laurencekirk and dropped at a desolate turn off. Luckily a red Porsche took me to Dundee. The Sally wouldn't take me and they sent me away to Comfort House on Bell Street, which sent me to the night shelter on Contee Street where there was the usual collection of loud drunks and vocal derelicts but it was bed and food for a couple of nights.

Day 133
Tuesday
Some of the day's drifting time was spent at the Wishart House Day Centre which had the usual facilities for the town's drifters and those with a poor man's troubles heaped upon them.

Day 134
Wednesday
Leaving Dundee I had some short lifts, but the main lift of the day came from a young lorry driver in his own car who had a penchant for motor bikes and computers. He dropped me within walking distance of Prince's Street. Edinburgh was buzzing with a huge throng of people and I had to escape to the relative calm of the Day Centre, but as it was closed, had to mess about in shops, including a perusal of better winter sleeping bags, before I could gain entrance to the City's sanctuary for dropouts.

Day 135
Thursday
At 7 o'clock I was waiting on George IV Bridge Street for a 42 bus to the A1. Also waiting was a Canadian groundsman, who worked on a local golf course and we had a long chat about Kentucky blue grass and Poa Annua, Torra mowers, fertilisers and other green keeping matters. We waited for an age, eventually discovering that the real bus stop had been moved and once there had to wait yet again for the real bus to get out of the town centre. At the by pass, adding to my frustration, I had to wait three hours for my first lift - from a 78 year old man who dropped me in the middle of nowhere. He had eleven siblings (7 sisters and 4 brothers), was a recent widower and had just visited Australia with his sister. Then a Jack- the - Lad, dealer took me to Alnwick and gave me a 2 oz. pouch of Golden Virginia and a lighter, part of his stock in trade. An ex-army lorry driver took pity on my lone form and delivered me to the outskirts of Newcastle. Lorry drivers rarely stop these days because of insurance risks, but he said he couldn't leave me there on New Years Eve!

After succumbing to a 98p bus ride into the city centre, I found the police station and the Salvation Army Hostel. The latter had recently had a £2m refit and was extremely clean and well run. It was like a hotel with showers and toilet in every room. I met Tracy and the Major who supervise a tight ship, but with compassion. Tea was at 5.00 in the canteen where I met Bill, Alan, Joe etc, old tykes, archetypical Sally interns. Then after wandering into town with its crowds of revellers I returned for an evening snack, a midnight service and an elevated view of the fireworks spectacular which was a practice for the Millennium celebrations of the following year.

Day 136
Friday: New Years Day
After breakfast the Major did a room check for living and dead bodies and I went for a stroll along the Riverside. This is a town 'improvement' and includes modern iron sculptures depicting past activities, simple river scene murals on new light buff stone town walls, and an obelisk to John Wesley who preached nearby in 1742:-

> Isaiah L.IV
> The Sovereign Lord has taught me what to say, so
> I can strengthen the weary.

Workers, on overtime, were busy dismantling barricades and cleaning up the mess of last night's celebrations, the smashed bottles and webs of expanded party poppers. The nearby impressive All Saints Church of 1786-96 stood tall and somehow set the tone for this Georgian Town!

Day 137
Saturday
Other features of Newcastle include the Cathedral Church of St Nicholas with its wonderful gilt pennants and clock, and nearby Queen Victoria on her throne.

Day 138
Sunday
This passed mostly in a futile attempt to escape town, as people just weren't giving lifts on a Sunday.

Day 139
Monday 4th January
At 4.30 in the morning I walked out of Newcastle to the Angel of Gateshead. This is spectacular, especially close up, and is now an accepted part of the locality after the early controversy. At a bus stop opposite, the remnants of a seat was sufficient for an hours sleep and when the first light came I moved to the main road roundabout and was soon in luck as an O. U. student, on the dole, picked me up and dropped me near Stokesley. A short lift took me to Great Broughton followed by a cattle lorry to Chop Gate Visitors Centre in North Yorkshire Moors National Park where I had tea. Back on the road, the area manager of the park picked me up and took me to Helmsley. After a quickie lift, a garage owner dropped me near Scarborough and I walked a few miles to the Rosette Inn, near Burniston, and began my enquiries into the whereabouts of Phil Taylor's abode. But as I asked, a van took me to Cloughton. The driver knew of Phil and he spotted the farm hand who had sheep on his plot. We gave hilarious chase of the fast moving muck spreader, but finally without any joy on Phil's location. Nevertheless the van driver gave me time at the village shop to buy supplies before dropping me near the plot further on along the road. I strolled across the field to the caravan and was able to relax over supper, by the light from some candles which I had carried many miles and at last had become extremely useful, before succumbing to the sweet embrace of sleep.

Day 140
Tuesday
After a tardy start I hitched into Scalby and started the search for Phil. The clues were few: name, half a road name, 2-3 miles south of Cloughton, a new house near 'Rosedene', a Discovery parked outside. After walking to various possibilities I had a brain wave and consulted the electoral register in the library. There they were: Susan Taylor in one district and Phil in another, but both with the same address. It was not far away but difficult to find in the maze of new housing. When found, only the teenage daughter was in and I had to wait two hours on the streets before their return. Part of this time was spent in

a local shop where I witnessed the drama of an escaping shop lifter - which was the day's main excitement. When the Taylors returned, we had tea and a good chat before Phil took me back to the caravan, deposited me and removed my car battery for recharge.

Day 141
Wednesday
Phil brought out a bottle of malt whisky and the restored battery so that I was able leave the sheep and caravan behind and head for Bradford, this time without petrol worries.

Day 142 - 148
Thursday - Wednesday
In the early hours I parked in Patrick's yard in Crossflatts and slept in the back - a return to normality before spending the next week eating, sleeping, writing up my diary on their computer and effecting necessary repairs to my frame, my equipment and my morale.

Days 149
Thursday
It was a damp cool winter's day when I abandoned the car, setting off for the north again and heading along the canal for Leeds. Past the five rise locks and Bingley, the rain started as a fine drizzle, at slovenly Shipley drizzle became rain drops which gradually turned to a drenching cascade and my thoughts of reaching Leeds, ten miles off, became blurred. At the next possible bridge I crossed to the south side of the canal and headed through the woods for the outskirts of Bradford. Two skittish schoolgirls tried to give me directions for the centre but I was more successful at a YMCA play group, where the leader took pity on my sodden appearance, gave me tea in the porch - protectively away from the children - then described my route into the bowls of the metropolis. In the city, I yoyo-ed between the police station at the bottom, the YMCA at the top of the south side, where I was too old, and the Sally on the north hill, which was full. Wiling away the time in the middle of town, I dried out a little and eventually, opposite the hostel in Leeds Road, found shelter in an old and derelict portakabin. It even had an old and tired mattress on which to sleep as the spurts of wind and rain blew boisterously past the unglazed windows.

Days 150 - 250

It was 8.00 am when I entered the Salvation Army Hostel and was immediately taken to breakfast. Afterwards the Major processed me, forms were filled and the sole vacant room assigned, luck being with me as one resident had just been ejected for not following the house rules. It was after eleven before the room was cleaned and ready and I was able to throw off my pack. This was a new 55 bed hostel and the modern rooms were more than adequate, each was equipped with a bed and plastic covered mattress, a bed side cabinet, a chair and desk, a wardrobe and wash basin - all relatively new. Luxury spread to carpeted floors, electric points and heated radiators. Two meals arrived each day in the canteen - breakfast at eight and tea at half four. A TV lounge on each of the three floors and a day room with pool table downstairs. Luxuriant accommodation for any male, off the street vagrant, for the homeless or those recently out of prison. Indeed it was home for a short while for a great number of people, though there was encouragement to move you on, the objective to gain self respect in your own place. The first floor was for older and less independent individuals who couldn't make it outside through minor mental or physical limitations. Serious addicts tended to be on the top floor while I was lodged on the middle floor amongst a mixed bunch of desperados.

My intention was to stay for a few nights and then continue my journey north towards Cromarty. Unfortunately the few nights turned into a week, which turned into a fortnight. Then a bright idea turned this into a month which became three. The comfort and routine making it more and more difficult to escape.

It cost £20 a week to stay plus housing benefit. Conveniently the DHSS had its offices next door and was the place I next visited for queue waiting, interviews and more form filling. To find funds for the first week I also had to request a crisis loan. This was done at another DHSS office on the other side of town at Manningham Lane, more forms, police checks and ID requirements. All rigmaroles of the NFA situation. By tea time I was ready for it.

My diary stopped on arrival as there did not seem much point to scribbling while in this suspended section of time. It was always tomorrow that I was going to leave by the front door and carry on walking - manana was a strong impulsive influence. I met so many people and heard so many stories that this whole episode could fill its own journal. The life was certainly an eye opener, a leveller and an insight into a world that many on the normal side of life seldom see or know much about.

I began to share my time between the hostel and its inmates, with the day centre in Edmund Street a mile away across the city centre and meanderings within the town itself. This became my world for several weeks and, in that time, I didn't tell anybody outside my whereabouts because of its presumed temporality. In the same token all the other residents were temporary - getting ready to move on.

The day centre, close to the tall and wasted empty edifice of the old tax office (!), was open six days a week, a place to rest for all the homeless and hopeless of Bradford. It was funded by the local council and everything was free with an urn constantly full of tea while free basic lunches, served on paper plates, were provided for nutrition. A surgery doctor came once a week for consultations and to provide connections to the local dentist and other medical facilities around the corner. Advisors for housing, health, drugs, sex and law were available for help at basic and higher levels while a TV catered for a line of worn out dossers slouched in the tired armchairs lining the lounge. A supply of cards was available for a continual rummy game and the occasional cribbage player. Washing facilities were there if you got in the queue early enough and a clothing store opened on Wednesdays. Up stairs there was a workshop open twice a week, which seldom had a client but kept Peter, the crafts teacher, occupied and half employed. Later I used it to make two crib boards and a pool table player marker for the Sally. The adjacent computer room was more popular and generally catered for the IT beginner, being available three days a week, while in Colette's kitchen you could learn cooking skills. A further small room was provided for tea and smokes which was far nicer and calmer than the frenzy downstairs. On Sundays there was a treat and after lunch several games of bingo were called, numbers were shouted out and small useful prizes were won - packets of food, soap and socks being standard rewards. The one thing to remember in this place was to be as poor as everybody else and not to put anything of value down for more than two seconds out of sight. Addictions drove the need for money and spurred the need for theft and prostitution, schemes and scams, for prison and probation.

Nearby, two blocks away and adjacent to the YMCA was the evening soup kitchen - the curry centre. Open at seven, it catered for a similar tribe of hungry people. In my first two weeks I used it frequently to supplement my Sally rations trying to increase my weight which had sunk below ten stone from its long term average of eleven. The staff had to be alert to quell any breakouts of the ever present tensions that the clientele brought with them from their 'on the brink' lives and the continual quest for smidgens of tobacco and the solace of stronger and more addictive drugs.

On Friday nights another voluntary soup kitchen operated behind the town's twin job centres (one small building for the big jobs and one large block for the menial jobs!). More free food and clothes were available and a few free cigarettes. It was apparently run by an ex NFA man who had made it on the other side in a big way and wanted to help those who hadn't or couldn't. It is a typical essential amenity, present as an integral part of big city life for that scion of skulkers that have riddled and squirmed their way for eons through the layers of the more industrious inhabitants.

The centre of Bradford has been cleaned up - the restorations since the war almost complete - what a time it has taken - and on a good day it's a fine place to wander. The City Hall is the focal point, the high eaves splendidly decorated with a whole line of elevated statues depicting British Kings and Queens while below, for the hoi polloi, lies the walk-about plaza lending space to the claustrophobic clustering of bold buildings generated in times of wool and textile wealth. In the middle of this pedestrian area lies a small poignant sculpture commemorating those lost in the football stadium fire while at night a gaggle of youths practice their skate board skills, bringing life to the ghost zone.

Along the Leeds road leading away from the centre, some half a mile away, past bright lit garages, a thriving mosque and the mixed mishmash of shabby shops and burgeoning businesses, lies the Sally. Red bricked, calm, warm and a temporary home. Staffed by cool but competent salvationists and lay workers. The office staffs behind the reception grill hand out keys, mail and warnings, then lock the doors at midnight until six the next morning. Next door is the chapel, with services every morning at ten, where there lies tranquillity and reflection for some, brownie points for a few - but is much more enthusiastic and lively on Sundays. In the hostel a crew of cleaners move in each morning for two hours of hygiene, to remove the mean mess of fifty men in the corridors and lounges, then to wash and iron the sheets once a week. The sullen kitchen staff find civil gestures remote in this menage of low social adequacy. It takes time to find their humorous side and for them to relax that tiny bit, to accept the residents idiosyncrasies and allow a little trading of civility. Perhaps an extra slice of toast or another cup of tea. 'Sorry only two sugars in your tea' a normal admonishment. The rations were strictly counted and a ticket system for meals operated - dark warnings prevailed concerning the loss of your 'meal ticket'. Faces would light up when the occasional free fruit was handed out - oranges, bananas, grapes and apples would quickly disappear. Sometimes late at night a tray of out-of-date sandwiches might be delivered from a local store or garage - and a horde of hungry residents descend like a flock of scavenging vultures awoken by an unheard, unseen signal.

Your room was out of bounds from 9.00 to 11.00 am. But if you over-slept it was best to stay put as room checks were seldom made. After breakfast the pool game began and continued, possibly till midday or might even go on all day. No smoking was allowed here, only out on the porch where a row of addicts crouched, almost oblivious of the fine view of the overworked (!) DHSS offices above. A constant movement of smokers and butts twitched around the doorway to the outside as the Major did his daily rounds ready with an acid remark for those he caught. You can play pool all day if you don't lose. But the probability of a run of over seven games is low. When I lost, I cried 'Aberdeen Rules', replaced the black and got booed off the spot. Other recreation is available in the lounges upstairs, TV being the main entertainment. But that can cause a continual source of argument through the variety of programmes available. There were also jigsaws, crib, chess and books, provided that some junkie hadn't had his fun and thrown the pieces out of the window. The occasional illicit spliff might be smelt with its characteristic rich sickly odour. These are invariably rolled double length from four Rizlas, with hand roll tobacco and a sprinkling of the black liquorice hash. The odd bottle of cider, whisky or can of beer also creeps in to satisfy those with the taste or the thirst. The room was invariably full of cigarette smoke as there are very few non-smokers in a Sally. The familiar cry is for a spare Rizlas, pinch of tobacco or both as they are always in short supply - though cheap price tobacco is usually available - through an enterprising resident. These lounges are not overly busy as several men have their own TVs in and other have more clandestine interests. Some just retreat to the quiet of their room away from the more rowdy elements or moods that can be strongly invasive.

One wing of the building is called the resettlement unit which had just started up again. It had been closed as the attempts to re-educate some addicts had simply led to the loss of all equipment. The two opposed sides of the Sally are not supposed to mix in the building. Although the 'resettlers' do have some privileges in the normal half, their side was taboo for everybody else; to prevent the incursion of drugs and the excursion of belongings and materials. They had to cook for themselves and go to all of the life skill classes. This sudden demand on their time made it difficult to last the 12 week course. Drugs or alcohol were the usual cause for return to square one. But for others there was the opportunity to find the way back into the main stream of modern living. The principal successes were probably those men that may have served time.

Apart from the bricks, the core of the Sally lies in the people. Such a diverse range of individuals, backgrounds, problems, psyches, addictions and needs. A rich tapestry of stories, some true, some lies, some imagined while others are peripheral and selective. On arrival it was a sea of new, unknown and nameless faces. Gradually the names attached themselves to faces and the faces told their story as the thread of personality was woven into the manufactured cloth of that society gathered there at that stage in time. An ever changing material that gains and looses fibres - all inter-acting - sometimes into a patchy ragamuffin fabric, while at other moments a strong group against a commonly perceived tyranny.

On my first arrival the man with the suitcase greeted me as a long lost soul.

Stan was forever leaving for a better hostel and carried his battered case everywhere, into the canteen, the lounge, and the toilet. It was nobody else's business and what was in it, lord knows. He always wore the same old ill fitting clothes on his shrunken frame and the same gaunt expression, having seen it all, as he went along his supposed seafaring way through life. His nearest contact was a veteran pudge from old industrial Yorkshire: Mike had a string of homosexual innuendoes that meant nothing. He loved to have a morning game of pool and would wait, in his chair, for his chance. But being one of the worst players on earth, you had to concentrate really hard to let him win - to restore his morale. Occasionally he might play an equally inept player, maybe George, who was practically unable to speak and the game might take an hour or more. George stared vacantly ahead his only sign of communication a slight twitching of two fingers suggesting the need for a smoke, and never having one, you always obliged. He had a guardian angel, Simon, an ex porter, a quiet drunk, apparently estranged from his alcoholic surgeon wife and always off - to the Nottingham Sally. Nobody believed him but one day he was gone. Gone with another resident who returned with a strange tale of an awful drunken spree. Simon shared much in common with Nigel who loved his whisky but seldom showed apparent evidence of it even after a bottle or more in his veins. An intelligent engineer he could still work out complex designs and calculations for estimation and construction. His forte was farm waste disposal, but his company had dissolved and his wife had ejected him. The thought of de-tox was ever there but the demon kept dragging him back. He might be tempted into the cider drinking circle of the Ethiopian Ali, a maths and engineering student at the local university. Always on the borrow for a pint of 'milk', he finally lost it and was locked up for sexual harassment. Another occasional drunk was Mick. A reasonable fellow when sober, but with two cans in him, he became a loud mouthed psychotic who was constantly wanting to go and see his son in Kirby, where he'd previously worked as a fork lift operator in the smelting works. On the resettlement unit he seemed to be getting it together, putting money aside, but alas something snapped, the booze took its bite and it was not long before he was back among the normal run, back to his mate Martin. This man was an ex-fairground operator from Blackpool who had done time for a PO robbery. I played innumerable games of crib with him and sometimes Mick. He had an amazing facility to beat me but this was evened up by my better skill at chess. Scrabble was far too argumentative, especially if the cannabis was in the air. The spliff ring extended to the duo of Trevor and Keith. The former an ultra thin ex psychiatric nurse and the latter a man of my age who was an electronic and radar wizard, who had gone through businesses, wives, cars, was perfectly stable and reasonable but now preferred to lose his money on girls a third his age. When Mick was expelled from the unit he left, behind him, two ex cons, previously jailed for murder and GBH. But you could tell from their determination that they were going to make it and learn the life skills for rehabilitation. I hope that adversity didn't force them away from their aims. The common currency all around was tobacco and the main supplier was Andy, who made a small profit on some fifty pouches a week. He waddled round on his short legs and extra belly, played pool with a cool even ability and had settled into the hostel for a long stay. The other commodity in demand by a few was for a bag. A bag of H. There must have been about a dozen on methadone trying to kick the habit, slipping back to the occasional use and those who clearly couldn't. The price was ten to twenty pound a day, the source of money - theft. Shop lifting, car theft, borrowing without return, anything that was not fixed down. Jason, Oliver, Alan and Clive were the shoplifters, with their own moral code. Big shops only were their main targets - in their view - these capitalistic enterprises 'could afford it'. They knew they would get caught eventually but the risks were small and the penalties minor and bearable. Desmond and his gang of three were the car breakers. A brick through the window and out came the radio or what ever else lay around. Again the demands were not onerous. Constant schemes were afoot for getting ahead of the game or for not slipping too far behind, crisis loans, housing grants, and clothing allowances, spent wisely or unwisely. The hard struggle to get off the drug. Daniel just not quite making it, waited for a rehab place. An ex dealer sucked in by the street culture about him, who really just needed that extra chance, a job suited to his ability and the thought of seeing his children regularly. A sad but common dream. During my stay he had helped a potential OD case but was not on hand to prevent another death, the constant threat to any user.

I slept, ate, played, talked, watched TV, walked, smoked and joked my way through that mesh of living fibre. At the Day Shelter I made cribbage boards and worked on the computers, had walks and waited as strength returned, winter snowy weather passed and time turned to spring. I'd had an idea, which should have taken 28 days but in the end this took three months. In early March I surfaced, contacted Patrick sorted out the car and it's MOT, while my brother paid for the Tax and Insurance. Legality returned. The idea had reached fruition, partly through a betting scam, and at the end of April, at last I had a positive bank balance and not an overdraft of £1700. It was time to leave. It was spring. The last yawns of hibernation were breathed and the rucksack prepared. All I had to do was to make the return to Cromarty.

Another sad event occurred during this period when my brother-in-law passed away - eventually heart broken over the loss of my sister. The visit down by coach to the funeral had its own personal twist when I overshot my destination in Dorchester and ended up in Weymouth and I had to persuade the driver to drop me in the middle of the night in the middle of nowhere. In the dark I tried to walk to West Knighton, sought help for directions at a house, set off again and was then offered a lift as the owner of the house came out and found me on the road. In the village I had to use more persuasion to obtain the key for the house. Next day it was wonderful to see all the extended family, relations and friends albeit in sad circumstances. The bus trip back was illuminated by meeting authoress Anne McCusker; talk of her 'Masked Eden' and her Papua - New Guinea experiences.

The momentum gathered pace and success finally displaced despondency and it was time for the off, the car packed ready for go.

The Salvation Army

United Kingdom Territory
with the Republic of Ireland

Social Service
Lawley House
371 Leeds Road
Bradford BD3 9NG
Telephone: (01274) 731221
Fax: (01274) 7388399

TO DOUG ALL THE BEST FOR THE FUTURE AND LOOK AFTER YOURSELF All The Best GRAHAM

Tony

GOOD LUCK
[signature]

Duncan Hobson

Good luck mate, Eric S

Get stuffed and stop hustling people
all the best nick

Martin xxx

GOOD LUCK DOUG AND DON'T WEAR OUT THE SHOELEATHER, I'LL CUT YOUR HAIR IN ABOUT SIX MONTHS (I'M GETTING SOME HEDGE TRIMMERS) ALL THE BEST MATE,
JIM

Have A good Life! Best of Luck. Trevor.

good luck Mitts Um Danny K- Rufus Take it Easy APot

Good luck from Ned best wishes

MDS Fisher (Rock Pleye)

GOOD LUCK FOR THE FUTURE Robert Ivor Johnson

It was a pleasure meeting you, thankyou for your friendship, all the best martin.

Good Luck Douglas

Tony [signature]

GOOD LUCK IN YOUR NEW ADVENTURE
BAZ

William Booth *Founder*
Paul A. Rader *General*
John Gowans *Territorial Commander*

A Christian church and a registered charity
—with heart to God and hand to man

- Chapter 3 -
Scotland in the Spring

Day 251
Monday: 26th April
After my last breakfast and game of pool in Bradford's Sally-Ann, all the lads signed me off with suitable pithy farewell epithets and I got away to arrive in Newcastle by mid-afternoon. At the Salvation Army hostel there I met the Major, Alan Austin, as well as other staffers, Les, Jack and Tracy who arranged a bed for two nights. Compared to my home for the last three months, small differences were apparent; here the staff was more professional and more proactive. There were fewer carpets especially on the corridor floors, meal times were earlier and there was smoking in half of the cafeteria. Each room had a toilet, shower, bedside lamp and better bedding. There was no chapel and services took place in the lounge. There was a quieter crowd with fewer young people.

After a quick tour of the town I spent the evening chatting, playing pool and watching TV - getting my comforts in.

Day 252
Tuesday
My first job of the day was at the DHSS (Saxon House), half an hour's walk away. Then after completing housing-benefit forms I returned via a scrap yard, bought a side window for the car and then spent 2 hours fitting it. Back at the Sally I played pool and slept for a couple of hours before dinner and in the evening had a bit of a spin round town before the 11.30 curfew.

Day 253
Wednesday
Soon after breakfast I was driving up the A1 to Morpeth, Weldon Bridge and onto the A697 past the Cheviot Hills with their pines and big eared cheviot sheep. Then on to Wooler, Coldstream and the Lammermuir Hills which is good looking walking country with plenty of monuments. The southern part is 'Law hill country: - Dunlaw, Hogslaw and Criblaw all at 1000 ft and whilst on the other side of the hills lay my Dunraw Abbey of last December. Edinburgh was reached in daylight with its dark bedraggled Gothic structures picked out by the splendid soft spring evening sunshine.

Day 254
Thursday
My departure for Aberdeen was delayed until four and I slept in some fields on the way.

Day 255
Friday
Aberdeen was abandoned in the early hours and again I used the car for sleep in a lay-by on the road to Inverness. In Tescos I spent £20 on supplies including a flask which was to remain with me as a faithful friend for the months ahead and a throw-away camera. Cromarty was reached at four in the afternoon. I spoke to a boatman, made tentative arrangements for crossing the water on the morrow and then waited for Helen to arrive back at her Chicken House home, an amazing depository of art work connected to her outdoor shows concerning the earth, elements, spirits and music. Her favourite efforts had been at Glastonbury as an attraction on the fringes of the festivals there and she was off the next day to do a show about snakes and plants in the forest on the other side of Cromarty Firth. She arrived back late but we had a chatter about her performances and work with her OU geology students and also about my plans. Then I slept, gathering energy for tomorrow's continuation of my walk.

Eleventh Stage
Cromarty to Fort William
Day 256
Saturday
What an excellent day to restart. It was wonderfully sunny with clear blue skies and only a little wind. At seven o'clock I walked down through the fields to catch the working Kathern Barge and with boatman Erwin crossed the Firth to the Nigg Ferry terminal. At long last I had passed that cold watery barrier of Christmas day and I was on my way again. It also looked brighter, to the west snow still hung in the hills but local gorse was out in yellow bunches and my first Scottish deer sprang into view.

After Castlecraig, Nigg and PicalnieI, I cut across to Balintore arriving by the Bar Inn at 10.30 half an hour before opening. This is good farming country and I saw many sheep with lambs and beef being reared in green lush fields. According to a dog walker, Balintore F C was playing its last vital game today against Golspie, some miles up the coast. Now, with the relevant OS maps, I was able to make better ground decisions and my hope was that this state of affairs would continue. From Balintore a path closely followed the coast to Rockfield, past rocks covered with cormorants and the soft sandstone cliffs gave way to very sandy soils inland. At Tarbat Ness, a splendid red and

white lighthouse was framed with bright yellow gorse while in the surrounding grass and forests, primitive patches of yellow primroses were sprouting through. Spring was definitely in the air. Tain was reached late, but just in the light, having rushed past the Morrich More danger area to the north. Fancying a B&B I trekked round them all but without any luck, and in despair ended up at the Police Station where the police also eventually arrived. They tried phoning around with a similar lack of success on a Saturday night. In the end they took me to an abandoned caravan on an industrial site and this made an ideal spot to sleep. Full marks to them - perhaps the chief constable had instilled lateral thinking.
25m

Day 257
Sunday
An early start after a good night. But it was main road again, which luckily, early on Sunday, was not busy, past the Morangie distillery to the long Dornoch Firth Bridge, opened by the Queen in 1991. At 890m it is one of the longest cast and push bridges in Europe. Once over there was a straight narrow B road past weekend houses to Dornoch. This town is graced with a 13th century cathedral outside of which is a prominent shrine to a county lady. In a high street cafe I objected, rather rudely, to the breakfast which didn't include tea and so had a simpler meal instead. A large overweight customer told me about the state of the world and his past life as a dairyman and lighthouse keeper before he drove off to sheltered accommodation in his yellow 3 wheeled Tippi. On leaving I apologised to the waitress for my earlier abrupt behaviour, which had left her upset, and this left me thinking about how my manner had been coarsened by the experiences of the last few months.

   The way out was slow and painful as my feet were blistered and objected to ill treatment. The grassy path and track went through a long established golf course then partially followed the disused railway on its way into Embo, which looked distinctly uninteresting. By-passing this village the train-track path and road continued to the 'Mound' over Loch Fleet. Opposite to Cambusavie Farm lie the remains of an old castle, labelled as a dangerous building and I didn't venture in, so instead I sat on the edge of the loch nearby and a 70 year old son of a railwayman told me of his birth in the house next to the castle, about the busy past of this area and the active part the line played in the war. He mentioned the London - Thurso troop trains, named after some WW1 general, which had priority and were pulled by double unit locos. For him it was sad to see the line now disused and at the lochside its remnants completely disappear, except for the Mound built, in the 19th century, by Telford and which now only carries a road.

   I crept into Golspie on my blistered feet and found a B&B in Fountain road,

which indeed did have a large ornate fountain as a roundabout. In the evening I visited Bruce Field who lived in the same road and who is Scrabble secretary for the area, loves mountains and plays chess. He warned me about the midges in NW Scotland. Back at the B&B I had a bath, especially for my feet, and watched Hendry and Williams play in the World Snooker Championship. The score at bedtime was 10-6. I also wondered how the town's football team had fared against Balintore on Saturday but never did find out.
21m

Day 258
Monday 3rd May
Leaving at 9.30 I visited the Ordovician Stone Company's sales room and exhibition with its fascinating display of local rocks and soon after Golspie found Dunrobin castle with its ice-cream cone topped towers, the former seat of the Duke of Sutherland. Half way to Brora I wasted an hour sitting by and paddling in the sea to ease my feet which had softened during my protracted lay-off. Last night, the bathroom scales indicated that my weight was up to 11 stone again but I felt very tired and weary. The sea remained calm but very cold, whilst the rain of yesterday had given way to occasional sunshine.

On a path by the sea, rounding a corner, I was surprised by the sight of a group of 30 seals on the beach. They were also startled and were quickly off and out to sea. Brora has a prominent monument to Queen Victoria, while the nearby war memorial had additions for the Gulf war. The track continued almost all the way to Kintradwell past a roadside plaque which declared:-

'The last wolf of Sutherland
killed by Polson in 1700'

From here it was road to Helmsdale. On the way I met Paul Wardle, an automotive engineer, one of the few people seen all day. The Youth Hostel here was supposed to open in May but sadly it was still closed so the police sent me uphill to a B&B which was full,however the landlady kindly took me to Mrs Smith in the town where I did get a bed. She was an ex-South African and so we had an interesting chat about our mutual experiences. Later getting fish and chips I met Billy, a Glaswegean cyclist doing the JoG to Lands End run and we exchange notes over a drink in the local. Back at the lodgings TV showed Hendry beat Williams (18-13) and I bathed my feet and body in a hot bath before an early bed.
18m

Day 259
Tuesday
It was a dour, misty day for the long four mile climb along the main road out

of Helmsdale but I was amused by some unusual grey speckled hens ina quarry and a well built by the Duke of Portland beside the road. Woods and moorland abounded while the underlying shale and granite was revealed in roadside exposures. A side road pointed to the deserted 19th century sea side village of Badbea, and a mile further on as it was warming up I found a grassy mound for a couple of hours of dozing.

On the way down the steep hill to Berriedale Bridge there was a prominent soft sand trap for runaway vehicles - there must have been some accidents here in the past! In this delightful little spot there is an impressive war memorial and a PO while the Duke's place is a huge white house set high up in the forests.

Another stiff climb led out, up the main road past, of all things, a llama farm. There were many crofts around and I stopped to chat to one local crofter who, answering a question of mine, said 'the difference is that a crofter names his animals whilst a farmer has price tags affixed'. At the Castle Hill petrol filling station I bought needles for my blisters, signed the bulging travellers log, intended for JoG -Lands End travellers and took a photo of the young lass responsible for this document. A short distance later, a side road (presumably the old main road) led me through a quiet estate, where I saw some outstanding red and white pheasants, and thence to Dunbeath. One mile further on at Tormore I found a B&B, the MacDonalds at Tormore Farm, pin-pointed by the heart shaped shrub on its wall. They let me in even though they were closed because they were busy lambing - 300 Cheviot ewes crossed with Sussex, some having triplets, giving a high lambing percentage. On the far side of the fields puffins sat on the high sea cliffs and rocks which plunged into the sea. On TV the hustings of the Scottish elections,two days away, continued.
17m

Day 260
Wednesday
Two miles from the B&B and just before Latheronwheel village there was a whale bone arch set as a gateway to a field, reminding me of Port Stanley, while in the hedgerows the last of the daffodils hung on. In Latheron I posted maps back to Roger and noted that the fire was still burning in the grate of this small rural post office. After Lybster (twinned with Fort Mackinaw USA), as the sun shone and the wind stiffened, my way continued along the A9 to the prominent chapel of Bruan to rest in a little hollow, soaking up the UV. At Ulbster, it was a scene of rolling sheep and cattle country filled with small crofts, many of which had newly built houses. I tried to get away from the main road here and found a track which petered out near the Mains, necessitating crossing the Hill of Ulbster with its trig point, bomb shelters and excellent views, while on the other side was an old burial ground for lunch in a small comfortable depression, accompanied by the sound of chewing sheep. After

Day 260 War Memorial at Latheronwheel, one of the many, to those that gave their lives in our defence

crossing boggy ground I found the track heading north, which passed many more crofts and the last house at Corbiegoe, where the track quickly deteriorated to a very boggy walk and I was soon sinking, up to my knees, in brown slime. This lasted for at least a mile before a more solid path developed above vertical cliffs crowded with seagulls and puffins. Then a maze of burnt cornfields further confused my navigation but eventually the ruined castle - the Old Man of Wick, appeared and the path became a track leading to Wick.

At the first B&B, the lady said she'd seen me earlier in the day, but was sorry she was not open. She indicated the whereabouts of two more. The first was full but the second, Quayside on Harbour Quay, was open. Brenda was in charge - it was non-smoking and full of rules, but tiredness overcame my opposition. Gratefully dropping my sack I went reluctantly to the bank for money for the bill but on the way back bought a needed pie and chip supper.
20m

Day 261
Thursday
Wick used to be the World's biggest herring port, now it slumbers in the sloth of modern housing estates - a mantle of urbanity - but now the harbour and bay were nearly empty. After Staxigoe I crossed sheep fields to Noss Head, where another path disappeared towards the prominent lighthouse while mine continued to the castles, Sinclair & Girnigoes, residences of the Earls of Caithness, which were silhouetted against the sea. One earl even locked his son in the latter for six years before murdering him. The sun still shone but was tempered by a southerly wind although unfortunately it was track and road for the rest of the day past Westerlock with its big pipeline fabrication unit where three mile sections are built and then pulled out to sea for the oil rigs, and onto Keiss. Here I indulged myself again with a night in a pub B&B, The Sinclair Bay Hotel, just affordable at £17.50
13m

Day 262
Friday
The quiet main road took me past Nybster, Auckengill and Freswick where I turned east for Skirza. Unclassified tracks took me north towards the cryptic Wife and Fast Geos and a view of Stroma appeared as I walked past dramatic stacks of sea lashed rocks. On arriving at Duncasby head and its lighthouse the sun actually came out and I wondered if this was the norm for round the coast walkers. Finally a seaside path took me to the disappointing John o'Groats, a take off point for the Orkneys and the ferry, Queen of Pentland, lay silently at its dock. The hotel was also in 'dock', awaiting planning permission for development, testament to the fact that JoG hasn't yet been overdeveloped. I'd had thoughts of taking off from here and doing the northern

islands, but it would have been an erratic and complicated route involving several more ferries and ending in Scrabster. Doubting my chances of obtaining free passages on all the crossings involved and not being moved to even start asking that question here, I abandoned the idea.

The museum at the Last House in Scotland does have an interesting collection of artefacts and the sad story of the depopulation of Stroma in the fierce Pentland Firth is particularly poignant. After doing the other usual necessary things at this point of the journey I took the A836 to Canisbay and found my first Scottish Youth Hostel (SYH), indeed my first youth hostel for over forty years! I was joined by one other hosteller, Michael, a lad from South Australia - and a chance for a good natter with another itinerant. But alas the local shop was closed and so it was hard rations for the evening meal.
15m

Day 263
Saturday
Trekking along the main road to Mey I passed an isolated maker of chess sets and bought a sheep 'pawn' for Liz's collection. A 'B' road took me to the track past Castle of Mey, the Queen Mother's northerly home - since 1952. All was quiet. At Brough I called into the cafe, Dunnett Head Tearooms, at the request of Bernard Heath, a founder of the MBA whose name was given to me by my brother, and left my bag there for a walk out to Dunnet Head, Britain mainland's most northerly point. On the way I met an interesting sound recordist collecting bird calls, which he sells. At the head, the lighthouse stands high on the 300 ft cliffs, with puffins parading down below. Since the route to the head was marked as the one and only 'in and out' track my next move felt justified - I hitched back to the cafe for tea with an egg sandwich while the owners gave me Bernard's information about bothies and also a certificate about my visit to the head.

Continuing my journey across these flattish northern lands of scattered crofts mixed with bigger farms, I went through Dunnet and then took the main road towards Castletown. This was by-passed by using the harbour heritage trail along which stood a number of dismal dilapidated houses. Cinder tracks led me to West Murkle where the road ahead was blocked by a gate warning 'Private - shooting - Danger'. But I jumped the gate anyway and found a way past Harold's Tower, a peculiar folly with phallic towers, and into Thurso and the Ormilie Hostel, which Michael had told me about last night and after quickly shopping up the road, had a good night with a dormitory all to myself.
23m

Day 264
Sunday
Not rising till ten o'clock I went along the A836, came to the Bridge of Forss, used the telephone there to report the loss of my bank card, so missing Crosskirk with its ancient monument of St Mary's chapel and instead went on to Dounreay, guided by the prominent landmark of the huge reactor dome. The whole station, especially the fast breeder facility, is in the long process of decommissioning at a cost £40m per year for fifty years. At the exhibition centre in an old airport tower I was the only visitor and spent nearly an hour talking to the staff who told me that another round Britain walker had gone the other way the day before. At Reay lies the most northerly golf links in mainland Scotland and it is here that the flat lands give way and the hills start while by the hotel in Melvich the road down grades to single track. The police informed me that there was a B&B in Strathy and I headed there in the gathering evening gloom, arriving at nine. Knocking on the door of the old post office painted with a 'ban the bomb' sign on an outside wall, and after asking about the nearest accommodation I was rewarded by the owner, Moss, inviting me to stay for the night. He normally lived there alone, amongst all his knick-knacks but his absent minded mother Lucy was staying for a few weeks and strangely she was tickled pink to see me. It was a wonderful unexpected evening of food, stories and home cures, especially those for my feet. The best he reckoned was to use primrose leaves. Moss had arrived here some fifteen years before, from the south with a horse and cart. The local Lord told him to stop and eventually he bought the place, living off the land using his wits together with bits of this and that - a genuine tinker!
22m

Day 265
Monday 10th May
We took a turn around Moss's garden, talking plants and fishing. When I got away it was along the A836 again across the moorland to Ladnagullin where I tried the isolated telephone but it didn't work! It would be nearly a year before I sorted out this problem through a cartoon and letter to the customer adviser of BT Payphones who sent a £10 phone card for the inconvenience. Continuing to Kirtomy, with road works on the way, I met a pedestrian going to Bettyhill and we talked and walked together. He was a bit of a wanderer, ex-London, and ex-Orknies. But before his full story unfolded he left me as I branched off for Farr. At rural Glaisgeo there is a transport graveyard where I met Robby and his two sidekicks, a hillbilly trio of wheelers and dealers running this scrap yard. Over cups of tea and an egg sandwich they told me how the local council were trying to squeeze them out because their image was alien to the rustic scene. Sure it was rather odd in that area, but it was not OTT and also kept them employed as well as supplying succour to walkers!

My way to Bettyhill was via track and beach. In the village shop was a man I had previously seen driving a tractor which he was obviously using for transport. He was one of the few people hereabouts and there were even fewer shops. A storm was brewing but it just missed me as I edged up river to the bridge over the Naver and then down river in order to pick up a vague track going up and up, past electric pylons and water pools until it emerged, over the hill, to the road for Skerray. It was getting late when I found an empty house at Crossburn, untied the door and decided to stay - especially as there was a mattress there amidst all the renovation work.
14m

Day 266
Tuesday

Again I slept well and late and after leaving a note of thanks, found a wooden bridge across the stream to the minor road leading to Clashaddy, Tubeg, Skerray, lovely Lamigo bay and then over the hills to Strathan Skerray, where the owners of a craft and cafe shop gave me coffee and sandwiches. A track took me down to a stream, the Altan Dearg, from which there was a track towards Sletell but I was soon on my own, on trackless open moorland with fantastic views of Rabbit Islands and Eilean Nan Ron. From here an unexpected track crossed rocky moorland to Skullomie and another took me to Coldbackie. After some more main road I slipped round on a minor one to the SYH of Tongue lodge and on the way had good views of the Bridge over the Kyle of Tongue. It was a wonderfully warm afternoon as I reached the Hostel at five o'clock and dropped my bag before walking a mile to the nearest shop. Gratefully a lady gave me a lift back most of the way to the hostel which was nearly empty, except for a fully equipped Dutch family with their large and heavily laden estate car.
11m

Day 267
Wednesday

My feet were slowly improving; Moss's remedy of primrose leaves may well have been helping them. The morning was overcast and damp as I left the hostel at ten o'clock for the long march to Durness. After the causeway bridge, the road rose up and up past the wet brown bog-land of the rolling countryside with snatches of the old road running alongside the new concourse. Past the plateau it was downhill to Hope on the double lane road which became single track towards Loch Eriboll where salmon were being farmed and fabulous views exposed. Around the other side of the Loch the loose gravel of the current surfacing programme made for hard walking over the last nine miles but the aches were softened firstly by the sounds of a lone piper practising on the loch-side, standing well away from his house(!) and then by the accomodation found in the quiet hostel at Smoo. 27m

Day 268
Thursday
Leaving just after nine I took the short route into Durness town, where there was mail from Roger and Liz. Grassland beyond the town led to WW2 shelters at Aodann Mhorand, and a track went back to Balnakeil, with its ruined church and past the exquisite lochs of Croispol and Borralie on the way to the 11.00 o'clock ferry across the Kyle of Durness. This was the only ferry where I had to pay. At £3.50 it was expensive, but wading across unknown rivers didn't appeal, even though it is possible. On the other side a mini bus waited for the other passengers, while, in good weather, I did the long walk to the bothy at Kearvaig, on the way crossing the army bridge at Daill and stopping briefly at the heavily boarded MOD cottage in the middle opposite Loch Inshore

At the MBA* bothy, my first, Stan, the elderly local shepherd, told me about the impending loss of the area's land to the MOD and the expected reduction in his duties. Later, soon after collecting wood and lighting a fire, Glaswegean Graham arrived from the south, tired and weary. It turned into a wonderful night of fireside chat, just like an idealised bothy evening should be.
13m

Day 269
Friday 14th: May Day
We left Kearvaig bothy at 8.30, Graham being first off, heading east while I, myself, went west to the Cape by way of a cliff top scramble alongside fences; how they must have toiled making these erections on such steep hillsides! On one side lay dark Torridonian sand stone and on the other glittering pink gneiss, picked out by the glorious sunny weather. Over the first headland, in the jetty inlet of Clais Charnach, was a stone shed with an open door and fire place; suitable for an overnight shelter? The stone jetty was hidden under the protection of a huge net overhead and one could imagine secret landings taking place here, but it's probably all to do with the MOD. A stiff climb led to Cape Wrath proper, first to the cairn and then onto the lighthouse with the adjacent disused Lloyds buildings. The view was excellent and the sea calm with plenty of passing shipping. The lighthouse is of course now automatic but a lone maintenance man was finalising details of a helicopter lift of the debris accumulated during its manned operation. It is now clean and clinical, not much different from all the others and another way of life has gone together with its folk lore and local knowledge.

After a short bit of road, it was map and compass to Strathchailleach bothy across this wild, remote and unspoilt place, although the actual land is impoverished heather with very poor grass and some very quaggy areas. No wonder

*MBA Mountain Bothy Association

it's better for military use rather than farming with sheep which were few and far between. It was heavy going and I was glad to get to the recently renovated bothy despite the short distance covered. The bridge over the stream has now gone, but stones and rocks brokered an easy passage as the water level was low. I dragged in peat from the much vaunted best peat bog in Scotland and which had sustained Sandy, the huts original occupant for over 40 years and who had attracted many stories of ruggedness. After bathing my feet in the icy cold water I was able to make a decent fire out of this peculiar fuel (eat your heart out, Graham, for doubting the viability of such fuel). The silence was absolutely magical and the views superb, while at my feet pink and white orchids together with violets lightened the dark brown heather.

Now, having pulled round the top of Scotland, I faced the West coast and the long haul to Land's end. It had been a short days walking but it was delightful to rest a little in this peaceful spot.
10m

Day 270
Saturday
It rained during the night and, due to the over-long roof nails of the recent renovations, the bothy leaked, necessitating strategic sleeping positions. I started off in a fine drizzle, as the sun tried to emerge during the walk to Sandwood Bay on a track reasonably marked with cairns and red flags. It was only two miles to the bay, and on my arrival the tide was way out meaning that a late start had been made from the bothy, though now I had no watch to check times. The smaller seaside loch had dried up and there was plenty of sand so the bay's name was even more apt. Nearby was Sandwood house in a derelict state but it still retains a quarter roof for some feasible shelter.

Glaswegeans were out in force - more walkers than seen in months - and one group were struggling along with cool boxes full of beer, declaring this to be the best place in Scotland, although others have expressed the view that there were better places and I wouldn't disagree, even though its good in Sandwood especially as visitors are not allowed to drive to this remote spot, being now under the dictates of the John Muir Trust

The path gradually improved until it emerged at Blairmore from where a tarred track south by-passes Oldshoremore and becomes the B801 at Kinlochbervie, which is said to be the fourth biggest port in Scotland. It was certainly busy, much more so than Wick, which when looking at the map is surprising. At Badcall I restocked at the post office, while at Rhiconich I found a police station and reported my unfortunate loss of two sheets of signatures lost somewhere on the cape. My apologies to all those people who signed and especially to those who gave me addresses and especially Graham's. How is it possible with so little luggage to lose such things? I popped into the pub here for a drink meeting a road worker who said he had spotted me on that pebbly road into Durness.

It was now the main A838 but with very little traffic and at every corner new views appeared, filled with hills of quartzite and schist and languid lochs. Hence to the important bridge crossing of the River Laxford, from where the A894 went west taking me to Badnabay. One mile later I left the road and headed NW into the hills in order to assay a short cut to Foindle. It was not too bad up into and over the hills by map and compass then down to the hamlet and its surrounding bogs in which optimistic new plantings of deciduous trees had been made. Camp that evening was in a sheep pen at Fanagmore Farm, where two lads, Angus and Christopher, were friendly and helpful. They guarded a salmon farm in the bay which, so far, is virus free. They promised me boiled eggs for the morning but they never arrived and my limited diet continued.
24m

Day 271
Sunday
Starting at 9.00, I was soon in Tarbet, but on the Sabbath there was no ferry to the nature reserve of Handa Island. Anyway it cost £7 for the trip plus £5 for the bothy. The path out of Tarbet starts well with cairns for the first half mile, but then you're on your own through twisting rocky terrain and many mini lochs. This was definite map and compass country until finding the path again on the last mile to Scourie. I went for tea and lounged in the Hotel - quite definitely worth the £1.10. There was a group of Gentleman anglers and walkers deep in their Sunday papers, but with humour I managed to extract some good natured sponsor money from them.

Back onto the A894, I soon branched off to Upper Badcall and had a lovely view of Harris. The path to Lower Badcall was difficult to find but, on arrival, a rest near the Eddrachilles hotel was wonderfully peaceful amidst glorious waves of bluebells and rich clumps of blooming rhododendrons. A long slog on the main road, past dark basaltic rocks and the view points at Duartmore Forest and Kylestrome, led to Kylesku, an important road bridge which was opened by the Queen in 1984 replacing the old ferry. Nearby a cairn commemorates the 50th anniversary of the XII Submarine flotilla:

> 'These silent hills remember the young men of his majesties
> X craft submarines and human torpedoes who were trained in
> these wild and beautiful waters'

In the back packers lodge I eventually found the Dutch owner and persuaded

him to take a cheque for a nights lodging and then proceeded to fill the place with the smell of fetid socks while watching the hills magically change colour in the setting sunlight, as the evening clouds dissipated.
16m

Day 272
Monday 17th May
The Dutchman woke me at 10.15 so I must have slept well! But I managed to cook a large mess of porridge before getting away. The twin peaks of Sail Gharb and Sail Gorm dominated the SW view, sharp, clear and painted with browns, greens and yellows. They held my attention for the rest of the morning as the route gradually passed to the north of them, along the twisting B 869 and past the crofts of Unapool. Today, again, every twist in the road brought a surprising new view, every up and down sprang a change of scene. At Eilean a Ghambhna I had a tea break and watched the salmon leaping in sea farm pens below. It is not surprising that the Norwegians produce cheaper fish when you see how many folk are employed on these Scottish farms. From here, as the road twisted and turned, delightful patches of dark-barked silver birch, interspersed with many wee lochs, contrasted sharp and clear with the clear blue skies, the only traces of cool air remaining were in the shadows cast by the castellations of metamorphosed shales.

Three miles later a sign pointed temptingly south to Tumore on Loch Assynt but I pressed on to Nedd where two men were repairing their shrimp boat with less than the best enthusiasm, as they said that the harvest was now low. At the neat little harbour a lady was delivering directories to telephone kiosks and, contrary to my own recent 'Street' experiences of petty vandalism and directory-free telephone booths, she reckoned they would remain there for a long time in this quiet spot. At Drumbeg I was able to phone Liz on our anniversary day, she had been working as normal but said that she was 'dog' tired and needed a rest. Then after tea in the hotel and supplies at the PO next door it was off to Clashnessie where the road ran beside the deep blue sea with one lone couple on the beach exercising their dog. In Rienachait I was offered two lifts which had to be refused and walked to the compact hamlet of Stoer, regretfully by-passing the point of Stoer, and then on to straggling Clachtoll. At Ailtanabradhan a clear sign pointed to Achmelvich with a good path all the way. This was fine, because of the expected bogs and difficult going for the last part of the day. The Youth hostel was full of Dutch, French and English students but the pragmatic warden found me a bed, with the compliment that you can't turn away a real walker. The hostel was only a stone throw from the beach though the water was only warm enough for paddling - the swimming was for the youngsters - not me.
21m

Day 273
Tuesday
There was an 8.45 call to rise and I faced a meagre breakfast but donations of bread, milk, cheese and oats came in from the students of cognitive science, language, computers and artificial intelligence and a Zimbabwean girl doing medical biology. These were hill walkers of Edinburgh University, all out on the loose for Victoria Day, a Scottish holiday and prolonging the weekend. Most of them were going to do Stac Polly on the way home.

   I set out on the pretty path to Lochinvar via Ardroe, Bhaile and Baddidarach and passed one pair of walkers and the yellow-pages lady of Nedd. The bracken was growing rapidly and a collection of spring flowers brightened the way. Sylvan woods abounded, gnarled oaks that had struggled with past winds stood guard while big horned, brown highland cattle with pensive forelocks grazed nearby. The harbour at Lochinvar was busy and a single track road climbed out to the south to Straithkirkcraig where a car stopped to give me charity money. The scenic route continued by riverside glades. Beside a wide gurgling river I sat at a picnic bench for lunch while a cheerful chaffinch shared my table and food. Eventually the road came back to the sea at Polymore and then made a slow climb up the valley of Alt Gleann ant Strathain. The reward for this toil was the prolonged close sight of a stag on the road and a view of Loch Buine Moire set in wonderful spread of hills. This is certainly astounding country and to the south the profile of Stac Poly stuck out amidst this sparsely populated and wild part of Scotland. I turned right at Badnagyle to the NW where the land flattens out beside Loch Osgaig and. surprisingly more lifts were offered, two by lady drivers. How different the attitudes are here compared to the south. On to the bleak Rubha Mor and a long gradual climb up to the summit pass, where I was rewarded by excellent views towards the Maryllins in the SE, towards the Polly National Nature Reserve. This euphoria was topped up with a magical view of the Summer Isles in the slanting evening sunlight, unfortunately the edge was reduced a little as I took the slow trudge through Altandhu, Polbain (with its 'smoke shack' for sea food), Achiltibuie (for a drink of the Orkneys), Polglass, and Badenscallie before reaching the Acheninver hostel, a quiet little rest place of only 20 beds, run by Peter. Also staying the night were two quiet girls, two less quiet Americans and a voluble South African Historian with the theory that the Queen ran the country by proxy. We stood outside and watched the evening sky as Peter pointed out Venus, Mars and Arcturus and told us of the sheep that kept the grass short. One in particular used to patrol the stone wall in front of the hostel but hadn't been seen since the previous year, perhaps it now patrolled elsewhere - possibly on a more heavenly sward! He also told me of a tall meticulous round Britain walker who three years before had passed this hostel as he took in every inch of coastline and bagged every little hillock on the way. But the name escaped him.
30m

Day 274
Wednesday
The Stornoway ferry from Ullapool steamed past at ten o'clock as I lingered at this lovely place, reluctant to make a start to the day and set off on the track southwards. On my right a calm, turquoise sea, sprinkled with islands and little boats while on my left the country brown with heather but alive with small yellow flowers. Idyllic! Though you had to watch your footing this was a wonderful walk along the easy to follow old postman's path, close to the sea and with fantastic views towards Isle Martin. A smattering of salmon farms crouched in the sea and to the south snow lingered on the north faces of the high mountains. At the end of this energetic and splendid walk there was a scramble down to the river plains of North Keanchulish and a wade across the river Kanaird to avoid the bridge two miles upstream. I continued down river along the wrack ridden beach, and took a track to the main A835, only having to cross two small hills on the way from Ardmair to Ullapool, which appeared picturesquely in the distance cradled between hill and loch.

The SYH was on the expensive side particularly as I missed the free breakfast next morning but my replacement bank card had arrived by post at the hostel enabling me to raid the local Safeway stores for supplies.
13m

Day 275
Thursday
The morning was spent in the bank, in the post office collecting and posting mail, and buying new boots (German**** Meindl) which thankfully were immediately comfortable - and for nostalgia's sake posting my old boots back to Bromley. Towards midday a start was made. In a cabin on the quay I had tea, with the maintenance man who spotted the ferry on the other end of the promenade. I promptly hoofed it there and was given a ride on the Mother Goose, a small cabin cruiser and private supply boat for the Altnaharrie Hotel on the far side of the loch. Once there a rough track climbed steeply away to the SW, while behind me excellent views of Ullapool gradually faded away. The track turned to road for a while as it headed for Badrallach where it dwindled to the postman's track, only suitable for four wheeled motor bikes! This followed the shore of Little Loch Broom into the small but thriving community of Scoraig which had been restarted by incomers. As I sat looking at the first house on the perimeter of the village, puzzled by it strange construction, a cyclist came along and immediately invited me in for tea. Davy and Susanna live with their two children in their half finished house which was coming along very nicely - Davy is a chippy and does some part time work across the water. I stayed for the night, sleeping on the floor, after a wonderful meal in convivial company.
11m

Map 4

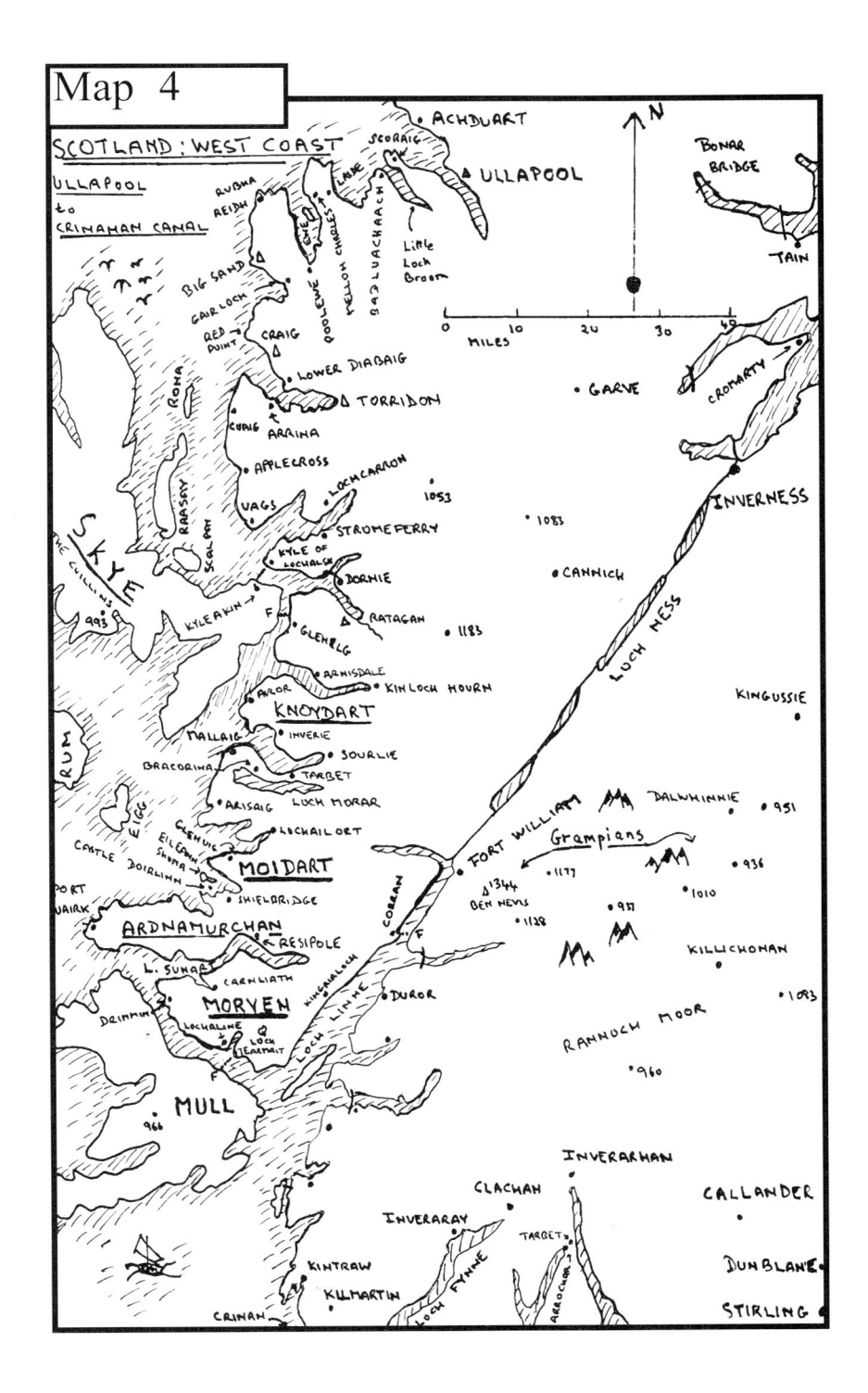

Day 276
Friday
There was a school in Scoraig with 12 children, one of whom boards weekly from the so called 'mainland' as this long cut off peninsular is so island-like. Residents also include a violin maker who uses simple methods and two wind-power experts with their work shop by the shore. At 10.15, in light rain, I was on the post ferry, with the postman and three school children, one of whom, under instruction, steered the boat and controlled its outboard motor, doing a very competent job in a rough but safe sea.

At Badluarach, on the other side, I took the NW track out of the village then struck off SW across boggy ground, in the rain and wind. Two miles over the ridge, I hit the A832 on the way to the trees around Gruinard House and the out buildings where I sheltered for a while not far from the corpse of a dead fox. The road continued over the big and little Gruinard Rivers, past attractive woodland and with a continual view of Gruinard Island, which is now, I believe, anthrax free, many years after a wartime experiment, and no warning signs were visible.

At Sand I had tea in the hotel watching a sheep roundup before a short cut across a caravan site led to Laide. Towards evening it was still wet and as there were no shops I managed to buy some beans at one house and had my flask filled at another. Thinking that Slaggan looked the best choice as a place to bed down, I was soon on the track there, which was declared unsuitable for cars, a classification which was not really true, and found the ruins of Slaggan which was true. There was not a roof in sight and the bad blustery weather continued. Though managing to light a fire in the ruins of one old house, after half an hour of wind and hail, I decided to battle against the weather and cross the pathless soggy ground to Mellon Charles, eventually finding lodgings with a hospitable retired hotelier Jim Slow, and was able to dry out before having a good evening discussing a variety of topics including Kosovo, fish farming, IUF and cloning. 17m

Day 277
Saturday
On leaving sleepy Mellon Charles at 9.30 I went SE through the croft suburbia of Ormiscraig with the sight of Isle of Ewe in its Loch. The wind of yesterday continued from the east. At first this was fine, helping me along, but as the day progressed it became more and more difficult to continue walking. The showers came and went. At Drumchork it was the main A832 again but it was not at all busy. The wind was very strong now and I was thankful for the leeward side of any hillocks, cuttings or woodland and had to stop more frequently to rest. A mile south of the town there was a MOD sign to NATO - Loch Ewe, an indication of the importance of this area for naval operations. In

the sea two circular salmon farms lay in the rough waters. At Tournaig Farm a man was struggling to start his car and I pointed out the faulty battery connections, he tapped them and roared off while I pressed on towards Poolewe passing big pine forests bordering the road and the Inverewe botanical gardens. These beckoned for a viewing but a bevy of tourists put me off while all around banks of rhododendrons were breaking into flower suggesting that it really was spring.

The battering wind continued on and off as I walked out of Poolewe on the northerly B8057 through Boor and Naast before finding an open shop in Midtown. Having misread the map and walked well past my turn off to Inverdale, I had to back track past the quaint tiny isolated PO, consisting of half a port-a-cabin, before turning right. The last house in the village treated me to cake, supplied hot water and gave me the hint of good news - the presence of an unmarked bothy at the end of the route to Rubha Reidh. A good, well marked path led away NW. This was quite variable in quality, gradually became more boggy and at least one of the streams was crossed with some difficulty. In the silver birch woods, half way there, I thought about shelter for the night. However the ancient forest trees and a herd of hinds lifted my spirits and so I pressed on. Near the loch on my right there was a possible shelter in a sheep dip shed but perversely I continued along the wet rough track and was rewarded with the real bothy, Ivor's Cottage, its roof held down by a swathe of blue fish netting. I hauled up logs from the beach far below and lit a fire with the dry wood that had been stored inside, the bothy quickly filling with smoke. However it was warm and dry - an ideal place to sleep in bad weather. Not far away, high above Carnu beach was a plaque to:-

Robert McGregor Innes Ireland
Scotland's 1st grand prix champion
1930 - 1993
And son James 1970 - 1992

19m

Day 278
Sunday
It must have been snug because I slept on and off till 11.30 next morning being awakened by a knock on the door and the appearance of two hikers checking up on the bothy's condition (Ivor's Cottage is an independent bothy normally kept in order by local people.) The coastal cliff path to the head over the top of the sea cliffs was fun, though the winds made care necessary. At the lighthouse of Rubha Reidh, set squarely in its stark surroundings, there was a unexpected tea room where a German girl served me with tea and also an Outdoor Centre which offers guided walking holidays but was closed. A tarred track continued south and eventually became a B road, through a rather dreary land-

scape sloping down to the sea and intersected by the occasional ravine. Wind, rain, sun, and hail were the order of the day.

I went through Melvaig, a crofter village, three house Peterburn and at Erradale passed through Mr Macgregor's garden - Rosalie (which he had been cultivating for 25 years) - but I saw no playful rabbits like Peter, Flopsy or Mopsy! Then farmland was crossed in order to reach the path for Big Sand and through the neat caravan site, with its mown grassy paths, to Carn Dearg. The first house there was open and inviting, but empty. Apparently it was a school's private hostel. The SYH was around the corner and a bed was available. A big party of polite, but insular, urban Academy kids were in residence, warming up for their D of E expedition on which they had to cover 56 miles in four days including camping for three nights.
13m

Day 279
Monday 24th May
The other hostel was still open and still empty; what a blow - an opportunity missed - although no welcoming bowls of porridge lay on the table. The wind had swung round to the west and today helped as it blew me eastward to Gairloch. The rain squalls still came and waterproofs were necessary but between the showers the welcome sun showed itself and a flock of black-faced, horned, west highland sheep and their horn budding lambs thought the weather was improving too.

The A832 wound through woodland with rowan in flower, past attractive harbours before running beside River Kerry where a bridge took me onto the B8056. The wind battering started again but this was compensated by the scenery of woods and hills. The road twisted through to Badachre and went on to Port Henderson, where I found a low stocked 'shop' and was given a beef sandwich in a caravan while sheltering from the wind. My host was a carpet fitter, Andrew Tallach, and his van had a poem painted on its side:-

We're friendly in Wester Ross;
We laugh and chat, and none of us is 'posh';
We share our joys and sorrows too,
And life is richer; because we do

Far from the noise and bustle of town
We live our lives without renown;
We do our work in a peaceful way,
Helping each other day by day

> Those from the south say we're dull, I fear
> But we find bliss in all that's here;
> And when our tale of life is told,
> Some of the pages may shine like gold

And so it was: a good chat and a rest. Across the yard was an old red telephone box housing a toilet and set down by their front door. This guy certainly had a sense of humour.

I struggled on through South Erradale and Redpoint in strengthening wind and occasional heavy showers of rain and hail quickly followed by bright sunshine. At silent Redpoint Farm it really came down but there was shelter in a shed. Back on the path the sun emerged as I crossed the machair (sheep greens) to the fishing station which seemed almost deserted although there was still some activity as indicated by fishing gear on the beach. From here a proper path started, a rock strewn route over several big streams, out in open country and with exciting views towards Skye. At the seventh river the path turned upwards past thin birches and over a bridge to the sudden appearance of the wee, welcoming and excellent Craig hostel, with Leslie in charge, a first time warden from Berkshire. This is a testing place to learn, simply due to its remoteness, with a three mile walk to the nearest road and her car before any thought of shops and carrying the supplies back to the hostel. Leslie made tea and we settled down for a good chat. The 14 bed hostel nestles in between hills and is warmed to the heart by a wood stove. The house was once part of an old settlement of sixty people, subsisting on farming and fishing, which at the turn of the century left for New Zealand. Now it's all in ruins, except for the hostel.

Having parked their car and walked in, two late arrivals appeared, friends of Bernard Heath (of MBA and Dunnet). Connections are forever happening and always surprising, though its probably birds-of-a-feather syndrome.
20m

Day 280
Tuesday
When I surfaced at 9.30 Leslie had already left and the other couple were off to the local water falls. By the time I was ready to go a Canadian arrived and this further delayed my departure in giving him the drill for the hostel.

It was a good track to Lower Diabaig, luckily the rain staying away nearly all day and more importantly the wind almost died down. I decided against last night's advice and took the coastal mountain path to Alligin. A sign said 'precipitous path' and indeed some of it was, but further positive signs pointed the way around Loch Diabaig. It was a strenuous walk but well worth the effort through the mountains with white quartzite cliffs everywhere. At Port Laire, on the edge of Loch Torridon, the path passed an isolated wee cottage with three boats all alone, what a precarious living in such a place, I thought, but on the path I found a ten pound note! Just lying there, waiting to be picked up. In Alligin, sitting on a grassy bank to rest and watching the sea, my surprise was renewed by a holiday couple, Wolf and Clare, from a nearby house, who came over, talked, and then gave me a welcome cup of coffee and a sandwich.

Refreshed, I continued using a mix of tracks and roads around the pleasant loch and a walk through old woodland of beech, limes, Scots pine with masses of blooming rhododendrons until coming to Torridon which lay minute in the cusp of the hills. Arriving just after seven the shop in the village was open and a bed available in the big hostel with a crowd of people staying all doing strenuous things like D of E, Munros etc: the numbers rather overwhelming me.
14m

Day 281
Wednesday
The hostel was emptying as I had a quiet breakfast over a quiet read of a book, though my hunger must have been apparent as a small group of mountain walkers gave me food for the day. In a slight drizzle, I eventually left at ten, passing the very busy hostel camp site, onto the main road for two miles before going up the driveway of the impressive Torridon Hotel. On the other side of the hotel a sign on a bridge declared:-

'Douglas and our Highland cattle are on the other side'

What would you deduce from that? What could I expect? Especially as the path continued through ever encroaching rhododendrons which gradually made the path narrower and the headroom lower and wetter with its canopy flowers only just beginning to show. To me this was a welcome, recognised, walker's path which, as it widened, had many of the characteristics of a Berkshire Ride, though it was punctuated by rapid rivulets and little waterfalls and suddenly, inconsistently, an unexpected silhouette of a stag sprang out of the scrub - the metal cut out for local target practise. The attractive inlet of Ob Gorm Mor appeared with its quota of big, solid, brown slabs of Torridon sandstone lining the water-side path. It couldn't last and I was eventually spilled onto the main A896 which took me into attractively neat Shieldaig with its hotel and shops. On the front sat an Armada gun, a maritime find of the previous year, pointing out to sea towards Shieldaig Island. This has its own special Scots pines, which, once used for the masts of local fishing boats, are now in some danger due to possible cross pollination with mainland trees. On the far side of the island lives a colony of otters, local trips are available and several tourists were being rowed over. I took advantage of the shops, topped up my supplies then had tea on the front, but the midges were starting to bite. On reflection the stage was set - to enter the fabulous and remote Applecross peninsular which once used to be so difficult to penetrate.

A mile further on from the village a busy one lane B road turned off right, scrambling its way to the NW, gaining a refreshing sight of the hills that I had climbed yesterday including that lonely wee house with its three boats. Two summer cyclists passed me which was notable since virtually none had been seen on my journey. After passing the busy little port at Ardheslaig and having a break beside a large Poclain Digger I managed to get off the road onto a path and as the trees disappeared had an energetic walk up and over A'Bhainir, across a wooden bridge over a fair sized, but unnamed, river draining into Loch Torridon and hence into Kenmore to rest beside the old post office, chatting briefly with a delivery man about bothies and other walking incidentals.

The path from here started on greens but soon wandered into an overgrown and derelict state. Escaping from the tangle, I watched the antics of some boys canoeing in the sea by the cliffs at Camas an Eilean, then a squabble of chickens rush towards me and I wondered why hens always seem to strut up to me. Are they demanding food? Or are they seeing me off? It was now only a short distance to Arina (shortened from Arinacrinachd or is that spider town?) and the old school bunkhouse. This would have cost £16 but it was not properly open! Instead I stayed in a delightful little caravan for £10, luckily it was empty because a Londoner was not due to arrive until the next day and he had been coming there each year for 23 years. An evening stroll to the local point was a partial failure as the view to Craig across the water was hidden in mist 18m

Day 282
Thursday
Unfortunately I'd had to read a book most of the night as a toothache had driven sleep away until dawn broke. On hearing of my misfortune, the caravan's owner, Mr Gillanders, provided me with some cloves, which though carried for miles were never used. I was off before ten with the wind now coming from the south - not really what was needed for most of the day. Initially the narrow road continued northward into the treeless Torridonian sandstone landscape. Then at Fearnmore the road bent south to Cuaig and released some excellent views of the Rona and Raasay Isles in the west. I found a hat on the road and later spotted a cyclist who was obviously looking for something and indeed had lost it. We chatted for a while before he, hat in pocket, pushed off south. There were big stretches of clean sand at An Cruin and busy MOD helicopters hovered nearby, disturbing the quietness. At Applecross, which was supposed

to impress but hardly made a note in my diary, the post office topped up my supplies before a slow walk took me to Toscaig where I tried to get eggs from the multitude of chickens but there was nobody selling.

A commando built wooden bridge led to a south-easterly path which petered out a mile later, though it was not too difficult to find the enigmatic dismantled stone houses at Shielings and then locate the proper path further on. I struggled somewhat over the hills and was thankful for Bernard's notes on finding the Uags bothy at the end of the peninsula, opposite the Crowlin Islands. It has a great location near the beach, within the arms of a wood of silver birch and enjoyed a special view of Skye, across a mill pond sea sporting one lone sailing boat. After collecting a scattering of fallen wood, happiness abounded with a fire to lighten the gloom of evening and good stocks of food for a decent meal.
22m

Day 283
Friday
Last night it rained and it continued all morning so finding a book I started reading and went on all day. It was the '39 Steps': gripping stuff, not read before. Having humped in a good supply of food allowed me to enjoy time off in this wonderful solitary little spot.

Day 284
Saturday
The stream was well up and it was still raining and another book was found: 'Inheritance', by Dennis Friedman, describing the Royals from Victoria to the present and their problems with parenthood. In the afternoon, as it cleared, a Lancashire couple arrived on a beautiful calm evening without midges.

Day 285
Sunday
Soon after nine I left to pursue the southern coast. There was a good path to start but it soon disappeared and my line became very precipitous on the way to Woody House. From here a beach route with its jumble of rocks exposed by a lowish tide, was okay, except at one point where I did get my feet wet, which was a small price for safety. It was a still, perfect day, and the scintillating water was grooved with channels made by the light breeze and marine currents.

It was slow work but a worthy walk after the rest at Uags, coming at last to the River Kishorn and a wade to Courthill House. I had negotiated a reasonable stretch of country without a properly marked path, come out unscathed and found that there was more to walking the coast of Britain than you could

imagine sitting in a chair in London. After putting on dry socks I walked to thickly wooded Achintraid, where two lady walkers said that the trail was boggy but quite easy to follow. This surprised me because I soon lost its scent and had to navigate by compass through tall pines and erratic streams until finding it again. At Ardaneaskan on the edge of Loch Carron, overlooking the picturesque Strome Islands, I had my flask filled, before continuing through the pines to Strome castle. There was no ferry here, and not really expecting one, I continued to Lochcarron, managing to get supplies in a Sunday shop and a little further on camped by the shore of this very pretty loch. My chosen spot lay beside a deserted grassy car park opposite a golf course which had an honesty box asking £40 /week or £10/day for a round. But I had no clubs! A fire kept the midges away and cooked my meal while sleep came slowly as I reflected on the day and my surroundings.
20m

Day 286
Monday 31st May
An early start saw me round the head of the Loch and from here I followed the main coastal road (A890) to the SW. On my left were sheer cliffs of hard shale climbing high above the road and swathed in great curtains of steel mesh. Carved on one of the road and rail tunnels near Attadale was the motto:-

'Dread God and do well'

At Ardnaff I couldn't find the lower loch-side track so instead took the railroad for the walk to Storme Ferry. At one point a train came from behind, tooted and then passed on. I walked on several bit of track after that, ignoring the possible £200 penalty and nobody seemed to mind the trespass. The hamlet of Storme is now almost totally derelict and burnt down, since the last ferry crossed in 1973. A little further on I sat in a huge chair that some humorist woodsman had sawn out of a pine stump, and enjoyed the view back up the loch. Walking a tad up the road I was able to get water from Alan and Helen, a doctor and his wife who were on holiday. Moreover they gave me tea with cake and took my photo which they sent to me several weeks later. At Achmore the busy rural West Highland Dairy sold me some tasty Friesland-Sheep cheese.

The road to Fernaig was lined with close-walled tall beeches on the left and 200 year old oaks on the right - judging by their girth. But soon I took to the rail track again unable to reach the road above and at Craig found an animal sanctuary and a rather tacky old highland farm before turning towards Duncraig Abbey. There was once a strong religious influence hereabouts and a nearby stone arch over a doorway again declared:-

Day 286 Strome Ferry hospitality: Helen (and Alan) provide, tea, cake and a chance for a chat after my request for water

'Fear God, work hard and do well'

The local landowners were probably in cahoots with the church to keep their minions under control, faithful, pliant and good workhorses.

From here, a lovely wooded track led to Plockton where I lunched, on my new found cheese, before walking the railway to Duirinish and the road to Drumbuie, Erbusaig and Kyle. After deciding not to walk around Skye I caught a bus to Kyleachin and its somewhat expensive SYH which was full of Japanese and Australians, most of whom were travelling around in small tour buses.
23m

Day 287
Tuesday
I was up at 8.15 and <u>still</u> missed the continental breakfast which made it an even more expensive hostel. Alas you can't win them all! But then I also missed the 9.15 bus! This gave me the opportunity to do my post in Kyleachin before catching the 9.45 shuttle back to Kyle of Lochalsh which left me rather down in the dumps: disappointed with my own logic, planning, impecuniosity and tired feet. Moreover it was back to main road again heading east up Loch Alsh.

At Scailpaidh I bought a map and note pad and saved 1p on the deal. This somehow made me feel better! One mile later at the Donald Murchison's Monument (1715-21), stopping for a break, it was just nice to look back at the inspiring view towards the new Skye Bridge. But afterwards, even after consulting libraries, I was none the wiser as to this man's place in history, until the 'I' told me that he had been the Factor for the Earl of Seaforth (6 years?) and had prevented the English military laying their hands on the local rents and was hence a bit of a hero. Now this snippet of information is my test of people's faith in the usefulness of the Internet highway - are the facts there?

Near Glaick I climbed over a high road-side fence into the woodland gardens and almost fell at the feet of some surprised child explorers on their woodland trail, although they remained relatively undisturbed by my Neanderthal appearance. This delightful, interlude path soon took me through a school and over a beach, back to the busy A87 which I slogged along to Kirton. A gang was busy digging up the land and laying a new, long and expensive water pipe. What price a drop of (chlorinated) water? A track leading south petered out near the headland beach and I had to scramble over the shore rocks to Avernish, where there were a number of dilapidated houses and a jobbing builder who signed my StC form. I continued by Nostie onto the A87 again and went quickly through Ardelve where I stopped for a chat with the pipe layers I had seen before. They were certainly moving along. At Loch Long there was a pier on the western shore but no boats! Presumably the boatman was made redundant when the bridge to Dornie was built.

The picturesque castle of Eilean Donnan with its connecting humped-back causeway was beset with sightseers. The man on the shop till said that if he'd have known of my coming he would have bought me dinner!! He was probably the present laird. Originally 13th century this castle was pounded to bits by a English Man of War in 1719 and only restored in 1912 by the Laird Macrae. Now the castle is a big tourist attraction because of its charismatic setting on the loch beneath the rising mountains on each side and the excellent display of exhibits inside.

It was then three miles to Inverinate along the shore of Loch Duich with the surrounding towering hills above me. After buying tobacco at the petrol station and taking a remnant of the old road I came to some impressive, open, gates and pressed the bell of the modern, flat-type, intercommunicator. Nothing happened. Not deterred I pressed on down the drive and noted the arrays of infrared security equipment. But there was nobody about and there was no sudden challenge as I strolled the next mile through these immaculate and delightful grounds, full of blooming azaleas, rhododendrons and tall trees by the loch. Later I learnt it belonged to a rich Sheik and security was usually high, abuzz with cars and helicopters. On emerging at Kintail I was back on the main road towards the head of the loch. High hills were all around, towering ahead and snow still lay in the high gullies. A large causeway carried the road over the loch towards the hamlet of Shiel Bridge and the store which sold me supplies. On the B road I had to refuse a lift for the short distance to the Ratagan SYH which was nearly full with mountain walkers and cyclists but hosted only a few late night midges. It is a good and popular hostel with a vast potage of stories in the log and with a Warden who could discuss my plans about the best routes forward.
19m

Day 288
Wednesday 2nd June
Unusually I'd had a bad night's sleep but the sun was out as my day began in absolutely calm weather on the road along the southern shore of Duich. Spring was changing to summer as May turned to June. Wild and cultivated flowers, including yellow poppies, were out in profusion while noisy oyster catchers were busy with the feeding of their young. I could see Castle Dornie in the far distance up the loch beyond the level coastal road. At Letterfearn, I phoned the fish research station that I'd learned about in Ellon many months ago and now found that I'd walked past it and so had missed another night's free lodging. Another blow to my pride in cadgeability!

The road ended at Totaig opposite to the castle over the water and the walkers' path began, going west into the forest, with a view overlooking the three lochs Walsh, Long and Duich before taking me into wilder places for a few days. The path rose gradually through the woods to a plateau and then plunged down to the beach and a field to Ardintoul, where there was another salmon farm. I was given half a cup of tea and told of the old talc mine in the hill above which had foundered years ago after their cargo boat sank off Skye.

A mile further on, as I snacked, in the sun, on a beach just off the loch-side path, several groups of walkers passed - it was turning into the hikers 'French Riviera'! The gravel path, undulating up and down, led to the Skye Ferry which could have been my alternative route through Skye, instead of around Loch Duich. Further on stands Bernera Barracks (1722), a dour square block fort with tales to tell, and spread-eagled Glenelg for supplies and its well kept and striking war memorial. At Eilanreach as I looked ahead at the prospects of the long road climb out, a couple offered me a lift and not wishing to turn a good offer down proffered my bag instead and asked for it to be dropped at the upper Sandaig Bridge. Unburdened, I continued walking the road, tracks and forest to Sandaig meeting another walker, a keen photographer, on the way. This place was a surprise as I had not realised that it was the place made famous by Gavin Maxwell (1914-69) with memorials to Edad (1958-69 - in Ring of Bright Water) and to Maxwell himself. His little white cottage still stands below the inland hills and near the shore, presumably restored after the disastrous fire. We walked out to the wonderful little Islands and, spellbound, nearly got cut off by the fast incoming tide. Preparing to leave this haven I reflected on Maxwell's epithet:-

'What ever joy she gave to you give back to nature'

After saying goodbye I made my way back to the road, but it was further than expected, losing my way on the twisting forest tracks, then walking along the road in the wrong direction and having to retrace my steps to my bag standing alone on the bridge. Trailing back down the road again into Arnisdale, a walker who was just off the Munro ridge above joined me and so we walked and talked into the village where he collected his car. On the road by the shore the first person I spoke to about barns for shelter was on holiday and soon offered me a meal and a floor for the night. We stood and watched the last light go as the outlines of Knoydart and Skye faded into the night. A magical ending to a long day with my confidence in providence restored.
25m

Day 289
Thursday
It was raining but calm passing through Corran as a herd of fifty hinds grazed

in lowland pasture. Turning out of the village, I re-met my bag helpers of yesterday and saw yet more yellow poppies. The path climbed into Glen Arnisdale gradually rising to 1000 ft, past woods by the river and up to two lochs which had dams that were now broken, relics of past enterprises. Thereafter it was a steep drop to Kinloch Hourn, an attractive isolated farm and estate. But even here, the ubiquitous and iniquitous spread of parking fees had arrived, although rather modestly at £1/night or 50p/day. The path continued westward beside Loch Hourn with three hills near the end to tire the weary walker even further. Indeed there were many walkers out and about, far more than the total number I had seen on the trip so far. One hiker, an Indian lad, even stopped to take my photograph and the fast strides into Barrisdale were with a walker, in the briefest of shorts, who was a master brewer from Keighley, setting a good fast pace. There was a bothy with four other hikers in residence but no fire. The plusher White House hostel, up the track, was full and the camp site had a horde of trekkers in tents: Piccadilly Circus in the sticks!
16m

Day 290
Friday: Entering Knoydart
According to the map the first five miles today was uncharted but I was told there was a deer path down Loch Hourn. Departing the bothy at nine, I proceeded around Barrisdale Bay to the Loch. To my delighted surprise, soon, after the first bend, I spotted two otters and it became compulsory to sit, watching them play in the water. It was fascinating as these were my very first wild otters and a pure magical moment. But at the same time it is sad to reflect that we have lost so much of our natural habitats, flora and fauna and we need magical moments to appreciate it.

Considering the ground, there was a fair path to the house at Camas Domhain and the ruin at Glac nan Sgadan. The cliffs ahead were too sheer for my liking so I climbed the steep gully of Druim an Aoinidh. It was exhausting work, clambering up over 1000 ft followed by a big drop down to the unexpected and isolated rich farmland beyond. Another strenuous climb followed before crags and sheep tracks led me to Rubha an Daraich where I found a two man stalker's bothy which had even had a telephone link to Inverie until some animals had eaten the cable. Machair pastures started here and these appeared to shorten the easy walk to Croulin and beyond. Knocking on a door at Ab Cnocgorm for water I met a fisherman and his teenage daughter. They had moved up from the south, from England, to get away from it all. With the nearest single lane road five miles away, they certainly were. But the farm tracks did gradually improve as they passed some caves and statue like rocks - pillars worn into shape by wind and rain.

At Inverguseran Farm I asked for water and the farmer, Ian invited me in for

tea, a meal, birthday cake and to meet his wife, Jo, their two children, Cawm and Anna, and the local stalker. For me it was a wonderful party complete with birthday cake, candles and such abundance of spontaneous hospitality. Coincidentally Jo had connections in Dymmock and they said they would knock on the door of my wife's shop next time they were in Herefordshire. Unfortunately I had to leave, evening was coming on and there was a stream to wade instead of the stepping stones which were awash. That night I stayed in Airor in the farm of Dave Smith who came out quite unexpectedly from his house and invited me indoors. We stayed up and chatted until well past midnight. Maybe I was a bit of a novelty in this isolated spot. But it must be the hospitality born of isolation and natural human gregariousness.
15m

Day 291
Saturday
Dave fed me on a full fried breakfast. What luxury! I was off at nine into the rain and appropriately, around the corner there was a Noah's Ark houseboat on the beach. From here a recently resurfaced single track road, with no passing places, led to Inverie through hilly ground full of heather and grass but no trees. After the pass I met two ramblers off the boat from Mallaig and learnt that this is a popular place for day trippers. Towards the town past the loch which supplies local water, I saw the ferry boat go in and out of leafy Inverie while beside the road the first yellow irises showed their faces together with three abandoned unlicensed cars, the last having come from Wales. This road is not connected to any other and is therefore beyond the 'fringe'. In 'town' the hospitable Old Forge provided free drink and sandwiches while the Keighley brewer (Worth beer), I'd seen in Barrisdale, arrived for a chat. Unfortunately I had missed the entertainment of last week - a Russian troupe of dancers - but could see them clearly, from Ian's vivid description when he told me about it at yesterday's birthday party. In particular the musician who played an energetic tune on a flute which gradually was reduced to its mouth piece and finally to nothing but his hands!

Soon after noon and two miles later, passing a house under construction I saw a huge rat which did not impress me. But the nearby footbridge suspended over the river did inspire although followed by a long wet walk up and up into the swirling mists of Gleann Meadailand and then down in the rain to Sourlie bothy of which I was expecting great things. The sand flats at low tide provided firewood on the way to the bothy which was busy. Four Glaswegean surveyors Pete, Eric, Ian and Chicken were in residence. But sadly no fire was allowed; they said it smoked too much. In the log I read that Emma Methelda Baker (19) from Kendal had also been here (31st - 1st) adding to her list of Scottish bothies, her tour a source of comment for other bothy men. Legendary epics could be built from such exploits! Two more hikers arrived, soaking wet

and living off the land. They said they did it for enjoyment and that 'paths were always placed where there was a stream'.
16m

Day 292
Sunday
Yesterday must have tired me, as I woke late and didn't get away until 11.30. What a sloth! My route lay directly west of Sourlie's along the southern shore of Loch Nevis. It was sunny and bright and feeling good after my prolonged rest and after farewells all round, I set out optimistically, my mood further boosted by the evidence of two girls and a boy who had just walked the route from the west and said it was not too bad. The path started on the shore line without difficulty and turned into a wonderful walk if somewhat slow. The water below was crystal clear, full of stretched out jelly fish filtering the sea for food. Little woods of birch grew among the rocks, while each of the small cliff bluffs that interrupted the path was passable. All this scenery boosted by the sunshine, in contrast to yesterday's rain, left me quite contented.

At Kylasmorar I met an Oxford couple setting out in their boat. Although they offered me a lift and recommended Frank's lodgings, a well marked rocky path took me to, their destination, Tarbet, apparently a name derived from a passage suitable for ten men and a boat, aq hamlet consisting of two houses and a bothy adapted from a church where I met Frank the owner. He was not at all welcoming and although it was only £1.50 a night I felt alienated and therefore decided to push on. Going south along a rutted stony track across the small pass to Loch Morar, I continued along the track to the west on its northern shore and just before Bracorina where a road starts found three empty caravans in rough condition. One was just right for me, with a fire outside to cook and even a Ken Follet novel to read. There were several walkers passing on the path but none disturbed me or questioned my intentions and my decision to leave Tarbet felt well justified.
12m

Day 293
Monday, 7th June
A lazy day was spent reading, finishing the novel, before I could make the effort to set out. The path upgraded to a road through thick woods but a mile after Bracora I turned north on tracks and did some cross country walking, past lochs, to Mallaig Bheag. By mid-afternoon, westerly roads brought me to Mallaig which is the place of departure for the Bruce Watt Sea Cruises to Inverie and Tarbet in Loch Nevis. The big, busy pulse of civilisation struck me and, although it might be bypassed, I had felt duty bound to go there and a mission (yes - even here) provided tea and scones for a nominal price. From a road sign I calculated that Fort William was now 33 miles nearer, after the last

Day 292 Progress down the deer path beside Loch Nevis, looking back to Sourlie MB

sign to that town, a weeks walking behind, in Kyle! - a slow crow's rate of five miles a day

The busy A830 headed south, reverting, after three miles, to twisty single track highway along an attractive shoreline. But it was several miles before I could make detours away from the traffic. Firstly to Gortenachullish and Keppoch before returning to the road at Arisaig. Then a circular route through estates to Glen Cottage, to refill my flask complimented with a gift of peaches, baked beans and eggs. Prince Charlie's cave was marked on the map near Arisaig House - a possible novel place to sleep. Though my search for it was without luck I made camp, nearby and close to the shore. The sea was calm and the sun was setting with all the shades of red and blue as I lit a fire and had my basic meal followed by peaches and coffee. What a peaceful way to end the day although expecting a cold night reflecting on the Enigma of the Young Pretender. He had gone from here in '46 following his epic escape of the manhunt which prevailed after his disaster at Culloden six months earlier.

Why do we revere such failure - is it pure romanticism of the underdog? After this last serious attempt at overthrowing the throne things settled down in Britain, science came to the fore after Newton's death in 1727, the Industrial revolution got its wheels moving and the British Empire expanded so that Victoria could watch it all with imperial majesty
23m

Day 294
Tuesday
The clouds came in the early morning bringing spots of rain but I still only managed an eight o'clock start, walking east, continuing to look for the cave. It could be one of many, covered by rhododendrons or beneath an oak amongst the grey shale rocks. Local knowledge was required, but I saw no one to ask. However two miles further on I did find the Prince's cairn on the foreshore:-

> This cairn marks the traditional spot from which
> Prince Charles, Edward Stuart embarked for France:
> 20th September 1746.
> So ended the last Jacobite rebellion.

This is wonderful country and it would have been nice to spend more time for exploration. There was plenty of bird life and even my untrained eye recognised eagles hunting and kestrels hovering. Alas, feeling very tired, I was soon on a smart new dual carriageway European road passing ambiguously through eye catching mountain scenery. At Lochailort I turned right onto the A861 and passed yet another salmon farm and it was six miles before get-

Day 294 Tioram Castle in Loch Moidart

ting off this road at Roshven onto a track. This did not do what I expected and consequently landed me in the garden of a natural-spirit healer who had been there for 13 years in his turf roofed Swedish log cabin. He uses Ley lines and works with a similar thinking group in distant Inverness. His garden was full of apple trees grown from seed but he was struggling because several trees had salt burn from the sea water spray. He showed me some steps and I was away again on a path thro' the rhododendrons and then back to the road. This continued around the Sound of Arisaig and through the delightful surrounding wooded country.

Passing the beeches said to be the Seven Men of Moidart, I found them less impressive than expected - just a row of assorted bedraggled beech trees - was this now more fitting to the memory of Charlie's supporters? After Ardmolich a series of paths led along the southern shore of Loch Moidart, finally emerging at the delightful castle Tioram near Doirlinn on the Shiel Estates, with its private bridleways. Sitting in Loch Moidart, the castle remains (13/14th century keep and 16th century tower) of the ancient seat of the MacDonalds are reachable at low tide. Unfortunately stark warnings of unsafe buildings precluded further exploration. Built by John Moidart, it belonged to the MacDonalds. The clan chief burnt it down in 1715 to prevent the Campbells getting their hands on it. The chief went off to help the Mar's uprising supporting the Old Pretender (James III) in the general Jacobite rebellions and probably ended up dead at Sherrifmuir near Dunblane. One useful thing emerged - General Wade was sent up to build a network of military roads and some forty bridges. In 1746 the Stuart's ambitions came to an end when the bonny Prince lost it near Inverness. Unfortunately the victor, Cumberland, became the butcher of Scotland.

On leaving the estate not fancying jumping across the fast flowing river Shiel or crossing the private bridge and grounds of Hydro House, I had to walk all the way back to Blain and Shiel Bridge before heading for Arivegaig and the ford at Gorteneorn. By this time it was late evening and on selecting a place beneath some oaks I found the midges, in their natural habitat, were rampant and so I was forced away onto a small knoll by the sea and where a fire drove the more persistent biters away.
29m

Day 295
Wednesday
Before dawn, I woke, up to find the sea all round me, marooned on my little island as the old moon rose over the still waters and lit the bay with a pale predawn light, it was truly magical! Not much later the sun also slowly rose adding further surrealism to the scene and inducing more lethargy. Consequently I didn't break camp until 11.30 before going up into the forest

and gradually climbing over to Gortenfern where a delightful country opened up. There was a good path and nobody to bother me until Ockle where a couple from Ebbw Vale took my photo and promised a charity cheque. In glorious sunshine I made my way to Fascadale through sheep country and across the stepping stones over the Achateny water, and then open country westward to Sanna. A further path took me to Portuairk where, on the shore, sat a low, solid built grey granite house:-

> Mr M E Donaldson: Author: In 1927 built this house to shew others how the beauty of the old highlands fashion; and its fitness in this scenery, can consort with every comfort needful in these days.

However it offered me no shelter that night and it was a rocky scramble into the village. In the last house, a family on holiday provided me with water, bread, biscuits and an apple and also gave me directions to May Beach a mile away, just short of the point. A roofless old house provided some shelter and with a fire I was fairly comfortable, although there was a strong possibility of rain in the night. The donation of the apple was an answer to my earlier thoughts in the day to improve my diet by eating more fruit and vegetables selected alphabetically and today's fruit was unexpectedly first on the list.
16m

Day 296
Thursday
Although cloudy it had stayed dry in the night and I was up and away early for a change, clambering over a couple of strong fences, some cliffs and a precipitous sheep path before finally making it to the Ardnamurchan lighthouse. Two old dears were renting the rooms and they were suitably surprised by my sudden appearance at their bedroom window but let me in for coffee. They had come from Staffordshire in a specially modified car with their paraplegic, astrophysicist son who, like Roger, had had a climbing accident on Triffan, but more seriously than my brother, had broken his neck many years ago in the fall.

On leaving I took the track and road south east, through the remnants of an ancient volcano, to Kilchoan, seemingly without a shop. Two miles along the easterly road out of this village a path started towards Ben Hiant but soon lost its way leaving me struggling over those hills through new forests to finally reach the road to Ardlignish. High above the Bay of Camas nan Geall I met a Swedish Christian enjoying a solitary sojourn with God and practising the beating of his drum. I joked with him about the power of the Druids being relevant to this area while below the bluff lay some ancient church ruins and graves. An information plaque declared:-

A fertile land

The hills around here are formed from volcanic lava which erupted 55 million years ago. Ben Hiant is the highest in Ardnamurchan at 528m and is the base of an extinct volcano. Recently these rocks have been eroded by wind, water and ice to form shattered rock, sand and clay and fertile lime rich soils for the nourishment of grasses and wild flowers providing food for butterflies and insects and finally man through grazing, trees and crops.

Scannchladh

Fertility has made this area attractive to settlers for thousands of years. The burial chambers on the valley floor are about 5000 years old and over the centuries stone structures like this one have lost many of their larger stones. Nearby is a single stone with early church carvings, being uncut it may have been erected 3000 years ago. Scarcely visible, for it lacks any monuments, is the ancient burial ground Cledh Chiano named after St Circan Marc ant-Savir who died in 549 and is said to be buried here. A recent burial ground was probably created in the 18th century for the Campbell's of nearby Ardlignish, a Roman Catholic family. Within it is a stone walled enclosure with two carved grave slabs dated 1733 erected in his life time by Alexander Campbell. For centuries Ardnamurchan has belonged to the MacIans. But in the 17th century the Campbell's of Lochneil gained control. In 1722 Ardnamurchan was sold to Alex Murray and later after sequestration was bought by James Ruddick in 1767. Until 1828 there were two flourishing towns, Tornamon and Bourblaige on the west side of Ben Hiant. They were part of an old system where clans may hold land from the chief in return for services. The houses and fields are on a plan by William Bold in 1806.

The clearance

Destruction of the clan system after Bonnie Prince Charles fled from Culloden in 1746, changed much. The economics of the time and area needed cash for improvements and hence tenants could be evicted at any time. Under financial pressure, Sir J Riddles let Ben Hiant to a lowland farmer, Jacksman Mc Coll, and by 1828 he had cleared the townships ready for sheep. So the tenants went either to Ardnamurchan or most to USA and Canada. Today BH and CMG are responsible for a large estate and many red deer, cattle and sheep and CMG has a sense of destiny

This is a big area of remote, under-populated, seemingly unspoilt and attractive country, worth getting to, especially on a hot clear day such as I experienced. The evidence of the ancient extinct volcanoes lies all around and was a characteristic of the unique landscape.

The coastal road led through the timbered loch side to Salen. Again there was no store, only a craft shop which had just closed but where I managed to extract some sandwiches, mars bars and sweets. Back at the village pub I chat-

ted with four Glaswegeans and also bought half a dozen duck eggs from a nearby wayside box. When passing the craft shop again, to collect my bag, I peeped in the waste bin for some fire lighting paper and found, instead, a treasure trove of cherries pickled in whisky. Three bottles were rescued! This was the 'C' on my new mental dietary list. My camp that evening was beyond Resipole under the shelter of some rocks by the beach with a breeze and a fire keeping the midges away.
25m

Day 297
Friday 11th June
In the night it became overcast but without rain and now the sea was still. I'd had a good night's sleep, helped by my survival bag stuffed with seaweed, ferns and moss and this had improved my back which had been considerably painful for the past week.

After a breakfast including the pickled cherries, I was off at ten into a beautiful, clear, sunny and warm day and on a road through woodland beside Loch Sunart, to Strontian. Oak forests were being restored as part of a millennium project. But what will happen to the seeds of the conifers that have been removed - would they not germinate? For now however a sprinkling of white flowered rowan and hawthorn were appearing in the woods with the reds and purples of rhododendron inflaming the undergrowth.

In Strontian I did get supplies and visited the 'I' followed by a light meal in the cafe. There were quite a few tourists about including some walkers and cyclists which was not surprising in this beautiful area, ripe for holiday exploration. There are several mountains around here like Ben Resipol (2750 ft) but none are over the 3000 ft mark and hence Munro baggers were elsewhere.

The A861 led to the head of the loch and then the A884 took me back in the opposite direction. The south side of Sunart had outcrops of grey granite often coloured yellow with lichen and despite the road walking it continued to be an attractive area. After three miles along along the main A884 there was a turning to the right for a coastal route around Morvern. Two miles along this track at Laudale house a herd of a hundred red deer, complete with antlers, were still grazing on the winter paddocks while fish eagles hovered over the loch. Towards late afternoon I reached the Nature Reserve of Glencripesdale. At the house the generator was going but there were no humans about, so, taking a liberty, I went into the unlocked house and boiled some water for my flask. Nobody appeared and I set off again through a maze of fallen timber having difficulty finding the path south, involving a stiff climb over Bealach Sloc an Eich. Bealach of course means pass, and once beyond this feature I quickly lost the path in a jumble of tracks on the other side - just as the first gloom of

evening was gathering. Heading in what seemed the right direction it was not long before arriving at Carnliath where there was an open house (Caro Ann) where, with cheek, I could have stayed but instead slept in a sheep byre opposite. A note in the house log had recorded the observation of 56 birds in 4 days.
25m

Day 298
Saturday
At 6.45 the sun rose over the hills and drenched the glen and its trees and the still quiet loch with that wondrous early morning light. The view was doubled by reflections in the water. Another absolutely magical place and all I could say was WOW! With the realisation that superlatives could do little justice to this place.

Around the head of Loch Teacuis, was the vast spread of Forestry Commission pines with new gravel tracks - money was being spent for the future? Along here I was walking happily and singing (!) in tune with the environment, particularly as my back was somewhat better. But it was a good job nobody could hear me! It was not too long before I emerged on a beach at low tide, and followed the rocky sometimes squelchy shore to Doirlinn. There was wild life here, including otters and possibly mink. Lunch was at Doplin while amusing myself breaking the code for the combination lock on the front door, apparently once freely open and available to travellers - something must have happened! Knowing the way in, I could have stayed but decided to press on. A good idea, since not much further on unexpected generosity was extended at the wonderful retreat of a Glasgow-London surgeon and his wife: being provided with a meal and a luxury cabin for the night. In exchange I did a very small spot of gardening - planting some trees. Many years ago this little area was used by wealthy picnickers, who would arrive on steamers from Glasgow, attracted by the safe anchorage and picturesque views to paint. The house was probably used by the crew for their own party. Further remnants from those days included the cast iron mile posts along the track of the next day.
7m

Day 299
Sunday
The track took me, by degrees, to dim Drimnin and then gloomy Glenmorven with its huge trees - beeches and limes. Or was their size a reflection in my mind of past barren landscapes? In the west, over the sound, the horizon had been filled with views of Mull. On to Lochaline where, in pursuit of supplies, I had a drink in the Inn, busy with Sunday drinkers. It was not the best day for stocking up and some holiday sailors were also on the same fruitless quest. I settled for a hot pie in a quayside snack bar, before setting off into the increasingly wet day. Just out of the village there was a big silica mine with white

powder everywhere; the silica is used for the preparation of high quality optical lens and this was particularly important during WW2 when there was a demand by the military for good lenses. Later I would see this quartz vein running further afield. At least the mine had financed some maintenance work on the track up to the head of Loch Aline. An uphill climb took me to Loch Tearnalt in the hills and to my relief I found the bothy, mentioned yesterday in Doirlinn, having been advised to come this way as the southern peninsula was very precipitous after the first few miles. There were several hours of daylight left but I wasn't going anywhere further, and so scampered around gathering a small amount of scarce firewood. Settling in for the evening, a man and his two sons arrived. They had all been fishing for trout, but not with enough to share out. This is a relatively popular angling spot for those who don't mind the hike and there is a useful but leaky boat on the water, although wood is in very short supply.
23m

Day 300
Monday 14th June
It was a miserable wet morning and I found half a book which absorbed me for several hours until a couple arrived and roused me from my reading. They also brought a break in the clouds allowing me to set off soon after two in the afternoon. There was a poor path across the wet soggy upland grassland and navigation was necessary. There were considerable numbers of deer, which seemed to mix well with the lochs and treeless grasslands and I suspected that there were even more in the expanses of the less accessible southern area. On the other side of this moor there is a vast quarry, mining road stone of bright pink gneiss. But all was silent, deserted and macabre. Great piles of chippings stood awaiting shipment while a conveyor belt rested silently in the dripping rain. One advantage of super quarries is that it only messes up one area but I would see that deep scar later.

The coastal path followed the pink and white pebbled shore to the northeast. It was not clearly defined and made a difficult walk to Kingairloch. There were good possible sites for camping combined with fine views across Loch Linnhe but out of matches I had to abandon that plan, not willing to try rubbing two sticks together. After making enquiries at the stables near Kingairloch House I continued just beyond the town to find the church and nearby tracked down Bill Davidson, church caretaker and local estate manager for 22,000 acres. With his help I was able to stay the night at the chapel in a side room where there was an electric fire that allowed me to dry out a little. Bill also brought some food and a tot of whisky - another minor miracle of providence.
14m

Day 301
Tuesday
It must have been ten before I left. Today my back was worse again but it is only a short trip along the coastal road to Corran and its free ferry. On the way I passed a group of red hatted outward bound students learning the art of abseiling down rocks. It always makes me smile a little when seeing the lengths taken for safety and remember the earlier 'sink or swim' learning regimes. But I am relieved to hear that it's now deemed 'cool' to be a little dirty as this winds up your immune systems! Just off the main road, at a cafe in Ardgour two girls were experimenting with a microwave, trying to cook meringues. I was welcome to taste the failures with my tea. But their final success remains a mystery.

After the taking the ferry across the Corran Narrows which separate Loch Eil from Loch Linnhe I began hitching to Cromarty in order to collect my car. An oyster man took me beyond Fort William before being picked up by a teacher of open learning and instructor for hand controls in cars. He thought he knew the paraplegic of Ardnamurchan lighthouse. He also explained that the economics of Scottish life demanded normal working in a number of part time jobs. A footpath officer, a lorry and three local cars saw me into Cromarty, the last driver being the local potter who knew Helen. After walking up the field to the Henhouse and finding that they were out I started the car (with its nearly new battery) and collected hot water from the flat below the local potters shop before camping next to Helen's house.
14m

Interlude Eleven
Days 302 to 308
This was an idle period driving around northeast Scotland and spending too long over R & R, mostly around Aberdeen, before returning to Fort William.

- Chapter 4 -
Summer in the West of Scotland

Twelfth Stage
Corran Ferry to Largs
Day 309
Wednesday

The last stage of my return trip was driving west into a spectacular early morning sunrise which illuminated the remnants of low cloud. With empty roads I was able to relax and enjoy a wonderful drive through the Tyrolean picture book landscape of Aviemore with its chalets, forests and clean sharp rock exposures. After shopping in Fort William and parking at the Corran Ferry, I continued my walk south towards Oban. Four miles of the main A82 led to Loch Leven at North Ballachulish and in the climb down from the bridge was a bizarre monument:-

> The Appin Murder- Execution site
> James Stewart was hanged here on 8th November 1752 for being 'Art and Part' to the murder of Colin Campbell of Glenowen. The murderer has never been identified, although most people believe Stewart's ward, a Jacobite fugitive, Allan Brock to be responsible.
> J.S. was tried and condemned at Inverary and then taken to Fahr to await execution on this site, because it overlooked the site of the crime. His corpse was put in gibbet irons and left hanging from the gallows until 1761 [9 years!] to serve as a dreadful warning to the people. The case is notorious.
> Stewart protested his innocence to the end and Jacobite sympathisers kept doubts about his trial and conviction alive, and the truth of the matter has never been settled.
> In 1911 this monument was erected to James Stewart.

The massed mountains of the Ben Nevis range, in the north east, lay behind me as I walked down the low-traffic road beneath towering vertical cuttings of shale rocks. Three miles beyond the monument at Kentallen a track branched off towards Ardsheal House and when the track turned into a water washed path I remembered the mountain sage of Sourlie and his path's epithet:- 'put it where the stream is!!'. It didn't really matter here because it was a hot still day. After exiting through Cuil and Duror the main road continued southwards and on which I gained a lift back to Corran with a paper maker, collected the car and parked in a secluded lay-by near Loch Linnhe.
10m

Day 310
Thursday
After sleeping for over nine hours I was feeling less tired helped by walking in my Clark's shoes and carrying only a very light pack. Along the main road the super quarry could be seen on the other side of the Loch, the pink polluted rivers etched into the side of the mountain and the view made me realise why many people dislike them. From North Dallens there was a side track around Loch Laich and the striking 16th century tower house of Castle Stalker, standing mystically on its loch mouth island, and once owned by the Stewarts of Appin. The path used the unusual wooden Jubilee footbridge to cross the water of the river while wedges of yucky sea weed littered the shore, a sight not improved by the dull weather. On the other side, Ardtur farm was set on thick rich silica veins, similar to those quarried at Lochaline across the water. The house itself was delightfully set in its grounds with copper beeches, shrubs and herb gardens. I passed the ferry port to Lismore Island and went around the head of Airds Bay where there are many natural arches and caves while a shag fished the silent waters. Then while wandering through the private grounds of Drumnel House I watched small red deer leap enchantingly across fences and off into the woods. At the exit, on the far of the estate, I found a locked and rusted iron gate with its 'private' label but the lower rungs had been worn smooth where countless feet must have climbed over. This is an attractive quiet peninsular with a fair number of settled houses on poor scraggy land with good views across Loch Creran. At North Shian two fence erectors said that putting in poles here was hard work because of the rocky ground but I didn't volunteer to stop and help.

Having circled round to Creagan I worked my way through an expensive pot of tea in the Inn watching Wimbledon on TV; (Greg was two sets up, Tim was one set up, waiting for the rain to stop and another British player came within an ace of beating Becker). Nearby I saw a sign for Glasgow - 91m away and I wondered how many days of walking that would entail with all the coastline yet to come?

After crossing the water of Loch Creran by the old rail bridge there was more main road to Barcaldine with its 16th century castle built by Black Duncan as the most western of seven defences. Three miles further on, past the tourist attraction of Sea World, there was a minor road to the right leading to Dalintober, and along this I stopped to photograph a colourful garden, full of a wide variety of plants around a natural stream. They invited me in for tea and cakes. The owner was an ex-forester, running his own nursery, who was an exponent of mixed forestry planting.

Afterwards I continued past the stronghold house of Barcaldine Castle, through Baravullin to Benderlochand and then more main road. Running par-

allel to the road were the remnants of an old railway which I had been trying to use but it wasn't until passing a couple of purpose built and rather sad gypsy camps that a usable track opened up all the way to Connel. North of the bridge I asked about parking then started hitching back to the car. A young lad took me to Sea World, followed by a farmer, in his 4x4, returning from the Edinburgh Show where his horses had won 1st class awards. From the Inn at Creagan I walked for a while before getting a lift from a Preston-based nuclear-fuel man. He actually turned back especially to pick me up. He was on a Munro catching trip and took pity when he'd seen my rucksack.
28m

Day 311
Friday
'Camped' in same spot as the day before, on the beach and after a beautiful sunset, I had slept well. It was a relatively early start at eight o'clock, my back was improving and the birds were playing in the misty, calm morning as I drove to the Falls of Cora and parked the car in the lay-by indicated to me yesterday.

After crossing the striking girder bridge to Connel, I climbed down the path to the A85, which was heavy with traffic and on the pavement survived five speeding cyclists who were reluctant to use the road, but who I scolded for terrorising pedestrians. Three miles later, by a large cemetery, a right turn took me to Ganavan Bay, where outcrops of volcanic rocks were riddled with caves. Aloof Dunollie castle was perched high above, while in a field stood an isolated rock pillar crowned with a cap of trees, and below, the ferries plied their way to and from the Isles. Oban was full of people (!), making me realise that I wanted to escape to the country away from the crowds and the tall elegant buildings. After buying a map at the 'I', I went to Tescos where the manager, Mr Rooney gave me a free breakfast before I did a piece for the Oban Times located in the industrial outskirts. Back to walking, I wiggled my way up Pulpit Hill high above the town and at the top noted in my diary that the hills around Oban were like droplets shaken from God's hand as he shook it out and said 'There! and that's Oban'.

It was developing into a hot day as a footpath, ablaze with foxgloves, led to the Kerrera Ferry and then a road to the diving school at Port nan Cuil, where I turned inland. A farmer allowed me onto his private fief for the route across to Kilbride. But at Gleanna Bhearradl the loch was flooded and my proposed route blocked. The previous night I'd had a dream about a boat taking me across water and there it was, a small rowing skiff, out on the loch, fishing. But, despite much hand signalling, they would not take me across; instead they directed me down stream for a struggle along the path to Ariogan after which it was road to Kilmore.

After four miles along the main road beside Loch Feochan and where the B844 branches off to the right, I abandoned frugality and bought tea and biscuits at the Salmon Visitor Centre. Three miles later at Loch Seil a cut across a field took me to some standing stones and a long ambling track through cattle grazed grassland to the Bridge over the Atlantic - Clachan Bridge which was over 200 years old, quaint and associated with Telford. Who else? But actually built by John Stevenson of Oban.

In the packed pub there was much talk of the highland games on the morrow at Dunmor Farm but at 7.00 I left for the walk to Auchnasaul followed by hitch-hiked rides back to car. A builder dropped me in Oban and then the father of a local radio DJ took me to Connel to move the car a short distance to a dead end back road for a quiet night's sleep.
21 m

Day 312
Saturday
After driving out to Shiel Island and picking up stores in Balvica, I was keen to see the highland games at Dunmor, finding them spread out below the road. But after driving into the car park, quickly decided that they were no more than an exaggerated village fete and drove out again!

At Auchnasaul I parked in a farmers yard and started walking at 2.30 heading south down a minor road. Two miles later branching off for Ardmaddy castle and then, pushing through tall grass and woods, I did not find the expected castle. Only one wall stood as the visible remains and even this seemed to use a natural dyke for its main existence. After Caddleton it was a long hike over to Degnish and then Kilchoan house. Apparently I had missed the wishing tree and some lime kilns, according to an estate worker picking up stones on the beach beside Loch Melfort. A road continued through the woods by the Loch to Ardanstur and Melfort emerging onto the main road near Loch na Cille. Four miles further along the quiet A816 at the bay of Traigh Nam Musgan a lift took me to the Kilninver Junction, from where I walked for a couple of miles before a Canadian tourist picked me up and dropped me off, back at the Auchnasaul farm.

Driving back down the A816, I stopped in a picnic spot near Traguaina where I'd been before, having said to the people there to expect my return. Ensconced in the lay-by picnic area was an archaeologist, Mathew and his friend Monica, a Polish lass doing a Ph. D. on Norse matters. They had started a fire and shared their cooked fish with me. We went to our beds, serenaded by the strains from a large and wild wedding party in Craobh Haven twinkling across the water.
14m

Day 313
Sunday
There had been overnight rain but we rekindled the fire for breakfast before I managed another tardy ten o'clock start, parking on the verge at last nights finishing point and setting off on the track to Craobh Haven, site of last nights six hundred strong party for Simon B and his bride. There were a lot of expensive boats here and an abundance of rich hangovers as well.

   Through Lunga I walked to Ardfern and while sitting watching the boats, a man in a truck stopped and said he had seen me yesterday. It was nice to know that people were interested in their surroundings, and were providing a loose insurance against disaster. The craft of chain saw sculpture seems to have taken off around here and there were several displays of these timber artists. Two miles took me back to the main A816 and then a further half mile to Kintraw Farm where retired farmer MacKae gave his permission for car parking.

   After hitching back to the car with a TV installer and driving to Kintraw Farm I had lunch before tackling two miles of rocky coastal clambering around Craignish to the cow grazed beach of Ormaig and, for an hour, looked in vain for some cup and ring rocks in the woods. A cycle path took me to Old Poltalloch through cool, claustrophobic spruce woodland with enchanting moist mossy 'snowball' rocks lining the track sides. Emerging into warm sunshine, the walk continued through cleared woodland areas towards Kilmartin and all the amazing druid cairns on this valley floor. It always comes as a surprise when you find something that you know nothing about. This is a renowned archaeological area and it is certainly worth a visit to these prehistoric circles and standing stones. It must have been a thriving community aeons ago. I continued on the valley bottom fields to Poltalloch, Barstoisnoch and finally Bellanoch across the Great (Sphagnum) Moss of the undrained marshes of Moine Mohr. Trying to hitch back, a lift quickly took me to Kilmartin. The House there had been changed to a museum and a centre for studying the local archeology, but was closed at that time of day. A walk of five miles back to the car came before my problems in finding a suitable spot to camp. Finally I settled for the car park at Carnassarie Castle, built by John Carswell, Scholar and Protestant Bishop of the Isles in 1565 and expanded in 1643 by one of the Campbells.
17 m

Day 314
Monday 28th June
After parking near Bellanoch at the Islandadd bridge I walked the mile missed out yesterday and then had breakfast before setting off in sunshine along the Crinan Canal, the old boating Gateway to the Isles and still full of a rich col-

Day 313 Art with a chainsaw in Ardfern, Loch Craignish: a tribute to Scottish trees

Map 5

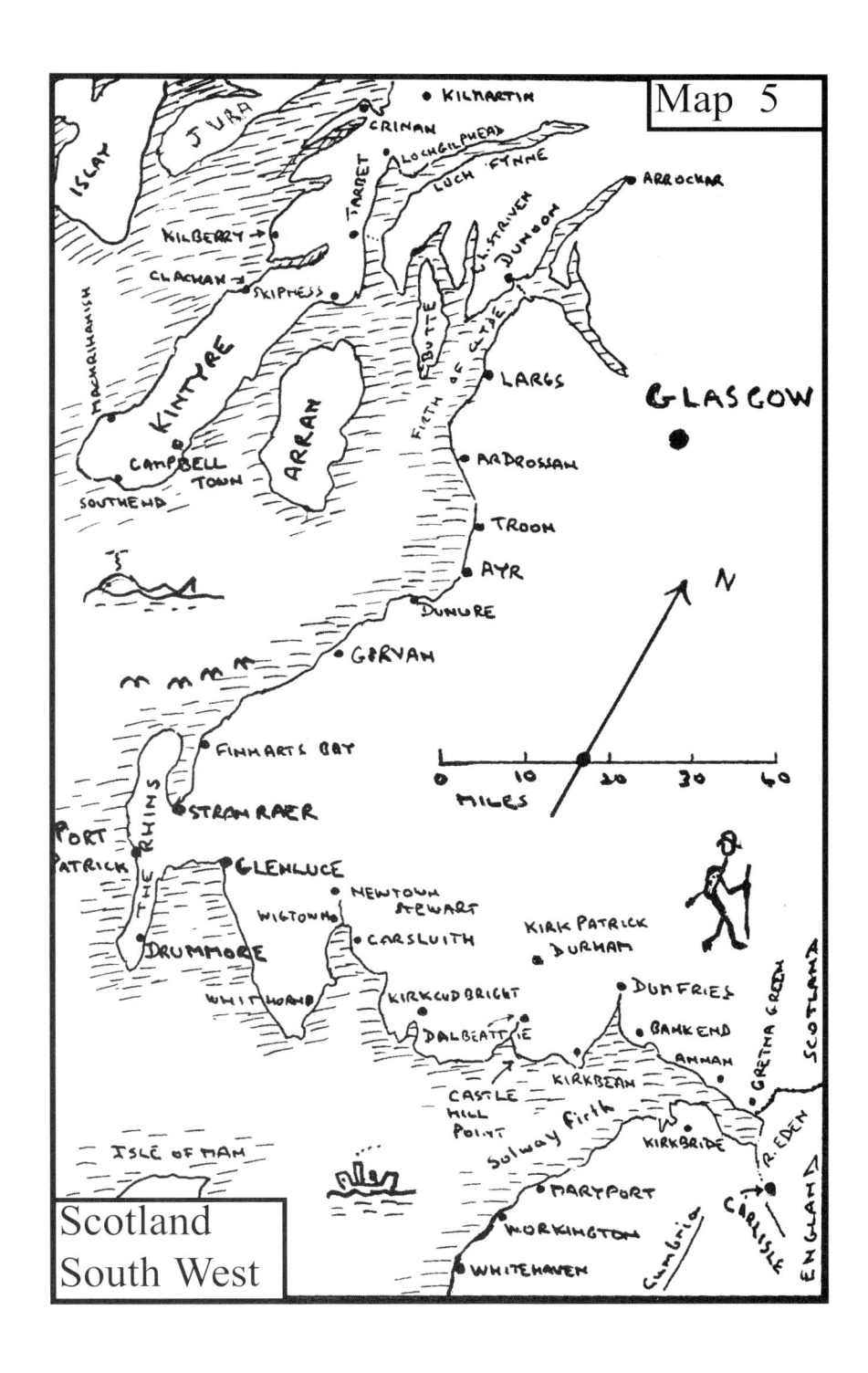

Scotland
South West

lection of boats and was soon at the last lock in Crinan, treating myself to tea and chocolate cake. A lady sitting by the lock gates, selling kippers, told me that she did this regularly. It certainly added a rustic charm to the place! Though she wouldn't have been out of place shopping in Bromley High Street! After walking round to the harbour and along the path up to Ardnoe point I stopped at the top to look at the spectacular view of the Jura and Scarba islands to the North West.

Great quantities of the wood had been cleared and huge piles of logs lay on either side as I progressed along deserted cycle tracks through Knapsdale forest to Dournie, Ardnackaig and Carsaig. The farm at Barnashaig was derelict and ripe for development and a turning point back to Tayvallich. An ex-forester, mowing his lawn overlooking the harbour, signed my form. As we stood and talked he told me that we were only 100m from his birth place. He had lived in the village for 64 years and amongst jobs had worked on the roads and the canal. Soon afterwards I had a pot of tea at the local Inn while watching the agile athletic Agassi at Wimbledon. From here a protracted woodland road took me out to the head of Caol Scotnish and then past the bottom of Loch Coille-Bharr, going a mile further than necessary to the side of a beautiful mini loch with delightful deer playing in the sun. After back tracking I found the path to Strone, the road to Craiglin, the forest track around Barr-Mor back to Seafield farm and the road to Acnamara. At the outdoor centre, Midge - the warden - agreed to my overnight parking. On hitching, a young couple, who were messing about with refuelling their car, dropped me at Bellanoch up the road.

Back at the centre, crowded with noisy adventure children, and with hot water from the kitchens I 'camped' in the rain. Settling in, I thought 'Oh for some quiet'!! Having walked all day I was now only three miles from my starting point that morning but it had been a glorious midsummer day in an area recognised for its excellent scenery as adjudged by the extensive cycle tracks hereabouts. Or was that the Forestry Commission's contribution to conservation and the countryside?
23m

Day 315
Tuesday
The overnight heavy rain had stopped by the time I started at 9.30, having shopped in the village store for Mars bars, and before setting off south-west along the road with grand views of the peninsular across Loch Sween. The formations there were made from the shiny micaceous shales tilted E-W and eroded into troughs and these had turned yesterday into a long walk. By Ashfield I cut off the road to the beach with its private houses, walked through Ashfield house and left via its big ornate gilded gates onto a delightful narrow

loch-side road. A mile later, a silly little diversion took me on the path through Sweet Charity Forest before I continued along the road to Castle Sween where the adjacent tea rooms gave me tea on the house. The MacSweens were of Norse origin and lost their title to the Earl of Menteith in 1262 and after siding with the English in 1300-1310 lost everything and beat a retreat to Ireland. The castle is surprisingly intact, open to the public, and is probably the oldest stone fort in mainland Scotland. In 1308 it was occupied by Alexander Macdonald but he was surprised and beaten by Bruce who dragged his boats across the isthmus at Tarbet (hence the name). It belonged to the McNeils for a couple of centuries before the Macmillans gained the Knapdale lands through marriage. The place finally plunged into oblivion in 1647 when the royalists destroyed it. But now its a great place for holidaying children to play.

I worked my way back to the road and on to Kilmory where there is the splendid little 13th century chapel of St Mary, which has a protective glass roof over the ranked tomb slabs of dead Norman crusaders. Within a mile the road ended at a locked gate but continued as a private track through the Stronefield Estates. The scenery improves here, is full of whitish hills, woods and views to the sea, while at the far end of the track two eye - catching circular lakes were ringed with coronas of white lilies. On the track I met a convoy of four cyclists each with a child sitting behind and strangely two cars which would have no escape. The track descended to the side of Loch Caolisport and as the rain began again, I followed a paved track to Ellary and Achahoish but some- how missed St Columba's Cave!

At the junction with the B8024 I soon got a lift with a fisherman of lobsters and crabs and he took me to see his his boat in Ardrishaig. A mason who had a badly cut finger after tangling with his cement mixer, picked me up before speeding through Lochgilphead to Bellanoch and beyond. Then a short lift led to Barnluasgan and its prominent roadside Celtic ring and cross. After walking some distance a mini driven by a local white haired man took me to Achnamara. It was supposed to be a simple drive back the same way - the reverse of my hitching but the entrance to the B8024 was stoppered by a police car as a lorry had come off the edge of the road and was blocking traffic. Consequently I had to wait in a lay-by for an hour before it was cleared. Eventually after parking in a wooded lay-by opposite Loch Caolisport I had the task of walking two miles back to the Achahoish junction and then return- ing, in the dark, to the car in order to provide continuity for my journey.
20m

Day 316
Wednesday
A ten o'clock start. It was overcast with a stiff southerly breeze, but there were masses of bluebells and other wild flowers to lighten the day. The gulls hov-

Day 315 The last of the Normans: effigies at St Mary's chapel in Kilmory

ered and I spotted a lone seal on a beach, while brown lambs played in the fields. It was nearly a straight road to Kilberry with its Inn and coffee shop, a fire, good food, a propitiatory landlord and flashy red fuchsias outside. This was a popular stopping place for tourists attracted by the hospitality and the cuisine. The road continued around the southern part of this peninsular and at the bottom end I phoned my mother who said that she was well. A detour took me through Dunmore Farm Woodland where I was soaked by the wet bracken and also saw none of the advertised ravens, owls and hawks! Increasing rain saw me through Torinturk, Stonfield, deer infested forests and the main road to West Tarbet. Sodden, I hitched back to the car.

My intention was to park at the golf course in Stonfield but as I asked for hot water in a nearby house a jovial girl and her boy friend took me in for a large gin and tonic and a long wet summer's evening chat. It seemed unreal as I was beginning to lose orientation with normal time and space as related to 20th century living.
21m

Day 317
Thursday
The day's action was debatable and the small patches of blue in the sky echoed my doubts. Would they grow or shrink? It was a question as to the necessity of the Mull of Kintyre in the itinerary of my journey. It all hinged on a four mile stretch of the A83 from West Talbert to Redhouse. The Mull lies suspended on the map like a large multi-gemmed earring, in between the Sounds of Gigha and Kilbrannan. Would I find an independent way up the other coast and back to Tarbet? I had plotted a possible circular route through the woodlands of the eastern coast traversing a trackless area of some 3 miles. Not finding a way would alienate my rule of the route that I shouldn't cover ground twice! However to leave out this area of Kintyre seemed preposterous, whereas I had willingly left out some other minor headlands.

It was a long hard walk to the south along the western main road - the only relief was at Clachan where there was a detour through Corran, Loup House, Portachoillan, Dunskeig Bay and then swooping back by the river to Clachan. In reassurance I learnt that the prominent legalist, Lord Irwin, lived somewhere on this loop! While back on the main road south a filling station shop sold me supplies.

The blue in the sky increased and a wonderful sunny day developed, in a complete contrast to yesterday. Having reached 'F' in my diet, I lunched on figs and biscuits in the cemetery south of Clachanand looked at the memorial to a 1st world war soldier complete with an idealised statue of an ancient warrior in a winged helmet:-

> To the loving memory of
> Duncan Mackinnon
> Scots Guard of Ronichan
> B A Magdalan College: Capt. of Bt.: Pres. of Oxford Union Brigade
> Born London 1887: Killed Flanders 1917
> Served in Calcutta Light Horse 1913-14
> Served in Gallipolli and Egypt 1915-17

This had been erected by the owners of Ronachan House, a mile down the road. But what a waste of a human life!

Beyond Ronachan Point lay a seal nature reserve with its quota of tourists and even some seals basking on rocks. In the car park a van screamed through its burglar alarm and I joked with the German owner that it 'sounded like a dying seal'. After another mile feeling hot I left my sweater under a caravan which was tucked away in a little sheltered bay and decorated with sea shells, thinking it would be just a few hours before returning to collect it.

At Lenaig farm, a big operation was in progress to make silage. Red tractors dashed up and down the road cutting, baling and carting and then automatically wrapping the bales in green shiny cling film. All about, the fields had had their grass cut. The mixed farming here is on the fertile flat inshore fields, the presence of easy worked soils evidenced by the outcrops of old red sandstone complete with little caves. The rocks and the mild climate have made this an affluent farming area. In 1647 there was a battle at nearby Rhunahaorine and the survivors fled to the local Dunashry Castle. It was hard to imagine the blood soaked fields now as the sun shone on this peaceful bucolic scene. However, on trying to check out this drama, all I found was the massacre of 299 Macdonalds (Catholics and supporters of Montrose) by General Leslie, the Covenanter, in 1647 at Dunaverty, near Southend lower down the Mull, with only one lad spared.

For a change in Tavintoan there was a little shop, while at Killean the chapel in a cemetery had a crypt, with a grill tomb slabs and the bones of a good family - the house of Largan. It was all very gloomy. Opposite was a long house bought by a wealthy Dane, with a lifeboat stranded on the road side. Near to Musdale I found a holiday park and watched a low roll of clouds gathering in the west in an outline about the island of Gigha, and continued walking south while at the same time trying to hitch north, but no lifts materialised.

I passed the war memorial monument just north of Glenbarr and carried on to Bellochantuy with its two inviting hotels before coming to Fangytavit with its craggy fore-shore. By a lone cottage, a lone man rowed out to sea, planting half a dozen lobster pots, hunting for his breakfast. On knocking at the door an

English lady emerged who was polite but unwilling to bend to my plight. She was no real help and gave a definite no to a derelict caravan up the road. I approached a farm set high on the cliff above and the farmer, another Mr McKae, was far more amenable. He insisted on driving me the long miles back to my car, just as the sun was setting in a most glorious spectacular style over the sea. Back at last night's hospitable house I was given more hot water and another gin before hitting my bed just before midnight.
31m

Day 318
Friday
It was raining again on my departure soon after eight. While getting supplies at the Clachan petrol shop I and the other customers were treated to a spontaneous ballad song by an old crofter in his grubby tam-o'-shanter hat.

   After parking at last night's farm, walking started at 1.30. Two miles of road were needed before striking off along three mile of beach in Machrihanish bay with its big sand dunes on my left. On the wave wet shore was a doctor messing about with a canoe. When I joked with him about getting to Ireland in 'that', he said that indeed was where he was going but not by canoe. He also invited me to stay on my arrival in Glasgow. As I marched down the firm sands a thick grey mist hung ominously over the southern headland. At Machrihanish I did a rather pointless gloomy little loop around the small headland in order to gain the minor road up to Little Lossit and an entrance into the damp forests. A misty track led to Killypole where there was a derelict and overgrown house, sadly unsuitable as a shelter from the wet so I set off to try and find a track one mile away to the south east, but without a compass, which I discovered had been lost! Soon in a terrible confusion of a maze of hills, fencing, mist and forests, I was completely lost stumbling around on wet boggy ground and vegetation and becoming wetter and wetter as I clambered up and down ravines. After an hour of these ramblings a stream, possibly the Lochnacreive burn, intervened and knowing that it must come out somewhere I followed. It was hard work but miraculously and suddenly I landed on a narrow road, a little to the west of my supposed destination. Thankfully I continued along this road, its correctness confirmed by one solitary driver who told me to back track uphill for half a mile for the strike off to Glenahanty. In the late gloomy evening I found a derelict farmstead with a roof and fireplace, gathered enough wood for a fire and was able to make a reasonable space for supper with a dry place alongside to bed down.
15m

Day 319
Saturday
Tiredness prevailed and sleep dominated the early morning. The thick mist

hadn't thinned, but it was calm and mild. A good track was laid past Gartnacopaig, Largiebaan and High Glenadale where I stopped in a dilapidated shed before borrowing a board to cross the stream without wetting my feet. There were a number of gates to pass through and the occasional sheep showed its black face through the fog. It was in this country that a Chinook helicopter from Ireland crashed with the loss of all those security men six years before. Seeing it, in its present misty condition, it wasn't surprising that such accidents could easily happen. Finally the path descended to Carskiey where I knocked on the door of a house which turned out to be the Estate Manager's. His wife was there and she gave me coffee and two egg rolls which were especially welcome; she told me that two days ago on Scottish Parliament day they had lit a beacon as a signal to Ireland! But although I could see Sanda Island, Ireland, which lies only fifteen miles away, remained invisible to me while about me lay an area of prosperous looking mixed farms with dairy cows, sheep and barley.

Back on the road to Southend (!) I passed St Columba's Chapel at Kilcolnkil and saw his supposed footprint in a rock. At Macharioch a decorator told me that the conical tower there should have been at Inverary, but that the surveyor on his horse had got the plans mixed up in the 1860s. Continuing coast-wise on a narrow road I noted a hill called 'The Bastard' on which was land belonging to the 'Glasgow Contest Group' bristling with antennae, generators, tents and camp-a-vans. But what they were contesting was unrevealed. By this time the mists had cleared as I continued through more forestry noting a hump of an island in the far distant sea and it would be some time before finding out what it was, as it wasn't on my map. A ferry and a destroyer passed by me as I walked on the high coastal road, enjoying the good views, including that of the Island of Davaar joined by a thread of shingle to the mainland. The tall clock tower of Campbeltown was still on winter time and beckoned me like a crooked finger. As I entered the town the mist rolled in again and the clouds gathered.

At 9.30 after an hour of fruitless hitching a B&B seemed wise, but it was Saturday and they were all full. Downcast I headed out of town to the east to look for shelter and rather perversely knocked on the door of the last, rather grand, guest house. It had one room left but it was £24 and I declined. Janet scurried away and had a hurried back-room discussion with her husband Trevor about the scarcity of B&Bs, my journey and the charity. This brought results with the offer of a free bed, a hot bath, a chance to dry some of my gear and breakfast in the morning. Heaven! Especially after last night's experiences. How easily and quickly despondency can change to delight through somebody's thoughtfulness.
24m

Day 320
Sunday
Away at my more normal 9.30, I travelled east then north on the B842. At Macringan's Point I sat and watched the foam-lashed sea and reflected that 'it was not all about walking' and what was all that nonsense of 'wearing a cap to school'. In the church yard there was a remarkably fresh marble tablet to Rev. John Snell 1747-1807, together with a rich mixture of names, dates, lives and professions deeply inscribed on the numerous tombstones, the earliest was dated 1692. Just up the coast was a WW2 fort - a collection of octagonal brick hideouts - as I continued through Peninver overlooking Ardnacross Bay to Bunlarie by Sandell Bay, and on the way talked to a shepherd, on his four wheeled Kawasaki, who reflected about the changes in shepherding, transport and the world. His world had changed more slowly than for most of us. At Torrisdale an organic tannery boasted the 'best sheepskins in Scotland' while after Bridgend I wandered round the flat Carradale peninsular with its caravans and bushes, then through the forests to the north and the road to Grogport. Some three miles further on by Cour I was given a lift by gardener, Jim. He took me to the junction with the A83. No lifts were forthcoming here but, surprisingly, a long-distance coach stopped and I was happy enough to pay the £2.70 back to the farm where I'd left the car two days before. Sitting on the bus next to me was an occupational therapist who told me she was just moving to a new job in Campbeltown. The coach driver said he knew the farmer and dropped me at the right place just as darkness came at the end of my day.
21m

Day 321
Monday 5th July
After waking at 7.30 I was due for a lazy day and while stretching and scratching the lady of the house opposite popped out for a chat and also gave me hot water and boiled eggs. The farmer, Donald MacKae also passed on his tractor and I was able to thank him again for his help. After driving to Campbeltown for the bank, tobacco, sorting office, a new compass and a report to the Courier, I was able to return to last night's pick up point and parked near a house boldly flying the Scottish flag. Soon after noon I walked the eight miles to Skipness along this delightful, quiet road perched on the shoulder of the coast, with views of Arran all the way. At the Claonaig Estate there is a nature reserve of the Aage V. Jensen Foundation, with a charming little path down to the sea. Near the shore there was a stainless steel viewing plaque, which had distances in kilometres and heights in feet!! - not knowing whether to be British or European. The Allt a 'Bhuc burn bubbled and twisted through the slanting slabs of grey sandstone while above crouched an oak woodland, gnarled and twisted by the relentless elements of weather - festooned with lichen and moss and hosting a wealth of insects - they were not the oaks for ships or houses. Down towards the fore-shore grew grasping layers of bur-

geoning bracken impeding passage and encroaching on the yellow green mottled rocks lodged on the shore, beyond which lies the dark hump of Arran with midget houses where the dark rocks met the sea.

The seaside B8001 continued into Skipness village and I walked around the woodlands of the estate before doing the three miles back along the shore. After a rebuff from some tourists, a young Tourist Board inspector of B&Bs and hotels gave me a lift back to the car. Then back at the Claonaig nature reserve I relaxed in the warmth of the late afternoon sun, finally staying there overnight.
10m

Day 322
Tuesday
After transferring to Skipness and its cafe car park I was able to leave at 6.30 (!) for the walk to Tarbert, finding a path by Skipness River and through the forest. Two estate workers on the way confirmed an earlier suggestion that a new track existed which joined the northern one shown on the map, so I continued with more confidence into the mist over towards the headland above Tarbet. It certainly was a new track built on thick cuttings of peat and the thought of having to navigate that tricky land in the mist faded away. Helpfully towards the end of the path two more track workers toting strimmers and chain saws indicated the path down to the town where I had breakfast (which at £4.00 was poor value), did the PO and caught a wee bus, which does three journeys a day, back to Skipness arriving in the early afternoon. On the drive out of Skipness, I gave a lift to a South African diver who was working here with some mates collecting Razor fish for a buyer and then drove to the caravan of Day 317. But my sweater had departed and despite leaving a note I had little hope for its return.

Tarbert is a port of call for the well travelled Waverley, the last sea-going paddle steamer in the world and which spent much of its time plying the Clyde and sundry other ports. After parking near the police station and walking to the pier to arrange a free passage on the ferry I arrived in Portavadie, across Loch Fyne, at 4.30. This was a ghost town with a swathe of abandoned MOD housing and buildings. With difficulty I found the path out and over to Low Stillaig, through bracken, gorse, bog, sheep ways, past standing stones and with another, different, view of Arran. There was a single ancient caravan on this headland to sit beside for a break while below, the indents of two bays could be seen almost pinching the headland into an Island. The track went north but after a short distance I took to the fields and headed for Stillaig farm and an interesting gap in the forest towards the east. This firebreak was heavy with vegetation and rocks: it was hard work but eventually it led over a couple of fences to Kilbride farm. On a park track to Craig Lodge I met a weary family group

who had been on the beach and were now trailing back to their car - the holiday season being on again. The lodge farm looked derelict and the farming not much better as I headed down the road towards Ardlamont point and the sweeping view at Camp cottage towards Arran and Corra. The farms are much better on this side of the peninsular, and they were too busy clamping silage at Kildavaig to help me. At Carry there was a caravan site and sailing school where I got hot water and begged some bread before walking on to a wonderful beach and camping on the shore just below Blair's Ferry. A good fire helped dispel the few spots of rain, although it remained still and warm. The beach was full of stranded jelly fish dehydrating on the beach, while oyster catchers continued their warning cries.
19m

Day 323
Wednesday
A pre- nine o'clock start!

Just above Blair's Ferry, which is now defunct, lies a slipway used in WW2 for loading tanks, yet another reminder of this area's war efforts. I stopped at the small 'I' in Kames but they didn't stock OS maps and it wasn't until Tignabruaich, after having tea in Susy's tea room, that I could buy map 63 in the local PO. The town sat waiting for touring coaches and the visiting boat but the peninsular, which I'd just passed and found attractive, appeared to be largely forgotten as a tourist area.

The road down graded from B to single lane and then to track, along which white foxgloves flowered and good views towards the Island of Bute appeared. Opposite Eilean Dubh there was a diminutive lighthouse and near here I met the Estate Manager from Glen Caladh farm. Neil, an ex-brass founder, had taken the job a year before when he found that at 40 he was too old. That is, too old to teach his subject, which he had previously done around the world. He had met his wife while making bikes in a local showroom, changed his job and now had 500 acres to care for - quite a lad. He told me all this while he sat with me under the trees - waiting for a lift to Ormisdale.

The path eventually disappeared in rocks and undergrowth, ending at cliffs which plunged into the sea. Luckily, as I rounded the sheer corner, a salmon farm boat was tied up to the rocks and they give me a lift around this seemingly impassable obstacle and out to Craig Cottage. Its time the path here was given a clean up!! Towards the head of Loch Ruel I tried to cross the wide flats but finally chickened out and gave up in the extensive oyster beds and consequently had to walk the five miles up to the bridge at Waulkmill before heading down the loch the other side on the A886. It was now very damp and starting to rain as I got hot water and started looking for a sheltered spot for a break.

Half a mile further on I found a three week old kitten that had lost its mother and which was going to do me a favour. No mother cat was visible while the kitten was soaked and losing a tooth. A sorry sight. It followed me across the road and the traffic would not stop! So with the kitten on a sock in the back pocket of my rucksack I ploughed down the road looking for advice, finally meeting a static-caravanner at Salthouse and after a conference with him decided to go to the vet in Dunoon, the caravanner sending me off with a sardine and milk for the cat in case he could eat. An elderly lady gave me a lift in her Combi to the B836, along which I walked for two miles before a Canadian and his wife in a smart red Mercedes (in explanation, he was ex Scot and it was a hired car) gave me a lift, in the now teeming rain, to Dunoon. The 'I' told me where the vet lived. After walking there, we had quite a chat and he said he'd find a home for the kitten.

As it was so wet I decided on a B&B which, after my third attempt, was Moncreif run by Frances and Billy Peel. It made a pleasant change to have a bath and a bed. A Shetland man, who was looking up his relatives, was staying together with two American tourists from Minnesota.
17m

Day 324
Thursday
With hot water and sandwiches I set off at 9.30 - again! - and tried to hitch. The first lift was last night's landlady herself but then a half mile walk before a hydroelectric fitter took me back to yesterday's caravan where I told the man the story of the kitten. It was a damp and misty start to the day but gradually improved as the road continued south. At Colinraine, from where the ferry for Bute runs, I bought supplies including a Telegraph but there were no cigarettes in this small shop, having only just made it, as it closed at 1.00 and it was then 12.30. After lingering over tea in the adjacent hotel I passed through the village and spotted ladies bowling on green plastic; how peculiar in this damp and fertile area!

The lonely single lane road continued to Strone point with its pebble beach on which a solitary seal was playing. As the road turned north I found a grassy spot for lunch, since it was now sunny and hot, and was entertained by gannets diving and flying up and down the loch looking for food. Further along, at the point where the road ends and the track starts two ladies were sunbathing and needed warning about the hole in the ozone layer. At the last house, Braingortan, I met an evangelist, who had been to Nigeria, and who now told me to read the Bible as he strode off. At Troustan there was an old stone shelter and an open caravan, but I continued along the path and up into the forest. Finally the path levelled out before petering out, as per the map, so I clambered down through thick trees to thick moist bracken and crossed a river to reach

Day 324 Loch Striven: one of my best camps, all because of a cat

the beach. It was a rocky climb along the shore in beautiful scenery while on the opposite side of Loch Striven a helicopter was spraying the hillside bracken with 'Aslam*'. One mile further on, early evening was starting and the waters of the bay trembled and fluttered as a shoal of racing fish twisted and turned. Were they trout? I sat down by a rocky projection to watch, and soon heard a seal trumpet. Entranced, as the bay became alive, I decided to camp although it was still early, collected a pile of wood and even found a piece of foam for a mattress for a relaxing evening. There was now not a cloud in the sky. A perfect evening. A perfect spot - one of the best on the journey. If I'd been here yesterday I would have been wet! Thanks were due to the kitten for distorting the time continuum.
13m

Day 325
Friday
It was a three hour walk along the beach beside the Loch to the head where the tree lined drive of a big house led up to the road (B836) which led to the track on the east of the Loch Striven. This was a good path but it had its own share of trouser-soaking bracken beneath the birches. At Glenstriven, on the beach by an ornate jetty, I met some people in a holiday cottage who gave me tea, holiday chat and a fond farewell. A good march took me down to Ardyne point but this was rather spoilt by the strong smell of rotten fish amongst all the jetties. It was a hot sunny day and at Toward I had my first swim in the sea just as a sleek black submarine manoeuvred past. Afterwards I walked to the lighthouse, set in a neat private garden, at Toward Point where some houses have some remarkable nautical characters carved into their sandstone walls.

It was then northward to Dunoon. The B&B used before, was closed so I continued to the ferry at Hunter's Quay and walked right onto the last ferry having the £1 fee waived. Furthermore a helpful ship assistant kindly refilled my flask and gave me a snack. On the other side, landing at Gourock, I walked two miles south, past the lighthouse at Cloch Point, before camping on the beach and gathering wood in the semi darkness for my fire. It had been a long day.
28m

Day 326
Saturday
Morning started at 5.45 with a few drops of rain and a scene from the rebirth of the world. Dark brown - black rocks littered the shore floor with the water withdrawn out to sea. Ducks were just being ducks, some wading, some quacking while other birds flocked and swept by, calling and feeding, while solitary herons stood aloof. The misty grey air hung still and silent - a new beginning - stark and beckoning.

After negotiating the path around Inverkip it was road to Wemyss Bay, where ORS outcropped and many of the big solid detached houses, made of the same stone, faced the sea, remembering past glories. Some had attached towers with conical roofs; marks of wealth in a bygone age. The station terminus with its ornate iron supports was also symbolic of that past era. Across the road the Sea-view-Cafe provided breakfast and also fed the men going to Rothesay, not to work but to fish.

Unfortunately it was main road to Largs where the 'I' wanted a story, which I promised on my return. At the post office there was no mail so I walked to the A760 and hitched to Glasgow, firstly with an ex-steeple jack turned guitar teacher and then a young couple took me straight into the city centre. After napping in a sun-filled park I did the necessary things in Glasgow before catching the long-distance bus to Tarbert and proceeding to 'camp' in the car park at Ardcastle Forestry commission, which boasted one of the best country walks beside Loch Fynne.
12m

Interlude Twelve
Day 327
Sunday
I took my time getting up, having breakfast, tidying the car and watching the hikers and bikers. A mountain cyclist said 'you cover bigger distances on a bike' before my drive to Glasgow.

Days 328 - 331
Monday to Thursday
12th July to 15th July
Four relaxing days were spent in Glasgow doing the sights while sleeping in a park on the edge of town, six miles from the middle.

Thirteenth Stage
Largs to Carlisle
Day 332
Friday
I took the wrong road out of the City but eventually arrived near Largs, parked the car two miles south, slept till 12.30.and then walked into the town. There was no mail and no Largs News to take my story for the 'I'. However I did buy supplies, film and from a charity shop, for a mammoth £2, a lightweight saucepan which proved to be a highly useful part of my equipment.

My journey continued along the Anchor footpath, sponsored by NATO

(Fairlie) decorated with a collection of large black painted anchors and sea floats laid out beside the way. Civilisation was obviously approaching as there were also plenty of little picnic sites along this coast. Beyond Fairlie lay a lagoon with a path for strollers but which soon rejoined the road. Part of this path was infested with a thick cloud of flies generated by a bushy stand of Leyllandii and it was a good job they didn't bite! The main road continued past the Texas coal terminal, built for the steel works that didn't happen, but was now being used for importing fuel into the UK! I followed the abandoned road, now converted to a cycle path, to Hunterston B nuclear power station, past Hunterston House, standing alone, grey, brown and half derelict in a dilapidated park, another reminder of past wealth. The path continued across flat land close to the shore past Hawking Craig pier before going to the 'publicly' owned 15th century keep of Portencross castle (a transit point for the bodies of Kings going to Iona) and then in piecemeal fashion around Arneil Bay and West Kilbride, before becoming a cycle track road to Ardrossan and I was now walking in busy traffic conditions: a real contrast after rural Scotland. However shafts of sunlight burst out and houses glistened with their white painted walls while in the west, black silhouetted Arran stood against the pale straw yellow sky with low cloud banks gradually changing to an orange sunset.

In Ardrossan after buying supplies and while walking back, through the town, looking for a lift or bus, Tommy, an old sailor, from the Ark Royal, talked to me and invited me to his house for a wee dram. When I left it was after nine and having missed the regular Largs bus I took one to West Kilbride, facing a long haul to the car. Fortunately, one mile later, a lift appeared from the darkness and saved me from the five mile walk. I moved the car to the dead end road of Hunterston power station where some rabbitters were using a gun and spotlight for their sport and it was midnight before they left and I could sleep.
15m

Day 333
Saturday
Slumber held me until eleven, then with my mobile base moved to Ardrossan, I walked round South Bay, while birds' calls abounded, two proud ducks paraded their brood, two swans bobbed along with their cygnets, three colourful wind surfers scudded across the sea and on the shore a raft of stranded jelly wasted away. The weather was overcast and windy, contrastingly different to yesterday's calm, whipped up a fury on the sea and dashed swathes of salty water against the sea promenades. One mile out of Saltcoats the proms stopped and an assortment of paths took me to the beach near Irvine, where I was assured of a crossing over the River Garnock, a view possibly shared by an enigmatic painting on the sea wall of Robbie Burns looking out to sea. Two

Day 333 Irvine Bay:one of the many faces of the ever changing sea

Day 333 Robbie Burns watches the sea in Irvine Bay, towards Aran and Ailsa Craig

miles later, at the other end of the beach, a millennium dome was being built, albeit the wrong one for me, and the footbridge access across the river had not been completed. The adjacent ICI land (used for making and testing explosives) was blocked, and despite getting a call through to their control room I couldn't use their road and had to retrace my steps two miles back along the shore before passing through Stevenston, Killwinning and Irvine to Fullarton. The compensation was a dramatic seascape as the moody sea beat on the shore. On the far banks of the river Garnock was a modernised quay area complete with Maritime Museum, a life-like statue of a horse, a leisure centre and adverts about this 'big idea'. The prom continued around the headland where a small modern sculpture 'all at sea' stood alone, while across the sea my unnamed rock-hump island was still visible south of Arran.

Grass paths and cycle tracks continued to Troon, which was reached as the sun was setting. I caught a 'free' train to Killwinning and then a blue bus to Ardrossan; trains are generally more expensive than buses but they don't always collect the fare, while one invariably has to pay on a bus.

After buying chips and getting my flask filled, I sat in the car and listened to the news. It was the 3rd day of the Open at Carnoustie, which I had passed through months before, and the game was a hotting up. Sleep came at midnight but I was awake two hours later having dreamt up an Operetta and then lay thinking of 'star and street light' photography - again - but eventually slept till ten the next morning.
15m

Day 334
Sunday
At midday I left Troon by a coastal path, past the Ballast Bank built by the Duke of Portland in 1840, across golf courses including the Royal Troon - while at the Prestwick, using a borrowed club, I even tried a 12 ft putt, which would have gone in if the pole had been in place! The wind had died down which was good for Carnoustie where a Frenchman was leading, seven shots in the lead. At sea, seven dinghies raced each other in light breezes and further out was an even better view of my granite rock.

A promenade and road brought me to Ayr where scruffy scrap yards around the lighthouse and docks greeted my entrance to the town while by the stark river bridge two large cormorants fished the river. The weather worsened as I looked for a Salvation Army hostel but on finding none walked around the headland to the Youth Hostel, a grand old house with its entrance beneath a tower complete with a striking conical roof. After making arrangements with the warden about parking and having a much needed shower I went to the station for a train to Troon.

At Safeways I spent a mammoth £17 boosting my stores and then sat in the car, listening to the golf open. Then, as the Frenchman began to falter and the tension increased, I drove to Ayr. The man was now in trouble with a treble bogey in a river. I found Robbie Burns' cottage and put the car into the adjacent car park for the night. The golf was into a play off now and eventually a delighted Scotsman - Paul Laurie - won on the last four holes of sudden death. Real golfing drama. It was wet there on the course and exceedingly so in my car park sitting and listening.
9m

Day 335
Monday 19th July
Having taken the car to the Youth hostel, I was away at ten o'clock. Coastal promenade parks continued to Cunning Park and the A719 main road walked until a minor road led through Dunure. I had tea in a quiet cafe by the stark cliff side ruins of the 13th century castle and ice tower overlooking the shore. In 1563 Mary Queen of Scots stayed here for a few nights at the start of her royal progress, while in 1570 the Earl of Cassillis took the lay abbot of Crosraguel and roasted him in soap to try to persuade him to give up the abbey lands. Albeit, despite the heroism, the abbey was dissolved twenty years later. In At Drumshang I found a path on the old railway to Croy Brae (Electric Brae). Wondering what was in the name I crossed fields and fences, trying to reach the shore, and in the trees found a convenient blue rope to descend, through thick clawing undergrowth, into a caravan site, finally landing at the feet of a surprised resident. The long beach below continued to Culzean country park with its delightful grounds crowded with tourists. In the house, a gift to the nation from the Kennedy family, I obtained an authentication signature and then meandered through the gardens, past the gun battery, ice house and lily pond before resting from the rain in the boat house while talking to a man and his wife exercising their Papillions in the park

The footpath tracks of the estate continued to Maidens with its seaside green. It was road to Turnberry, dominated by a white hotel and smart gardens. In the town I bought a map for the next stage and continued down the busy A719 to Girvan. By now it was very wet, but, even so, golfers were still playing their game. After four attempts I found a guest house with a room, a bath, tea, TV, a chance to dry out and a landlady who washed my trousers and shirt. Out at sea, directly west, was a super view of my little island and it dawned on me at last that this was the mountain of Ailsa Craig from whence that potato variety got its name.
21m

Day 336
Tuesday
An amble through the lower parts of Girvan and by the shore took me to the A77 and Kennedy Pass where I was reminded that this is Kennedy, or Earls of Cassillis, country with a string of crumbling castles and coastal watch towers while the actual castle Kennedy lies in the extensive gardens of Lochinch Castle just east of Stranraer. Also at this time another Kennedy died in an air crash in the USA involving a long sea search. Seven miles of main road lead through Lendalfoot to Ballantrae where the bank was closed! In a nearby thrift shop I bought a memento programme, full of songs, for Liz's birthday and took tea in the PO, talking to a Canadian teacher as the rain continued outside.

At 3.30, making a move I realised, half a mile down the road, that I hadn't paid the cafe bill. Dropping my bag by a post I walked back to redress the mistake, but on returning to the post, my rucksack had gone. Disaster!! Retracing my steps to the town again, intending to find a police station I talked to someone about my predicament when suddenly a car pulled up and the young driver said 'have you lost a bag?' Honour had been restored to the district.

Out in the country again, with the birds and hares, on good farm tracks which led past Dove Cove to Finnarts Hill, I foolishly decided to take a short cut down the side of the hill through head high bracken and a dense plantation of fir trees and I got thoroughly wet on the way down to the path below which led around Finnarts Bay to the A77 heading for Stranraer.

At Balyett Farm I took a bed at the backpackers hostel - Sally's house - a port-a-cabin - where, strangely, 'Pat' was the landlady. The only other occupant was a free-wheeling Aussie motorcyclist, Lloyd, who had come from Bangkok and was now touring all the British Isles. He gave me an interesting talk about the Australian free settlers of 1839 as opposed to the previous convicts and government servants. It's all on microfiche he said.
26m

Day 337
Wednesday
About to enter the Rhinns of Galloway I had another reluctant start and although up at 8.45 a slow breakfast meant my arrival in Stranraer was delayed until eleven. At the Salvation Army having coffee and cake, a large, rotund and garrulous lady of some 55 years told us all about her 50 cc moped trip from Norfolk and on through the coastal towns of the eastern coast. It was entertaining stuff compared to the rain falling outside.

Out of town the concrete promenade suddenly disappeared near a wood, and progress therefore continued by beach, fragmented path, a golf course, where the players were still busy, and back to the road as the rain started once more. There were few birds around at the West Galloway bird sanctuary but a lone stag stood high on the cliffs above and watched as the high speed ferry to Ireland passed causing waves which washed and eroded the beach below.

North Galloway seemed like a little bit of Ireland: neat green fields, white painted houses, sleek black cattle and attractive Charolais bulls with brown cows. The walking was attractive along the west Galloway coast though my enthusiasm was somewhat reduced by the wet conditions. In Kirkcolm I passed through the grounds of a run down house, with its complement of two big fat peacocks parading around. Why is it that these two things, ruins and beauty, seem to go together?

After spending all day walking to Portpatrick, which used to be important for sailings to Ireland but lost its status in the middle of the nineteenth century when steam arrived, I found no B&B in the town, but with the advice given at the Commercial Inn, went one mile further on, in the dark, along the wind swept path to find the local Dunskey castle perched high upon the cliffs. It wasn't a complete ruin and I found a dark, airy, dry and dirty room for a night's sleep on the hard floor, sheltered from the wind whipping across the sea.
25m

Day 338
Thursday
By contrast it was a glorious sunny morning but the uneven coastal cliff path disappeared at Knockinaam Lodge. Unable to find the continuation I had to scramble across the last 100 yards downhill through and over a bank of small hawthorns bushes, brambles and gorse and once started had to continue. At the bottom I emerged thoroughly scratched, torn and full of thorns. But the sun warmed my body while the grassland hills rolled beautifully around me as the waves broke on the golden beaches beside this green and vegetated land.

Using minor roads I arrived in Clachanmore at eleven to have tea and cheese-cake in the picture gallery cafe of an old school, sheltered from the strong northerly wind. In the attached gallery the work of seven 'professional' artists showed seascapes and still life pictures while outside modern metal sculptures stood their ground. It seemed a strange place for a gallery but they obviously did a reasonable trade. I continued to Ardwell point where there was a lovely empty cove and an unlocked empty house, obviously a holiday place. Not finding the earthwork castle at Grennan point, I cut across to Drumbreddan for a track to Port Gill and from there a very minor road leading south. On the way, a dead cow lay in a ditch and further along a runaway cow lurched across the fields with erstwhile cowhands in hot pursuit - perhaps these farmers were amateurs? Then a woodland path took me to the fish ponds of Logan Bay which are worth a visit together with the sands.

In Port Logan the pub served soup with bread and I met a group of Irish cyclists which emphasised the cross water connections. A track took me to Clanyard Castle, which had only one tower left standing before crossing rolling farmlands full of cattle, fields of barley and white washed farmhouses. At Knockencule a man was busy making silage as I walked round to Inshanks where a lady gave me a cupful of tasty raspberries. Across to Auchneight and fields to Knowe, a view of the Mull of Galloway sprang into sight. In the hot sun at Cairngaan I was given tins of tomatoes and tuna by a barley farmer. In Drummore there was no B&B, so I went into the pub for a drink, crisps, milk and a chat. At their suggestion I found another caravan site where it was thought they might have caravans for nightly hire. That idea was incorrect but they gave me permission to camp plus logs for a fire. However not fancying any of their spots I continued for another two miles, carrying the surplus wood, to camp on the shore below the trees of the Grennan Plantation and finally settled in with stacks of fire-wood to a wonderful if not spectacular sunset. This is indeed a pleasant part of Scotland which seems to be somewhat overlooked by tourists.
26m

Day 339
Friday
A few drops of rain woke me making me rise early. Feeling very tired I decided to have frequent stops and went picnic site hunting up the A716, stopping briefly at Ardwell where the tea room was shut. At Drumantrae Bay the site had no table but at Sandhead there was a shop for chocolate bars and a Daily Telegraph for the crossword and to light fires. From here to Glenluce the sea disappeared beyond the broad flat scrubby belt of MOD firing ranges - danger areas, the red flags were flying, the guns were firing and the smell of cordite drifted around me. On my left lay the airfield of West Freugh showing little sign of activity but amusingly its radar silos looked like giant, teed-up, golf balls. The sun got hotter and at one point on this road I lay back in the grass and fell easily asleep. Further along, forests appeared interspersed with fields of maize in the fertile fields around Piltanton Burn. Turning right for the minor road to Stairhaven I left my bag by a roadside bench while shopping in Glenluce which has an abbey and a motor museum, and after lunching on my seat, without a care in the world set off along the coastal road. But I'd had a lapse of concentration and had to drop my bag in the picnic site at Stairhaven and hitch hike back for two miles in order to retrieve my hat and lighter which I'd left behind when stopping for lunch. This was really crazy as usually after getting up after a break and putting on my pack I normally take another turn around my stopping place to check that I have not left anything. It was a longish wait for a lift, but it was a lovely day for relaxation and the couple who

did help did so in double measure when they brought me back again after rescuing my lost property and I was then able to walk the track to Auchenmalg, via Laigh Sinniness, where red deer stood below the cliffs. A couple in a seafront bungalow filled my flask, told me that otters were common here and gave me a SGM biblical text to read. They also told me of a cave in the cliffs further along where an old lady used to live and which might suit my needs.

Although I never found the cave nor saw any otters I camped near the cliffs amongst seaside rocks and grass with plenty of drift wood to cook my meal, using 50% sea water as an experiment in salt intake. My only reading material was that SGM New Start Text including Mathew 11:28-30:-

> 'Come to me, all you who are tired of carrying heavy loads, and I will give you rest. Take my yoke and put it on you, and learn from me, because I am gentle and humble in spirit; and you will find rest. For the yoke I will give you is easy, and the load I will put on you is light'

23m

Day 340
Saturday
After a comfortable night I cooked porridge in more sea water, just as the first beams of sunlight came over the hill to liven up the yellow limpet encrusted rocks of this rugged shore which lay exposed at low tide where signs of otters were apparent, but I had no actual sighting. To the west lay the silhouetted Rhinns of Galloway, to the south the Isle of Man and in the far distance lay England across the Solway Firth. I set off down the main road, the A747, passing a field where white Charollais played with black steers like animated chess pieces. On the shore lay isolated cottages in rural gardens while flocks of black cormorants stretched and dried their wings as they perched on the boulder strewn shore. At Corwall Port lay the ruins of Chapel Finian which honoured Celtic St Findbars and had been rebuilt, long ago, for pilgrims, who arrived by sea, in the early part of the second millennium, and were going to Glenluce or Whithorn. At Changue Farm a man, strimming the verges, also told me that otters and seals abounded here but for me they remained elusive. I was in Port William at eleven when it started to rain while at Monreith the sun came out again and I went into a one acre garden arranged around the old mill, with a wide variety of plants arranged in sections between stands of white fluffed rowan. The owners had worked on it for 25 years, and I voted it best in the west!

A dead badger - my second - lay in the verge as I made my way to the Point of Lag. On the way out to the golf course stood a sculpted memorial to Gavin

Maxwell (1914-1967) and his celebrated otters:-

> 'Haec Loca Puer Amavit -Vir Celebravit'

After passing the course I found an unmarked coastal path but looked in vain for the sea mammal wildlife, instead a feast of debris washed up by the sea lay on the raised gravelly shore - enough for a hundred camps and a few huts as well. In my reverie I passed St Ninian's cave and had to walk back a short distance to see this enigmatic 5th century retreat with its contemplative view of the south east. Unfortunately the neat early pilgrim crosses are rather dwarfed by the rapid spread of more hastily scratched modern contributions. St Ninian, the first British bishop built his first Scottish church in Whithorn, around the corner, in the last part of the fourth century to tend the local spiritual needs. And when I left my bag on the beach while visiting the cave, somebody left £5 for StC in my map case. Was the saint still in action?

From the beach a spectacular cliff top path continued to Burrow head and onto the Isle of Whithorn, a lovely village in the evening sunlight. White washed houses lay around the curving harbour, while a fox strutted in the nearby cow meadows. Leaving my bag with a gang of boys, who were drinking 5.3% white beer, I walked to the quayside shop which was a leaning wooden shack. Alas it had just closed so I retreated to the pub for a drink. The boys, beyond the call of duty, brought my bag back to me before my walk to Portyerrock Bay for a camp near the beach. Again there was plenty of wood and even though the ground was hard and uneven I slept well on a mixed hash of rice and beans.
21m

Day 341
Sunday
A few spots of early rain woke me. The sky was restricted by slow moving grey clouds to a narrow streak of blue in the east, and pillowed by short columns of white nimbus which gradually expanded as the morning grew into shape. The tide was out entailing a walk across jumbled rocks to collect sea water for my breakfast porridge before continuing up the B7063 through farming country to the ponds of Palmallet Farm. The remains of Cruggleton Castle were a silhouette on the shore cliffs across the fields and nearby, isolated, in the green and yellow streaked fresh cut grassland, stood a solid church set amongst tall trees of sycamore, ash and beech, and circumscribed by a well built seven foot wall. A high stone stile led me over the wall to this 19th century rebuilt Kirk, but the old doors profusely embossed with rusty seven-petal studs were resolutely locked, hiding the preserved Norman Arch inside. One service is held here each year and the keys were available at the nearby farmhouse. Close by, a field was thick and heavy with ripening wheat, at least four

tons an acre, while a flush of barley waved in readiness for an October harvest. The farmer's wife told me of the numbers of peregrines hereabouts and how they would sit on the grain silos teaching raptor tricks to their young.

A thickly grassed field, a derelict house and a walled area of regenerated woodland led me pleasantly to Rigg Bay, in which lies a part of a Mulberry Harbour that hadn't floated and remained as a reminder of the WW2 activities here which led up to the Normandy Landings. Mulberry supposedly was another code word - plucked out of the air - for the serious business of landing supplies using these Lego type docks, which were floated into position. One was smashed up in a storm while the other, more patiently assembled, at D+12 unloaded a stream of vehicles onto the beachhead for the breakout. An old cattleman told me of his local experiences during that time: the manoeuvres of the 'magic carpet', the nearby convalescent home and the airfields. Now, this area is a peaceful idyll with its pleasant views, scenery, rocks, sand and picnic sites. Having a break in one of these recreational areas an elderly man and his wife from Carlisle told me of his mushroom farm, its temperature requirements and their ability to make a reasonable living even in these troubled times of low farm prices.

Continuing through the woods and grounds of Galloway house to Garlieston I bought my day's rations in the SPAR shop just as it was closing and had tea next door, looking across the salt burnt harbour green. Inside Ben and Hilary from Castle Douglas, with their children, were also having tea and out of the blue they invited me to stay at their house when passing.

From this bay, a very overgrown path continued for the most part through woods of beech, ash and sycamore but a sign declaring 'No Path and No Dogs' pushed me to the rocky shore where a spasmodic trail ran from one grassy bit to the next, through barley fields and ankle tugging rye grass. Then the woods recaptured the path and reduced the sea to occasional glimpses of shore rocks decorated in yellow lichen and the occasional tiny bay. There would be plenty of places along here to camp in solitude. The tall sycamores by the path stood like cathedral columns, bare bolled and lofty while the signs that habitation were not far away showed as wayside raspberries sprouting in the side growth. At North Balfern Farm, a horse farmer told me about the path which led to the Crook of Baldoon and the airfield, where I was offered a lift by two young men. Declining I crossed the disused aerodrome to Bladnoch and followed the road to Wigtown and sat in the middle of town under the clock tower, watching the evening game of bowls. A minor road went up the River Cree passing near the Martyr's Stake commemorating the two local Margarets, Covenanters, who, tied to a stake in the river, were allowed to drown by the incoming tide. Later a 71 year old ex-CSI insurance man accompanied me to St Ninians Well, a figment of a map maker's imagination as it has now vanished.

A bridge on the A75 took me over the river, away from the possibilities of the Newton Stewart Youth Hostel and I began looking for a place to shelter. At the next cross roads a sign said 'B&B a quarter mile' pointing towards Carsenaw. On arrival the lady was just about going to bed and the lodgings were full with two long term guests - two tourist board girls. I pointed to the caravan in the garden and, although she thought it was dirty, she responded positively and allowed me to use it and so I had a wonderfully comfortable bed for the night for nothing except a chat. The caravan was due to be towed away to the scrap yard in a few days!
24m

Day 342
Monday 26th July
An unexpected hospitable and long breakfast did me no harm except to delay my departure until eleven. With a few diversions I followed the main A75, through Creetown (source of Liverpool Dock's granite), Carsluith (the castle was home for Abbot Brown of Sweetheart Abbey) and Skyreburn. It was a pleasant and not too crowded road. At Knockbrex house I found a route to the shore where the sea was locked in by islands and camped at the site of an old, ornate, stone-built bathing hut on a quiet beach, and even had a swim! There was not a cloud in the sky; a heron came to fish as the sun set with an orange glow and the full moon rose. The evening cry of bird flocks broke the silence of the deserted shore. Then two oyster catchers picked and pecked the beach as the sea in subtle shades of blue and grey merged with the colourful sky.
21m

Day 343
Tuesday
A good fire, but a poor sleep on uneven ground gave me an early start to Kirkandrews, where the simple 19th century church had been built by a local farmer. I found a way to Muncraig, and then the Graplin caravan site where a regimented crowd of holiday makers found it hard to raise a smile. A young man strimming the grass told me the problems of living on the minimum wage of £3.60/hr and how this had led other workers to leave, his sole helper now being a girl assistant. After Brighouse and Rock vale came the delightful Ross bay before wending my way alongside Kirkcudbright Bay. In the town I found the ruins of McLellan's Castle (1582), overlooking the harbour happy in the summer sunshine and at the PO I met Darryl who, after some banter, led me to his house for tea and tasty raspberry jammed scones and with his wife we all shared tales of coincidences in travel. After a lovely relaxing hour in his garden, I left town and found the site of the demolished 13th century castle originally begun by Alexander III of Scotland in 1264 and completed by St John Comyn in 1288. In 1291 it was transferred into English hands. King Edward stayed there for ten days in 1300 and then placed it in the hands of puppet King

Day 343 The warrior warden of Kirkcudbright

Day 343 Dunrennan Abbey, Solway Firth: Mary's last stop in Scotland

John Balliol. After it fell in 1306 much of the castle stone was used to build houses in the town. John Austin, exercising his dogs there, filled me in with the local geography and history, finally wishing me well for my journey. Afterwards I wandered though a housing estate past a wonderful garden full of giggling gnomes before going round the peninsular of St Mary's Isle, sitting in the middle of the Dee estuary. Half way down I dropped my sack by some logs to complete the circular walk, through the wooded isthmus, without the load. After recovering my bag an hour later, it was back to road work through Park House, Mutehill, The Lake, Balmae, Townhead, Balig Hill, Chapelton and finally to Dundrennan, avoiding a huge MOD area of firing ranges on the land and sea. Dundrennan Abbey, founded by the Cistercian Order in 1142, was abandoned but the remains were well preserved, walled and locked. I phoned Ben and Hilary to arrange a lift to their house near Castle Douglas and while waiting met Darren and his wife Miriam, an unemployed ex-Lincolnshire couple, who told me, over a cup of tea, about life on the dole and their whippets that they used for rabbitting.

Waiting by the Abbey, the sun dipped lower and the air cooled appreciably so I was glad when Ben came and took me to Kirkpatrick Durham for the night. He was a craftsman and they had made a lovely house from a single story derelict wreck into a two story abode with spacious rooms. But now alas they were selling it to return to the Hereford area as they'd had enough of the parochial country life in Galloway.
23m

Day 344
Wednesday
Hilary took me to Dalbeattie, a 200 year old purpose built town of grey granite houses. It used to house the work force that had quarried and exported the local high quality stone. I was at last able to find a bank before taking the eleven o'clock bus back to Dundrennan through rolling countryside full of views at every turn - deciduous woodland interspersed with conifer forests and hiding quarries, castles, fortified houses and archeological remains. Back at the abbey I was reminded that the shaven headed Mary Queen of Scots stayed here before sailing to England (1568) and spending twenty years in the restrictive sanctuary of Elizabeth's prisons prior to her execution at 46 years old. Walking, under an overcast sky, I made my way to Balcary Point by a variety of delightful minor roads, tracks and a cliff top path. At the point sat three houses behind a barrier with the look of a penal colony. A wooded track took me to Auchencairn where I sat in the small public garden largely constructed by local school children who had left a highly decorated totem pole as the chief centre-piece. The main A711 led to Douganhill and then a minor road took me to Orchardton Mains and an unexpected, attractive and well preserved round tower house (Orchardton Tower,15C) - which was the best find of the

Day 344 Unicorns in Dumfrieshire: gaurding the estates!

day. I continued down to the Horse Isles and the private Almorness House before heading north again for Dalbeattie arriving soon after six, but had to wait an hour or so for Ben to arrive to take me back to their house. They were off out for the evening to a farewell party and so I spent a relaxed evening with their two children and the baby sitter.
21m

Day 345
Thursday
Ben took me into the town of Dalbeattie again and soon after 9 o'clock I was walking out along the relatively quiet main A710 for first three miles of the day. Branching off to Kippford I enjoyed the scenery of twisting grassy granite shores extending out to Rough Island and its causeway and at Rockcliffe, in the tourist filled tearooms, shared a table with a Yorkshireman who was exploring this part of Scotland. As luck would have it, half a mile further along the shore, past a line of 'root sculptures', I was invited to lunch in the home of Bill, a Prof. of Medicine, and his Australian wife, while their dogs played on the lawn. In the house new lino was being laid while we sat in the sun looking across to Rough Island which according to Bill constantly changed colour, through the mauve rose bay willow herb (bomb site weed), heather and bracken. They told me of the local sport of flounder stamping and of the annual Cadet races of the Solway Yacht Club in Kipperhorn which was always followed by more serious sailing. This was their holiday place and normally they live in London's Whitechapel or Glasgow. I stayed for an hour of chat, mostly about GM food and its dangers, a debate which promises to go on for a good time yet.

My next stop was Castlehill Point sporting wonderful coastal views. A mile later a monument sat as testament to a local sailor, Capt. Sam Wilson, who, in 1866, had saved his crew at this spot before his ship, The Elbe, was swept away and sank in the west at Rascarrel Bay.

There was several walkers out today some of whom I saw repeatedly as we passed and repassed on the way to the views at 'the Torrs' and onto the holiday beaches of Sandyhills Bay. The tide was ebbing and exposing a vast stretch of shallow yellow sands. At a cafe I enquired about walking to Southerness Point but was advised that an intervening burn was too deep and muddy for a safe trip and so had to take the now busy A710. On the way a stone waller said that you could walk the sands but by then I had committed myself to the road route.

Two miles past the village of Caulkerbush, near Mainsriddle, I returned to minor roads and stopped at the Reith tower, which was marked on the map, and had lunch, borrowing a tin opener from the cottage opposite, which had been built of stone pinched from my picnic site ruin - the age old process of recycling resources. Zig-zagging to Arbigland I passed the lighthouse of Southerness and a number of golf courses. From Powillimount a coastal path started but quickly vanished in a small rocky cove where I met two young boys, aged maybe 12 or 13 sitting and smoking. I chatted to them and helped them light a fire about which they had little idea.

In the undergrowth ahead I found the path only to lose it again on the rocky beach which crossed over to Abigail beach house, where some more children pointed me in the right direction. Just short of Kirkbean, passing a lone house, I was taken in by Terry, Gilly and Susan, ostensibly for tea, which never arrived, and was eventually led to a caravan for that night's bed. But Terry, high on something, wanted to chat, about whisky, dope, flying saucers and the existence of the mind. Some hours later I did get some hot water and was able to make some supper.
20m

Day 346
Friday
Terry, back to a normal state with the effects of last night gone, woke me from nine hours sleep and made breakfast. So it was another late start before I set off for photogenic Kirkbean followed by main road to the floral town of New Abbey and its 13th century well kept Sweet Heart Abbey, built of ORS, surrounded by a huge graveyard containing many big memorials. The abbey was founded by Devorguilla Balliol where she was buried in 1290, with her husband's heart still around her neck, twenty years after his death. John Balliol himself was chucked out of Scotland and then fought for Henry III. He established scholarships at Oxford and with his wife set up Balliol College. After tea in the adjacent cafe I re-met the Yorkshireman I had seen in Kippford the day before.

Trekking out to Airds point, the path deteriorated and vanished near the river, which I knew I had to cross and which was rapidly deepening as the tide came in. But a fallen tree allowed a precarious crossing of the water to gain access to the isolated point which appears to be an unofficial bird sanctuary with large flocks of sea birds on these vast estuarine flats of the River Nith. However this was only the tip of an iceberg, the official reserve lay spread out on the other side, eastwards towards the Solway Estuary. A meagre path continued through overgrown woods and over big granite chips, past poachers (?) nets hidden in the brush, to a pair of circular silos (stores for what I do not know). It was a quiet secluded spot and as I had some lunch, the only sounds were those of busy oyster catchers, distant traffic and the tide creeping in. The privacy of the road, going north, allowed deer and rabbits to play in freedom and only one car passed, the driver staring at me suspiciously. At Kirkconnell house an elderly trio, possibly also surprised by my exit from the private woods, asked if they could help and gave directions to the minor road for the Dumfries main road. I tried to get water at Woodside without luck and was spurned by a lady driving a four wheel drive vehicle. However an unattended farm tap at Gillfoot was sufficient, so that I could sit at the entrance to Mabie Forest to cool off. It was another two miles before breaking off to the riverside path into Dumfries and near the town; I sat and spoke to three children who were polite and interested. They showed me a place for paddling across the river, but I went on into the town to buy a map and cakes. Eating more carbohydrate I sat in the busy centre close to the ornate cupids' fountain and the mausoleum, not feeling inspired to see the town despite its history. In 1306 Bruce murdered Comyn, a Balliol Stalwart, and thus started the long war of independence which raged on and off for nearly 400 years. The town was sacked and burnt by the English at least three times in the 15th and 16th centuries and Robbie Burns lived here for five years before his death in 1796. Instead of lingering I walked down the eastern bank of the Nith to Kingholm Quay and spoke to a barman just walking back to the main town for his night shift.

After making a small navigational error here before taking the B725 south, in the late heat of the day, I reached Glencaple and lingering in the pub tried to slake my thirst with a pint of shandy. It hardly touched the sides! The estuary marshes of Caerlaverock National Nature Reserve start here while across the river were the silos where I had walked earlier. A bird watcher on the marshes told me a little of all the birds that frequent this place: the black necked swans, geese and so on. In the evening gloom, I continued to the 13th century Caerlaverock Castle, which looked complete and interesting but was locked up for the night. It was surrounded by grassy moats and siege guns and would provide an excellent family day out. This stronghold was built by the Maxwells in 1290, taken by Edward I in 1301 but back in Bruce's hands in 1312. In 1640 it surrendered after a thirteen week siege to the Covenanters those Protestant Presbyterians wanting Reformation simplicity. Unfortunately I couldn't find a suitable place to camp for the night and instead set off in the warm night along the road to Bankend and eastward for Annan where I wanted to be the next day for a nine o'clock start. A mile past the edge of my map (OS 84) a car pulled up and two youths, Jack and Rod, wanted to talk. We sat on the road in the dark and of course had a smoke and shared my scarce coffee. They sobered up as they told me of their student experiences and their night's pub troubles in Dumfries. At 11.15 I was off again until I found a field near Cockpool and slept in the grass without supper.
28m

Day 347
Saturday
Despite a relatively early start around eight o'clock it took me nearly five

hours to reach Annan which lay only eight crow miles away. At Stanhope I passed Brow Well, a haunt of Burns, but now a mud hole with its modern flagged surrounds. Ruthwell is a one street floral village that had won the award for best new entrant for villages in the national flower competition. It also hosts a museum based around the cottage where Scotland's first saving bank had been established by a local Reverend in 1810. On to Priestside, East Howcreek and the neat caravan site of Powfoot the path continued beneath a fireworks factory on its way to Newbie Cottages and Newbie Mains, before skirting the factories at Newbie and Barnkirk point. It was a very hot day and I stopped frequently to quench my thirst before finally going under the rail bridge and into Annan, a compact town but not pretty. The fire brigade were deployed, collecting charity money from a crowd of short sleeved shoppers while I bought some stores including orange juice and coke for cooling off while sitting and lingering on a seat beneath the town hall, but not for long.

As I wandered south out of the town a car load of boisterous youths directed me on to the route for a hot walk to Waterfront, where I sat chatting to a 101 year old lady from Crewe and her 'young' offspring carers. We were seated paradoxically on one of those new recycled plastic benches next to an old cairn commemorating Burns and his local customs duties, especially the supervision of imported rum from Antigua four thousand miles away.

The six mile coastal walk to Browhouses was hot, tough and tedious, with mud and many tidal hollows. At Dornock I was driven inland, almost to the village, by a river ravine and its mud and on the road back to Dornockbrow fell asleep in a field of thirsty sheep. From here the path was even worse, through rank weeds for two miles beside the MOD green mesh fence. Starting at the small hamlet of Browhouses good tracks took me to Redkirk, Rigfoot and Old Graitney before coming to the modern housing estates of Gretna. I stayed a short time in this tourist town, amused by the huge car park for passing coaches, and escaped on the B7076 past the first and last house in Scotland.

Soon after crossing the border into England at 9.15 I found a farm, secured hot water and slept beneath a hedge on the old road, dulled by the drone of constant traffic on the nearby trunk road.
24m

- Chapter 5 -
Car-walking in Cumbria and Lancashire

Day 348
Sunday
It was an early start and I needed frequent stops to reach Carlisle in the increasing heat of the day. The frantic A74 took me to the bridge over the River Esk at Metal Bridge Inn, Telford's 1815 idea - the bridge not the pub, and on to the Cumbria coastal Way (CCW). This was very poor at the start, overgrown with stinging nettles (often at shoulder height) and the crossing over the railway was half blocked while at Haltown I missed a bridge and had to struggle over water ditches in order to procede. A very truculent herdsman informed me that the local villagers had walked the path recently but, to me, there was little evidence of this. However the information spurred me on through Rockcliffe Cross, Demesne and to the river, where it did improve. At Rockcliffe I sat beside the church and nodded to the vicar before taking the River Eden Path upstream, past St Ann's Well which, although marked on the map, remained hidden and only an empty house, a possible night shelter, was visible. Near Cargo, a solitary fisherman was casting flies for salmon and trout in a bonny reach of water where wrens and other small birds flitted to and fro while in the river wild life burrowed and swam.

A mile before Carlisle an old brick rail bridge crossed the river. This had been blocked off by developers and safety men, but locals had obviously objected and torn railings out of the metal fence which was supposed to bar the way. I crossed over here and went through industrial waste land to the infirmary where a 60 year old watchman was reading his book but welcomed me as a change of routine, and although bemoaning his recent redundancy he was otherwise cheerful. In the city, past the castle and cathedral built of distinctive red sandstone, I found the SA Temple where a captain directed me to their hostel, which was found after some difficulties with his directions. It was self-catering and I booked in for two nights before finding an open local shop for stores. As it rained in the afternoon I snoozed while listening to Gloucester beating Yorkshire in the cricket Super Cup and later walked round Carlisle which is somewhat decayed on the edges. The centre is better having retained much of its old character with interesting small alleys and robust historical buildings despite the modernist's attempt to change things. There was a tall statue to one J. Steel associated with the nearby letter box proclaimed as the first mail box in the UK.
12m

Day 349
Monday 2nd August
Back at the infirmary I soon found the CCW and after a couple of miles met a priest also doing the walk as far as Beaumont on Hadrian's Wall, opposite St Ann's Well and we went there together. The way was perched above the river under shady trees with occasional visits to the banks of the river and the priest had a path guide which was useful when the signs were poorly displayed. After we parted I continued west along the course of the 'Wall' into the rambling little old village of Burgh by Sands and at midday had tea and a sandwich in a pub housing a wonderful local wood carving of an eagle. Sadly, in hindsight, I left out a visit to the memorial to Edward I, who died (1307) around here on another of his skirmishes to subdue Bruce and the natives of Scotland and Wales. It would have been a link to all his castles and battlefield sites. After his death things went down hill as his son Ed II, a weaker king, began to lose the plot.

The Cumbrian way follows the arrow straight Dene Street across the flats of Burgh Marsh to Drumburgh which used to have a castle, but which is now gone. On the road an array of signs indicated depths 'when the water reaches this point the maximum depth is 1, 2 or 3 ft', but most traces of Hadrian's Wall have vanished and now only a stone or two remains of the various forts.

On the way to Port Carlisle I met a soldier, loaded with a rucksack, going to the east coast. He said that walking was his way of earning a living! Further on a fledgling flock of bird twitchers had arrived, enthralled with the sight of arctic birds. The coastal road continued, with Annan a tantalising short distance across the wide river Eden, through Cardurnock and past a field with 13 tall radio masts, just as a cyclist, head down and with radio earphones plugged in, nearly ran into me as we passed each other - my nearest road accident. At Anthorn the foot path sign pointed temptingly towards the marsh on the far side of Wampool River, but as the tide was high and knowing the dangers of bog side banks, I continued along the road. In Kirkbride at 6.15 spots of rain began falling and I was struck by a lack of generosity hereabouts. Was it more depressed than Galloway? I was reminded of Hilary's diatribe about the lack of hospitality around Kirkdouglas. Perhaps I had been treated too well on other parts of my walk, but then to confound my uncharitable vision while hitching back to the city, a cab driver had second thoughts about stopping and took me into Carlisle. In the half-price Sally I found that my general theory of basic human honesty had been dashed. My room had been raided for milk, tobacco, sugar and my treasured flat-pack tin opener had been stolen, so upset, after a longish day, I had a cold bath to cool off.
24m

Interlude Thirteen
Day 350
Tuesday

I caught buses to Ayr via Dumfries and Cumnock and as the wheels gathered momentum, back through the previous week's country, Galloway rolled towards me. Green and gold-brown farmlands, etched with lines of hedges and trees, slept under the hot humid still air, stretching lazily to the distant, haze shaded and eroded volcanoes in the west. Dumfries lay hugging the flat valley floor, squat like a sleeping dog with feet splayed, an attentive raised eyebrow, questioning the intent of an intrusion into its dreams. As we approached, the scene dissolved into reality. The details came into focus; the centre of the picture became the ancient crossing for the river Nith. This old stone bridge spanned the water with six arches remaining out of the original nine (the other three having gone in modernisation work). The bridge was buttressed, at the western end, by the old cooper's house which contained stories of the town and had been kept as an intriguing little museum. A pace down river lies a modern DIY simplistic statue - the footprints of two rubber soled boots - dedicated to the Cumbrian Hero. In the town above, the basic structures of old houses still stand as a reminder of the civic past, but now despoiled by the standard fronts of a range of modern shops, little different to the same named shops in other towns across the land.

Having left my bag near the bridge while shopping for film, scissors and a tin opener, I returned to find it being searched by a man who was probably an unemployed, alcohol-addicted NFA and I had to tell him, in a way that left no doubt, that such behaviour was inappropriate. Fisticuffs were not far away.

After a late arrival in Ayr I checked my bank account to discover that my small DHSS allowance was not being paid, consequently funds were low and action necessary. Picking up my car from the Youth Hostel, I thanked the hostel assistant and then drove to Glasgow arriving just before six while sleeping later in the Garnheath Wood country park at Coatbridge.

Day 351
Wednesday
Back in Glasgow during mid-afternoon, seeking sustenance in a city chip shop, an outspoken young lass tried to pick my pocket and she was another person I had to reprimand.

Day 352
Thursday
On the road towards Carlisle a Road Chef was my stopping place for the night.

Fourteenth Stage
Kirkbride to Knot-End-on-Sea
Day 353
Friday

At 8.30 I arrived back in Kirkbride, nine miles west of Carlisle and while looking for a place to park, stopped to help push another car towards a garage: my good deed for the week. Leaving the car in a haulier's yard by the old railway near Angerton, I set out along a poorly designated footpath to Longlands Head and then road to Newton Arlosh to pick up the CCW and walked to Salt Coates and Abbey Town across these flatlands. The country here, and even the ports, reminded me of Norfolk! But the difference was the sea sand as opposed to eastern mud, little in the way of sea defences and the absence of windmills!

The sun took its time to emerge through the sultry mists of the morning leaving the rest of the day hot and sticky with only the minimum of rain. In Abbey Town I bought supplies including cheap over-ripe bananas and a hot pie, before winding my way down the River Waver and after lunch on the banks I continued to work my way across the flat estuarine marshes, having to make guesses as to the route, as the sign posting was poor. Wandering cows have grazed these grasslands for eons and their hooves had pockmarked the paths in a mad chaotic pattern and altogether it was a bit of a scramble until I reached Skinburness to recover by having tea and a chat in the local hotel bar with its expensively carved light fitting on the ceiling. The path now improved, gathering purpose, and I was able to stride towards the south, across sand dunes and embankments, the path tight between the shore and the road. A stark but photogenic multi-tiered promenade led to Silloth where a detour into the town was necessary around the docks. A garish red bouncy castle on the town's common was in action, and formed a strange contrast to the stone church. Beside the local golf courses there were empty sandy beaches, many parking places and an abundance of drift wood. After by-passing Mawbray I entered linear Allonby where a crowd of people were out for a stroll. A caravanner with two splendid donkeys told me that this was common land for grazing and that he came each year to preserve his rights. At Blue Dial, a shoal of bass, fins just exposed, skimmed the water, while a fisherman taught his child to cast and the sun lowered itself in the west - an idyllic picture. I departed along an old and empty promenade, much like a deserted Blackpool, which took me to Maryport. Missing the train by 13 minutes I had to catch a bus to Wigton and set out in the dark for the five mile walk to Angerton but was again lucky getting a lift for most of the way, having to walk only the first and last miles. The householder owner of my parking place gave me hot water; I got food in Wigton and a hidey hole near Aspatria.
25m

Day 354
Saturday.
After driving through Whitehaven to St Bees and leaving the Escort in the station car park, I caught the 11.30 train along the antiquated squeaky railway. I was trying to look ahead so as to avoid the necessity of walking back to the car in the darkness of evening. From the Maryport station a path meandered around Motte hill, missed the sludgy high tide mark and ended at the town's bridge where an attempt had been made to improve the town's looks with the erection of a sculpture of three fishermen and their dog, which seemed rather out of place in this dour town.

It was a simple matter to follow the defined path, past Flimby and the seaside wind farm to Workington, beside a mix of limestone, coal measures and volcanic lava beds (or more probably steel production waste from The Bessemer converters which used to produce so much pig iron). After Harrington the CCW moved inland to the road at Distington. At Locwa I met a gang of school children who entertained me after I had used their local store. They were polite if vocal and interested in my trip, giving me their 'luv' as I departed. This area must once have had a very busy coal, steel and chemical industrial community, but is now a very depressed area and much of the housing reflected this. Because of dereliction the path did occasionally lose its way, particularly near the big wind farm at Workington. In Whitehaven past activity was remembered:-

Kings Pit: opened in 1750
In 1793 this reached 160 fathoms

From here a busy and more attractive path led past a quarry to St Bees Head nature reserve where the scene improved dramatically as it passed over the high sea cliffs. A little bay lay below, sea birds swung past the tall cliffs and excellent views opened out northward, only partially marred by inland chemical plants and mines, the landscape softened by the deep blue-purple heather. Wandering towards St Bees I met a family of four, all laden with full rucksacks and looking for a nearby camping barn and realised that this was also the start of the Wainwright Coast to Coast walk across to Robin Hood Bay. I had come the long way round!

My plan had worked out well and after obtaining hot water from the friendly restaurant staff I retired to a beach car park for the night. The previous evening there had been much wireless discussion of the prospects for the three teams promoted to the premier league and as to which would most likely go down again. Today Bradford beat Middlesborough 1 - 0 and I cheered as the new football season started, already in August. Time was flying by!
21m

Day 354 Maryport improvement

Day 355
Sunday
At 10.45, out of St Bees the path went initially alongside the actual railway track and its new embankment and then proceeded tightly between the shore and rail line to Nettleton. I tried, but failed, to get tea at the country club and continued along the road to Braystone - back to the CCW proper. This crossed the Ehen River and passed Sellafield BNF processing plant complete with rail trucks for carrying radioactive waste and a high protective mesh fence. This had evolved, via Windscale, from the old Calder Hall, Britain's first nuclear power station and was soon to be much in the news for falsifying safety checks. Although this is not a great sight my urban mind flipped by and moved on to more natural delights.

I took the alternative path across the golf course into Seascale, bought a map from the closed portion of a half open shop (Sunday Trading!) and went up the village to find the local Scrabble organiser, Mavis. We had a wonderful hour of talk, mostly about her travels, firstly about her adventures in Jamaica, Guiana and Brazil tracking down her father's grave and her godparents, and then about her proposed trip to Russia in 2000. You would not suspect this type of audacious tripping in such a solid looking citizen.

Rested and relaxed I started again in the hot sun, back to the CCW, around the Rolls Royce factory, on to Carl Crag and then inland to Drigg. After crossing the River Irt by the small old packhorse Holme Bridge, I stopped for an hour over a late lunch on the grass and in the sun. Afterwards the path straggled along very minor roads into Ravenglass and went across the shore of the Esk. I missed the Roman Fort but found the railway bridge convenient for crossing the river and once over took the road to Stubbs Place, where unable to find the path I took the road to Bootle Station and Annaside. Finding no barns for the night my camp was on rough ground behind a stone wall near Gutterby. So says my diary if not my mind: there are black spots as well as bright ones in our memories but if I went back to that place recollection of thoughts would probably flood in!
21m

Day 356
Monday 9th August
I was away before eight as it had been a poor night but at least it hadn't rained. A mile further on there were shelters which would have been better! But you don't win every time. I continued inland to the level crossing and main road to Silecroft, where somebody asked me the way to Wasdale and the cafe, advertising an all day menu, was not, at 8.30, yet making tea. Crossing a wind farm to Haverigg Prison, a path ran beside the lofty grill fence around the prison fields of cabbage and potatoes, while inside I saw and heard inmates working

to the sound of music. In Haverigg a cafe served me bangers and mash while a lady told me of the dangers of the estuary and Duddon Sands.

On leaving it was drizzling but this would clear as the day progressed. I took the sea wall around the large old mine reservoir which had been turned into a nature reserve lagoon, and passed the desolate lighthouse. The wall had been built in 1905 to protect the mine whose shaft head towers still stood across the water. The CCW now meandered across flat lands to the YH at Duddon Villa which was closed and without a soul in sight. Apparently a suitable homely hostel, in a fair location, it had views of distant Lake District hills and in the grounds lay the blue hulk of an old fishing vessel. But it was too early to wait around.

Past Millom, a footpath beckoned to cross the sands to Askam, but I heeded the warnings and took the dyke to the north east towards the Lakeland hills and against a stiff breeze. There were thousands of sheep grazing on the flat, channel pocked marshes and by Green Road Station a large flock were being gathered in but I could find no local knowledge about paths across the sands. Instead I crossed the River Duddon by the rail bridge to Foxfield, avoiding two trains that passed rapidly on their ways. Struggling out of a wet field on the other side I stopped to chat at the first house and met an ex-farmer, John and his wife Ann. They gave me tea, hot water, cigarettes, and their opinions about farming, politicians and war.

The CCW rambled along a minor road to Wall End where appropriately a man was building a large and solid wall of thick slate which he had acquired from the quarry on the hill, of Kirby Moor, towering above. There were many such walls hereabouts but none as good as his. After the footbridge over the railway at Kirkby-in-Furness, a poorly trod but delightful path took me to Askam-in-Furness via the sands, which lay in vast expanses as the tide was out. In the town there was no room at the Inn and so I continued to the beach and dunes of Sandscales Haws, Nature Reserve. This was an enthralling place and camping on level soft grassy ground in the south eastern side, with cows grazing contentedly about me and a glorious setting sun, I fell asleep.
24m

Day 357
Tuesday
Luckily there were only a few spots of rain in the night but, without breakfast, I quickly worked my way out of the dunes around to Scarth Bight. The path was washed away and I had to cross fields to a prominent pill box before finding the CCW at Sowerty Lodge as it rose to the main road. At Cocken tunnel I dipped under the railway and found a brand new path which took me to the Dock Museum in Barrow. This is free but on Tuesdays is unfortunately closed.

Map 6

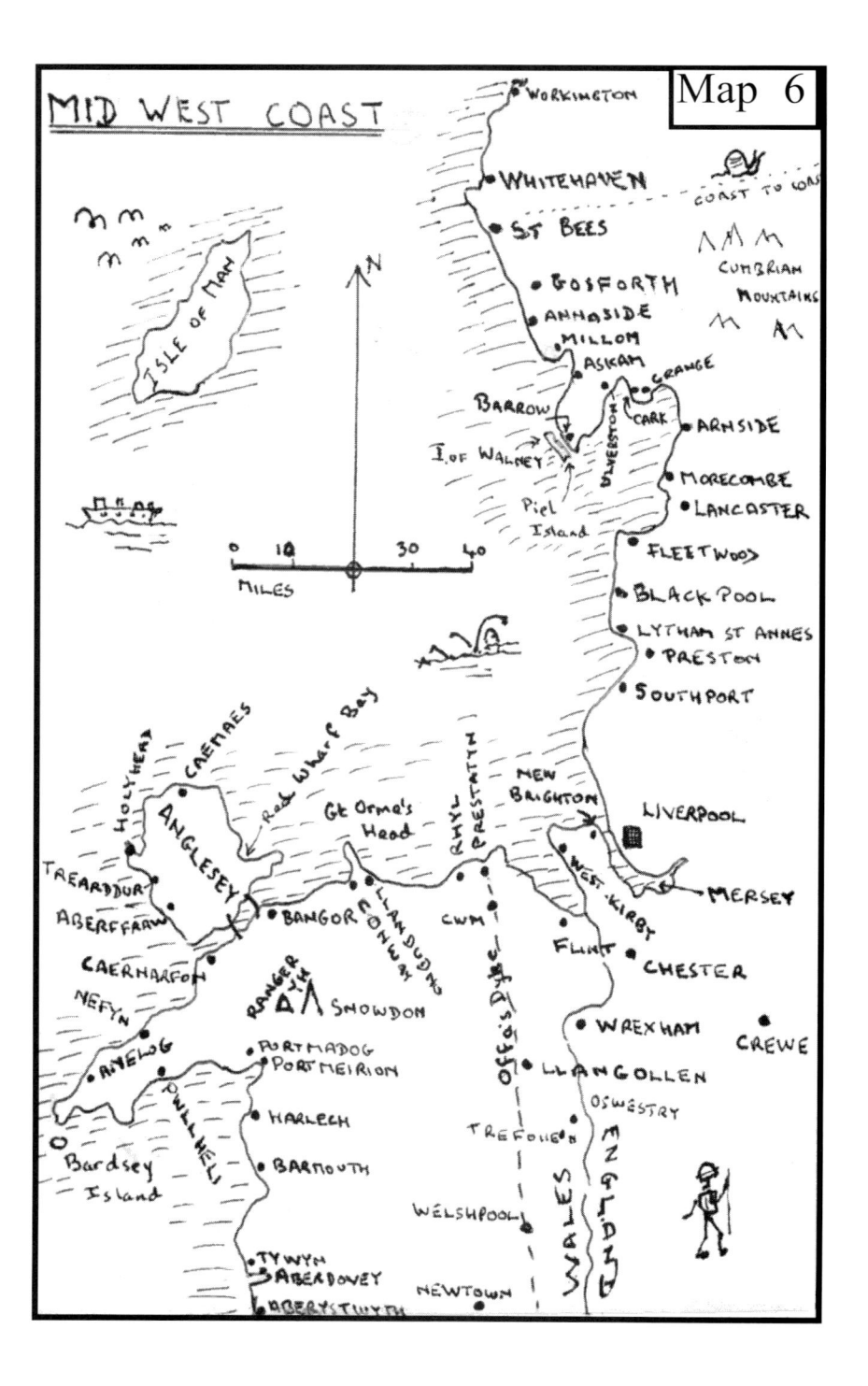

MID WEST COAST

- Workington
- Whitehaven
- St Bees
- Gosforth
- Annaside
- Millom
- Askam
- Barrow
- I. of Walney
- Piel Island
- Grange
- Cark
- Ulverston
- Arnside
- Morecombe
- Lancaster
- Fleetwood
- Blackpool
- Lytham St Annes
- Preston
- Southport
- New Brighton
- Liverpool
- West Kirby
- Mersey
- Flint
- Chester
- Wrexham
- Crewe
- Llangollen
- Oswestry
- Trefonen
- Welshpool
- Newtown

Coast to Coast
Cumbrian Mountains

Isle of Man

N
0 10 30 40
MILES

- Holyhead
- Caemaes
- Anglesey
- Trearddur
- Aberffraw
- Bangor
- Caernarfon
- Nefyn
- Red Wharf Bay
- Gt Orme's Head
- Llandudno
- Conwy
- Cwm
- Rhyl
- Prestatyn
- Ranger
- Snowdon
- Ayelog
- Portmadog
- Portmeirion
- Harlech
- Barmouth
- Pwllheli
- Bardsey Island
- Tywyn
- Aberdovey
- Aberystwyth

Offa's Dyke

WALES / ENGLAND

As the tide was high I crossed the lifting bridge to Walney Island rather than the footpath across the sand and at the first pub had tea before leaving my bag with the barmaid. It was noon when I set off around the northern part of the island and the sun came out bright and hot. Walking the shore, as the tide fell, a bird watcher mistook me for the new reserve warden. He told me the path was okay and so I crossed the marshes to the nature reserve at the northern tip. It was as good as last night's dune area, which lay across the Scarth Channel. There were thousands of oyster catchers and extended views to the northern coombes and the Lakeland peaks. At my feet a carpet of flowers, yellow, white and purple, heathers and thriving grass cropped short by sheep (including Jacobs) and rabbits. Ragwort and sea kale were also abundant, while butterflies, bees and dragonflies busied themselves. It is also home to Walney geraniums and natterjack toads.

I walked down the west side and headed across, through purpose built Vickerstown, reaching the pub soon after three and collecting my bag before marching south along the road to Biggar and then along the Cistercian Way to Snap Point and Rape Haw. Thankfully, I found the track on the sand and began the walk across to Piel Island becoming reassured that this was right when a tractor came towards me with a trailer full of children. There were little reflector markers all the way across but also a number of car wrecks littering the sands - those that hadn't crossed the quick sand bits. I arrived on the island at five and went to the Ship Inn, to meet the King of the Island - the landlord - and some campers, one boy giving me a fresh mackerel wrapped in foil for my supper. I camped in the grounds of the castle, collecting wood and dung for a reasonable fire and cooked my evening meal while surrounded by flocks of honking geese, grazing sheep, and children playing hide and seek in the ruins. All beneath a fine red sunset, this was, I reflected, a magical place to find. Originally called Fotheray (Foundry) the island has an important past, first in the 12/13th century as a food warehouse for the nearby Furness Abbey, then strengthened by the 14th century Motte and Bailey castle, smuggling became routine and an integral part of the economy. In 1487 a wannabe king of England, Lambert Simnel, landed before marching to defeat at Stoke but his audacity is remembered still as the Landlord 'King'. The island saw the flow of troops and ships in the civil war and a customs officer soon arrived to impose taxation. Then as shipping, trade and industry increased harbour pilots were also housed on Piel.
21m

Day 358
Wednesday
It had been a starlit night and remained clear for the first hour of day before clouding as I ambled about and waited for the ferry. At 11.20 there was an 89% eclipse of the sun and a dozen of us were there to watch it. Wonderful!

While waiting it was an opportunity to talk to some residents. Near the pub stands a row of three houses and island resident, David, an ex-Vickers man, who now worked as a carer, told me he had moved here two years before to his 1875 house and was looking after three lads. But now repairs were being made as they'd had a fire in the middle of one night.

When I spoke to the King, he was working on the bearings of a trailer which he was going to use to take cattle to market. He farms the island and pays a peppercorn rent of £1 per year on a 25 year lease. He had lived here 13 years, made many improvements, had recently sprayed his ragwort which is rife here due to lack of council maintenance, and he also had an embryonic zoo of guinea fowl, ducks, chickens, peacocks and sheep.

Eventually the ferry arrived at high tide, just after noon and I was given a free ride while other passengers were going to their boat in Piel Channel. We landed at Roa Island and I continued on the CCW and cycle-way towards the NE alongside Morecambe Bay, through Newbiggin to Aldingham where I had lunch by the church. Then it was road through Baycliff and Bardsea. Over a field and a wall I headed for Conishead Priory, which I entered by the 'back door' across a field and through a host of tents. A Buddhist convention was in full swing and the place was full of marquees and campers, while monks wandered round in their saffron and yellow robes. But there was no succour for wayfarers and I was thrown out by a security elder. A yew tree hedge lined the track away from the grounds to the main road which went to Ulverston where I bought fish & chips and had my flask filled before eating and drinking beneath Oubas Hill and its lighthouse monument.

Then came Next Ness followed by the grounds of Plumpton Hall in order to cross the Leven Viaduct. Two boys said the nuclear train had gone through so I walked briskly across the three quarter mile gap, with the River Leven below me, slipping down the valley from Lake Windermere, a short eight miles away. On the other side I swung precariously on a pole in order to cross a water filled dyke and look for a sleeping cave in the cliffs of Barker Scar. But after that effort I was without success despite its location marked on the map. Using a number of paths thro' woodland and around ponds, startling a multitude of wildlife, I eventually recrossed the well embanked railway to find a good route on the southern side across flat land filled with more grazing sheep and any amount of driftwood, but despite the later decided against camping there.

After leaving the Barrow Peninsular I was now on that of Cartmel and at Cark regained the CCW as it turned off to Sandgate and Canon Winder Farms. There was no room in the barns - they were worried about thieving - and I continued for another mile in the dark before finding a place to camp beside a wall. It overlooked the marshes with a fine view across the bay towards the

lights of Morecambe. Although having walked for eight hours I had only covered eighteen miles but nevertheless relaxed with a big fire and a stomach filling feast.
18m

Day 359
Thursday
It had been cold and cloudy in the night, so I was up early and soon on the sea defences near West Plain Farm, which had been last night's objective but proved to be something of a dump with lots of scruffy horses. A road took me round Cark airfield to breakfast at Holme. Near Wyke Farm I found an Outdoor Centre and left my sack while I walked, unladen, around Humphrey Head. It was a good cliff top path across the 'karst' limestone with a vast panoramic view of the bay and you could imagine the last wolves in England howling to the moon and the surrounding sea. I went back on the eastern side of this splendid little peninsular, picked up my bag and found a path on the shore side of the railway into Kent Bank where I stopped for tea. Some people from Ilkley joined me, chatted and contributed £2 to StC. Then it was a pleasant walk into Grange-over-Sands (from-Hest Bank). Forsaking the remote possibility of accommodation at the Hospice on Hampsfell above the town I began my return, but the train fare to St Bees was £11 so I decided to hitch back instead. My first lift was with a retired engineer, who now collected litter and rubbish on a six day / 37 hr. week. Then I was picked up by Mike, a catering manager with five children and two houses, and this turned into an excursion. He was towing a trailer with a settee and was going to do a good stretch of spectacular scenery over the hills. Ascending one steep hill in Netherdale his clutch packed in, necessitating a complicated reverse down hill to a phone. We waited by the tea rooms in the heart of 'horse trekking' rural dales for the recovery truck before ending the day in remote Neston Carsdale at his cottage, which he had renovated superbly and had great plans for the overgrown garden. We nattered well into the night, about his Alvis and world-wide classic motor rallying: the next adventure - to motor around the world in eighty days from May 2000.
9m

Day 360
Friday
After a good night's sleep we had breakfast of tea and toast. Mike went off with his friend Tim to pick up his trailer and then on their return we went to Gosforth where we parted. I hitched to St Bees and after collecting the car went round to see the local Scrabble lady to trade ideas and get water before driving to Grange.

After parking in the station car park I walked beside the railway to Arnside,

crossing the water at Milnthorpe Sands by using the Kent (rail) Viaduct, wondering about the dangers of this short cut. I booked in at the Youth Hostel and caught the 8.13 train back to Grange, a free trip - BUT in Grange station tripped and slipped - sure that I'd broken something when my leg crashed down on the hard raised kerb stones. But fortunately there were no breaks though I was bruised and stiff for a week from just a 6 inch fall. After driving a long route back to the hostel and suppering in peace it was bed by 11.30, which for me back in civilisation was an early night.
12m

Day 361
Saturday
A good meandering path by cliffs and through woodland took me to Silverdale and Jenny Brown's Point as the Cumbrian Coastal Way turned into the Lancastrian route. As the tide was coming in and the weather was very squally I decided against the track across the main marsh and instead went to Crag Foot where, waiting in the phone box for the rain to pass, I phoned to find out about possible accommodation with Patrick's stepson in Morecambe but without luck.

A rising road, through woodland with views of Warton Sands, took me to Warton, before descending to Cotes Stones and Carnforth. High tide lapped the rim of the saucer shaped shore and many of the marker posts were out in the sea as I walked the estuary fringe around to Hest bank. Later, after taking tea in the cafe of a health complex I took the road to Morecambe. The sun came out, a stiff breeze blew and the tide receded leaving curving furrows in the brown mud. I hurried through Morecambe and pushed on to the 'End of the World' caravan site and then past the dilapidated Butlins Holiday camp. There was an abundance of blackberries here and I had my day's dessert early. Under a painter's sky I continued round Sunderland point to Overton and as I passed through Oxcliffe the sun sank as a golden ball, highlighting a flight of swans. The sky was full of threatening dark heavy cumulus which the sun illuminated in strong relief, while a bright rainbow formed above Lancaster. I crossed the railway footbridge at 8.45, walked straight onto the train to Arnside and rested my aching legs before collecting the car to park near the M6.
27m

Day 362
Sunday
As it was Sunday the shops took their time opening but eventually I found a map at the outdoor shop Ultimate in Lancaster. For all its importance this is a small quaint town. The solid castle is a HM prison, the market has an interesting sheep mural and the Penny hospital is a throwback to times before the NHS.

I left the car near the station and at 11.30 escaped from the town, setting off on the Lancashire Coastal Way (LCW) along the banks of the River Lune and through Glasson with cycle ways and horse ridden bridleways constituting most of the path which was made for easy walking. The main feature was the small locked remains of 12th century Cockersand Abbey. and tea at Bob's path-side mobile cafe. I arrived in Knott End-on-Sea in the dull lonely evening. and as there was no ferry caught a bus to Blackpool, took the 10.15 train to Preston, changing to the free Virgin flyer for Lancaster to pick up the car, before droving to Skipton in the early hours. A local quiet spot provided a place to stop for an extremely good sleep after averaging over twenty miles walking per day.
21m

Interlude Fourteen
Day 363
Monday 16th August
The DHSS was a priority. Then after other visits, sleep was by the golf course at top of Leeds Road.

Day 364
Tuesday
Bradford; 8.00 to Blackpool; 11.30.

Fifteenth Stage
Knott End-on-Sea to Preston
Day 365
Wednesday
At the once important port of Fleetwood, where two old lighthouses testified to its former maritime significance and trade, it was a sunny day and the crowds were gathering as I spoke to the ferry man and arranged a free passage both ways. The first to re-establish contact with my last stopping place at Knott-end-on-Sea, the second to make my coastal walk continuous. The fare used to be tuppence ha'penny representing the 2d walk upstream to the ford plus the half pence for the half mile across the water. After parking the car in a suitable side street I waited for the departure of the Wyre Princess. On the other side jumping off the ferry I raced up the quay to the bus stop and ran back in order not to delay departure but with time enough for the embarkation of other passengers. This exercise was abhorrent to me - a man not used to running! As we docked a big P&O ferry, dwarfing our little boat, pulled out of the Wyre on its voyage elsewhere. Back again on the southern side of the River, I proceeded down the long concrete promenade into Blackpool. The beaches were empty, sandy and groyned waiting for the incoming tide while the occa-

sional small, isolated group of holiday makers played in the sun. All the wooden groynes were numbered from G76 to G1, but the G5 projection was unmarked and without a 'summit'. I passed Roger's Rossal school (where he had boarded during part of the war), set back from the shore in spacious playing fields, its old outdoor swimming pool now lying defunct and almost forgotten in this new age of improved safe facilities. The coastal suburbs passed me by - Clevleys, Little Bispham and Bispham as Blackpool Tower grew into significance. Hotel after hotel jostled for a view of the sea and for passing trade. After reaching Star Gate I caught the tram, complete with two jovial conductors and a driver, back to Fleetwood. There are a mixed assortment of trams all doing the same job - the Walls Ice Cream unit being the most eye catching.

Back with the car I added petrol and noted it had risen another 3p a litre, while crude remained at $20/barrel. With a hot pie for supper I drove slowly through the town where the streets were strangely quiet and illuminated from the glow cast by the multi coloured lights decorating the piers, the big wheel and the huge big dipper. Sleeping and dreaming in the car park at the end of the tramway I wondered what a Waverley was, there are so many things named after it or him? Perhaps the well-spring was John Anderson Waverley (1882-1958) who introduced PAYE and after whom the Anderson air-raid shelter was named but somehow I doubt it, Scott's Waverley novels being more likely.
12m

Day 366
Thursday:
A whole year had passed since I first set out from Bromley and on waking at ten o'clock it was a horrid looking day. Having eaten and parked the car at Palace road I started walking, soon after eleven, straight towards Lytham St Anne's, where I did some banking. The road and promenade took me to the windmill and the adjacent museum of Life Boats, which is worth a visit, while on the sea-side grass a holiday game of cricket was underway. The day got better but the path deteriorated and began to reek of mucky mud and dilapidation. A cafe at the point where the main road crosses the Main Drain sold me tea and apple pie for a mere £1.15 and I talked to a solitary schoolboy who would soon be doing his GCSEs. He wanted to become a landscape gardener and so I told him that he should learn one plant and its Latin name each and every day - my recipe for impressing clients.

The LCW continued around twisty muddy creeks full of impoverished boats as both the path and the weather slowly improved. At Warton aerodrome I was bombarded with the roar of noisy jets on the runway and taking to the air. Nearby, a local man and his mallards told me about the shooting rights on Warton Marsh and what you have to put back to keep the stocks up. He reck-

oned that the official mallard population was only at the 120,000 mark whilst at least one million had been released locally. Nearby drilling for oil was under way and lights were being installed for this operation on the marshes. After cutting across a field to the main road beyond Freckleton, I walked two miles of tarmac before using difficult paths to Preston arriving just after seven. It was now sunny but feeling extremely tired I caught the 7.30 train back to Blackpool, five hours later than planned.
19m

Interlude Fifteen
Days 367 & 368
Regenerating energy I spent two relaxing days around Blackpool and St Anne's.

Sixteenth Stage
Preston to Rhyll
Day 369
Sunday
Beside the river, the banks heavy with driftwood, I walked the Ribble Way from Preston to Southport, a rather dreary walk across the marshes beside the Ribble and River Douglas which was crossed appropriately by illegally climbing a structure carrying a large pipe over the water. Farm tracks took me across Hesketh Marsh to an unmarked bridge leading to Banks Marsh and finally Southport with its concrete promenades and endless stretches of sand. During the whole day it was difficult to crack out a 'hello' from the dour passers-by. Perhaps it was because our cricketers had lost a test match again.
21m

Day 370
Monday 23rd August
After buying a map, my day's journey started soon after eleven and Southern Southport was almost empty as I walked towards a group of sand dunes. Some of these were substantial and slowed my progress around Ainsdale until I found the railway-side path. After this, there was a short cut on metalled roads through a caravan site to the relatively soft paths around modern Formby. Drifting sand had half buried many of the trees I saw and old Formby itself had been lost a hundred years before under a deluge of shifting fine grained sand. At least it was a warm sunny day with little cloud although I missed out on seeing the red squirrels of these parts and the MOD ranges of Sefton were also a no go area. Consequently it was the rail side path to Hightown followed by more sand dune paths to Crosby where the white sands were empty, except for one man on a bike. At Waterloo, further coastal progress was blocked, so I

went into Seaforth and at the cafe in the park had a chat over a coke and signed their visitors' book! The walk through the suburbs of Liverpool was not attractive; at one place stones were being thrown and I thought that this was the capital of Ireland! The most eye catching object was a tower block painted with the outline of a house although the city skyline was attractive in the evening light. On arriving in the City centre, at seven, I found it difficult to get directions because of the local accent but after wandering around for a while I caught the Metro back to Southport.
21m

Day 371
Tuesday
My night was spent in the car park on the vast sands of Southport, where the sea seemed so far away. Part of my breakfast was a Mr Whippy ice cream reminding me of days as an ice cream salesman. After buying supplies in Safeway's and driving through the Mersey Tunnel to New Brighton, I slept in a sunken car park by the sea which was better than parking in the city.

Day 372
Wednesday
It had rained in the night and now it was wet and damp. Leaving the car I walked to the station and caught the eleven o'clock train back to Liverpool and its large clean robust buildings while in the mist large ships were passing the busy pier. I arrived at the water front just after noon, obtained a free ride on the ferry and while waiting studied the immediate surroundings: the statue to Edward VII, a memorial to Capt. F J Walker (1896-1944) killed in the Battle of the Atlantic, and a statue of Sir Alfred Jones with a pigeon on his head, ship owner and founder of Liverpool's School of Tropical Medicine - the fine big white building on the other side of the square. Once across the Mersey on the ferry - a real corker of an old boat with a pictorial history displayed in its lounges - I walked the promenade to New Brighton and for a short time had the company of two young boys who wanted to talk, as we passed the statue of a black Labrador commemorating the founding of Guide Dogs for the Blind. Continuing alone along the interminable, near- empty, concrete promenade it started to rain and the sands remained determinedly devoid of humanity. In a seaside shelter I sat watching the rain and met Peter, a young, unemployed apple picker. We walked together into West Kirby, and he directed me to the Red Acre Convent in Abbey Road where, for my troubles, I was given a rather miserable looking sandwich and this provided some sustenance on the journey by two buses back to the car.
12m

Day 373
Thursday
After sleeping on West Kirby sea front and moving the car to Safeway's car park, where the manager allowed me to park for the day, I walked around the big Marine Lake on the shore, a very popular stroll, which was almost like walking on water, the retaining wall being so low. Beyond this I found the old railway which is part of the Wirral Way with its views restricted by hawthorns and ragged hedges and only occasional glimpses of the sea. The way continued through the fringes of Neston, across Burton firing ranges to the modernistic single pier suspension bridge spanning the River Dee. The main road (A548) took me into Flint where there was a modern sculpture of a Big Foot at the Station which seemed appropriate to my walk. I caught a train to Shotton to change lines and had to wait two hours for the next train which had been delayed by somebody pulling the communication cord. It was strange waiting all alone on the platform with the grass and weeds growing between the tracks. It felt like a ghost line until I was joined by two girls going the same way. There was another train change at Bidston for the last train to West Kirby but the conductor didn't charge us - compensation for our inconvenience. After getting chips and water, I took the car to a quiet spot, seen earlier on the path near Neston, and after supper, listened to the radio till one o'clock.
17m

Day 374
Friday
In the morning I did Chester (!) and at midday drove to Flint, parked at the Station and started walking to Rhyl. A mile out of Flint a path went out to the shore and continued on short cropped grassy clay banks, heavily eroded - with great chunks were being washed out into the sea. Further along, a big boat - The Duke of Lancaster - had been beached many years ago and lay there as a slowly weathering old relic - perhaps nothing would be left in a thousand years time. Then it was main road all the way to Rhyl but I should have stopped at Prestatyn as will be explained later. The fare on the 8.12 train back to Flint cost a staggering £4.40, ugh! After driving to Crewe and parking near the 1644 Battle Site at Acton I was about to get to sleep when the police checked me out - again!
19m

Interlude Sixteen
Day 375
Saturday
Unfortunately I awoke too late and when I arrived at the Mornflake factory in Crewe Mr Baxter, the site manager, had gone home. Consequently I was unable to get fresh supplies of my staple food - oats. This firm had been help-

Day 373 West Kirby: a holiday sailing lesson

ful in sponsorship and supplied a substantial amount of their oat products (given away to other needy people due to my tardy start), tee shirts and sun hats before I started the charity walk. Having hoped for more, I somewhat disappointedly drove off south - heading for Ledbury, where I intended leaving the car while walking around the coast of Wales. In the early hours of the morning I stopped in a favourite lay-by high on the Hereford side of the Malvern Hills.

Days 376 & 377
Sunday and Monday: 30th Aug
Having reached my latest objective - a resting place for the car - I spent an extended two days gardening, washing, relaxing, feeding and sleeping.

One of several post cards sent to relatives

- Chapter 6 -
Free Fall Around Wales

Seventeenth Stage: Llanymynech & Rhyl to Bristol
Day 378
Tuesday
In order to continue my journey I intended hitching to Rhyl. So soon after nine Liz dropped me at Trumpet and I started walked towards Ashburton, soon getting my first lift with a lady from Kent with her two young children in an estate car. She dropped me in Bodmin and at the garage I bought chocolate bars. A retired vicar took me to Leominster and after walking through the town a farmer gave me a ride to Ludlow. A lorry diver from Cardiff went to the A5 where I was picked up by a young quarryman - a stone dealer who dropped me on the other side of Maesbrook. He told me that the Offa's Dyke (OFDP) was close by and following a suggestion of Roger's I decided that it would be a good idea to trek along the Dyke to North Wales and this was why it would have been best to stop in Prestatyn the previous Friday, as the OFDP finishes there. Out of Llanymynech I paused for lunch at the first Dyke sign which indicated the path leading off the main road. My only map of the path was a page from a road atlas, but perhaps adequate as the route should be well sign-posted. I had no idea of what would be seen, the places to be passed nor the people to be met.

   A long climb took me to an old quarry hacked out of the hill which overlooked the town. From here a series of delights awaited me as the path continued its rambling way along the ridge overlooking the peaceful, undulating, green patchwork border countryside of hedges, trees, fields and grazing cattle. It was amazingly quiet as the hills cut off the sound of traffic. Passing over a weed encroached railway, which unbeknownst to me was a rail-link for quarries to Oswestry, and I wondered 'Quo Vadis'. My path climbed up Nantmawr, surrounded by a spectacular panoramic view in the evening light. After becoming a little lost as the path crossed roads I found a way-side pub near Trefonen. The B&B was £20, camping £2, and so I carried on in the dark along the now well routed path and a mile later found a suitable nook in a wall which came complete with a stone seat, made camp and lit a fire under the dark canopy of a sky full of brilliant stars.
7m

Day 379
Wednesday 1st September
Soon after sunrise I was up and away on to an old racecourse and common land where a statue of a two headed horse stood near the grandstand. Was it a win-

ner? From here the sign posts were poor but the views were excellent. Above Craignant I had my flask filled by a lady in an old cottage and feasted on the valley view to the Wrekin. I said 'I hope you don't get too many walkers bothering you' and she replied 'Oh! we get a few — but as long as they're enjoying themselves!'

Once over the next hill, to the north, I saw Chirk Castle surrounded by woods. The path rose up past giant ashes and oaks to this NT site. It was 10.45 and the castle was not yet open as I spoke to Patrick, a gatekeeper, guide and general factotum. He led me to the office to meet other staff but I was too early to tour the well restored buildings. He took me back to the car park in his wagon (for transporting disabled people) and in the Tudor barns there, I was able to use the toilets for my ablutions. New gates led me through the country park festooned with fledgling pheasants growing wings for the gun, ripe blackberries full of vitamin vigour and holy hordes of red rumped sheep grazing - keeping the grass short.

The next land mark appeared to be a distant Abbey but, more immediately, on coming out of the trees I found the Shropshire canal filled with speckled brown water churned by the slow moving hulks of holiday long narrow-boats. On the other bank I came to Telford's narrow aqueduct (built 1795 - 1805) carrying the Canal over the River Dee and leading towards the busy port at Trevor. Here I made some map reading mistakes and it was a while before I corrected the errors to get on the correct westward arm of the canal. But then the path soon left the waterways and went up to Garth on the way to Valle Crucis Abbey whose 16th century Abbot was prosecuted for highway robbery. What a splendid place this would have been for banditry and I hoped that I wasn't set upon.

The sun was out, just right for shorts! As the day was too hot to think about a long walk I spent some time enjoying the warm rays and the views, sitting on a bench by the main road. This saw me chuckling as gawping motorists drove through - rubbernecking to see what a tramp was doing enjoying the sun while two big busted girls strode past, hair blowing in the breeze, oblivious to the world and cocooned in their own conversation. Unfortunately this inaction conspired against me, the clouds began to gather and my lack of supplies started demanding attention. Time to move.

After passing some security cameras staring down menacingly over the path I went into the cool shade of the fir forests for the long upward climb, and suddenly and without warning, burst out onto the bright limestone moorland. The designated route to the west hung below the summit of the ridge. At first it was tarmac, but the path soon gained full hill-walking status as it wove past the ruins of the abbey and drove on to the rigours of the North West. On my right,

Day 379 Path surfaces varied: this was planking on Offa's Dyke across bog heather towards Llandegla

high cliffs with climbing potential crowded in, while below, rich green pastures riddled with ripening livestock vied with yellowing arable fields and their burgeoning harvests.

At a small ford I soaked my hat to cool my head while hiking up the next hill and was offered a lift which like a fool (?) I turned down, not needing to be in this wonderful bit of country. Using a pathway partially made of sleepers I crossed three miles of heathland and pine forest to Llandegla. The Crown Inn was closed, but the shop had just re-opened for evening trading and I bought a good stock of food to weigh me down. Way up above Ruthin, a family walked past adding a human touch to the scene but then at the last trees on the ever ascending path, high in the hills, I found a ditch to protect me from the strong breeze and prepared to camp. A stunning colourful sunset etched the sky as I collected wood for a fire. My newly acquired saucepan at last fulfilling its full role. Lying back to watch the star studded sky I fell contentedly asleep to the chant of bleating hillside sheep.
15m

Day 380
Thursday
I made a tardy start and climbed to the top of the ridge, rich in a swathe of purple heather and below a lone figure plodded behind me on the path. After descending to the sleepy Motel on the A494, I couldn't find the path so climbed the hills, using instinctive directions northwards in order to regain the OFDP further along. On passing a dry sheep water trough with a tied down valve and stopping to fill my flask with clean water, I glanced back: the persistent figure behind me was also making progress. I had breakfast at the top of the first cairned hill and then descended to the busy car park beyond. It was there that my pursuer caught up with me, Roger from Malvern and Hanley Castle School, where I had done a couple of days of supply teaching in the 90s. We shared tea, water, Roger's camp stove, food and tales. At one o'clock I set off for the top of Moel Fammau with its even more spectacular panoramic vistas. To the west lay Snowdon and I thought 'I'll be there in a week' although it took eight days as I went the long way round. A wonderful walk along the ridge, crossing two roads allowed me to stroll into Bodfari just after six. At the SPAR shop on the main road I had tea and obtained more supplies. It was a stiff climb but at the top a local man showed me the best places for mushrooms. While sitting and resting there to admire the view I discovered the loss of my new red sweater, which had only recently been retrieved from my Ledbury cache! Positives and negatives balancing out? As I walked towards evening the first view of the sea appeared, in the sunset, beyond the silhouette of a cross, which presumably indicated the monastery I sought and a possible bed! When I finally arrived there in the dark it was private, a retreat house that had no room for wayfarers. However the guardian who gave me the news did

have some mercy and found me a sandwich and an apple for my sustenance. Within a short distance in the deep evening gloom I found a derelict farm and buildings, ripe for conversion, overlooking the busy Motorway (A55) below and made camp with plenty of wood for a grand fire. Musing over my meal I thought of Stephen King's - 'The Shining' with its final section: here the sky was studded with stars, the hell's hole lights shone below me and devilish noises gnawed at the silence about my camp.
14m

Day 381
Friday
It was a lingering morning over the fire, porridge and tea before I crossed the Highway where a mobile cafe was flying both the Union Jack and the Welsh flag. I passed through Rhuallt and up to Cwm having a break on a stile, where I left a note to Roger, trailing behind me, enquiring about a lost sweater (!). From here it was only four miles to Prestatyn. Indeed, soon after passing above fields where fertiliser was being spread onto the green clover pastures, the town became visible by the sea but the path meandered lethargically round a quarry and then steeply up the last hill before descending to the town itself. In the station I reprimanded some boys for throwing paper down and strangely they didn't seem to mind my admonition! Wonderful!, as in London I would probably have got a mouth full! But then we were soon on the westward train.

> 'Have a thrill
> In raw Rhyl
> But use skill
> Take the pill'

I start walking west along the road and at Towyn saw the sign advertising:-

> Kings 'Greatest Circus on Earth'

Resting between acts were three immature elephants and some tired camels with the hump.

Just after Pensarn I was able to leave the main road and use the modern footpath and cycle way by the sea where jet skiers were enjoying speed in the sun. On reaching glowing curving Llandudno in the growing twilight I shopped for supplies and hot water before walking out of town in the night air up towards the light house of Great Ormes Head. At the top shelter was provided by a cafe wall and, feeling a bit like a fugitive, my supper was eaten as the old moon rose and the lights of passing cars swept by the boundary wall.
25m

Day 382
Saturday
The sun rose as a big red disc in a slightly cloudy sky while high above the vapour trails of jets dissected the heavens and on the hills, Kashmir (mountain) goats roamed freely. As I walked the high public coastal road, the private lighthouse road wound round the shore below. To the south lay Conway Castle in glorious sunlight whilst the broad cut of main road crossed the harbour. In Llandudno West stood a distinctive Memorial to Lewis Carrol while further along a small plaque read:-

> Lost but not forgotten
> Fishing Vessel   Katy
> Conway 16.1.99
> Sam (22) Cochin (30) Robo (20)

I crossed the river Conway to Edward's impressive fortress Castle, rested briefly on the harbour quay by the citadel walls and then went through the town and council streets to the main road, for a mile before coming to the shore-side cycle and foot way. By a road tunnel, mountaineers from Yorkshire were climbing the rocks and on the beach below a troop of horse were galloping gloriously with hooves splashing in the shallows, while above hang gliders swooped past as if in salute. I was soon down on the beach myself and walking the sands westward and where a man from Liverpool, was recovering from a recent heart attack, getting recuperative exercise while walking his massive dog on the beach.

After Penmaenmawr a sketchy path continued beneath the railway and I had lunch on the sea wall before crossing the sands to Llanfairfechan where I stopped for more tea and cake in the sea front cafe. From here the coast path was erratic and eroded. There were possible camping spots but I carried on to Penrhyn Castle, having to perilously scale an eight foot wall to gain access to the park. The mock castle (1860) lay in sweeping grounds which I negotiated by navigation, past spacious well kept gardens, to Maesgeirchen, the main road. At the Youth Hostel, after booking in, I met Alan, a NFA, and he led me to the night stop, St Mary's, for hot food while he kept me telling of the hut he had built from slates on the beach. But more importantly he told me that the unemployed could get a reduction in hostel fees - useful information!
21m

Detour Around Anglesey
Day 383
Sunday
Through Bangor I passed the ornate Victorian excursion pier pointing into the

Day 382 The broad flat sands of North Wales are a natural habitat for lugworms and this lugwormer

waters of Menai and this was a signpost for me as there were two ways on and off Anglesey it became compulsory to cross the Straits. After finding a route more or less beside the water my entry to the island was by the magnificent Menai Bridge, built by the Engineer Thomas Telford (1757 - 1834) and opened in 1826.

> 'High fortress above the sea -
> The world drives its vehicles over it
> And all the ships of the ocean -
> Go underneath its chains'

Getting the chains across with the use of barges was an amazing achievement.

This island used to be the granary that kept the olden day Welsh princes fed when they were pressed by the English in the continual battling for these lands. But, now the ferries have gone and the bridges built, the Island providing a simple link to the ferries for Ireland and because of this high speed road connection many of the beauties and much of the history of this province is often overlooked. Walking NE along the shore road (A545) overlooking the Menai Straits I spotted a motorist snacking in a lay-by and tried my opening ploy, 'just in time for tea' I said. To my surprise the lady, with her two lads, responded with a refreshing cup of brew together with a slab of cake. In Beaumaris I met a motor enthusiast from Wigan and we walked to the car rally further along the shore to meet his father, Peter, mother and their classic Riley. Photos were taken and signatures written. A semi-coastal path took me to Penmon where the priory was abandoned but still standing together with its splendid dovecote. Near the headland lighthouse, which stood isolated out in the sea, was a cafe for yet more tea and cake before wandering through an abandoned quarry towards Pentir. Roads and tracks took me to Red Wharf Bay and Pentrellwyn as the sun dipped and set a red path down on the sea. As darkness came to the beach, holiday makers were lighting fires while I found a little flat recess in the marram grass and set about making camp, scraping wood together from the shore and from a pile of logs in the grounds of an empty house under sale nearby. But I found no fresh water in the dark and had to use sea water for part of my extensive meal of soup, potatoes, beans, oxo and plums.
15m

Day 384
Monday 6th September
I watched the dawn break as the twinkling stars died and the new moon rose while jet-trails raced across the slow blue sky. The route's scenery was as variable as my accident prone day. On an early start I came away from the shore into woods and forests, past wheezing horses and then through bracken to the

shore of the marshy estuary to Red Wharf. The continuation track took me to a sandstone headland where I had to worm through hawthorn tunnels ending in a near sheer drop. But I scrambled down to a caravan site and crossed the beach to Benllech. From here a cliff path took me to Penrhyn, crossing the sand of the bay as the tide went out. It was then only a short distance to Moelfre. Along the way, on a cliff, a redundant sign said:-

'Congratulations Di!'

It was a day of minor mishaps, included burning a hole in my long worn cotton shirt, losing 40p in a telephone box and upsetting the contents of my flask. But to compensate there were wonderful views of rocks and bays along this coast, with all the signs in Welsh as well as English. At Moelfre I had tea at Ann's Pantry and went to the post office just before one o'clock to buy chocolate bars, cigarettes and envelopes but couldn't get stamps as an aggressive Welsh Postmaster alleged that the alarm was about to go off and he brusquely manhandled me out on to the street. This was my first real antagonistic encounter. Fortunately stamps were available in the machine outside (!) and I posted my films.

On the way to Lligwy Bay there is a memorial to the Royal Charter Steamship which succumbed on the rocks in 1859 with the loss of 400 lives. After crossing the sands to Dulas Bay I had to wade the river to reach Portobello. Out at sea, cargo boats were 'racing' to Liverpool passing the rocky island of Ynys Dulas highlighted by its tower. What a glorious coastline this is and to me so unexpected. As well as the natural scenery, little multi-coloured cottages, farms and lighthouses improved its rural character. In Amlwch I visited the SPAR shop before walking into the gathering gloom for the main road to Bull Bay and a path to Castell. After passing an old factory I lost the path and had to navigate to the minor road for Llanbadrig with a rank of wind-farm power masts whirring on the skyline, before arriving in Cemaes at eight, dead tired, to find a B&B which I do not now remember but one which sheltered me from the night's rain.
22m

Day 385
Tuesday
After the BNF Magnox Generation power station and visitor centre a NT way led to Cemlyn where the shingle beach protected an inshore pool of a nature reserve and splendidly the sun came out. On the far shore of the bay lay an unpretentious house within the bounds of a high long brick wall which once belonged to Capt. K Hewitt, millionaire, landowner, and brewer (Hewitt Breweries) who was the first to fly to Ireland, but crashed and afterwards had a steel plate fitted in his head. He used to give tramps one meal a year but now

it is NT and the garden is overgrown while nearby a plaque commemorated the 150 years since the first life boat was launched in Anglesey in 1828.

The path to Carmel Head and Church Bay was fitted with dull factory built flat pack stiles and gates - all rather flimsy. But then three jolly walkers masquerading as wardens joined me on the way down to the car park before I continued southwards on coastal tracks to the Stanley Embankment over the water to Holyhead arriving just before eight. In the 'Ten o'clock' shop, the girl was helpful with stores and also filled my flask. The weather had deteriorated but my luck improved as I searched Soldiers Point for shelter. In the grounds of a hotel under demolition I found a solid hut - empty and open - where, inside, I ate my supper by candlelight, sheltered from the wind raging outside and slept on top of a solid wooden workbench thoughtfully provided inside!
19m

Day 386
Wednesday
It was very windy as I wound around Holyhead (Caegybi) Mountain by the footpaths above the precipitous cliffs. The wind beat up from the south but it kept the rain away as I passed through heather and gorse - the purple and yellow scenery. Down on the road great gusts of wind sucked the papers from my map case and blew them away over a field. Pulling off my rucksack I jumped over the stone wall to retrieve them but on getting back - my bag had gone! A lady in another car said she saw someone pick it up, putting it into the boot of their car and she gave me a partial registration number. Walking forlornly into Trearddur, I dialled 999 (my first time ever). 'They' said that a car would come and while waiting I phoned my other brother Owen and chatted to Helen his wife for consolation. Eventually I was taken to Holyhead Police Station to retrieve the bag where it had been taken by a thoughtful motorist! The police even gave me tea and a ride back to Trearddur - they must be a better class of bobby up here, trained in lateral thinking and courtesy.

After this strange interruption I continued on a very overgrown coastal path around Ynis Gybi (Holy Island) and had more tea in Rhosneigr before entering the sand dunes where it started to rain. Combined with the wind it made a lousy day. After passing the motor racing circuit at Llangwyfan I saw a chapel on its own island but couldn't reach it because of the tide. Wet and weary I reached Aberffraw at eight, found the Prince Inn and booked B&B for only £15 and after luxuriating in a hot bath, sat by a warm coal fire over a revitalising whisky.
25m

Day 387
Thursday
Dawn and Bryn served me a huge breakfast and then gave me a packed lunch. I was off at 9.45 on a full stomach and entered the dunes of the local Nature reserve. Losing the path I mused that it might have been stolen by a local landowner - a lordly knight perhaps. On a narrow road through this domain I saw an estate wall which had holes in it, reminiscent of a castle's battlements, and doubling my thoughts on the owner's preoccupation with status and land.

It became sunny but the wind increased as I reached Malltraeth to raid the shop before crossing the river Cefni by the main road bridge. A causeway led to the extensive Newborough Forest, planted in the dunes during WW2. Prophets of doom had said it would fail but it has survived, much of it open woodland and not claustrophobic. It was traversed on good tracks and trails built for walkers and cyclists and in its depths I passed a lone forester with two mighty and expensive forest clearing machines. On the western side lay the long firm beach towards Llanddwyn Island with its lighthouse and church. This was a lovely stretch of sand with a splendid view past the island towards Snowdonia while the sound of the surf on the sand pounded my ears and scores of sea birds rose and flew off as I approached, regrouping and settling again behind me. Past the Island I briefly rejoined the tourists and re-entered the woodland. But I was soon alone again on the path round the perimeter of the pine woods and then struggling across the sandy heath to Pen - lon. In the distance, set in the sea, was Abermenai point but I didn't venture out there, even though there was a supposed footpath. It was the A4080 briefly before a track led to the stepping stones across the river Braint. At Rhuddgaer I met Jenny mowing her verges. She stopped, thankful for a break, and took me to the farmhouse for tea. We had a fun filled hour of gossip about OU, money, farming, history etc. and I was reluctant to leave. This is Marquis of Anglesey country and the paths are difficult to find, but I passed onto Cae Mawr and then through the closed Sea Zoo for a grand view of Caernarfon and its castle across the intervening water. Further along in Plas Porthamel the widow of an ex-Shell man fed me on tea and biscuits, filled my flask and held my attention until sundown. A mile beyond lay the church at Moel-y-don with an open outhouse but I pressed on to an unoccupied house on the shore and camped on its lawn, lighting a fire from an abundance of seashore wood.
20m

Day 388
Friday
I'd had a great fire but a poor night's sleep and dawn suggested an early start. Going through the strictly private grounds of the Conway Centre I passed the slumbering commonwealth college inscribed with a poem by John Masefield (who was born and bred in Ledbury and went to its quaint old wood framed

Grammar School). Out of the other side of the estate I came to the less impressive bridge, the Pont Britannia and crossed on the A5 to the modern Travel Inn for refreshments.

By road and path I made my way to Llanberis. Initially my planned route was fine - but one path (between 550684-548680) had disappeared and I had to scramble down into a ravine through trees and thick undergrowth before climbing out the other side, like a sheep, up to Garth Farm. The hills of Snowdonia began to gather about me and sun drenched Snowdon grew larger. The best view was at the foot of Llyn Padarn, a land locked lake, a relic of pre-glacier days, in which arctic charr swim and the lake-side railway's trains of yellow engines with trailing green coaches plied their way along the far shore showing off with cheerful 'Thomas-the-tank-engine' hoots. At Llanberis with its scores of shops and crowds of tourists I did a little shopping and then took the easy track beside the railway up Snowdon. Little red engines pulled up and down and a vast crowd of people were walking the path; everybody saying 'Hello' to everybody else. It was as busy as a London square, but far more friendly on a glorious warm sunny day with views worthy of the effort. At the top I had my form signed by Neil, who was down from Manchester for the day as he often did, just to walk the hills. My descent was by the path to the Snowdon Ranger Youth Hostel and on this route I saw nobody at all, in complete contrast to the ascent. Arriving at the Hostel fairly early I met two Tennesseans, Reagan and his young buddy, who were video makers working on a script for their own film. They had missed the bus twice and so stayed an extra night. Later a crowd of police-people arrived to make an attempt on the seven peaks the next day.
22m

Day 389
Saturday
It was a late start after sleeping till ten and waking to a gloomy day with threatening rain. At the head of Llyn Cwellyn I cut off the main road and climbed up through the forest on the path over to Drws-y-coed, where walking along the road was a crowd from the Welsh Miners Association inspecting the Owls Foot, a 500 ft shaft used long ago for mining copper, part of the complex workings around here. Prosperity never came because of the copper found at Ormes Head in Anglesey but the relics of past attempts of mining remain. Further up the road a farmer told me about his scratching stone standing in his field and which I had mistaken for a neolithic artifact. He said the cows used it after winter to have a good itch at the winter's parasites. I passed many more dismal obsolete mining operations including slate quarries on the road to Llanllyfni via Penygroes. In the village the youth football team were gathering and they pointed the way to the road for Clynnog Fawr, where I arrived too late for the shop which closed at noon. Somebody said there would be a shop in the

Day 390 There were many coastal golf courses. This one had a glorious setting near Dinllaen on the Llewyn Peninsular

next village so I hot footed it to Trevor and arrived just before five. Unfortunately that shop had closed at four. Thwarted I retired to the local social club and bought Mars bars, cigarettes, crisps and was given hot water. An hour later I set off into the mist which shrouded the old granite mine and walked up and up into that deserted, swirling mist covered, hell hole, taking several false tracks before gaining the top plateau. Away down below the sound of surf drifted up to me as I walked in a south-westerly direction. There was a sudden break in the clouds and the sea showed itself far below verifying my approximate position. At Mount Pleasant (it wasn't that day) I was told not to take the path south and so took the road to Llithfaen where there was no B&B, through the small hamlet of Pistyll and finally to Nefyn. I went into the Off Licence and Lamp Shop for advice and met Dawn and Ross, the owners. She had pity on me and took me to their house across the road to meet a miscellaneous group of friends and neighbours. Much later I was able to sleep on a mattress on the floor.
23m

Day 390
Sunday
After being given breakfast of sausage and toast in the Lamp Shop I set off at ten to follow the coast path to the Dinllaen peninsular. At the headland by Porth Dinllaen I met Lancaster students who had sailed from Ireland on a 35 ft ketch and who were now enjoying some walking in the excellent scenery along seven miles of the Lleyn Peninsular coastline. The path ended there and my way was into the hills on roads until cutting cross country to Bryn Mawr and finding shelter from the heavy rain in a barn. Later the farmer, enquiring about my activities, gave me permission to stay but soon after six I set off again, to Anelog and then headed into the hills. At the headland another storm belted past, right over the Coast Guard hut as I stood in a slither of its doorway shelter. Descending in the darkness to Garreg Fawr I knocked on a door. The response from the lady 'You can't stay here' rang in my ears until, a mile further on, a sympathetic farmer found me a tidy barn for the night.
21m

Day 391
Monday 13th September
In Aberdaron I bought supplies taking roads and tracks to Bryn Penrhyn, Cadlan and Ysgo, where I was given two cups of coffee by an ex-Rhodesian iron worker from Que Que in his caravan home tucked away on a farm. Refreshed I crossed to Mynydd Penarfynydd and its trig point with fabulous seascape scenic views looking back towards the Cape and Bardsey Island. A new path that was not on my old OS map, led round to Rhiw. At Treheli the path was in poor condition and I tripped over, without apparent damage, before descending to the beach with the help of a rope ladder. On the crescent beach

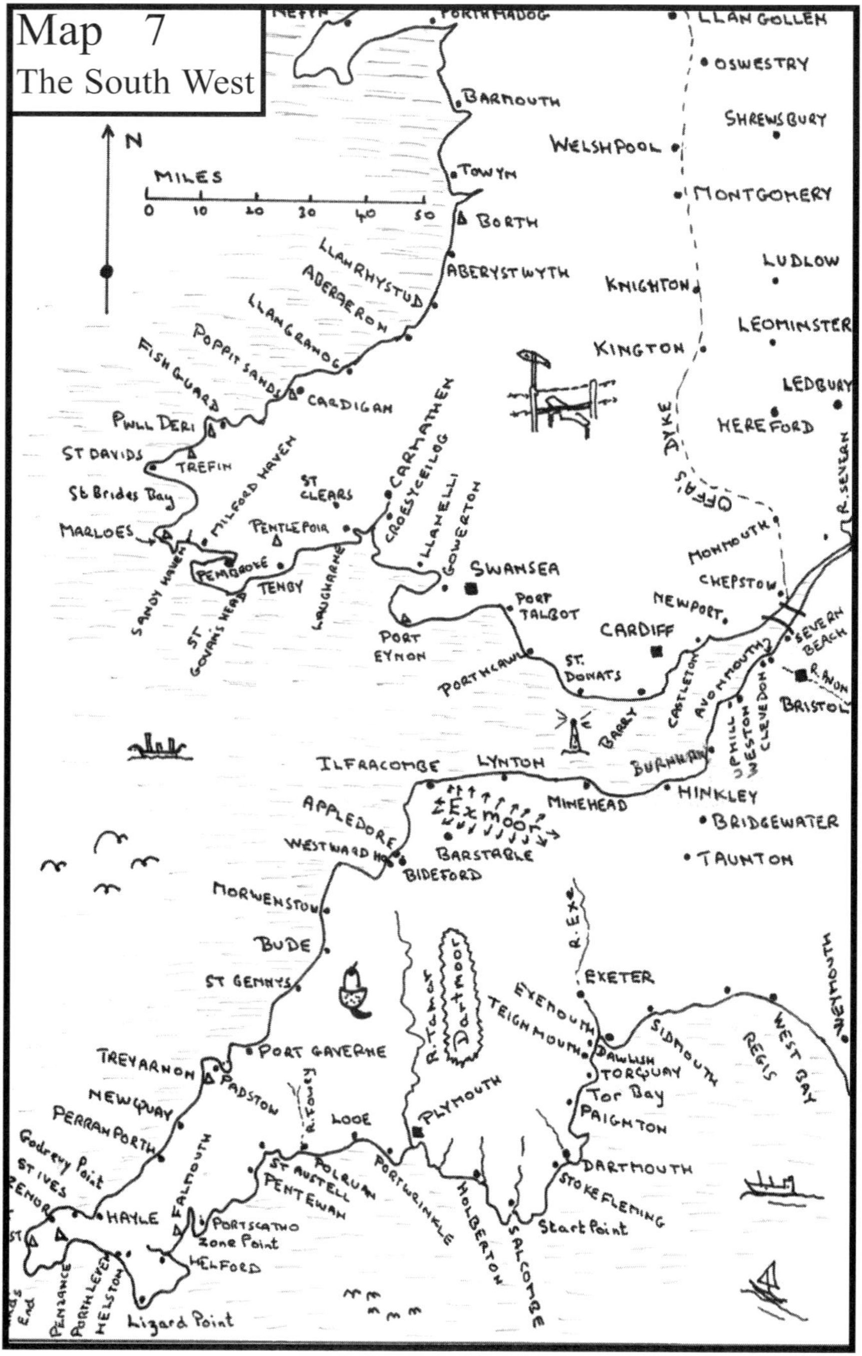

Map 7
The South West

of Hell's Mouth I sat watching the waves until the tide was on the turn at midday and then walked the three miles of shore, dodging the incoming waves breaking on the mixed gravel and sand. At the far end surfers were 'doing their own thing' and following suit at the next headland, I relaxed and took in the scenery. An easy grass track led to the top of Llwyngivril but deteriorated from there to Corm Farm and Porthtocyn. I reached Abersoch at 5.30, walked the beach to Trwyn Llanbedrog and then pressed on to Pwllheli where, expecting rain, I stayed in an inexpensive B&B.
24m

Day 392
Tuesday
At seven o'clock the sun came through the window - it hadn't been a wet night after all! I made a slow move for breakfast and watched early morning TV thinking how selective this medium was in its superficial portrayal of the real world. Sauntering around town and find nothing of great interest, I posted maps and bought a new sweater (£3.25) from a charity shop and in a splendidly old fashioned ironmongers enquired about all-purpose throwing knives for capturing rabbits and general camping, was offered sheath knives and told that a good carbon steel blade was needed for my outdoor activities. But I didn't succumb.

It was a glorious warm day as I set off, at ten, down the main road (A497) for a mile until a path led over the Afon Erch to the railway and a couple of pubs near the shore. On the two miles of beach which followed I thought about a swim but was too lazy for that. Up and over Penrhyn I had to negotiate three layers of barbed wire fencing to gain access to the holiday camp before walking to the concrete-block sea wall which allowed an escape on the other side. What the resident inmates thought of this strange apparition in their midst I do not know! Maybe it was part of the overall entertainment.

Black cormorants were fishing as I crossed some grass onto the railway and its bridge to cross the Afon Wen and at the Afon Dwyfor I pulled the same trick. On the far bank an old farmer and his son were erecting new fencing, improvising with a tractor mounted bucket acting as a mallet to drive in the posts while holding them upright with a useful homemade iron loop on a long handle. I strode off along the east bank of the river towards the Welsh castle of Criccieth, wondering if the river was wadeable. I didn't linger at Criccieth and took the path beside the railway out of town. On the headland a geography lesson was in progress, the young children very attentive - their summer break having done them the world of good. I myself had lost track of time and had forgotten that the schools had just started business again. On the beach, below Black Rock, there was a crowd of holiday makers with their cars scattered along this vast stretch of flat sand and some sat on wheeled seats, sailing along,

pulled by their bright billowing spinnakers. It was a steady march on this firm ground around the duned headland to Borth-y-gest and Porthmadog, although it looked tempting to cross the estuary to the headland on the other side. Trying brother Roger on the dog and bone there was no reply and no Poste Restante either. I crossed the long straight causeway of the Ffestiniog Railway and on the other side wandered around the Station with all its sidings and sheds, where enthusiast drivers were checking their locos while I found hot water in an unattended canteen. Walking on the marsh and soft sinking sand around the headland of Penrhyn-Isaf, I began to wonder if it was advisable, but under the cliffs by some old fallen trees found a cave just above the high water mark and made camp. Feeling like Robinson Crusoe I collected wood and built a fire under a beautiful evening sky as the distant sea caressed the shore across this extensive stretch of sand. In case of rain I had the cave and a small cliff to climb in case of a big tide! As I contemplated my position, man Friday walked past and peered at me before passing on without comment - whence he came stayed unknown.
18m

Day 393
Wednesday
Dawn wakened me and sunlight rushed in. The fire was still alight and the tide hadn't reached me. With a breakfast of tea, porridge and honey I felt in tune with the world and ready for the day's revelations. After a few steps across the soft sands I came to a staircase footpath, which rose quickly and suddenly to the astounding fairy tale village of Porthmeirion, which was being explored by American tourists. I knew then where that man Friday had come from. The gatekeeper told me that camping wasn't allowed around here but laughed when I told him about last night and he explained the way to the 'real time' village which was to be mundane in contrast to the Italian village I had just passed with its fountains, exotic shrubs and statues. Started in 1925 as the brain child of the architect, Clough Williams-Ellis, it took fifty years to complete and is now in the hands of his grandson. Like the Prisoner I made my escape on the road to Penrhyndeudraeth. Beyond this I crossed the causeway over the estuarine river of Dwyryd to the toll bridge where the keepers gave me tea as they collected money from motorists. Once past this motoring obstacle I was able to take the slate dyke across the flats to Llanfihangel-y-traethau with views back to the mountains of Snowdonia and across the estuary to last night's campsite. A good track downstream petered out near a farm where a man was sitting contentedly. He had been coming there for twenty years and told me that I had to walk around the farm by the shore. There was a path but in parts it was ankle deep in mud and I floundered through reeds and dodged overhead trees before escaping up a bank and over a fence to find a firmer path for Harlech across flat farmlands through the forests of the Morfa. A horse followed me through one farm and seemed to be offering me a ride but I declined

and at midday met two forestry workers from Welshpool and Betws-y-coed who were having lunch. We discussed timber and its low price; now £30 a ton compared to last year's £50, which made mechanisation essential.

An hour later I quickly found the path cutting straight towards the 13th century Harlech Castle which stood high on the skyline above its town and bought chips, consuming them just beyond the town limits. From here a track led, within two miles, to Llandanwg and beyond to the snug small church of St Tanwg, lying behind a protective stone wall, which announced a lamplight service at 6.30 every 3rd Sunday. After crossing the small river of Cwmnantcol by using the railway bridge I found a way around the small headland and set off across the beach, at low tide, towards Shell Island. Unfortunately there was a stretch of water in the way and I had to walk across wet mud flats to gain the southerly path on the other side of the airfield. It was then a hard walk threading through the sand dunes at the Paradise camping grounds to Llanenddwyn, even having to use the compass to keep on course. The solitude was broken by jets practising landings and takeoffs on the RAF landing strip to the east. There was no clear path here and at one stage I stumbled across private land and spoke to the farmer, who condescendingly allowed me to cross his land to the main road which took me to Barmouth. At eight it started to rain as I crossed the wooden foot and rail bridge, luckily finding, on the other side, an isolated byre with only a couple of bedraggled sheep and two horses for my company.
24m

Day 394
Thursday.
There had been heavy rain in the night . Glad that I'd had a dry place for sleep, and still sheltered from the rain outside, I took my time over breakfast, cleared a frog out of my sleeping bag and got going at ten o'clock. Out on the sea dyke I continued to the narrow gauged Fairbourne Railway which apparently still connects with a ferry to Barmouth from the head of the peninsular in the Mawddach estuary, but I had seen no sign of it in the town in the gloom of the previous night. Southward along the coast road I arrived in Llwyngwril around noon with the sun coming out and good views back to Barmouth. Three miles later the road turned inland and while I was sitting at this bend a farmer stopped his Landrover for a quick word, coming back 15 minutes later in a JCB to give a £5 donation. It was at his farm half a mile further on that I was able to escape the main road on a path to Bwlch and then take a narrow track road all the way to Towyn (Tywyn) - or so I thought. Unfortunately there was no road bridge over the Broad Water of the Afon Dysynni. Not wanting to walk the six miles around I resorted to the railway bridge trick, except that this time there was a difficult high fence to climb, while on the other side it was necessary to walk along a rough rocky embankment before finding a gateway access to the road. Being protected by metal spears, I don't think the bridge

was supposed to be used!

Tywyn was unremarkable except for its Talyllyn Railway, its long stone beach and for me memories of Happy Valley in the hills. It is filled with modern housing estates. I did the 'I' and took the footpath to Aberdovey (Aberdyfi) across reclaimed grassland, home to hardly any livestock. Nearing the golf course I met an out-of-work clown who was about to look for golf balls. He retrieved his hunting stick which he had hidden in some bushes and we walked together across the links. At six o'clock I arrived in Aberdovey and stocked up at the shop which was still open. On the front I met Beth Richards, an aunt of my first wife, in the same old house where I'd last seen her forty years before, and we had a chat while she filled my flask. Half a mile beyond the town I tried the Outward Bound School but it was full. However two miles later an empty house had a log shed which made a suitable shelter for the night.
18m

Day 395
Friday
There had been some rain in the night, but in the morning the air was crystal clear, like champagne and it remained sunny for most of the day. Two and a half miles along the road, in this lovely soft valley, I found a path across a caravan site, and had a wash in the unmanned toilets, before finding an exit into woodland and fields. But there were no footpath signs at all, and it was therefore difficult to find a way to the rail bridge over the river to Dovey Junction Station. On the crossing was a house which I thought was unoccupied but where Bill lived. Seemingly incongruous in this rural spot he stood there dressed in a suit and tie waiting to catch the Aberystwyth train. After one train passed across 'his' bridge I followed and then walked along a track to Glandyfi and main road before striking off to the Ynys-Hir nature reserve, boasted as one of RSPB's best, and possibly the quietest. There was a good mix of woodland, marsh and estuary and in a hide nearly opposite last nights shed I stopped and was able to write up my diary before continuing by track, dyke and rail towards the west beside the Dovey marshes as storm clouds gathered about me. At Ynyslas the road south led to long-strung-out Borth. The wind rose and short sharp showers were unleashed bringing clear short lived rainbows while, nearby close to the road, determined golfers struck their balls or waited patiently for me or cars to pass before making their resolute drives. The straggle of houses slowly coalesced to the resort of Borth and with some surprise I found myself passing a Youth hostel not seen on my map. As it was five in the evening and the weather very unsettled the decision to stay was not difficult to reach. With one traveller from Oxford and a couple of Americans, it was almost empty. At £6.20 it was also cheap accommodation.
17m

Day 396
Saturday
At ten o'clock I found myself going through the heart of Upper Borth and up above the town to a black dioritic war memorial which had been struck by lightning on March 21st 1983. From here the path switch-backs along the cliffs, which are impressively high but not especially dramatic. Black sentinel cormorants stood guard awaiting breakfast in the dull green sea below and they stirred restlessly in the south easterly breeze. An old lime kiln at Wallog provided a land mark in this otherwise empty coast and could also have provided shelter with its adjacent grassy patch for sleeping beneath the stars. Somewhat tired I stopped to drink coffee and sat in the warm bracken, looking at the two long arms of Cardigan Bay stretching away in the distance and in sympathy with the empty sea, scratched gently at the bites under my arm pits which had been itching for a few days. What trivial things filter though our lives! Continuing southwards, the outline of Aberystwyth suddenly appeared, just as I came to a run down cafe with the Camera Obscura above and the electric cliff railway both out of action. Further decrepitude was apparent on the town's edge, the first large building being run down and disused. However, despite the rain and rot, the central area was abuzz with people, since it is of course a serious shopping place for mid Wales. The 'I' sold me a map, the bank gave me money and food was provided by a cafe on the front which had been opened especially for the benefit of drug and alcohol addicts:-

> John 4:::: You knew the gift of God, and who it is that
> is saying to you, 'give me a drink,' you would have
> asked him, and he would have given you living water'

The young woman helping to run this cafe was having difficulty explaining to her daughter the sacrifice necessary to help people and when I left she gave me a blessing!

In the rain I visited the castle and the Ceredigon Museum in an old theatre full of historical artefacts related to the sea, mining and agriculture. By then it was time to escape on to the coastal path which climbed and dipped steeply as the cliffs became bigger and more dramatic. Heavy rain pounded down at the caravan site of Morfa Bychan and I found shelter in the workshops, meeting two maintenance men, one of whom had worked at Wellington College when I was there as grounds superintendent. He had been a film technician, working on the film 'Lords of Discipline'. Now he was happy to have left behind the modern technical film developments and spend his time using his hands in this rural area. After buying some Mars bars at the shop, and as the rain eased to a drizzle, I walked another five miles along the path as it followed the coast, crossed the Afon Wyre below Llanrhystud and in the gathering gloom of evening found a lone barn below Maesfron Farm. It was straw filled and there

were four playful kittens for company.
16m

Day 397
Sunday
A road stroll took me to Llan-non and one and a half miles further on I tried the coastal path but this needed a great deal of guess work all the way to the tidy town of Aberaeron. From there the path was easy to follow most of the way to New Quay but the last section was on the beach and the tide beat me, so I had to climb the steep mud cliffs which at the top had a protective thorn barrier that was extremely difficult to penetrate. Eventually I emerged, scratched, on the cliff top path and went into the bustling little town which was like so many others along this coast, with its harbour and all the paraphernalia of commerce and tourists that now replaces the bustle and noise of past shipping activity.

In a high part of town I bought some food and sat on a bench for a snack after phoning from an adjacent call box, but getting no reply. Continuing to eat the phone rang, and out of cussedness I picked it up - it was Roger calling back after his bath. Surprise! But alas alack he had posted the relevant maps to Aberystwyth! And so I was reminded of the proverb 'Make haste slowly'. Two o'clock saw me climbing on the path out of the town up to the headland and beyond. The scenery improved gradually and little sandy coves appeared as jewels in a crown though progress was slowed by the undulations. From the beach at Cwmtydu a road rose up out of the village and I walked with a man wheeling a baby, on hearing of my trek he informed me that 'people are too lazy these days'. He told me that he was a driver for the Bass brewery and frequently delivered in Cornwall and I said that we'd meet again there. The road climbed up towards the south west and two miles later I turned right to the Urdd Centre, a strange name for what was only a holiday village with its neat chalets, seasonally tired horses and a ski slope. The continuation path led to Traeth-yr-Ynys of the NT with a spectacular peninsular and craggy cliffs rich with white quartz veins, sea caves and green grass - a neat and tidy place. At Lochtyn Farm, 500 sheep were gathered for clipping, but the farm lady from Liverpool still bore the scars of Merseyside and appeared to know little about sheep.

Not surprisingly there was no room in the barns for the night. Down in Llangranog there was no room at the B&B. But in the pub I had my flask filled by a tired barmaid, quenched my thirst with a lager and lime and chatted to some walkers met earlier on the Traeth-yr-Ynys headland. On leaving, a lady ran out after me and gave me a donation for the cause. After half a mile came the cliff tops and, feeling tired, I decided to camp in a bit of bushy shelter high over the sea, and gathered enough wood for a decent fire against the cool of

the strong evening breeze. The stars came out bright and clear and contentment settled in despite of having to change my position several times to avoid the tear making smoke swirling from the fire.
20m

Day 398
Monday 20th September
Surprised by the arriving clouds, by morning the rain had given me a soaking despite my survival bag and I was therefore already wet on departure at 7 o'clock and it rained all day! Soon in Penbryn, I sheltered briefly in the farm's public toilet before climbing out on the road past an old church (which was open) to Tresaith and on to Aberporth where, while talking to a retired man from Basildon, delightful, unexpected, dolphins played in the calm sea below. Avoiding the town by walking across the harbour sands my visions of breakfast disappeared as the cafe was closed. Above the town a DERA base for missile testing lay concealed behind a high fence; this base, depicted in a mural on the harbour quay, was obviously an important part of the town's economy and way of life.

Soon it was paths again, but poorly marked and I had to cross fields and fences before gaining the road to the unmarked NT water wheel at Llwnysgaw. At the startling white ancient church in Mwnt two ladies were making arrangements for a harvest festival on Tuesday. The Holy Cross Church is a 13th-14th century structure on a 5th century site and through which 20,000 saints may have passed on the way to Bardsey Island. Many years ago they used to celebrate January's first Sunday as Bloody Sunday in memory of beating a Flemish attack in 1155. The ladies invited me to the harvest thanksgiving and when I apologised for not waiting for the service, in compensation they gave me a twisted carrot as a parting gift!

Another climb led to Crug Farm, and then I traversed grassland to Clyn-yr-ynys, where Park Farm had a notice saying 'strictly private' referring to the lands just crossed. A host of geese grazed in the wheat fields of this derelict farm while a notice advised me to wash my hands if I had touched the animals! The rain increased gradually all morning leaving this sorry and sodden hiker trudging into Cardigan and after withdrawing money from the bank I bought two new pairs of dry socks at the local market with jovial help from the stall holder. Further on at St Dogmaels I stocked up with food before hauling myself to the Youth Hostel at Poppit Sands and on arriving at 6 o'clock couldn't believe my eyes. It was closed. In frustration I searched for and found the warden, a relief worker, and on seeing my plight he let me in, made tea and turned on the heat for me to dry out. He was a lawyer from Hereford studying for more exams and making use of the quietness of hostels at this time of year. I hung out my clothes, papers and sleeping bag all over the place and finally

made myself a big meal.
18m

Day 399
Tuesday
A 9.30 start and on a path straight away, for it is from here that the Pembrokeshire path starts. Fifteen miles to Newport - an easy dry day I thought! But it was all up and down, quite the most arduous part so far, with lousy footing, to boot. A jovial group of nine walkers, on holiday learning Welsh, passed and re-passed me until I eventually got ahead and left them behind. The cliffs here are dramatic with castellated layered strata truncated by erosion. The sea was calm, while down below seals stretched and scratched on the rocks and sand. An occasional flock of birds added to the natural beauty of this area of low habitation, coloured by the yellow flowers of toadflax. But in Penbryn a flock of mohair goats stood wet and bedraggled not at all impressed. In my enchantment I spotted Newport but it was several miles before eventually arriving at the YH. Two volunteer wardens were on duty and a well informed YHA man was visiting. He told me that hostelling actually started around 1909 in Germany and didn't come to Britain until 1930 which surprised me since as children we had been taught that the British invented it. The Scottish association had gone its own way in 1932 he said.
13m

Day 400
Wednesday
A change in the weather brought a wet day and after only a mile I had to put on my waterproofs as it continued to rain, on and off, all morning. At Cwm - yr - Eglwys, in a neat little bay, I sat and rested amongst the remains of an old church (St Brynach's) and its graveyard built on the shore line and further along on the trig point on Dinas Head was a vantage point for glorious views of the coast as well as the boats heading in and out of Fishguard - ferry boats, the Stenna and Lynx together with a flotilla of fishing boats picking their way through the sea. Then the squalls battered me as I hauled to the main port of Fishguard. Although this is a wonderful coastline, the path sometimes, seems to follow the cliffs too conscientiously. That is until a road is inevitably reached, as on the way to rather dreary Lower Fishguard (where Under Milkwood had been largely filmed) and the road climbs up to the main town. In the 'I' they wanted to charge £5.75 for a map and so sent me to a book shop for the purchase at the normal, but still high, price of £5.25. What a contrast to the cost of some my other older maps, the lowest was five shillings! The helpful book shop sent me on, pointing up the road to Jean's Tea room for a snack.

Climbing away from the port up a long flight of steps I regained the path at the top and continued walking into the evening, pausing at Carregwastad Point

where the French had landed in 1797. What a craggy stupid place to land! No wonder they gave up to a Welshman! Some thirteen had even been rounded up by a 47 year old woman cobbler - the 'Pembrokeshire Heroine' with nothing but a pitchfork. Today, on the rocks below, a squad of honking seal pups were waiting for their busy mums. Two brick sheds offered shelter but I clomped on and completed the next couple of miles in the dark with the light of Pwll Deri hostel beckoning me forward. Luckily there was some moonlight and I safely negotiated the rocky path. There was a big crowd of walkers here, and the warden, Mandy, made me welcome.
20m

Day 401
Thursday
This hostel placed high up above the sea has some marvellous views and as it is such a wonderful place it has attracted a great number of people. Memorial slabs recorded those who 'stayed':-

David Selynn Birch 1922-1990.
From a gorse clad hill to a clear blue sea
That timeless view where he'll always be

and

Dewi Emrys 1879 - 1952
'A thina'r meddilie syn dwad ichi
Pan foch chin ishte uwchben pwllberi

and

Bill Williams 1917 - 1982

and

Cromech Carreg Sampson
Mae clogwynni'n llad
Cadwch at y llynybr

All bearing testimony to the simple pleasures of the sea, the land, the air, the sun and the black crows playing in the warm southerly wind, tumbling up and down the cliffs, oblivious of the FT index, and free in the elements.

In the hostel, last night by the fire, I had briefly chatted with Martin and Ian, a walking duo (M&I), today we met on the path, exchanged greetings and again in the pub at Trefin. We were destined to meet several times more. They

were going to stay in the landlord's room up the street and I also decided to call a halt, booking in at the hostel, sharing it with a Belgian walker, camper and cyclist and an American lad who worked in a BT think tank at Ipswich. Housed in the former village school, the friendly part-time warden lived in the village and just to confuse things further her office was detached from the main hostel in the building opposite.
8m

Day 402
Friday
Walking out of the village I met up with M&I, but they had a different route to mine. My first stop of the day was only a mile down the road at the stone circle of Trohne which was a surprise to me. Although close to the path it must be of relative low importance as I found no mention of it in guide books. At Porthgain there was a harbour and the remains of a slate quarry with its obsolete sheds, the remains of a short rail track leading over the headland. When the slate failed, dolerite was mined and the whole enterprise was probably never profitable. The only person to make money was the entrepreneur who imaginatively boosted its productivity and viability and then sold it on, a timeless procedure for making money. I met up with M&I again and we walked together. At Abereiddy the rocky coast continued with pods of seals and flights of dancing birds. The twin peaks near St David's Head, which could be seen from Strumble Head, now started to dominate the skyline as the hill grades of the path reduced their severity. Yet another short storm burst upon us and when it passed a sharp double rainbow appeared, as I enjoyed a companionable walk with M&I. But eventually I shot off on my own to St David's Head following the spoor of horses, the culprits a group of Shetland ponies used here with Soay sheep for selective grazing to assist the increase of natural vegetation. Then I re-met the walking duo at the White Sands cafe where we said our farewells. A grand pair of companionable lads and I wondered about seeing them again on another path somewhere else. They were off for the delights of St David's hostel but as it was only 4.30, too early for me, I decided to press on. At Pen Dal-Aderyn, the headland opposite Ramsey Island, I sat and watched the sea, which at high tide was fearsome, full of currents and whirl pools, accentuated by the slanting evening sunbeams. It is said to be one of the most treacherous stretches of water in the UK. A boat was making trips across this water, racing in and around the rocks of Ramsey Sound. The occupants were obviously having a grand time, but it looked a bit dangerous and foolhardy to me, a mere landlubber. At Porthllisky I had my flask filled, in the evening twilight, and started looking for shelter. A number of abandoned kilns looked like possible candidates but none seemed quite right. Interestingly and paradoxically there is no lime here. Apparently the church used to let out the land and insisted on liming so the enterprising monks imported the raw material from the Tenby area and burnt it in the kilns before selling it at a profit.

In near darkness at St Non's Bay spotting the silhouette of a barn, I passed the remains of a chapel in a field and went through two gates to the relics of a holy well. And it was from here that a minor miracle occurred which epitomised all the amazing incidents which had already happened to me and would happen again. Approaching the barn, thinking it would be an ideal shelter against the threatening rain, I realised that it was a chapel but still thought it would be suitable. I could sleep on the grass and if it rained, could retreat into the church. In order to add weight to my idea, I tried the door which creaked open, revealing burning candles. Wonderful! However I decided to let the adjacent house know of my intentions knocked on the door and was greeted by two nuns! 'Come in' they said. On telling them of my trip and intentions, without further ado, they had me sitting at a table to give me food. I had nearly eaten a mound of egg and toast when Sister Mary said she had found me a bed in St David's, but would I mind walking there in the dark. Later she relented and took me in her 'angel mobile' - a sedate red Metro. The place was a Pilgrims rest established by a vet and his wife after their pilgrimage to Spain and we had an interesting evening of gossip before a late bed.
18m

Day 403
Saturday
Eight o'clock and as nobody else in the house stirred I could say goodbye to neither the owners, their children nor the lodgers so after grabbing a quick bite, avoiding certain designated lodgers' shelves, I left. St David's is a very attractive town and the Cathedral is suitably impressive with its little chapels and historical relics. In the town I did a little shopping and some photocopying at an engraver's before walking back to St Non's and continuing to Morfa Common. There was a new track cut through the heather, presumably to reduce erosion. Enjoying myself, I sat down to rest in glorious sunshine while past me walked the 'silent man', who I had encountered in Trefin Hostel, dedicated to his task - the Pembrokeshire path. At Gewni, watching the multicoloured rocks, a black feral cat raced across my path. Then suddenly, around the next corner, picturesque busy Solva appeared.

Dinas Fach is reputed to have a spectacular blow hole and after dropping my bag I tried to climb down to it, but discretion took the better part of valour and I decided to retreat. Climbing back up I spotted somebody fiddling with my luggage - but they were simply leaving a contribution in a pocket. Having been away from traffic for several days, the seaside road at Newgale Sands looked like a race track. At the cafe a man and his grandson displayed his two pappillons which naturally led to a natter and an exchange of pedigrees. After Nolton Haven I reached Broad Haven only to find the hostel throbbing and full, but the phone told me Marloes Sands had a bed. They said it was thirteen miles and as it was already late the road seemed the best option, which was a shame

because the coast is supposed to be splendid. Indeed I found out much later that it is and that St Brides has night recesses in the church and an old lime kiln. At Little Haven passing a block of apartments that Liz and I had visited briefly some fifteen years before to investigate time sharing - I knew instantly that we'd been there before. Memory is a marvellous thing! I arrived, in the dark, at the excellent little hostel, with its piggery, hen house and cow shed sections, demarcating the various facilities and a welcoming warden. It was nearly full with a crowd of boys on a wind surfing week and there were dripping wet suits everywhere.
21m

Day 404
Sunday
Repacking for the day showed that somehow I'd lost a yellow shirt and one new sock, but this was a minor set back and I left my bag at the hostel to walk around Wooltack point. In Martin's Haven a group of divers were preparing to go to sea while at the headland numerous seal pups squeaked at the bottom of the tall cliffs and boggled up while just as many tourists watched above and peered down. Walking back towards the hostel I met the two German hostellers of last night and they were really enjoying themselves in the coastal delights. Having picked up my bag and said my farewells I got back to the coastal path where my old friend ORS rocks appeared and this explained the colour of Marloe sands. By degrees I gained St Ann's Head with its light house and then busy Dale, crossing the river by the shingle to Musselwick, without using the normal detour inland. Dale is where a Tudor landed in 1485 (from Brittany), only a short distance from his birthplace. He picked up Welshmen on the way to Bosworth, where Richard III was killed and Henry VII picked up the crown and then became a successful king. Hence ended that Norman thing. At Monk's Haven, a dropping off place for pilgrims, it was starting to rain and as I was getting wet I sat, for a prolonged coffee break, in the porch of a church, built on an old 6th century site. Walking inland to St Ishmael's I learnt nothing of the village but got hot water from a local council house as it continued to rain, rain, and rain. So much, that at Skerryback Farm near Sandy Haven I knocked on the door of a farm B&B and the landlady, Margaret (Williams), somehow took pity on me and gave a 75% reduction. After a bath I could relax and sat watching TV - Ballykissangel, Greengrass, Earthquakes in Taiwan, Troubles in Timor, USA wining the Ryder out of the blue, while we beat SA in the Davis cup.
17m

Day 405
Monday 27th September
Most of my clothes had dried out in the night but every inch of the creek at Sandy Haven was filled with water, which meant a long detour by road around

Day 403 Minor miracles occurred frequently: one source was the holy well of St Non near St David's

the head. Passing the church, envisaged as a stopping point for the previous night, a Baptist chapel, it was barred and shuttered, and I was doubly glad I'd stayed at the farm. Still a wet day I made my way round the creek, through Herbrandston to South Hook Point. The easterly path then took me up the Haven, past two large jetties, into the clamour of civilisation of Milford, a busy place steeped in naval history. It also processed large quantities of sperm whale oil for the lighting of London street lamps and therefore shares part of the responsibility for the decline in whale numbers. On the water front was a plaque (of 1994) commemorating Operation Overlord: part of the Normandy Invasion and a sea mine was planted by the path and used as a memorial:-

6th Brigade, Parachute Regiment
Lost at Taranto, Italy
and on HMS Abdiel lost on 9th-10th Sept 1943

The way over the river was blocked and the swing bridge was not open so I sat down on a riverside seat and read:-

Our spirits left our bodies as we slept
and walked along the shore
and when we came to this place
where we lost you forever

We knew we would walk no more
and as we sat and watched the harbour
and the darkness claimed the day
The water whispered to us
We took his breath away

Anon.

A touching testimony to an unnamed Milfordian.

    A scruffy path led away around the river, past Castle Hall and its stainless steel works and then by road to the top of the hill where the path continued again, crossing a field, followed by a walkway of sleepers and passing over a stile. At this point 'Disaster' hung in the balance as I slipped off the top of the stile right onto my back and lay there for a full minute wondering what had happened. Somehow my bag had saved me and softened my fall but I was sore for a week after that.
    Crossing the pink and rusty bridges of the Oil Company I saw the Pembroke Bridge and the townships on either side and through Neyland came to Brunel Quay: a small park, with an obligatory statue of Brunel wearing a top hat - and this was presumably the docking berth for the great Great Eastern. There was

good view of Ceddan Bridge, over the Daugleddau, which is slim, and functional but not, I thought, beautiful. Okay for Brunel! There was a short walk up the adjacent creek before the bridges could be crossed to Pembroke Dock. After getting supplies two boys followed me out of town and begged for a cigarette. As they departed I told them to look to the heavens for money and then while sitting on a seat up at Llanreath contemplating their antics and my next action, I looked down at the ground and there on the floor was a £1 coin! In the council estate of Pennar some local assistance showed me the path which leads by the muddy river side to Pembroke town and its magnificent moated castle. Crossing by the sluice bridge a group of kids told me that it was used by Edward VII and Henry VIII but after that all the kings went to London. Started in wood in 1093 it became an impressive castle on the river Cleddau and was the birthplace of Henry VII, nephew of Jasper Tudor, who finally turned it all around.

At 6.30 I was in Monkton which was being invaded by a stream of cars escaping the maintenance programme at the local refinery. Someone told me there was no chance of a B&B here so he invited me in for tea and hot water. Setting off three quarters of an hour later left me wondering about accommodation on such a damp dull evening but two miles later I found Brown Slate organic farm with its hooting owl. A request for a barn produced an old whitewashed kitchen, used as a meeting room. Otherwise bare, there was a table and some chairs and a folding bed that kept threatening to collapse. But I was dry, there was light and they even gave me some chips.
20m

Day 406
Tuesday
A mile from the farm the path dipped to a creek gripped by high tide and I found a lime kiln with firewood close at hand and which would conceivably have made a camp - but I'd had the better deal on that folding bed! The path continued to a silent power station strangely surrounded by artificial plastic grass and Pwllcrochan with a church, displaying an ice cream steeple, which was deserted, locked and surrounded by an overgrown graveyard. Around the refinery the woodland path clung to a bank above the shore lined with piers for unloading crude oil. Beyond several more abandoned houses further testified to a number of explosions that had occurred at the refinery, after which much of the local area had been evacuated and not resettled. Not far away lay Fort Popton, one part of nineteen similar defences, built in 1859-64 at a cost of £85,000 as a protection for Milford Haven which is said to be one of the finest natural harbours in the world and which has been used by the navy since 1539. The fort now houses a well protected and hidden RSPCA seal sanctuary where I met some of the staff - but they were too busy for a break.

It was a wet and dreary walk around Angle Bay. At every hedge there was a double set of new rambler's gates - somebody had money to spare! In Angle hidden away from the world there was a Norman Church and an old Tower, Gyda Chym Moult, which was closed by a heavy modern oak door. The path wound around past Chapel Bay to West Angle Bay where to my delight there was a cafe. I was served tea by a tired waitress while we talked to a window cleaner who was waiting for the rain to stop. But it didn't all day. Extracting myself from the comforts of the cafe I climbed up to Rat Island Head and waited for a while in a concrete gun bunker, also hoping the rain would ease off. Across the water, near St Ann's Head, a disaster occurred a few years ago when an oil tanker - the *Sea Empress* (21st Feb '96) - went aground, lost its load of crude and contaminated 100 miles of coast. One would hardly believe it now, nature had returned with all traces of oil apparently dispersed. I pressed on in the wind and rain to the beach at Freshwater West, where there was a toilet and a mobile tea wagon for even more tea. A road took me to Castlemartin, where I phoned Roger, before carrying on towards Merrion. The path struck off south across the MOD land of Castlemartin Ranges where a group of soldiers were having fun with transporters and loose cattle. I didn't stop to help but continued to Flimston church which was locked, porchless and with no viable shelter. The key was available, a notice said, at the main gate two miles away!

A steady march took me across firm flat limestone grassland to St Govan's Head, where it was then too dark to find the Chapel hidden below in the rocks but somehow I stumbled along, making it to Star Rock car park and the toilet block there provided respite for a brief rest. Nearby a farm advertised B&B but nobody was about. Nor could I find any suitable barn shelter, but as I was about to leave the owner came back and persuaded me to go to the village of Bosherston where another farmer offered the use of a caravan which sheltered me from the strong buffeting winds outside.
27m

Day 407
Wednesday
It was a squally morning as I walked back to last night's toilet and crossed Broad Haven to Stackpole Warren and the headland where ORS meets carboniferous limestone. On the way a girl was doing the path solo and systematically - she had stayed in the B&B where I couldn't find room last night. The sea, whipped up by the wind, was a picture of turbulence as it lashed against the cliffs and beaches. On the far side of Baracundle Bay a white limestone wall had been built and the stepped path wound up and through this barricade. The next part of the route went across dunes, by-passed Freshwater East and then twisted its way to the decayed Norman castle at Manorbier. This was the birthplace of Gerald the Welshman (de Barri) in 1146, grandson of Nest (Helen

of Wales) and who wrote a vivid Description of Wales under the Normans. At Old Castle Head the RAF were playing games with flying drones and powerful guns, presumably trying to shoot them down. Lydstep and Bubbleton followed. The danger area marked on the map appeared to have gone and I crossed Giltar Point to the The Burrow and thence across the sands to Tenby. Phoning Roger's friend, the pastor at Hebron Baptist Church in Saundersfoot, I only got the answer machine but undeterred pressed on along the path to find the address given - alas no one was in. The lady next door knew little of their movements so she kindly phoned the youth hostel at Pentlepoir and they had a bed. After shopping in the town, I unsuccessfully tried the darkened Baptist church then, in the rain and dark, headed for the hostel two miles away. Passing another church in Hean where the Harvest Festival service had just finished, I was invited in for supper, feted as the bedraggled stranger, and was given a feast of good food before they sent me forth with a bulging doggy bag. Consequently it was late when I arrived at the hostel but was still welcomed. The only other occupant was a Path walker from SW23 and we chattered by the fire well into the night in this satisfying old fashioned hostel. It had its own little idiosyncrasies inherent in the conversion of old buildings but although these were consistent with low cost accommodation other travellers used to more perfect conditions could find them difficult to live with, said the warden.
19m

Day 408
Thursday
The day started slowly and we both took the bus to Saundersfoot where I collected mail from the PO. The path faded away on the promenade road, ending near Amroth castle with an official plaque:-

> Llwybr hir arfurdir sir benfro
> Track Poppit 180 milltir
> agorwyd gan
> Wynfrud Vaugghan Thomas
> 1970

Why does Pembrokeshire path end here? Is there a border? Where is the control post? Saying good bye to last night's hosteller and the Pembrokeshire Path I thought, on reflection, that the second half was the most interesting although not the prettiest.

The road and a footpath brought me to Telpyn Farm where I had to walk through busy stables trying to find ill-defined paths. Using my imagination again I cut down through the hillside gorse to find a coastal path which led down to a stream in full spate, swollen from the recent rain. A stiff climb was required to the prehistoric Mapp's Camp (100 BC) and the outline of the Motte

& Bailey of Top Castle, before the path dropped down to Mapp's Farm which appeared to be a holiday home in a smugglers cove. Crossing this private land I descended by rope and ladder to the deserted beach and at the far end climbed out to Ragwen Point but disappointingly I could not identify the chambered cairns shown on the map. This was followed by a descent to Pendine and its famous, supposedly solid, firm, sands which have been in use since Victorian times. The most famous users were Donald Campbell with his Blue Bird and Amy Johnson with her Sea Fever plane. The sands looked indecently wet and squelchy to me so it was three miles of the main A4066, past Plashett, before I turned south. Avoiding the coastal military area, I walked round the heavily wooded ORS cliffs of Sir John's Hill where a TV camera and production crew of nine were filming a novel sequence. It's not surprising these projects cost so much with so many people hanging around. At Laugharne I found Dylan Thomas' home - the Boat house and his writing garage. Both were closed, but the simple stark writing conditions in the garage overlooking the river were memorial enough to a great man's writing, but what a shame that alcohol can be such an addictive and destructive poison as well as an artist's prop. The track led to Delacorse before emerging on the main A4066 up the river Taf to St Clears. In the ensuing darkness I couldn't find a B&B that was open so bedded down in a house under construction which had half a roof to keep potential rain out. But rescue was at hand some two hours later when Tracy, a girl I had met earlier in the street, called through the portals and took me in to sleep on her floor.
18m

Day 409
Friday
The weather was dull, the vegetation and ground wet, as my route continued along the Pilgrim's Path towards Llanybri. The initial footpaths were not well marked and were difficult to find but further on the minor roads and tracks were easier so that I was soon in Pentowyn, on the road to Llanstephan, with a detour to St Anthony's Well, preserved in the garden wall of a big house.

Dedicated to St Anthony of Egypt (251 - 356)
First Christian hermit, who was influential
in the initiation of the Celtic Church in South Wales.
Another hermit, Antwm, also settled near here in the 6thCentury
and used this well for baptisms.
Since then
it has been recognised as a point of healing and pilgrimage.

The well preserved Castle at Llansteffanon standing on a mound was set away from the river and was open to explore, free of charge. It would have been better on a fine day which is what Turner thought when he included it in a landscape of 1795.

On the B4312 to Gilfach and in spite of the electricity pylons being in the wrong place on the map, I found the newly made rocky track to Hendy farm and Llangain, where the church was locked. A path through thick woodland eventually led back to the B road near Cwrthir and a dismal river path brought me under the railway to Carmarthen, which was very damp. The police were helpful with advice and hot water, but there were no hostels. After shopping in the adjacent supermarket I set out over the new bridge and headed for Croesyceiliog, to ask about barns and was told about farms along the road. The rain was increasing in the dark when one mile further on, an obliging farmer allowed me into a barn. As the storm raged outside of this vast dry shed holding calving cows, one calf was born during the wild and wet night. But I slept too soundly in the straw to hear it arrive.
21m

Day 410
Saturday
It was a glorious morning, with the sun just hidden below the hills, a blue sky and a few sharp starched clouds. It's amazing what wind will do to the weather. Underfoot it was still very wet but this was not a problem as most of the route was along tracks or minor roads with one footpath from Towy Castle to Coed. I was given toast at a roadside farm where I sat on a bright whitewashed wall before continuing via Branyn to a track by the railway into Ferryside and breakfast in a bus shelter. The last ferry across the Afon Tywi had left years ago but there was a good view across to Llanstephan Castle and you could imagine Turner painting the scene from here. At St Ishmael there was another locked church. What are pilgrims supposed to do on this route? The minor road continued to Kidwelly, the path over the railway bridge looking extremely muddy, I substituted a river embankment for the last half mile. In the town, according to the village clock, it was 11.30 as I passed the unexpected and neat little mediaeval castle. Then, having a snack in a central cafe, a girl invited me to her birthday party that night. This was strange as I really thought it was Friday. I had also seen a few wedding parties during the day and had thought how odd to see weddings on Friday. It took me two days at least to realise the truth. 'You can see the castle, have a bath and sleep on the sofa' they cajoled. But I gave my regrets and walked on, thinking you should never, never, look a gift horse in the mouth.

A track through the town took me across the railway to the quay, which had been well used in the past but was now a relic. A nicely mown path led away around the little peninsular to an embankment, a rail bridge and fields onto Route 4 - Sustran cycle track. This wound around a disused airfield with all its WW2 defences showing, then into the rambling Pembrey Country Park before

eventually arriving in Cardiff and beyond somewhere on the south coast. The park was neater than the airfield but even some of the pines looked a little passé and could do with replacement (?). There were innumerable paths about and as they went in all sorts of twists, curves and directions it was difficult to decide which to follow as the only signs were numbers that were meaningless unless one had the plan. The cafe in the park was closed but I stopped there for a snack anyway getting my bearings and on the other side I was able to cross the golf course before going into Burry Port. This was undistinguished so I hurried along the main A484 to Llanelli, turning off right to Gowran. I didn't twig that this meant Station. But this was of no matter as I took the new coastal road towards Swansea and after Yspitty and Loughtor Bridge I jumped down an embankment for the minor road route into Gowerton arriving in the dark shortly before eight. I searched in vain for a B&B and sought advice in a couple of pubs with no joy but that of meeting a lass called Tina. For a mere £3, we shared a taxi to Swansea, where the police directed me to the night stop near the fire station. The 12 beds were all booked but I had a warm evening inside with something to eat. At midnight they chucked me out with a blanket to sleep on the concrete ground of the open porch!
28m

Day 411
Sunday
There were no early buses or trains so I hitched westward out of town. One single lift with a Welsh steel-man, who talked colourfully of this once bustling area, took me back to Yspitty. I walked out of this little town, over the bridge towards Loughton, a minor road to Gowerton and a path on an old rail route westward to Crofty. A road lay beside the marshes to Llanridian, with a view of the hillside castle to brighten the landscape and a line of competing anglers by the sea before a coastal path continued through grassy fields to Leason. I found an unofficial way to Weobley Castle, a well preserved 13th century fortified manor house, and, on having lunch within its protective walls, I reflected that its namesake in Herefordshire is a ruin. On leaving by the official front way a notice said that you were supposed to pay at the farm house but the absence of people allowed me a free escape.

The ridge road took me to Cheriton and Llan Madoc as it started to rain heavily again. When it slackened I took footpaths through Broughton Burrows to Burry Holms head and then walked three miles on the firm sands of Rhossili Bay to the steps up to Rhossili itself which was busy with day trippers. After stopping for a while on a bench, out of the wind, by the tea shop and a bit of a chat in the adjacent tourist shop, I ventured out to the Coast Guard Lookout at Worm's Head. It was open, with information displayed inside. Dylan Thomas had been here before me in 1933:-

'I was trapped on the Worm's Head once. I had gone on it early in the after noon with a bag of food and going to the very very end, had slept in the sun, with the gulls crying high over me. And when I woke the sun was going down - the tide had come in. I stayed there until midnight, sitting on the top grass, frightened to go further in because of the rats and because of things I am ashamed to be reminded of.

Then the tips of the reef began to poke out of the water and, perilously, I climbed along them for the shore with an eighteen mile walk ahead of me. I saw enough on the way, from snails, lizards and glow-worms and hawks to diaphanous ladies in white who vanished when I approached them.'

The westerly wind helped me along this wonderful coast with all its glorious views. At Paviland I passed above the famous Goat's Hole where Dean Buckland, an Oxford Geologist, had discovered, in 1824, the remains of a Cro-Magnon youth (the Red Lady) buried 15,000 years ago - an illumination on our past. But darkness had fallen on arrival at the Port Eynon Hostel and it was CLOSED with nobody about. Up at the adjacent and empty caravan site a student of maths in the office was doing end of season things and persuasion allowed him to let me sleep in the toilets and he also gave me water and packets of food. On inspection the toilet block was not suitable according to my standards (!) but at that moment a light appeared above the hostel. So I trundled back down there and, almost on my knees, persuaded the lady warden to let me stay. She could not bother to get out the books and so it was gratis with a wonderful relaxing night all to myself and even the decadence of watching TV while eating.
24m

Day 412
Monday 4th October
It had rained in the night but the morning was fine and sunny as I set off straight across the beach, beside sand dunes to the limestone cliffs across the bay. Then up to the headland of Oxwich point and into an oak and ash woodland walk and yet another locked church just above the beach at Oxwich Bay. Two miles of sands took me to the rock of Great Tar and a climb over the headland to Parkmill. Out in the Bristol Channel cargo boats plied their goods as in the John Masefield Poem.

> Dirty British coaster with a salt-caked smoke stack
> Butting through the Channel in the mad March Days,
> With a cargo of Tyne coal,
> Road-rail, pig-lead,
> Firewood, iron-ware and cheap tin trays

Over the water, the Somerset and North Devon coasts appeared and I cogitat-

ed on the short and the long distances to get there. On to Pwlldu Head and a steep drop to the rocky bay where I had to jump across the river before coming to Caswell Bay. Suddenly a concrete path appeared beneath my feet and I knew that civilisation was fast approaching! Sheltering from a burst of rain I met two guys also going to the Mumbles and we walked and talked together until arriving around 3 o'clock. It was now sunny and hot but I made a forced march into Swansea arriving at the Lodge by 5 o'clock in time to claim a bed - 5.15 would have been too late - the queue too long. Out of the usual mixed bag of drifters a couple of German lads stood out, they had very little English and were into war games, but I could not extract anything of their raison d'être.
21m

Day 413
Tuesday
At Millets I bought a map and yet another new map case, which don't seem to last very long, before the young assistant showed me the way to the bridge over the River Tawe. It was a crystal clear morning after a slight ground frost as I walked eastward for some four miles along the main A483, past docks, motor works and other industry and, after a deviation through a golf course, crossed the River Neath. On the A4211, I passed more docks, steel works and a huge oil refinery. Although these are not pretty sights they always make me marvel at man's audacity in building such intricate technical constructions, dragging in raw materials, turning out shiny new products and spitting out waste. Men working like ants inch by inch laying a labyrinth of pipes and snarling nozzles, chimneys and walkways amid a cacophony of sound. Not far away the serenity of nature was kept at bay waiting its time to re-invade lost territory.

At Baglan Moors I headed for the beach of Aberavon Sands and the outer edges of Port Talbot. On the front, in the play area, a rank of white and blue concrete penguins languished with the heady air of sea and factory intangibly entwined. All these artificial intrusions on nature did not make for a restful day and I cut it short by catching an early afternoon bus from Aberavon back to Swansea.
12m

Day 414
Wednesday
It was another sunny day as I caught a bus from the Kingsway back to Port Talbot bus station. The road through the steel works to Margam Sands is a private way and I had to use the busy main A4211 trundling past rows of houses, docks and the gargantuan steel works. As an indication of my walking pattern I enumerated and demarcated each stop for a smoke, a cup of coffee, a rest or merely contemplation, as progress was made along the route. Feeling some-

what tired I stopped frequently - at the Tollgate PO opposite Margam Country Parc, the golf range under the motorway standing aloft on its huge concrete pillars and Kenfig Castle where the remains included a few walls and a small knoll. At last I had escaped from the industrial necromancer of Swansea Bay while Monday's tired legs had almost recovered. It was back towards the sea on a maze of twisty paths across the wet and undulating burrows towards Kenfig Sands. This was a place of renown years ago but in the late sixteenth century was ravaged by sand filled storms and now lies near forgotten. A feeling of space descended amidst these spreading sandy burrows with acres of low quality grass with no sheep and a good grass track, Haul Road, ran southwards between the burrows and the sea which remained hidden behind the dunes, only a faint whisper betraying its presence. The reason for this track was not clear to me but was probably a past connection to the steel works? At the far end Sker House was under renovation as the new club house for the adjacent golf course and suddenly there were lots of people about, the first seen since the main road, several miles back. I spoke to two ladies sitting on a wall and asked for authentication of my passing. The glimpses of sea had now become a full blown view; the sun was bright and hot, while behind me the steelworks belched smoke as sharp cut-out clouds in the still air.

After the dismal amusement park at Porthcawl and the adjacent seedy caravan site, I found the coastal track to Black Rocks where a local bird watcher advised me to head for Merthyr Mawr castle and a certain patch of trees on a distant hill. His suggestion led me through the Merthyr Mawr Warren maze of high dunes and ponds to the River Ogmore where a fisherman told me to cross the bridge and not the stepping stones at the castle. The bridge was the official entrance to the Peny Bont Sewage works and the crossing required scaling the high fencing. Bent wire indicated that this rather unusual unofficial route had obviously been used before. A lovely walk down the banks of the river took me to the green swathe around Ogmore-by-Sea but there were no, urgently needed, shops. Sitting on a seat looking out to sea I watched a woman in a cloak standing silhouetted on the shore and wondered where the Lieutenant was? The path continued gently on limestone to Southerndown where I asked two lads if they knew of any shops for supplies but the answer was 'no', then on reaching Dunraven Park they came past in their car, stopped and gave me a packet of sandwiches! In the country estate there was a heritage trail which included an ice tower but I hurried along passing a string of little coves and cliffs. At Cwm Nash the path disappeared as deep ravines bit into the Liassic limestone - overlying that softer rock of the carboniferous age. On a stile, peering down into a vegetated valley, I ate my gift of sandwiches while the evening gloom quickly descended and an invisible noisy tractor was doing something important. Galvanized into action again I headed inland up the cwm through a wood, a herd of cattle and a gate to a farmtrack. Making for a light I found a friendly farmer's wife in an ex-council farm and she gave me milk, buns, cig-

arettes and hot water. Then the farmer himself arrived on his tractor, - the noisy one. He told me to try the church for accommodation but first to go into the Monkash pub which had hosted the Argentinean Rugby team that very day. And on arrival it certainly was a grand cheery place with a big fire and so with a whisky I sat by the warmth. 'Twas then I met Ian and Jackie who within a few minutes offered me a place to sleep in St Donats, two miles further on. They caught the 9.25 bus while I walked and we arrived at almost identical times! A wonderful vibrant couple, who washed my clothes, fed me and warmed me up. Jackie worked in the Department of Health, while Ian was a RAF technician and they were about to buy this unusual modernised barn.
26m

Day 415
Thursday
Just as the first bus of the day passed I set out from St Donats, its castle is now well known as an arts and education centre (Atlantic College) and was the place where the Duke of Windsor fretted away abdication day. It was a dull day with a westerly wind which assisted me, rather than hindering my progress. Along this coast the villages and small towns hang back safely from the sea on the table top landscape of hard Jurassic limestone, which at the edge gently weathers and slowly crumbles to the sea.

The good path which started the day deteriorated as it approached the strangely quiet coal power station at Gileston. Wet clear puddles had to be negotiated until I reached the sea wall revetments which helped ease my progress to Pleasant Harbour, a place somewhat misnamed. A dead end on the beach looked inevitable but suddenly a path appeared in the undergrowth and accessed the road above. At Rhoose, I found a small shop and a path along the cliffs around Rhoose point, Wales' most southerly point, and then through a caravan site to the Iron Age Bulwarks Fort, started in 200 BC and used till 50 AD. But little is written about its history. It was only a short distance to Porthkerry Country Park stretching down to the pebble and rocky beach where two groups of children, secondary and primary, were having geography and geology lessons, limbering up with some stone throwing. I crossed to the Knap, with its pond of ducks, before finding my way on to Barry Island, where all signs of gaudy family fun seemed to have died an autumnal death. I thought my route lay this way through the docks to Penarth but was advised against it and so retraced my steps across the bridge. How I hated going backwards! Although I was compensated a smidgen by walking on the other side of the road of the bridge. After plodding through the straggle of Barry, a large town with its usual collection of sounds and buildings I exited on the A4055 and the B4267 to Sully to join the eroded coastal path. In Swanbridge, because of fencing, I went up to the B4267 and passed under a dismantled railway that was too overgrown for walking. Suburban walking carried me through Penarth to

the Cardiff Barrier but I was not allowed across without a hard hat! They had a lot of work to do before the opening at the end of the year and they were busy at it with their Dinky set of mechanical diggers and JCBs. I arrived in Cardiff at seven o'clock and booked in for two nights at the Sally Ann which was under an extensive refit to conform to new regulations concerning the amount of space necessary for a sleeping man - so the number of rooms would be halved.
25m

Day 416
Friday
To escape the entanglements of Cardiff, I set off north east, as indicated by the sun peeping through the watery early morning sky. Snatches of blue, in a wet white sky, poised ready to dissipate or expand, waited, feline like, to improve the day or squeeze out the sponge over unprepared walkers. There seemed to be no decent route towards Newport, but a walk in that direction was essential. A somewhat random walk through a town is never without interest. A rich mix of buildings, houses shops, offices and factories has its own fascination and when this is laced with the variety of people, ethnic changes, gardens, decay, opulence, parks and general bustle it brings the walk alive with the promise of the unexpected. It is not always pretty but towns and suburbia of the older type have their own surprises. Maybe I would spot a man whistling his way down the road in happy contentment. Alas such simple pleasures rarely happen these days.

I made my way to Splott - what a name! Then on main roads to St Mellons where I sat at a bus stop listening to the roar of traffic on the M4; that continual characteristic sound from rubber on tar and the parting of air by rushing steel. Pressing on along the A48 I stopped near Duffryn before taking an expensive bus ride back to Cardiff, with the driver having to ask the other passengers for change. At Castleton we picked up a tribe of Chinese and the problems associated with their fares before finally bumping, swaying and jolting into the city. Why are buses so uncomfortable? Or is this the fun of the new integrated public transport system? Whatever, I arrived back at the hostel just in time for lunch and time to develop a Crozzle****.
9m

**** Five by Five Crossword: all answers five letters long
    Across 1. Hitchers aid 6.Rocker! 7.Bastard wing 8.Fruity acid 9.Site
    Down 1.Nomad 2.Muslim meat 3.Throat flap 4.Greek poem 5.Pair

- Chapter 7 -
The Bristol Complex

Day 417
Saturday
Leaving a bustle of restless rugby fans behind and catching a bus back to Duffryn on the A48 I started walking soon after ten. My first objective was the transporter bridge across the river Usk. A wonderfully different type of structure of 93 years standing, the suspended piece of road whisking me to the other side without charge. After walking around Solutia, the spread eagled petrochemical factory which produces advanced elastomers but for what I do not know, I found myself again on Sustran route 4. Where would this lead? The lack of signs was disconcerting so I used the road again and thought of the 21 miles to the Severn Bridge as nearby a large hoarding sign claimed that a £70 million project was in progress to clean up the river! Indeed I crossed the newly reconstructed marsh lands adjacent to the power station on my way to the lighthouse of Uskmouth on the newly constructed sea wall. It seemed exceptionally quiet here, after the frantic city bustle behind me. The empty space was occupied by quiet, docile, nibbling sheep and by wild white swans commanding the flat watery wastes with their powerful wing beats.

It was sea wall most of the day with the first port of call being Gold Cliff Valley, a small inlet backing up to the hamlet of the same name. But it was here that I walked around in a two mile loop back to the same point, simply because the newly constructed paths lacked sensible direction signs. Spend that £70m quickly I thought! Recovering the situation I made my way to an interesting house (Gold Cliff) at the sea's edge and climbed a gate out the other side only to discover it was the exit of the entrance to private land! Suddenly, by the rays of the afternoon sun, I saw first one then two Severn Bridges far to the east. The image of these goliaths pulled me forward, pointing the way across the dull brown waters of the Severn estuary. They sparkled white and blue as the distance contorted the vision of these true green structures with a spectral shift of light. The riverside path pressed on along its grassy groyne, behind a continuous concrete rampart against that rampant river and on towards those distant bridges. A few fishermen appeared as minute black dots on the banks, the first was a solitary man, walking and looking for a good spot for all his tackle. On passing, I joked with him that he couldn't be a Rugby supporter or fan as he was well away from all the TV coverage of the World Cup - he agreed and said he was after cod or whatever he could catch, which gave him plenty of choice out of the eighty - odd species of fish available in this river. The sun began to set, the bridges turned red and the sky exploded in a riot of colour, the peace only mutilated by that distant motorway drone.

At seven o'clock, as darkness descended, I came to the first Severn bridge (Caldicot-Severn Beach). An investigation revealed an unadvertised path separated safely from the traffic by a barrier, so after a cigarette and a rest I set off for the three mile crossing and walked in the black night across that vast structure with the roar of head-lamped traffic thundering past me. Once on the other side as I stood at the M/M junction pondering which way to go, a passing patrol car pounced. The police told me I was in an improper place and should not have walked across the bridge's maintenance path. But now it was done they whisked me away and ejected me near to Avonmouth where after a short walk I found a bus stop and waited for a bus only to be assailed by a small group of loud mouthed, stone throwing, spitting and bored 12 year olds, one of whom went home and returned to tell me to go as her mother thought I might be a murderer! Eventually a bus arrived taking me into the heart of Bristol where the police station directed me to the night shelter, which was busy feeding the homeless drop-outs of the area. After food and a shower we were all locked in and lying in my dormitory bed I thought that I'd now passed beyond the thrall of Wales and was about to roll down hill towards Land's End.
23m

Day 418
Sunday
The early shrill reveille of the fire alarm woke us all and breakfast was a bowl of soggy cornflakes, tea and toast - devoured by a scavenging horde. Later I stumbled around Bristol to find transport back to the bridge, firstly going to the station and then to the coach depot. In between I visited Millets, bought a map and looked at tents, particularly asking for a single person tent. The response 'No sir, you're not supposed to walk alone, and so we only sell two man tents'! A little late on the advice - I thought, as I caught the 11.10 bus to Severn Beach and found myself the only person aboard. After spotting the pick up point of the previous night I walked past empty housing and newly planted trees to make renewed contact with my route, and then made my way along the Motorway embankment to the visitors' centre, which was open and where a signature was given. The Severn-side path was overgrown, damp, bramble wracked, hardly used at all and not a nice walk. Pushed out to the road by the vegetation I strolled into Avonmouth and continued on the streets to Shirehampton to find the Motorway bridge, with its cycle track, spanning the Avon, and waited in vain for a bus while the protracted bridge maintenance work continued above me. Apparently they had been at it for at least eighteen months. A local man suggested another bus route a mile away where I did catch a bus back into Bristol. The night stop was not open on Sundays and after rejecting the YH I found shelter on the quay side under the canopy of some shops which made warm accommodation for a homeless night on the streets.
7m

Interlude Seventeen
Day 419
Monday 11th October
In the night I was awakened by a fellow vagabond with a well cared for mongrel dog. We shared stories, milk, bread and cigarettes before I returned to my slumbers. At 7.30 I was awakened by a tap on my shoulder.
'Good morning' said a voice. 'Yes' I replied sleepily.
'Would you like some tea?' as lucidity began to flood in.
'Would you like a hot dog sandwich?' whereby full wakefulness arrived. The Good Samaritan had arrived on his rounds of the Bristol vagrants. It was enjoyable to wake up with a free breakfast and watch the city rise and unfold for its daily toil. After packing up I caught the bus to cheerful Chepstow, walked out over its lower bridge, up the hill and then started to hitch being glad it was a sunny day as I had to wait some time before a maker of solid tyres picked me up. Then a parson, a continental walking enthusiast, took me the next stage. A Cardiff lad going to meet a group of apple pickers took me to Gloucester and a lady with a four wheel drive vehicle to Corse. While Alex Shade, a Hereford Bridge player delivered me to Ledbury. The Fair was on, the town busy and so was Liz in her dog grooming parlour.

Part of my reason for returning was dental and I phoned the dentist for an extraction, but couldn't get an appointment until Wednesday. With time on my hands I arranged the printing of some publicity cards, gave a report of my walk to the Ledbury Reporter and then went to the house to do some weeding as it was a lovely day. In the evening Liz cooked a wonderful meal and we talked until it was time for a real bed.

Day 420
Tuesday
Another beautiful day and we went for a walk on the Malvern Hills. A training session for Liz, and her new boots, for her Moroccan Walk in November. We went up Ragged Stone Hill with the three dogs, through the woods and up to the shaven top, with all its wondrous views of the three counties, Hereford, Worcester and Gloucestershire all bathed in bright sunlight and then returned with just the right amount of exercise. Liz went to choir while I relaxed in front of the television.

Day 421
Wednesday
The dentist thoroughly reprimanded me as usual in his customary brusque manner but pulled my tooth anyway and charged £15 for the privilege. In the garden shed store I had a good sort out and threw away 50 years of life by dumping all my career junk and notes, exercise books, books and computer. The sun shone and it was hard to believe that it was October, except for the

tints in the woods and the nip in the air as the sun went down, while I continued with the gardening.

Eighteenth Stage
Bristol to Lyme Regis
Day 422
Thursday
After driving to Bristol and Shirehampton I parked beneath the Motorway bridge. Access to its cycle way was up a bank and over a fence, a route rapidly becoming a path by custom. On the other side of the river Avon it was difficult to find a route continuation until I asked a local man, who said it did require local knowledge. Following his directions I passed under the bridge and found my way to Sheephouse Farm on barely used paths across a rather scruffy nature reserve. This was followed by negotiating wild life corridors, industrial developments, new car pounds, assorted roads and tracks to Sheep Way and Portbury Wharf. Not trusting the crossing of lock gates I went into Portishead, up the hill on the western side of the docks, around the headland to Battery point and to the Royal Inn at Eastwood which retains remnants of ancient coastal forest. It was past this point (in 1509) that Sebastian Cabot sailed on his trip to discover Newfoundland, and Brunel promoted the place as he wanted it as a terminal for the Great Western Steam Ship. Incidentally he was responsible for three important ships - the Great Western (1837), the Great Britain (1843) and the Great Eastern (1858).

After completing the day's walking at a car park near Kilkenny Bay I made my way back to the town and, after struggling to get a lift, finally resorted to bussing it into Pill, walking back over the Motorway bridge to collect the car and returning later to Portishead.
9m

Day 423
Friday
The weather was overcast and my legs were inconsiderately tired as I progressed along the coast marked with many lighthouses, not surprising considering the currents, the mighty 40ft tides and the amount of shipping which passes by. On this Friday empty cargo boats were speeding down the channel on the ebbing waters, all the blackberries had been picked and a cow had lost its way on the path. Was life dwindling when I still had so far to go and less than three months to be in London? Not that it really mattered when or even if I finished! The cliffs stood forty feet high on this gentle Somerset coast, bracken and brambles were the main vegetation while the hazy Cardiff coast lay far across the grey sea - apparently now a distant memory. There were traces of sun in the early afternoon, which made for a pleasant stroll with no

hills and just a few gentle slopes before coming to Clevedon Pier just as a twin funnelled paddle steamer, the Waverley, was about to dock bringing back memories of Scotland and the Clyde Estuary. After reaching the big pond on the sea front at Salthouse Bay I caught a bus to Portishead, and drove back to Clevedon for the night.
6m

Day 424
Saturday
Following the purchase of a map and parking of the car near the outdoor sea front swimming pool I went out to Wain Hill. This had a picturesque elevated view over the coast lying in the lazy weekend mist - warm and still. A Tarmacked dyke leading south was sea-washed and only partially covered in mud making access easy for the scores of bird watchers who were out and about. Near the confluence of the Yeo and Oldbridge rivers the dyke became a more familiar grassy bank protecting the land of typical flat riverine plains. I didn't fancy trying a low tide crossing of the River Banwell and instead walked into Wick St Lawrence. The church was open and it was such a lovely place I actually spent £1 on Christmas cards. Via Ebdon, I went to Woodspring Priory which was open, an attractively simple place and worth a visit. In the main museum room was a picture of James Greig Smith - a Professor of surgery and founder of the local Octet Golf Club in the 19th century.

Passing round Middle Hope I tripped to the tip of Sand Point, a rocky ridge full of walkers, before climbing down its southern edge to the Weston road. This passed beside Sand Bay where the tide was out having left the shore in parallel mud furrows like a ploughed field. After the long sweeping arc of the Victorian Weston front I escaped the crowds and walked the muddy paths of the small Uphill peninsular before returning to the village pub. After getting parking permission at this local I took a bus to Weston, a train to Yatton and a four mile walk back to the car.
20m

Day 425
Sunday
Parking at the pub under Uphill church and discovering the loss of my current note book I had to sit rewriting some memory jogging notes before starting the day's walking. From the Norman church on the hill, with good views of the marshes and the Bristol Channel, I followed a new cycle path which took me to the sluice on the Bleadon Levels to cross the river Axe on the way to Brean. There used to be a ferry hereabouts to cross the river but I was not aware of its availability or schedule. Unfortunately the gates across the sluice were closed and were not opening until the spring for the future continuation of the 99% completed cycle way. But a man standing there with his wife said he had

climbed across and so, braving the barbed wire and the drop into the river, I clambered past the obstacle. At Brean the road went south to Burnham-on-Sea, a far cry from that on Crouch! The route then merged with a golf course and an official told me that I was off track and should depart but they nevertheless allowed me to continue. In 1607 this whole area had been devastated by a tidal wave of biblical proportions and this had caused a corresponding amount of damage - not now visible. In Burnham, full of amusements, sand, boats and sun, I decided to walk on, in the late afternoon, to Bridgewater. It was sea wall all the way by the open spaced Somerset flats with the low tide exposing even bigger areas of sea washed mud. It was a wonderful setting, on a still evening, with a glorious sunset and its light illuminating flocks of slow moving fat sheep in the flat fields with gaggles of happy gulls gathered on the river.

Arriving at Bridgewater in the dark I just missed a train and had to wait for the next while sipping a whisky in the *Commercial Inn* and using the time to phone the family. After taking the train to Weston I caught a bus which was fortunately passing and just by chance going to Uphill from where I drove to my stepdaughter Amanda's place in Stoke Gregory, had a bath, supper and slept in their caravan.
23m

Day 426
Monday 18th October
Amanda gave me a lift to Bridgewater where we arrived at noon. With a full pack again, I set off on my route immediately, promising to return in six weeks. After extricating myself from the town I followed the path which hugged the River Parrett, slowly escaping from the traffic noise coming from the Motorway and the A38. It seems that you need a space of at least two miles before the sound dies below the audible.

My first stop of the day was opposite the Down End precast factory which I had passed the previous evening on the other side of the river. At Pawlett a group of children dressed in red were having a lesson on the river bank. They must have been really keen on their work because they wouldn't even wave back at me! - the summer holidays had done the business here as they were gripped in the responsibility of gaining an education. Red and green toy tractors wove through the fields ploughing with discs and drawing seed planters sowing winter wheat in the rich brown moist earth soaking up the autumn sun's energy - a modern day country scene, but the motoring noise from modern tarmac still persisted. I reached Cannington Brook where the farming continued on these flat fertile estuarine soils. Near the pretty village of Combwich a gaggle of young children were coming out of school, and an ex-Watford man, who was waiting for his wife, kindly took my letters to post. A mile further on, at a fork in the path, I chose the seaward dyke, which was reasonably good but

required jumping a couple of fences, before reaching Fenning Island bird reserve with its chain of hides I stopped at the main centre a rather grand bird watch tower - a new three-storey wooden affair. There was nobody about and hardly any birds either so I soon continued through the car park of Cox's Farm to Dowdon's Farm near the Hinkley Point nuclear power station. After getting water I walked another two miles, found some shore-side bushes as shelter against the strong breeze, collected wood from the darkened beach in the evening gloom and slept beside the glowing embers of my fire.
17m

Holiday season at Ilfracombe, a surfing break: Day 430

- Chapter 8 -
Free Fall Round The South West
(FOLLOW THE ACORN)

Day 427
Tuesday
An early start in sunshine soon saw me at RAF Lilstock. Nearby a farmer was planting wheat in his 100 acre field on the rolling downland overlooking the sea and he told me that rain was due on Thursday come Friday. Meanwhile it was misty with a south-easterly starting. Having decided to take short cut across fields of stubble through to a caravan site I had to fight with barbed wire entanglements and a gully filled with thick brambles, losing a little blood in the process. On the other side a man said 'this is private land you know' and my 'old map' explanation didn't cool his apparent rage. However he did give me directions to the road for Watchet where I treated myself to tea, scrambled eggs and left-over scraps. Another walker warned me of eroding paths on the way to Blue Anchor but the path improved and I survived. In the village as I phoned Liz, I had the strange sight of a red steam train pulling two old wagons through the fields - the popular preserved West Somerset Railway in action! The wind had dropped as I walked a pebble beach towards Dunster, round the coastal golf course, past the mediaeval 'tented' pavilions of Butlins holiday camp and thence into Minehead.

    After stocking up on supplies and walking out towards the harbour a sign said 'Poole 600 miles!' I was about to follow the acorn sign along the South West Coastal Path. The start of this path zig-zagged up the hill out of Minehead, and it was hard work at the end of the day, as it continued to rise inexorably for three miles. In gathering darkness, high on the hill a stag stood silhouetted against the sky as if welcoming me to his kingdom. But I could find no decent shelter from the stiff breeze in this seemingly wild place. Eventually at the top I gave up, parted a thick stand of bracken and laid my sleeping bag out to have my supper by the light of a spluttering candle. On this unusual occasion I had no hot water and had to wash my cold meal down with fresh milk before bedding down in my new bag** that Liz had given me in Ledbury. 19m

** Vango Ultralite 1100

Day 428
Wednesday

An excellent night's sleep but I was away early. At ten o'clock I went past the picturesque pink cottages of Bossington and in Porlock had my flask filled, using the hot water to make tea and porridge in my normal fashion. Coleridge apparently composed part of the 'Ancient Mariner' here and I came across this poet's footsteps many miles later. Having missed Porlock Wier I passed a toll house and met the lady who had collected the fees for the past 35 years. The path wound through black wooded hills, pungent with the smell of decaying, rotting vegetation with fleeting visions of witches riding broom sticks through the shaded open woodland glades clutching at my imagination - I was in Lorna Doone country, ripe for fantasies.

It was just starting to rain at Culbone but there was a totally unexpected, unmanned, refreshment hut where I was able to make tea and heat some Irish stew on the stove for a welcome break. At the nearby tiny parish church a lady was out rambling the path, only noteworthy because I wouldn't see many other walkers. Soon the path was lost and stumbling onwards I ended up at the Visitors Centre of County Gate where the manager gave me tea and cake as the rain and wind continued outside. He told me of the *Alan Titchmarsh* charity walk from Boston to Hope which had passed through here. He also sold me a copy of *Lorna Doone* for £1, but after carrying it for miles I never read a word (!) and eventually, somewhere, left it behind. Sweet chestnuts were falling and lay scattered among the dominant oaks as I walked down to the shore. The path levelled out with splendid sea scenery even though the rain and wind detracted from my enjoyment. More importantly it wasn't cold.

After Devon's most northerly spot - Foreland Point - at Countisbury, high on the ridge, two miles before the disaster town of Lynmouth, a Saxon foundation church was open for shelter and meditation but I stopped only briefly before walking downhill. It was in the opposite direction that in 1899 the local men had hauled a life boat up over the 1000ft pass to Porlock Weir to a dramatic sea rescue. After slogging up the steep hill to the Youth Hostel in Lynbridge I found the lady warden was working hard, with a hostel almost full of students, and entreaties about my missing hostel card, wetness and NFA status brought only a bureaucratic response. So I walked out in high dudgeon into the town of Lynton, bought chips and started, in the dark, for the Valley of the Rocks. However within a short distance I spotted the retreat of Poor Clare, knocked on the door and thankfully found a compassionate Nun who after a few minutes reflection on my plight found space for me in the adjacent community hall complete with toilet and other facilities that made it an excellent place to stay. 19m

Day 429
Thursday
Just after mass, having talked to a couple from East Sussex, I set out through the Valley to Lee Abbey, a Christian holiday farm, where there was a sign in a field which made me chuckle all morning:-

'On this Site on 1st April 1780 Nothing Happened'

To add to my good humour, at the bottom of the hill a weighted honesty box requested 50p for the toll from May to October. It didn't look over-used and it was only my quirky sense of humour.

My next stop was in a woody bay on the edge of West Exmoor country. There was a lot to see, but the weather remained dull and the predicted rain had started as I walked through oak forests patched with beaten bronze bracken while two walkers came towards me in their striking matching green jackets. October was a good time to walk with few people about, the silence disturbed only by the occasional shock of an overhead plane, the wind in the tree tops and the surf far below. After stopping briefly at Cow and Calf Bay I went on to East Cleave, the open spaces of Exmoor stretching before me, as three runners passed me and dwindled in the distance climbing the paths ahead on their charity run to Combe Martin. Although there was a wind, the steep slopes made me very sweaty and I seem to be stopping rather frequently. Soon after two o'clock I was in Combe Martin, enriched in Tudor times by the trade in silver and lead, for a late and free breakfast in the Harbour café. After passing the mock castle tourist attraction at Watermouth I arrived in Ilfracombe and at its Hostel just after five. According to the wardens, John and Liza, the hostel was not officially supposed to be open but they were very helpful as this was their hostel on concession having their own ideas about opening times and the provision of services. The only other guest was a technician from Teeside.
16m

Day 430
Friday
The town is largely Victorian, opened up by the railway in 1874, but this link has now gone. It was raining again as I set off in mid morning after non productive visits to the PO and DHSS, and climbed the headland of Tarrs Park while the view of Ilfracombe below improved under the clearing skies. Towards Lee Bay the wooded hillsides sparkled with the mica filled rocks and at Bull Point there was a prominent lighthouse. Morte Point provided fine views southwards and the sight of slate rocks reaching treacherously into the sea. In Woolacombe the bank was closed but I had coffee, amidst the crowds still thronging the seaside resorts, before walking across the popular and splendid sands as the waves beat incessantly on the shore and black 'skinned'

surfers enjoyed their sport in warm patches of autumn sun. Beyond the Bay was Baggy Point which inspired Henry Williamson to write Tarka the Otter, Salar the Salmon and A Patriot's Progress after moving here in 1921. Hence also a well named trail out of Barnstaple, yet to be seen.

The minor miracle of the day was picking up water at the last house in Saunton before entering Braunton Burrows. The local couple gave me tea and wished me bon voyage before I wandered across the common in increasing darkness, missing much of its natural history, towards the southern beach on the north of the River Taw, looking for camping spots. But it was two miles beyond this before I found an isolated open stone barn near the road in Braunton Marsh and with hot water was able to have a reasonable supper. Straw allowed me a warm comfortable bed and I fell into a contented sleep as the moon rose and cold snapped the air outside.
22m

Day 431
Saturday
Within a short distance I was on the toll road towards Braunton as the sun showed itself. The town was by-passed by turning right to Wrafton and using the path beside an RAF training ground. This airfield at Chivenor had been the source of the low flying Hercules seen over the last two days and is also a helicopter base for coastal rescues. The path had just been re-opened that very day having been closed for five days for improvement repairs. Even today it was still being finished off while I was the first person to try the mile length of new tarmac. It led towards the easy, though not very attractive, walk up the Taw. On the left was a parallel main road while on my right glimpses of the river were visible through the trees. I stopped at Ashford Lime Kiln which had been restored in 1986 and on the path met a round Britain walker from Gravesend. He was doing it in bits on weekends and holidays and promised a cheque for StC. At eleven, amidst small rain showers, I reached Barnstaple, one of the oldest towns in England and mentioned in the Domesday Book, now a busy walled conurbation which has retained its central character. The 'I' man was very helpful and directed me to Settles for 'the best coffee in the southwest' as voted by the BBC. I had a cup on the outside terrace and reflected that the 'Beeb' must have had friends there as if this was the best then you would shudder at the thought of the quality of coffee elsewhere. My disappointment was matched by Barry, the owner's concern, since he gave me a second cup. On reflection the real problem was probably that my taste buds had been shot to pieces by my rough eating. He also told me to expect big tides because of the full moon. To escape Barnstaple I crossed the 15th century multi-arched bridge, which had been widened in the 18th and 20th centuries, and set off on the old railway - the Tarkaline Trail - towards Bideford and the Atlantic. Because of my daily search for shelter I noted that some of the track-side

workmen's shelters had been retained and had remained relatively dry. By the first bridge over a small creek there was a memorial to:-

> 'John 'Dinger' Bell, drowned at 55,
> a fisherman and a character'

The showers continued through Ilsey Nature Reserve but I was able to stop for coffee by an isolated pier before the sea wall path swept me round towards Bideford. A high new bridge carried the re-routed A39 across the River Torridge and this provided a short cut, by-passing Bideford which I could see below with its long 24 span 15th century bridge. This was once a busy sea port which in the past had shipped in a wealth of tobacco and it has at least two famous sons - Elizabethan Sir Richard Grenville and author Charles Kingsley (of Westward Ho!). Apparently there is also a short cut summer ferry route across this waterway which I knew nothing about. On the other side of the river I regained the walker's path which split into high and low tide routes and was just in time for the lower of these, the incoming water snapping at my heels. Fishing from the banks were two men from Stoke - who had returned to their 'roots', and wanted a chat. Afterwards I took the path inshore around a big working boatyard, producing computer designed quick fit ships, into the quaint town of Appledore which had an unusual curiosity - a Mermaid Shop. I did not see Hink's Boat yard where wooden ships were built, many being replicas of famous craft like the Golden Hind. Walking around the Northam Burrows Headland and across the golf course I came to the western Pebble Ridge shore. The sea, at high tide, was pounding the beach with waves crashing through the shingle and retreating with that characteristic menacing hissing sound as the stones fell, rolling and abrading, in the ripping undertow. One wouldn't stand a chance against such forces and they had been right about the tides in Barnstaple!

In Westward Ho!, named after the book, I obtained hot water at a chippies before walking out past beach houses, many of which were almost derelict and some would have provided a good night's shelter if the town had not been so busy. Continuing along the Somerset and North Devon Coast Path as the moon rose, it was a few miles before I climbed away from the sea across darkened fields to find shelter at Cockington Farm. There was nobody about and so I left a note on the farm door and settled down in a well lit stock barn with shuffling snuffling young calves close by.
26m

Day 432
Sunday
The sound of cows woke me and after thanking the farmer I set out on the road to Farm Cross and Halls Cross with its old country coaching tavern, the Houps

Inn. Noting that one footpath to the coast was closed and not to open until April 2000 I continued along the road to Bucks Cross and Dyke 'filling station', where a car salesman was fitting out his sales booth and apologised for his lack of a kettle. In Highford an Australian, lady working in her garden, gave me water and biscuits so that at Highdown Cottage I could sit on the roadside verge for a warm breakfast break. It was tarmac all the way to Hartland point where a car park attendant was still collecting fees and a crowd of people were busy sightseeing even though the lighthouse was closed with apologies from Trinity Lighthouses and I borrowed one tourist to take my photo against the background of this 'wrecking coast'. The path was up and down across the valleys dissecting this spectacular scenery while the crowds continued to jostle each other at the tourist spots like the Old Inn at Hartland Quay as the day became dry after the morning rain. Much of this area used to have well to do estates and the gateways were often decorated with crests or the stone heads of unicorns, lions or other animals. I had kept to the roads this morning, forsaking the coastal path, and so had missed its delights and that of Clovelly - the result of walking without a proper map.

At Elmscott the youth hostel was closed and although the Saxon church (dedicated to St Nectan) at Welcombe, was open I pressed on to Mead along macadam tracks. It was now dark and I had to ask the way at a house where the lady indicated a bridleway dipping steeply downwards before it rose up again through the dark gloomy wood. After more asking at an isolated cottage I reached Morwenstow to have a drink in the friendly Bush Inn where the landlady gave me another on the house. A B&B was arranged at Cornokey Farm which had already been passed. It was £17 but at least the hostess came to pick me up. There were three of us there. But there was no smoking, TV or drying facilities and an inadequate breakfast - a bit of a poor deal!
23m

Day 433
Monday 25th October
The vicarage, the Galton, nestling quietly in a wooded copse on the side of a hill, was built by parson Robert Stephen Hawker (1804-1875), each chimney constructed in similar style to the towers of churches that he knew. In the graveyard he had buried many of the dead from the numerous shipwrecks on these shores and on the cliffs nearby he'd built a small wooden hut in the rocks. This was where he spent much time watching the sea and smoking opium to inspire his poetic visions. Today it was open and just big enough for a sleep perhaps, but rumour said that it was locked at night. My luck seemed to be running out, as even the local church of St Morwenna (alias John) was open and two potential stopping places had been missed! I put it down to tiredness and lassitude brought on by the two whiskies. On the positive side I'd had a good night's sleep and was now in Cornwall, although not yet into the Cornish.

> And have they fixed the where and when?
> And shall Trelawney die?
> Here's twenty thousand Cornishmen
> Will know the reason why!
>
> Hawker - Anthem

The first squall of the day was followed by clear sunshine and a bad signpost left me wandering until finding a cleft in the rocks through which was seen Sandy Mouth. There were good views to the north but fabulous ones to the south. Green capped, black rocks swathed in mist, projected into the surfing sea edged with tiny clean gold-yellow beaches. If my brain had not gone into hiding I would have walked along the beach instead of sticking to the path and enduring its climbs and descents. The weather and scenery induced the crowds to visit and surfers to ride the waves: it was the half term holiday. I asked somebody if they were happy: 'yes' they replied and when asked the similar question, lamely replied 'yes' too instead of replying 'I was miserable, until I saw you'. My mind was obviously elsewhere, thinking about buildings and the modern rock - concrete fortresses now standing, new and proud and the perplexity archeologists will have in five thousand years from now.

Then suddenly, in broad sunlight, Bude appeared around the corner and I stopped to look. It was such a lovely day for relaxation and reflection - the empty sea with its muted roar of surf stretching away out of sight to the south. There was no mail at the PO and my business cards from Ledbury had not yet arrived even though they had been sent five days before. Apparently the correct procedures had been followed which had slowed the process down as compared to the normal method of just posting the package direct. I shopped before making the cruel mile's climb out and up to Cleave House Farm for water and food and arrived in St Gennys in the dark, to find a church porch for shelter from the expected rain but was not in a state to admire the wonderful setting of this place nor the forethought of the Celtic saint.
14m

Day 434
Tuesday
My waking meal was coffee with biscuits and sunshine before leaving St Gennys to take in the spectacular coastal views along the path to Crackington Haven. My reward was a free breakfast in the Haven Cafe, courtesy of a couple from London who had taught at St Pauls Choir School and had recently taken over the cafe for a change of environment. High cliffs passed beneath me on the way to the viewing platform of Cam Rock as the sea turned blue in sympathy with the sky while lonely Lundy Island swam in the distance. The cliffs soar to 700ft here - some of the highest in England. Two miles before

Day 431 Appledore, North Devon summed up in the town's wall mural

Boscastle I sat on a seat dedicated to:-

Paul Heard (1944-94), the Council's faithful servant

This path seems to attract 'Pauls'. In the town at the harbour, just above the water, lay a Youth Hostel which had been 'open yesterday but would be closed tonight' said the lady warden as she passed me hot water through the window. I walked on with Tim of Bideford who was out of work since he left Bowaters five years before and was now enjoying his freedom. On the path to Tintagel I met two cats, one black and one ginger that apparently do the walk each day, and was left wondering what witchcraft still lingered around here, not understanding their miaowed Cornish reply.

The Tintagel headland throbbed with a throng of trippers drawn by the spell of Arthurian legends and because of the congestion I didn't cross the bridge to visit the castle but instead pressed on up the hill where a lonely old slate church sat drying its grey roof in the sun. In Port William there were more crowds and I climbed out up the 194 steps, as the sun started to sink. Three miles short of Gaverne I found an abandoned mine with a patch of grass with no crowds, a good camping spot, except for the shortage of wood and water. For supper I used sea water precariously collected while standing on the slippery rocks by the surging sea. Unfortunately this gave me a thirst and although I had a fire, warm bag, moon, clear sky and the caress of breaking waves - sleep was difficult, partly due to a low mileage.
14m

Day 435
Wednesday
I was off at sun rise, and reached Port Gaverne at 9.30 to buy milk, from a store that had opened at seven, quaffing it down to quench my thirst and then having tea at the Old School Hotel and funnily was given £5 by a lady who thought I was a tramp. She'd said 'I don't do this often but have a meal on me'. I thought she was contributing to StC and it wasn't till later that realisation dawned - I had been the real target of her charity. The path from Gaverne and adjacent Port Isaac went to Port Quin and was lined with new posts and four rail fencing - there must be a wealthy land owner hereabouts. There were many walkers out today including some from Bristol, Brighton and Canada. In Quin two lobster-catchers told me they had just lost £400 worth of catch as it slipped from the boat and fell to the bottom of the sea and they were not happy about the day or the general state of fishing. But I raised a smile when telling them of my earlier charitable lady and they replied that you didn't see many men of the road these days - I must have been looking trampish! My dirty yellow jacket with barbed wire tears exuding thermal filling not helping my appearance.

On the head of Rumps Point the dramatic scenery continued as I walked the sands of Polzeath, where a multitude of surfers and beachers were busy in the warm October sun. Back on the path walkers abounded and a passing lady said 'I'll be happy when I get to the top'. I retorted 'Sorry there is no top, it was removed last week'. The sands of Padstow Estuary took me to the ferry and fortune was with me: since, once aboard, the packed craft set off. Although the ferry man gave me a free passage he wouldn't shake my hand on the other side.

Stepping on the gas along the cliff top path, I headed for Trevone and beyond and on the way out to Trevose Head saw this apt sign:-

'The sleep of a labouring man is sweet'

Pounding round the headland, looking forward to a night in a bed, I arrived at Treyarnon after seven, when it was dark, but alas the Hostel was full. Other ideas were necessary. The warden was friendly although too busy feeding his masses to be able to think. Out again into the night left me wondering about my options. Fate intervened and a hundred metres away the solution appeared - a shore shelter with bench: an annex to the annex! And back to the hostel I was given hot water and candles for a reasonable night's stop.
21m

Day 436
Thursday
Another sunrise start in the clear dawn air, the slowly rising sun working its magic on the blanket of morning mist. Big sturdy black faced sheep grazed the downland and docile brown bodied cows contentedly chewed the cud. Underfoot the cobwebbed grass sparkled and danced in the early light as the white painted holiday village of Trevorrick came into sight where the houses were being packed up for the winter. Having tea in the shop I reflected on the spectacular coast that I had passed, a coast sprinkled with NT properties, bought up as wealth had dissipated. Perhaps there would be many more to buy soon, as farming continues in its economic doldrums.

After passing through Porthcothan, Park Head and Carnewas Island, Newquay became visible in the distance. Cutting down to Mawgan Porth at Trenance I crossed the sands and then continued on the switch-back to Newquay - the golden gateway to fun and surfing and was reminded of Peter Sellers' Balham - 'gateway to the South'. Above me occasional demonic bangs rent the air which were probably sonic bursts from Concorde on its way to the States. In the busy town I found mail at the PO, visited the helpful 'I', lunched on chips and bought some stores including candles. After crossing the small footbridge over the Gemmel River and walking across the estuary sands, I climbed over to Pentire passing old mines surrounded by strange metal hoops

on sticks. The army training grounds forced a walk through sand dunes before I came to popular Perranporth - named after the sixth century St Piran, patron of tin miners and soon found the Youth Hostel on the hill out of town. It was closed but Red, the volunteer caretaker warden, let me in together with an American from Philadelphia. We had great time and started a companionship that lasted almost to Land's End.
16m

Day 437
Friday
Setting off with Jeff from the hostel mid-morning we chatted all the way to St Agnes past the dominant old mine workings of this granite coast and disused mine shafts blocked off with their 'conical hats'. Tin, tungsten and copper extracted in the middle of the nineteenth century, had supplied some two thirds of the world demand. Jeff wished to hitch to St Ives and, saying farewell, left me by the old Tudor harbour Inn. The day was dull and windy, not ideal walking conditions, as I continued roller coasting to Portreath beyond which the flatter downs gave some relief. By a scenic mix of bays, valleys and harbours I passed New Downs of St Agnes Head, the prominent Wheale Coates old tin mine, Chapel Porth, and Porthtowan, where beach bums, vacant eyed students from Falmouth, were sitting round a fire smoking spliffs. Near the path at Portreath a white pillar stood as a memorial 'For the Fallen' written by Laurence Binyon in 1914, one verse is particularly well known:-

>   They shall not grow old as we that are left grow old
>   Age shall not weary them nor the years condemn
>   At the going down of the sun and in its passing
>   We will remember them

It was then easy walking to the headland of Navax Point, past the tourist attraction of Hell's Mouth but then darkness began to overtake me at Godrevy point and in the glimmer of twilight I made my way to the only farm around to find shelter beside some cauliflower planting tractors. The timing was perfect as the heavy rain set in for the night. After a light supper, the farmer then presented me with hot chilli con carne together with some malt bread so that I went to sleep - bloated.
19m

Day 438
Saturday
How changeable our weather is. At dawn it was dark and miserable but then the rain passed as the strong westerly wind blew the clouds away and released the sun from hiding. I crossed all the Towans - associated with the sand dunes - firstly across the beach and then below the army training grounds and the car-

avan sites before finally reaching the end of the peninsular near the River Hayle. In the once busy town it began to rain again and so I had breakfast in a cafe and sat with a reticent diner who was about to set off for the Falmouth beer festival. Braving the wet conditions I proceeded through Lelant, past the wonderful warm church of St Uny and onto bustling St Ives with its quaint old streets. But today the town was far too crowded for me and I noted that my return would be when it was quieter. Lunch was in a park shelter, sitting with a young family and looking back at St Ives. It was six or seven miles to Zennor along the big dipper path over granite rocks and scenically one of the best in Britain. I battled against the strong wind which blew away thoughts of St Just and at five o'clock found Zennor church and its open porch which would do for the night. But on investigating this tiny village further I discovered the back packers' hostel and rang the bell. Who should answer but Jeff? The managers were away for the night and we made an 'executive decision' to sneak me in for a night's stay. The nearby mini museum, founded by F C Hirst (1874-1938), was closed but looked interesting and outside were artefacts, that indicated the sights inside - including a water wheel and a plague stone (1834-45) which had held vinegar to sterilise coins. In the evening we went to the Tinner's pub for a drink, before I slept on the hostel sofa.
16m

Day 439
Sunday
Rising early, I spent the last two hours of the night in the church porch, in order to avoid trouble for Jeff, and then walked out to Zennor Head, given to the NT by A B. Nearby was a seat also donated by A B to 'those who had sustained him' and on the trail of this mystery person it materialised that he was Arthur van Bagel, a local farmer. The sun came out - spring like - turning the sea blue, lighting up the rushing surf which filled the bays, but leaving the bracken brown. Another day for reflection. The coast line was almost above description - a rugged granite buttress to England, bleached white by the wind and rain, ripped at endlessly by the sea and holding a nest of secrets best left unturned. The buffeting strong southerly wind continued and I stopped at a coffee shop in Movah with an Internet connection and I thought 'Is nothing sacred?' It was slow progress along the fine path to Pendeen Watch as the rocks changed to shale and disused, derelict, dreary mines appeared. At Porth Naven I met a Paul leaning on a wall and writing a poem. We walked together to St Just, debating the meaning of 'Hostel open till the 31st', the day's date. He went to the church and after shopping I wended my way to the YH to find it not yet open. While I waited, surprises jumped out. First Jeff turned up and then so did Paul. We sat and debated tactics. At five I found the warden, recovering from recent hospital treatment, who said the hostel was closed but she relented to some extent and we were able to use the kitchen where we had a wonderful evening of eating, sketching*, stories, Islam and music. Jeff and I

slept on the floor while Paul had his tent outside. Apparently Bob Dylan had been here and when asked if he wanted to stop, he had said 'Too many rules' and quikly left.

* The Sea - Paul Ceivers (1999) *

The ribs of the body of the ocean
are laid bare near the shore
They spill with her white blood
the gush and flood pours over
the chocolate and rust bucket rocks
She breaks her breath - she ruptures her death
Her great heart thumps like a fist,
hits the chest of the ragstone cliffs
She is in a state of bliss - she is in glory and grace
and in her face run the salt taste of tears

12m

Day 440
Monday 1st October
We had an early rise and breakfast but Jeff and I didn't start walking till eleven due to the lousy weather and long farewells. We set off into the wind and rain across wet fields to Gazick a mile away where Jeff gave up, to leave, he said, for the Lizard, London and Morocco! The rain continued as I lost the path and had to ask for directions at a farm. A joiner from Penzance was busy fixing a garage door and he gave me a route which I followed but was soon in thick brambles. Extracting myself by walking on top of an overgrown derelict stone wall I lost my footing and fell off, flat on my back, a rock followed and crashed onto my leg and bounced off. How my leg survived without a break I don't know, and it was also a struggle standing up again, extricating myself away from the clawing brambles before climbing over more walls and thorny vegetation to gain the proper path to Sennen Cove. This was all closed - half term having passed - with the exception of the Life Boat shed and the adjoining gallery, where I rested briefly before going the short distance to Land's End, cluttered with Peter de Savary's theme park. I did not feel a great elation at getting here, at England's most westerly point, but had my form authenticated by two newly weds from SE London. Knowing that Botham, on his last long walk, was not far behind, I did not linger too long in this disappointing place and, after phoning Liz to tell her of my arrival, walked out to the theme farm and beyond. A slow walk with the scenery becoming softer and trees starting to appear, the coast-hugging path continued around the headland to St Levan, Cable & Wireless Porthcurno, and picturesque Penberth to the neat little harbour of Lamorna. I arrived there in the dark before pushing on uphill to Kemyel and Mousehole. The coast road led me to Newlyn and a pub where a

chatty lady, smoking hand rolls, wished me well as I set off later for Penzance and the Hostel. This was open and, due to my status, cheaper than the nearby YMCA by nearly £3.
20m

Day 441
Tuesday
An Australian lass sent me off with a pithy farewell motto:-

> 'You can't afford to ignore salvation'

In Penzance I visited the excellent geology museum which is struggling to survive financially. Nearby stood a memorial to Capt. Sir Chris Cole (1770, Marazion - 1836, Lamelas, Glam.) who had gallantly captured the Island of Banda Meira (Bandanaira,The Spice Islands)** and the working gilded clock in memory of Eliza Trevelyan which woefully struck one. The town also boasts a statue of Davy, of miner's lamp fame, discoverer of sodium, potassium and a wealth of chemical innovations. He finally retired to Rome and Geneva where he died in 1829. His effigy is set squarely against the high columns of the Lloyds TSB front while the surrounding pavements have recently been repaved with relief curlicue slabs that must be the road sweeper's nightmare - especially after the pirates of Penzance may have escaped from the local Meadery. Eight miles later, along St Michael's Way (which leads eventually to St James's Cathedral in Santiago, Spain), and after passing St Michael's Mount with its Benedictine chapel, and the granite church of St Piran & St Michael at Perranuthnoe rich with grey, yellow and green lichens of some 90 species, I had lunch at Cudden Point in gorgeous sunshine, as a Sea King helicopter flew overhead. Afterwards I proceeded past the remnants of old tin mines which abound along this coast, to the coves of Prussia and Bessy which looked like the smuggling places they used to be - the former being named after the vigorous John Carter proprietor of the King of Prussia inn. At Bessy's Cove I met my next Paul, a part-time gardener from Cambridge enjoying the southwest path while at Praa Sands the surfers were out in force. At this time of the year there were very few birds on the coast as I headed for Porthleven and finally the minute village of Winnianton, where in the dark stood an unlocked church, close to the beach of Church Cove. The porch had a bench and the place was protected by the effigy of St Winaloe on patrol in the church yard. I could have slept inside the church but every time I entered the lights came on and this might have attracted too much local concern.
18m

Day 442
Wednesday
Rising with the sun I was soon at the Marconi Memorial where the first wire-

** G Milton's interesting Nathaniel's Nutmeg; Sceptre Books

Day 440 Farewell to the poet of St Just's Hostel

less transmission was made across the Atlantic in 1900 but the wireless station work hut designed by John Ambose Fleming, which used to lie close by, has long since gone. A mix of paths took me to Mullion Cove, where an outspoken lady of 77 (she said) refused to give me water, the one and only person to do this. She was an ex-coxswain of Plymouth too! I had mistaken her house as being part of the closed cafe next door so I forgave her. On Predannack Head horned sheep, 'burnt' black-brown, grazed alongside ponies, modelling blond locks over their eyes - Soays and Shetlands selectively grooming the grasslands. Nearby I met yet another Paul and we sat on the grass, chatting in the warm sun. In the 70's he had wandered Europe and found work in Germany and Finland installing HiFis and then after working in London returned to Cornwall to meet and marry a local girl who had also travelled for three years, but in the USA. We come back to our roots so often!

The path ran down to the beach at Tor Balk where there was extensive amounts of pretty serpentine. At low tide I crossed a pebble beach below the cliffs and, misjudging the incoming waves, moved too soon and had my feet washed by the sea. Two miles later having reached England's most southerly point and its cafe at the Lizard, I had tea at the Wave Crest Cafe just above and met the Atkins, a happy couple from Devon, and their dog Badger. They told me stories of the area and took my photograph as we enjoyed the glorious weather and view. This was a much better 'turning point' than Land's End and it was only slowly that I picked myself up and set off again, around the peninsular to the Lloyds Signal Station. Another path-walker, Dave, was on the move and he told me he was a robotics engineer from Leicester. I saw him again at the Devils Finger as he walked back along the path to his car at the Lizard. Almost immediately I met another man, strimming the path and had to talk to him too. Consequently it took quite a while to reach Cadgwith and it was in the gathering gloom that I reached my objective of Beagle Point on Black Head. On a nearby farm I was directed to a barn by a farmer milking his cows and who gave me hot water from his steriliser. Unfortunately the stock were rampant in the huge shelter and I transferred to a grain barn with a concrete floor but, having promised not to light anything, had a problem making my bed and eating supper in the dark, the only light coming from the repetitive flashes of the nearest lighthouse!
16m

Day 443
Thursday
The morning started with cold porridge and was not improved by a badly prepared EU path which I first used to reach the coastal path leading to Coverack, arriving there at nine. Trailing along the path having trouble obtaining hot water, it wasn't until near St Keverne that I was able to have breakfast. In returning to the coast at the quiet fishing village of Porthoustock with its

thatched cottages I went through a farm with an auction sale of the worn agricultural machinery of a retiring farmer. How sad it seemed that a hard working man's life was reduced to so little. The path climbed out of the village and carried me to Matilda's Cottage with its attached Cider Press Barn and large herbal sundial - a tourist attraction that hadn't quite made it. In Porthallow an old lady told me that 'in the war she could see Plymouth burning but this place was saved from the bombs.' She gave me a donation and at the PO there was a letter from Roger.

A few incident free miles followed, walking without much thought, until I was shocked back to life by an electric fence and had to evade an inquisitive bull. On the road, away from the bull, a man, behind his barbed wire gates, told me he had been burgled three times and had had all his power tools stolen - the spread of rampant crime even reaching this remote area. He gave me directions to the ferry across Helford River where I arrived in mid-afternoon. There was no ferry, the season being over and I sought help in the adjacent Boat House, a super cottage, occupied by Steven Cotton. He and his lady friend were very helpful, gave me a snack and made suggestions but back at the quay, Anthony the fisherman was in a hurry and the yellow boat which came next didn't want to take the non-existent trade away from the closed ferry. So I dithered around until I met Piers Alder who had just rowed up to the shore with his family in a wee dinghy. While he was giving me water and bread I met another neighbour taking her child home after school and she showed me the way to Nigel and Jude (Davies) who did B&Bs for walkers. Generously they took me in for a free nights lodging. He was an ex-warden of the Lizard NT, retired through acute migraines and they were still living in their NT house. I had a wonderful night all round and learnt that their daughter, Robin was a world-class Windsurfer - No 33.
10m

Day 444
Friday
After a light breakfast I said farewell, stepped onto the large porch and on seeing the day said 'rain, rain go away'. It was wet. In the village, I shopped at the PO and saw Piers again to thank him for setting in motion the previous night's kind hospitality. The tide was out and there were no boats about so I began the walk up river just as the rain stopped. A mile up the road a stream in full spate crossed my path and it was lucky that there was a wall acting as a footbridge. Further on a lovely old lady told me how she was brought up on a farm in Cornwall and had to raise the rest of the family when her mother died. Then afterwards she had married a 'wonderful' London man. At the ford by Forest Lodge, a couple washing their car told me to cross the footbridge and take the road opposite to Gweek and its bridge over the River Helford followed by a picturesque undulating road to Helford Crossing. Working without

Day 442 The most southerly spot: the Lizard

Day 441 St Winaloe takes care of the beach church (and me) at Winnianton, Cornwall

an OS map I tried to stop a passing motorist to ask the way; instead of stopping he nearly ran me down. The next one did stop and I was able to bypass Helford Landing and go by path through the local tourist gardens. There were few people about except for a lady in Dugan, who gave me more directions Otherwise I hardly saw anybody all morning.. Stopping for lunch by a boat house in a small bay a storm passed as did a local man, who was down from Norwich seeing his sick father and he offered me a lift to Falmouth which I reluctantly(?) declined. At Rosemullion Point, ships painted black, red and white rode at anchor, a picturesque scene with the stormy sky lit by the setting sun. Nearing Falmouth the rain came on again and in a sea-front shelter sat a drunk who was quoting Keats and reflecting on the power within the frigate anchored off-shore. After a cigarette I escaped for the short distance to the youth hostel in Henry VIII's Pendennis Castle, arriving in darkness at 5.30. It was Guy Fawkes night and up in the castle we had a grand view of the fireworks below. There were two other residents, Peter a rambler and Joe an enthusiastic Australian cyclist who had just completed a wet, one day round trip to the Lizard.
16m

Day 445
Saturday
A fine day lay ahead with only two showers, no wind and the air washed clean. There were farewells from the castle before I crept around the fortress ramparts towards Falmouth. The one-way high street curved through the town with a variety of charming shops it seemed like a place well worth exploring. A free ferry took me to St Mawes but there was no ferry to the next peninsular and I had to walk all the way around the Percuil River, taking the A3078 to St Just and at the bridge finding a path leading to Zone Point. It took me most of the day to get there as I continued beside the scenic creeks through Percuil and Place and past St Anthony's Chapel to Anthony's Point. On one creek I encountered two men discussing the village cricket team for next season while at the Point two workmen were arduously carrying ladders up the path having just finished painting the lighthouse. From the car park the route became less strenuous along the 'Mediterranean Coast' to Portscatho and a couple of miles farther on, behind a hedge, I found a beach-come-summer house that was empty but locked, denying access unless one broke a window. Nor did I have the inclination to pick the lock. As rain threatened I slept conveniently in the adjacent empty 'garden' shed which at five and a half foot square was just big enough - diagonally!
14m

Day 446
Sunday
It had not been a comfortable place for a good sleep and I rose at dawn, ate

cornflakes with milk and then set off beneath a beautiful sunrise in a clouding sky. My first stop of the day was at Pendower beach, by a 16th century hotel and then at Nare Head where it was so still that even the sheep slept, rested and contemplated the coast. At eleven in Portsloe, which lay hidden away in a cleft of the cliffs, I sat on a seat designated for village 'dignitaries' and spoke to Joe and Rose Trudgeon who gave me hot water and noted my passage. I had another stop in Portholland, a small village typical of this coast, and then continued, in the rain, on the rising and falling path to Dodman Point. The rain stopped while sitting on the base of the large granite cross and talking with two social workers from Truro. The cross was built in 1896 as a navigational aid on this treacherous coastline. To give it further spiritual assistance the Rev Martin slept by it for a night but apparently without much effect on shipping losses. The path continued along this splendid rugged coast, indented with small coves holding beaches of rock and sand, to Gorran Head and Portmellon. Mevagissey, bigger than the previous villages had many shops that were still open and an attractive harbour with a substantial flotilla of fishing boats. While buying supplies at a store in the village, the sales-girl said that, unlike Australia, this place was difficult for back packers and low cost accommodation was hard to find. In Pentewan I could find no suitable hidey-hole shelter for the night and so looked for a B&B. The first I tried was £30 and the second was full, though the man was reluctant to turn the 'vacancies' sign around to 'no vacancies'! Perhaps he could smell my socks! Next I knocked at the house of a man who was on a mission; going round Britain in different ways. He had cycled round, sailed round, was now going to power boat around and to provide funds had put his house on the market. He phoned the only other B&B in the village and soon the owner, Ed, appeared to escort me up the hill. He and his wife got organised and I had a quiet relaxing night. They suggested a visit to the local gardens of Helilant, noted for their uniqueness in local co-operation. It was a pity that I didn't - next time round perhaps!
19m

Day 447
Monday 8th November
At Black Head there was a memorial which said all that needed to be said:-

A. L. Rowsech
1903 - 1997
Poet and Historian
'This was the land of my content'

The sea lay still, the sun shone and clouds began gathering as the white houses of St Austell appeared together with its prominent conical mining dump. I must have been tired as I counted 137 steps down and 89 steps up to the Points of Glendra and Phoebe where there were good views of Gribbin Head. In the docks at Charlestown, named after one of the local Rashleighs, three impressive tall schooner ships were being repaired and readied for sea - the days of sail having not completely passed. The climb from these docks brought me to a muddy path around a golf course and to a WW2 shelter that would have made an ideal bunkhouse, remembering a thought I'd had months before about converting pill boxes into concrete bothies for coastal walkers. Passing the large china clay works I wondered where the hole was - to produce all that kaolinitic clay. I found out later that over thirty square miles of countryside had been destroyed by this mega tonne operation supplying 20% of world wide demand for this clay in paper making and ceramics. William Cookworthy (1705-80), a wholesale chemist, read about Chinese ceramics and scoured Devon for supplies - which eventually led to the devastation at Hensbarrow.

On the way to Polkerris I went through an up-market caravan site and by the beach-side Rashleigh Inn, related to the entrepreneurially successful 18th century family of that name, and on towards the next head of Gribbin past the 'red and white beacon for ships', a Daymark established in 1837 for ships entering Fowey Harbour. At the Grotto ruins there were swans on the lake and a notice saying: 'Sorry no water (for walkers) at this house'. But apparently it was an inspiration for a Daphne du Maurier novel. After rounding the head and walking into Fowey I caught the ferry immediately on arrival and again there was no charge for this charity walker. After supplies, there was a steep hill out of Polruan and at the top, behind a wall; I found a small empty cow shed which seemed a reasonable place to stop. Dumping my bag and walking back down the road to an unlit caravan site, I was lucky to find Ray and Andrew packing up for the day. They filled my flask and gave me sugar, milk and biscuits. Back at my stall, I barricaded the entrance against animals and settled in for the night.
15m

Day 448
Tuesday
A restless night led to an early start. It had been a dry night but there was dew on the ground as a good path took me across the rolling downs to Pencarrow Head. The autumn tints were splashed with green and the winter greens daubed with brown in a landscape crisscrossed with stone walls running to the grey cliff edge; with the sea's calm broken only by the great boats plying the shipping lanes while droves of gulls swung to and fro searching for food. There was not a soul in sight. My boots, which had carried me from Ullapool, were well split now and my socks easily got wet which didn't help walking although the paths were generally good. Writing my diary and contemplating the view and life I sat on a seat dedicated to Les and Geoff Hicks, wardens:-

'Thank you for caring'

Below the headland lay an isolated and apparently empty house on its own footpath without roads. Was it a bothy? On the hill lay the square towered church of Llansallos and would have been my second church to try last night according to the map. Instead of visiting it I dropped gently down to the NT Llansallos Cove, a special isolated place suitable for a camp with wood and running water, and then climbed past a white obelisk to the headland above, just as the melancholy bell of the church rang out the hour.

Another three miles took me to Polperro with its delightful twisting streets and hints of past smuggling activities. Two jovial men were delivering half a boat to a hotel and they said 'its half price' and 'suitable for half a journey'. A yellow sign said 'Rabies': 'no smuggling'. A little over the next hill I lost the acorn, a sign which I had been following for so long but I managed to negotiate fields, barbed wire and descents to Talland Bay in brilliant sunshine. It was a pleasant day for walking and indeed brought out a string of hikers. Out at sea lay Looe Island, looking attractive, particularly in the day's sunshine and where one of the Atkinson sisters, in her nineties, still lives. The book 'I Bought an Island' was an astonishing record of their survival and success on such an isolated piece of land which appears split in two with trees in the east and fields in the west while the beach of the island is apparently very good for bass. Looe itself seemed dreary and weather beaten but there were many boats and much activity. The most outstanding sight was that of an Australian War Veteran complete with medals and scout hat, standing near the bridge, selling poppies - a grand looking chap who gave me one to stick in my hat. I started up out of the town but soon stopped for a cup of tea with a lady and a tree surgeon sitting by the road and they gave me the local news. Then it was up and up to the suburbs of Seaton and Dowderry where I had tea at St Nicholas church as their prayer meeting ended and was given water for my flask. Continuing to Portwrinkle I tried various locations to camp but in the end the only suitable place for shelter seemed to be the toilets. These were clean, dry, not locked and set high above the beach, commanding a good view of the coast - a definite candidate for toilet of the year.
19m

Day 449
Wednesday
It was a poor night's sleep on the hard floor but perhaps 12 hours of walking had been too much! As the day cast off the cloak of darkness the sun rose for a brilliant day. A happy cleaning man came by and not a word of admonishment was uttered as I gathered my pack together for the day's walk. He had been a boat builder who liked wood and not plastic and so now did this work for the council and was happy to be with the elements of sea and sky each day on his morning duties - seeing foxes, gulls and birds of prey as he moved along the coast.

The path was hilly and the dewy grass soaked my feet as I progressed across the local golf course. The silhouettes of morning stood sharp and clear and a man walked his dog on the skyline symbolising a new day. A firing range forced me away from the coast to a road for Wreath. Holiday and residential chalets were tucked away on the steep hillside sloping down to the sea and the path swung up and down, twisting in a seemingly haphazard fashion through this peculiar collection of habitations. Eventually it emerged at Rame Head with its dominant 13th century chapel on the headland. Long ago it was used by hermit monks who were paid 1d a night to keep a beacon alight. Later it transferred to private hands before finally ending up as NT property. At the Coast Guard Watch Station, set back from the headland, the watchers were observing the sailing boats and navy vessels passing by in the placid sea. In Cawsand a man was building impressive eight oar wooden 'rigs' and he decried the lack of elm for his work. This village and the next, Kingsand was apparently an attractive place for Lord Nelson, especially for romancing in the local pub. I rambled along and entered the lovely Edgcumbe country park, full of swirling red tinted autumnal leaves, which led to Cremyll and its the rather fine ferry house to await a free passage on the two o'clock ferry. After arriving in Devonport I went to the Salvation Army Hostel only to find it full and instead went to the YH, dropped my bag and spent some time in Plymouth. Later back at the hostel I booked in and cooked supper.
16m

Day 450
Thursday: Remembrance Day
After my first YHA made breakfast, fair value at £3.10, I tried to catch a train to Castock to visit my cousin Nicholas Cole who was renovating a tin mine. But having missed the 9.50 train and not wanting to wait for the 11.30, I walked instead back to the Devonport ferry and around Plymouth. I love cities in early winter sunshine when there are few people about, ambling through interesting back streets, past old and new buildings and - in this naval port - all the barracks. At eleven o'clock I stood still for two minutes while the busy city noises continued around me. Along the streets lay many curious little sculptures and in the pavements plaques commemorating Sherlock Holmes and Arthur Conan Doyle's association with the city, each had a pithy saying ascribed to the author. One clever set of steel railings had been indented so that a scriptural text only showed at an obtuse angle. Thus I wandered to the Hoe where the water was very quiet with only a few sailing boats tacking in the light breeze. A placard proclaimed:-

> Across the sound the ships of war
> with cannons blazing at our shore
> have tried for centuries to tear apart
> this unyielding spirit - the Plymouth heart'

Day 448 Nearing Remembrance Day: an Australian veteran does the business in Looe

The water taxi, beyond the Hoe, had an owner, amenable to a free trip but the much labelled SW coastal path continued to the bridge, through the industrial part of the city, with its twisted metal junk, slabs of concrete and brick and permeated by pungent chemical smells. OTT, every lamp post carried the sign of the acorn and the south west path slogan. After crossing the bridge over the River Plym I caught the bus for the short trip back to town where I found the Shekinah Mission (radiating God's imminent presence) in Bath Street and had a free meal before returning for another night in the hostel.
2m

Day 451
Friday
Coffee was in the smart Theatre Hill Cafe and dinner at the Mission. Leaving my bag at the back packers' hostel, I returned at six to find it was full of girls and no beds available. Hence my night was spent in a shelter on the Hoe even though it was getting decidedly cold at night.

Day 452 Saturday
Sleeping was in fits and starts before I moved off and took my free trip on the taxi ferry to Ballant Hotel and a short walk to Jenny Cliffe for coffee and pie. '175.5 miles to Poole' (and the end of this LDP) proclaimed a signpost. Meanwhile it was a lovely path and in the afternoon I reached Wembury and Warren Point on the River Yealm. The seasonal ferry was not to be seen and there was little river traffic as I sat on the shore for an hour having a snack and a smoke. Eventually an obliging Welsh yachtsman, who had been doing repairs on his boat, substituted for the ferryman and rowed me across the water in his dinghy. This was both kind and helpful as I hadn't fancied the long detour around the Yealm river system. Over at Noss Mayo the pleasant walk continued especially the easy stroll along Lord Revelstoke's carriage way, built to impress his guests. The remains of old buildings lay along the path but too many sheep were using them for my liking. Ignoring these shelters and narrowly avoiding a down hill plunge in the dark, I headed for a light across the fields to find a road which led me to Caulston, Battisborough Cross, Mothecombe on the River Erme, and then back to the few houses near Bugle Cove in a night-time search for an elusive B&B. It didn't appear. However out of nowhere, heaven suddenly arrived: a car stopped and whisked me away, taking me to the pub in Holberton, The Colours, associated with horse racing and the Grand National. But I declined the offer of a £30 bed reduced to £16 and said I would rather sleep in the church. porch Splashing out on a meal I met builder Dave and his girl friend Lisa. Talk about my walk engendered an invitation to sleep on the floor in their newly converted house across the street. Once there I met Canadian decorator Bob and local carpenter Andrew and we had an entertaining evening watching old recordings of 'men behaving badly'.
18m

Map 8 The Heel of England

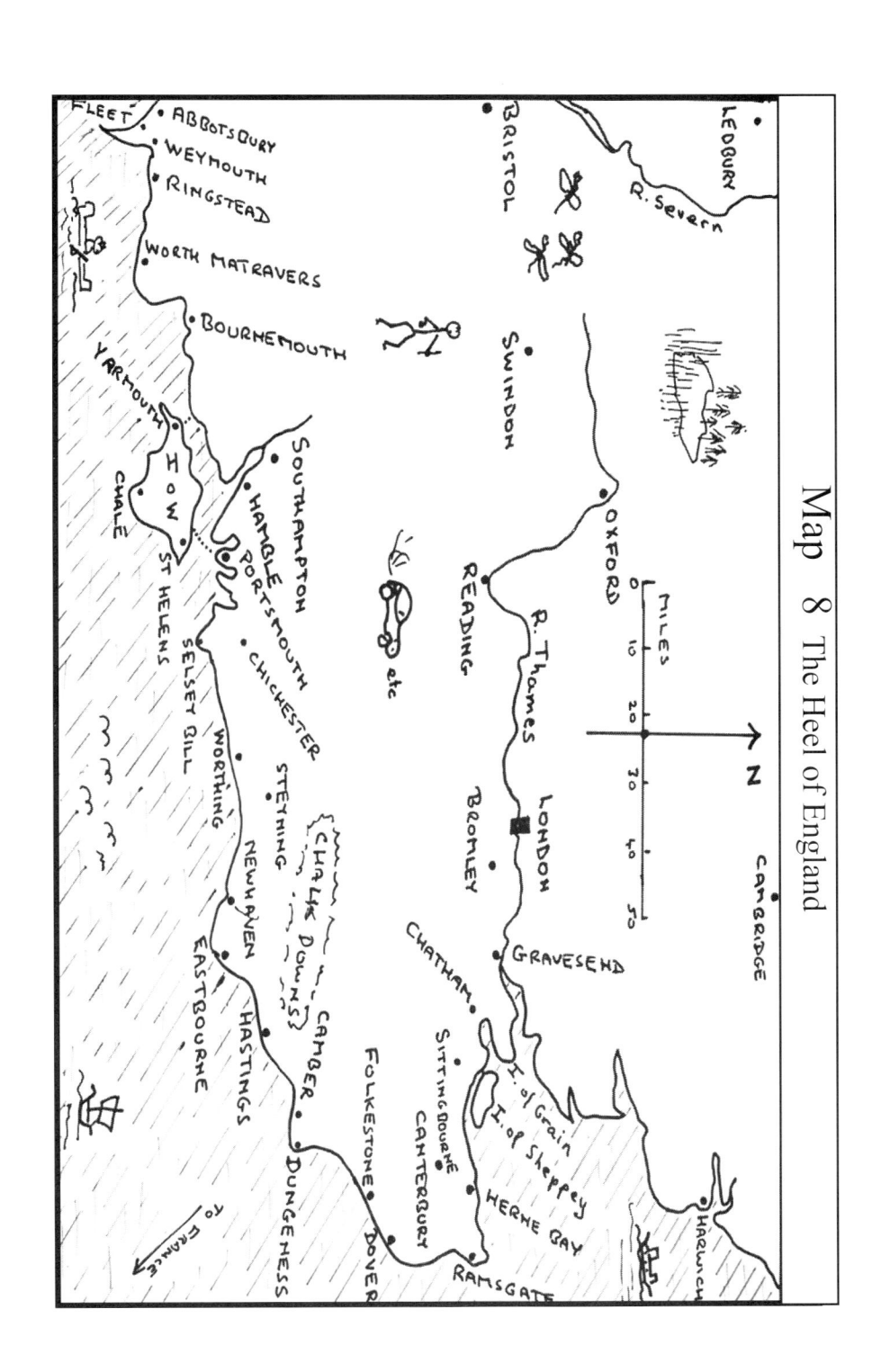

Day 453
Remembrance Sunday
At 8.30 the household was stirring and we had tea with beans on toast while Bob played the blues on his home-made guitar but it wasn't until nearly mid-day that Bob and Andrew with his dog took me to the river through the autumn woods, past the marsh reeds and the swan ponds while we threw sticks for the dog's exercise - Sunday morning strolling. The weather was good and there was a crowd of people out walking so that the path was busy. Having bid farewell I dropped my bag on the beach and walked up to Mothecombe, in order to continue my journey. When I got back to the river and retrieved my bag luggage I found that the water was only ankle deep to the other side. By luck and good judgement the tide was right. At the next river, the Avon, I had to walk upstream and then, with the tide still low, wade thigh deep across to the boat house on the far side before continuing to the SSSI of Hope Cove. It was dark as I went into the pub for hot water and the barman kindly gave me hot soup as well. Refreshed I soon found myself further up the village, at St Clement's church just as the Pophams were locking up. We talked and they offered the church rather than the porch for my night's sleep.
12m

Day 454
Monday 15th November
Dawn broke as I rose from the crypt and faced a cracking day with a super coast of rocks, bays and few houses. There was some cloud in the east trying to strangle the sun, but after an hour the sun won and gradually drove away the frost while I happily stretched out along the first seven miles to Bolt Head, past the treacherous rocks below that have claimed many ships and hundreds of lives. Next came the estuary at Salcombe with the question of how to cross? The first ferry, at the mouth, was closed and I had to go upriver to Salcombe itself for supplies and the town ferry with the ticket lad paying the fare - was this free? On the far side, back on the coastal route, I walked and talked with some Birmingham jewellers and their wives rambling the path. We separated a mile later; they to the left and I to the right. They were on a circular walk and consequently we met again later when they were keen to take a photo of my dishevelled state - or was that rugged state?

Out at Prawle Point, Devon's most southerly spot, I sat down in warm sunshine with the owners of two Alsatians and a spaniel, sitting high up overlooking the sea. What a grandstand view and the water was so clear. While on the land below the sheep were fat and sturdy with late summer lambs growing apace. Was this November I asked? Even my socks on the back of my pack had dried out today. Apart from giving me hospitality and a donation they also gave me an old local OS map which was handy. What more could you ask for than the sound of the sea breaking gently, the blue sky, the curve and grace of stratified shale with green gneiss, brown bracken and near solitude whilst the sun warmed my back and generous people assisted one's journey.

After Start Point, at Bees Sands, a Sherman tank sat as a reminder that this area was used in 1943 as a practice ground for the Normandy invasion, and a sign said 'Poole 164 miles': there was something wrong somewhere - I must have walked more than 11 miles in two days. Later in the Plough Inn at Strete I talked to the landlord and thought about joining the darts team for the night - they were one short. It reminded me of how the 'king pretenders' had come to England in days gone by and then had to rustle up their troops on the way to battle. Things hadn't changed much to this very day - we were still rounding up 'troops' on an ad hoc basis. Finding nowhere suitable to stay, neither the church nor the campsite looked inviting, I made a nocturnal walk along the road and felt like 'An invisible soul entering the devil's kingdom, nobody bothers you, or speaks, but lights shine stark bright as a continuous cacophonic stream of cars and buses sweep around you'. A bus stop was a possible shelter and the next church a feasibility. These were my thoughts when on my left I spotted a dark building, partially hidden under trees. I climbed over the roadside gate, crossed the field to investigate and found some barns, part of an old farmstead, unlocked, dry, sheltered and with a soft peat floor offering a good place for sleep. Perfect! The only distraction was the flashing beam from the lighthouse at Start Point many miles back.
20m

Day 455
Tuesday
Up in the village of Stoke Fleming I found a toilet and an open shop. Providence had been with me again as the church, which I'd aimed for last night, had no porch and the bus stop was right on the street. My curiosity satisfied I walked into Dartmouth past the castle and gun emplacements that used to guard the naval port but which now make up a heritage museum and one old cannon with a two mile range still pointing out to sea. It was an attractive busy town, new cobbled pavements were being laid and a young energetic violinist played her instrument in the high street busking up money for her keep. After a free passage across the Dart, making my way uphill I passed the locked and barred MOD huts high on the cliffs. From these a convoluted path took me to Coleton Fisham House but its gardens were locked and barred. The path went along thickly vegetated slopes to Froward Point, entailing hard work but breath taking in every way. Black islands stood stark in the clear blue sea, rippled by the wind while in the distance the shadow of cloud turned the scene to a painter's picture. I passed an abandoned holiday camp with its broken-windowed huts, and then suddenly spread before me was big and boisterous Brixham down below. This was where William of Orange landed in 1688 and marched to London. A funny place to land for such a long march. But of course

he had to drum up his troops and darts players on the way! Probably offering them boots, booze and a spot on TV, giving them time to dust off their lances and pikes and load up their muskets. In the harbour sat the ancient sailing ship, the *Mayflower* replica, that hadn't moved in 15 years since I was last here.

As Tor Bay began I was back with my old friend ORS and its associated red soils colouring the path, on my move northwards towards Paignton, but which was not attractive as it passed conglomerations of houses, lights and sprawling litter. Arriving at 5.30 I knocked on the door of my long suffering Aunt and Uncle, who had first put me up 45 years ago during a more youthful adventure. We chattered away the evening, ate some wonderful food and then I slept in a warm comfortable bed.
22m

Day 456
Wednesday
My boots were in a seriously cracked condition and I went into Paignton town to look for more, but without making a purchase as in the end I decided my comfortable if leaky boots would have to suffice a little longer. Apart from buying film I achieved little else there and in the afternoon walked to Torquay past all the built up housing, parks and pounding traffic. There were very few people about and little of interest to see. Torquay itself was an unexciting place under a wintry, watery and patchy blue sky and I caught the seven o'clock bus back to Paignton for a supper of delicious shepherd's pie. We watched a poor game of football, as England lost 0 - 1 against Scotland but won on aggregate 2 - 1 to allow them to participate in the European Cup.
5m

Day 457
Thursday
Dehydration had now passed, having remained hidden from my knowledge until finding my constant need for another drink. The tanks were full again and I felt like a camel. These were short walking days but the batteries needed recharging helped by reading Paul Theroux's 'Kingdom by the Sea' - his tour of the UK by foot, train and bus. As an American traveller he makes pointed observations of the English at home particularly those who live by the coast.

After phoning Liz and wishing her Bon Voyage for her charity walk in Morocco, I caught the Torquay bus and found the ladies aboard were all stony faced and stalwart. Back at the harbour I was off again past the Imperial, staring out to sea, and then climbing through false fortifications to the graceful curving Regency buildings erected by T. Wallace. My route went through pinelands and along the damp Mediterranean English coast past the evocative conical Thatcher's Rock as the sun struggled out of its cloud cover. The path climbed to the high road above as I moved towards Anstey's Cove and on the way rested briefly on a seat to:

>Pam J Bundle
>Where she found tranquillity:
>Where the land meets the sea

At Shaldon a Londoner, Mark, from the Elephant and Castle, and now working hereabouts put me in the right place, on the beach, to wait for the ferry to Teignmouth. He told me he had a gammy leg otherwise he said he would also be walking somewhere exciting. The ferry man spotted us on the beach and came to collect his fares, but when I told him my story he was very happy to give me a free lift over. After spending some time in Teignmouth I made my way back to and through Torquay. As this journey had taken much longer than necessary, my concerned relatives had called out the coast guard service, which found me walking on the promenade at 4.00 am and then returned me to Paignton in a police car.
10m

Day 458
Friday
A visit to former home of the Singer Sewing Machine Magnate was the main interest of the day: - an intriguing collection of old machines with their mechanisms improving from the first to the more recent models.

Day 459
Saturday
With a packed lunch and a repacked rucksack, Uncle Jack took me to Teignmouth and sent me off for a long contemplative walk through Dawlish up the River Exe and past the deer in the Manor Park of Powderham Castle. The first ferry at Starcross wasn't running, and I sat for some time on the pier waiting to see what the river traffic was like but it was practically non-existent. After continuing another four miles upstream, past the Turf pub (which sat at the entrance to the Exeter Ship Canal, where the nearest car park was 1 klick away and the customers had to come by foot or by water transport), I found another ferry at Topsham. A small boat with a cheerful boatman who took me over for nought and told me the council had kept the ferry open as part of the local amenities. After walking to Exmouth where I couldn't find a B&B that suited me, a chip shop provided me with food and hot water for my accomodation in a seaside shelter with a seat wide enough for a reasonable bed.
20m

Day 455 A hard way to earn a living: Busking in Dartmouth

Day 460
Sunday
There was frost in the night and it was a dawn start out of Exmouth. At 8.30 with the sun low in the sky I was at Sandy Bay and its empty caravan site, where the only occupants were rabbits and chirpy fat blackbirds. At Littleham church just as the service finished the cheerful Reverend, in response to my long distance walking, said 'he should be paid in theory, too' and I said that I'd have tea with him when passing his house. Indeed I did see him again with his wife on the promenade at Budleigh Salterton but he hadn't left any tea for me. I photographed two fishermen alone on the large shingle beach - they were from Gloucester for the day which left me feeling that home waters were approaching again! A short diversion was necessary here, away from the coast, up the River Otter, through the nature reserve and past the old salt pans, with a loose array of Sunday walkers, to the salient peninsular of Danger Point before rejoining the Devon path. The fields were still red here but in Sidmouth white limestone filtered in and gradually took over, beginning to dominate the cliff strata as the new rocks took hold. Along the coast at three Rocks Inn, in yet another Sandy Bay, the number of ramblers increased and some even gave me donations. At Jacobs Ladder a greenhouse, full of carnivorous plants and cacti, nestled in the gardens above the sea. It was warm and inviting but pressed on to Sidmouth, knowing I was on a mission - to find Bridleway 92, an address given to me during my Bristol meanderings.

For directions I tried the police station but with no success - there were no police on duty, only an answer phone with a disembodied voice that had no local knowledge at all! Heading for the area between Harcombe and Sidbury and stopping at a farmhouse under restoration I gained a possible sighting of my target. Setting off in the direction indicated and winding up to the woods I unexpectedly found the start of Bridleway 92, as if by magic. A weary trek to the top through thick woodland brought me to an open field and suddenly there it was, the encampment that I sought. Ben was there with his three oxen Bodin, Axle and Dolphin, saved from the butcher's block and now grazing contentedly on the rough grass of the flinty soil. Luckily Kath, the girl I'd met in Bristol, was also there, having only returned a couple of days before. When I saw her she was bent down, planting broad beans in her patchwork garden. She finished as the gloom came down and we retired to her bender, built from hazel branches and a tarp, with its neat wood stove exuding warmth. Over a meal we had a long chat about alternative medicine and the protesting community, before going to bed in one of the gypsy caravans. It was a privilege to be there despite the longish detour a pain which continued in my side and boots that were even more decrepit.
16m

Day 459 A long awaited welcome in Paignton: my veteran uncle and aunt Jack and Joan Quarendon

Day 461
Monday 22nd November
It rained in the night and I rose late, kissed Kath goodbye as she lay reading in her bender and walked down the hill. On the country tracks in these forested hills I had some difficulty finding the way to Knowle House and Weston. In Branscombe the 15th century Fountain Head pub provided coffee and a lively crowd for some repartee. Down the road was a well known spring but the Water Authority had declared it contaminated. With what, I wondered?

   I was finding that the uphill climbs were painful to my left side and again thought about walking without my pack but that was a few days away. Back on the coastal path I went through Beer, known for its whitish building stone, to Seaton before taking the bridge across the River Axe. The next track climbed uphill, across the golf course and then over downland to Lyme Regis where I arrived in the dark. Supposedly this was an awkward bit of walking and it was just as well I couldn't see much of where I was going. In Lyme, I saw a man getting into his car and asked him about buses. He immediately offered me a lift and without much thought I agreed to go with Dave to Chard, where his wife gave me a welcome cup of tea and then their daughter's evening meal which I hungrily devoured. Phoning Amanda, Andy agreed a meeting in Hatch Beauchamp and Dave took me into the middle of Chard to catch the bus we had seen in Lyme! Hence I arrived back in Curland (Stoke St Gregory) some six weeks after leaving for Bridgewater and the West Country. 16m

Interlude Eighteen
Day 462 - 464
Tuesday
The day began slowly, the car needed a jump start after its lay up and needing a rest because of my side I drove to Bristol.

Nineteenth Stage
Lyme to Ringstead (Weymouth)
Day 465
Friday
After driving to Crewkerne and sleeping with the aid of an aspirin I was up at eleven before moving to the upper car park in Lyme where I had been on Monday. I walked through, down and up out of this steep town. From the main A3052, the acorn path led off over the hill to Charmouth and back to a road past the Queen's Armes where the Queen had slept in 1501 and King George had also stayed. A minor road took me away from the village past Newlands before I regained the path through Westhay NT land to Gabriel and Golden

Cap, the highest bit of the south coast at over 600ft, and all the glorious rolling countryside of Dorset. Young November lambs played in grassy fields, enjoying the late autumn sun while the white flecked frothy surf fringed the restless grey sea. This bucolic scene stretched out before me to the east and disappeared under the overcast sky but it was a blustery day with strong gusts tugging at the body and feet, frequently changing direction, first behind me, then against me and then sideways - keeping my senses alive.

After Seatown below Fossicking Chideock, in gathering gloom, I reached Eype Mouth and then West Bay in the dark. From here I had to walk to Bridport and catch the bus to Lyme Regis, collect the car and drive back to West Bay. I obtained hot water in a waterfront hotel and parked near the harbour while a cold wet rain lashed down.
11m

Day 466
Saturday
The water front of West Bay has been remodelled and, together with the village, has been used for scenes in the entertaining TV series 'Harbour Lights' and the changing weather seemed appropriate to the TV drama.

Crossing three hillocks I slowly made it to the golf course while my cold filled chest plucked at my constitution and was thankful when the hills reduced in size. After losing the path on the caravan site near Freshwater I picked my way across fields to Burton Bradstock, from where the road led me to Burton Beach, the starting point of Chesil Bank. Three men with a four-wheeled motor-bike, heading east, were busy on the shingle and picking up litter - if they were going to do Chesil Beach - they had a long tortuous way to go! A view of Portland Bill swept to the right before me, the distant vista broken by the outline of naked winter trees, now stripped of their summer foliage by wind and rain - new beauty silhouetted against the sky. At West Bexington, weekend anglers tested the waters and on the track an army of walkers appeared - the place was coming alive - with human intrusion. I avoided Abbotsbury by going over a fence and through the swannery then exited on the road to New Barn. The hunt was out and I briefly joined the supporters while the 'antis' blew their discordant horns elsewhere. Leaving them to it, I soon found a path for Langton Herring but afterwards was resigned to the B3157, passing the Victoria Inn (Knights in the Bottom), before making an abortive attempt, in Chickerill, to find Roger's friend Ron James, who was away enjoying himself in Bournemouth. Thwarted, I hitched to Abbotsbury. The van driver of my first lift thoughtfully told me that the whole of this area was owned by one family but this hadn't left a big chip on his shoulder. On leaving the village I walked up the hill and was picked up at the top by a Shell worker who took me, out of his way, direct to West Bay, allowing me to drive to a field in New Fleet for

the night.
15m

Day 467
Sunday
In Fleet the small attractive church was open. It had been rebuilt in the mid 16th century by Maximilian Mohun and was also associated with the novel 'Moonfleet'. I popped inside for a brief visit before following the shore around the inland lake of East Fleet. Large groups of swans, ducks and water fowl paddled the water facing into the strong wind from the south while on the opposite shore of Chesil Bank a mishmash of fishing huts was built into the pebbles, protected from the sea winds. Further on, sheltered in low lying inland coves, I passed two camps of holiday homes. They were ghostly, almost completely empty, closed and silent, though in the second, a solitary bird watcher told me of the importance of this marsh area with its bird population nearing the 20,000 bench mark - a requirement for an international recognition of importance. Around the corner was an army training school full of lads manoeuvering speeding landing craft across the lagoons - on their weekend exercises, and after this the slippery path went to Ferry Bridge. In the dull weather of the day Portland Bill stuck out, waiting for exploring, but as there is only one way in and out I turned instead towards Weymouth and, on arrival, crossed the Harbour Bridge instead of trying the ferry which did not run on Sundays. In the harbour I went on board a fully rigged Topsail Schooner, a training ship - the Malcolm Miller, built in 1968 for £75,000. The lady captain signed my form and she told me that it had just been sold to an Australian outfit. A very unpleasant man was disembarking with his spare booze which he didn't want me to touch - I was only going to take it to his car. He was probably rich! On the other side of the town things were quite different with a splendid wide curving promenade and a beach of pale sand. The next bus for Chickerill was an hour away so I walked with the buffeting wind to Osmington, having tea in a cafe, and then on to Osmington Mills and Ringstead. It's wonderful sweeping scenery here and you can imagine John Constable with his new bride sitting down and painting the view towards Weymouth. On reaching the glitch of Ringstead it was time for me to turn round and start hitching. A Dorchester man took me to the main road but I had to walk back to Osmington before fortune smiled on me and two ladies from Stoke took me all the way to Fleet. Water was obtained in the house opposite my parking place before driving to Weymouth to get supplies eating in a sea front cafe and parking at Ringstead in the no-camping car park. But nobody bothered me. On the radio Bradford 0 — Chelsea 1: for me rather a disappointing result.
12m

- Chapter 8 -

Isle of Wight - Detour

Interlude Nineteen
Day 468
Monday 29th November
It was raining again - a miserable morning and when I tried to move the car it wouldn't start and so I had to roll it down the slight incline to jump start it into action, just making it with only a few yards of slope remaining. At the top of the hill, I kept the engine running, waiting for the charge to build up. As the rain was continuing incessantly I decided to use the day to transfer the car to Southampton. But it was after eleven in the evening before reaching the village of Hamble-le-Rice and then, with my memory playing tricks, I had trouble finding the home of my niece Jane and her husband Martin. The long lost uncle had returned after 25 years.

Day 469
Tuesday
A lazy morning sorting out my rucksack was followed by an afternoon visiting the bank in Southampton and using the toll bridge which was much shorter than my route of the previous night. In the evening we all watched cable TV and Roger phoned, having tracked me down again, to give me the latest family news

Twentieth Stage
Ringstead to Portsmouth
Day 470
Wednesday
It was a predawn rise at 6.30 and Jane took me to the local station in order to catch the early train to Southampton where I transferred to the Weymouth line travelling to Moreton. After walking a mile, luck happily returned as a passing motorist in a 4 X 4 picked me up, a sales manager with some walking interests, who went out of his way to help, taking me to the car park in Ringstead. Consequently I had a reasonable start to the day and was soon strolling across the chalk downlands. My first stop was at a tall pyramidal beacon - probably a landmark for shipping - but, uncharacteristically, there was no tourist information attached. It remained a misty day with rain approaching from the east while the wind was blowing from the west!

At West Lulworth Church there was a home-made visitor's information display concerning John Keats, rocks and village life - just right for an interesting read on a wet day. In 1868 a sum of £50 was given to rebuild parts of the church with the proviso that the seating should be free! Inside a beautiful stained glass window showed St George slaying the dragon. In the village lies a charming 16th century inn where, charitably, I was given soup and coffee while the echo of distant gunfire reminded me that the MOD ranges were out of bounds today. Later high on the downs I looked across the plains to the north, spreading towards Salisbury and Stonehenge while nearby a quarry pit of Cretaceous chalk was designated as a SSSI. At Kimmeridge nestled the local steepled church thick with yew trees and solitude, far away from those booming army guns. After by-passing the village I entered Smedmore country park with its solitary square country house and a high road took me to Chapman's Pool. Making my way without an OS map navigation was more luck than judgement and it was dark by the time I found the pub, the Square and Compass, in Worth Matravers. There was a small museum here, started by the landlord Raymond Newman containing a homely collection of fossils and ship artefacts. They sent me to a B&B, the Haven, up the road and after a bath I returned to the pub with the owner, Ian Taylor, who was thankfully retired from the management of pumping local Dorset oil from the largest inshore oil field in Europe, he had settled for catering to tourists. It was a hilarious evening, with a half dozen locals and a group of archaeological students from Bournemouth. We played name-guessing games and talked of pheasants, fossils, stone and scrumpy.
17m

Day 471
Thursday
A knock awoke me for an earlyish breakfast in this friendly boarding house and I was away before nine with directions for regaining the path, but after a quarter of a mile had to return - having walked off with the keys! At last on my way across the rolling downs to the sea, following the acorn mark of the coastal path, I soon came to Dancing Ledge, one of two grassy patches cut out of the chalk by the sea where you could imagine a big party with music and happy dancing local yokels relaxing after quarrying and harvesting. It was a fine day and from here I could see the IoW in the distance. Near the lighthouse stood the first of the oil field derricks associated with drilling and at Whym Farm a plaque showed that BP had removed 100 million barrels by 1993. Nearby I passed Purbeck Quarry, testimony to the importance of the local stone which has been used at Westminster, Salisbury and many other places with outstanding buildings. I was walking well but a pain in my left shoulder continued. Out and about were several walkers who were unusually conversational for the south, at Peveril Point two stopped, signed my form and gave £5 for StC.

On Swanage sea front I found the 'I' and then followed the promenade towards the cliffs at the end. The Marines were pottering about in power boats and landing craft sailing around the Foreland to Poole Harbour and as I walked north along Swanage beach they were also busy on community duties, cleaning the shore. At the far end the steep white cliffs threatened to block my way and therefore halfway along this beach I scrambled up a large steep grassy cliff bank to find the path above. The sun was now hot, the trees had shed their leaves and that 'old man's beard' was dominant. With wonderful views all around I headed for Pirlene Point and then Harry Point which had its own white needles opposite those of nearby IoW while in a cliff cutting coloured sands were also reminders of IoW formations. Beyond this the flat lands around Bournemouth lay before me. At Studland, on losing the path, I went down to the beach and, as the tide was out, rounded the headland before walking a long stretch of firm sands to the chain ferry across the mouth of Poole Harbour. I caught the 2.30 crossing on the 'Bramble Bush' and, for once, did not have to ask for a free passage since in this direction there was no fare! I had come to the smart suburbs of Sandbanks and to the end of the South West Path!

The road and promenade took me to Poole and then to Bournemouth where I spent some time before leaving for Southbourne along the sea front. By chance I asked a runner the way and he sent me immediately up the embankment where I found the Commodore Hotel and Seaview Avenue. I had come to meet the Tanner family, a name and address given to me at the Colours way back in Devon. They were not expecting me, as the young lad had forgotten to tell his parents of Dave's suggestion. However after the initial shock I was made very welcome. James told me of his work in a school catering for the autistic condition of Aspergers Syndrome and of his 17 years in the auto-trade in London. On going to sleep I realised that I'd now finished the 600 mile south west coastal path in some 589m strides but alas I never did see that Bass driver who'd been wheeling a baby in Cwmtydu near Newquay in Wales!
22m

Day 472
Friday
The Tanners*** gave me breakfast and I was away by nine on the road to Christchurch, a nice quiet town, twinned with Christchurch in New Zealand as well as towns in Germany and France. I wandered through past the 900 year old Priory, the town walls and the associated parks on my way to Ferry Port. Here the wind had really picked up and was causing a horrendous wailing in the rigging of the sailing boats on the hard as I battled to the fish shop at the end to verify the non-sailing of the ferry from Hengistbury Head that was available in better conditions. With the wind behind me I went back along the promenade to Steamer Point Nature Reserve, crossed fences and fields before

Make me too brave to be unkind
Make me too understanding, to mind
The little hurts companions give to friends
The careless hurts that no one quite intends
Make me too thoughtful to hurt others so
Help me to know the inmost hearts
Of those for whom I care
Their secret wishes, all the loads they bear
That I may add my courage to their own
May I make lonely folks feel less alone
And happy ones a little happier yet
May I forget
What ought to be forgotten; to recall
Unfailing, all
That ought to recalled, each kindly thing
Forgetting what might sting
To all upon my way
Day after day
Let me be joy, be hope, let my life sing

***Later James sent me this delightful thought
from an un-named poet

Day 471 Sparing a thought, in Swanage, for the departed Danes

finding the beach road to Barton and here sheltered in a bus stop until a heavy storm had passed and hence missed all the local fossils. On hearing that the IoW ferry had been cancelled I worried over ideas about the next stages of the journey, as my path continued eastward. The beach was all brown shingle with the crashing sea surf causing a constant roar but the wind surfers were still out on the water and I saw one that completely lifted off from the waves and performed a spectacular somersault before restoring contact and on meeting him by his car I congratulated him on his stunning solo act.

A shore path continued past Milford-on-Sea towards Hurst Castle which, I had been told, apart from its massive Victorian guns was not worth visiting and so I turned left across the small river and made my way to the estuary road to find a twisting dyke path to Lymington across dull flat marshes and past the Salterns, which once supplied large quantities of salt for naval rations. There was a host of bird life here and I could see that three ferries were operating, plying their plodding way to and from IoW. As I came to the town the sun began setting, the glorious winter colours illuminating a flotilla of yachts and other boats straining at their anchors. After walking through the town and over its bridge to the ferry terminal, I talked to the staff who kindly gave me a free open-ended return ticket, normally costing £8. Night time had arrived and the trip across seemed to go by in a flash, which was strange when previously the ferryboats had appeared to troll so slowly across the water. Yarmouth was a ghost town at this time of year and there were no B&Bs. Nor did I fancy a night in the shore shelter and so decided to walk to Freshwater where at the Colwell Bay Inn I asked for suggestions and eventually found a lady to take me in for £10 - as they were not really open. Afterwards back at the Inn I treated myself to a gammon supper by their fire.
20m

Day 473
Saturday
After an unexpected breakfast at my lodgings I set out along the road, bought film at the local PO and struggled to escape from the Freshwater area but eventually found a coastal path to Headen Barrows. Over this hummocky headland, cropped by rabbits, the Needles suddenly appeared while cross the water below lay Hurst Castle and Lymington with the broad sweep of Bournemouth to the west.

On the way a bus driver, commenting about the lack of people said that 'it was nice and quiet for a change'. At the far western headland there was shelter from the wind behind a concrete buttress which formed part of an old rocket testing site. Next came the Tennyson Downs, named after the poet who escaped here from his more urban society friends. The wind blew me around Freshwater Bay and down to its pebble beach. Eastwards these pebbles

changed to sand in the shallow offshore seas while the path continued over the rolling grasslands, between the cliffs and the road, past Compton Down and Brookgreen with its old lifeboat shed and on to the IoW Pearl and Coffee shop, which dispensed tea and free seasonal mince pies with a glass of sherry. After the holiday camps of Grange Chine the sun began setting behind the only cloud in the sky portending a cold night. It had been CHINES all the way from Bournemouth, the southern dialect word for deep fissure which were characteristic of these chalk landscapes. Late afternoon found me at Chale church where the children were practising a charming Christmas play about creation and the verger agreed to my idea of sleeping in the porch. A big sausage supper beckoned in the nearby pub, the 'Clarendon' named after the 1936 wreck of that name in which 25 people had perished and three survived. While eating the verger suddenly appeared over my shoulder and invited me to sleep in a friend's caravan at Tutten Hill Cottage, but not until 7 o'clock when the children's party finished in the CE primary school, the best small school in IoW. At the farm, in the van there was a radio and a drum kit to entertain me.
18m

Day 474
Sunday
It had been a frosty cold night and I crawled out for the walk back to Chale under a clear sky and with only a light breeze. Beyond the village erosion had cut the path necessitating a staggered route across fields and fences to Blackgang overlooking the Fantasy World complex below. A path continued above slipping cliffs with several scattered properties below - it seemed that IoW was a retirement home falling into the sea. At least somebody with imagination had routed the path high up so that good views could be enjoyed and below me lay St Catherine's Point, the southern most place on the IoW. After descending to St Lawrence with its well, 12th century church, rare breeds farm, the house of Alfred Noyes, poet and author (1880-1958 - 'Drake' and 'Two Worlds for Memory') and the Botanic Gardens, a snicket of a path took me down to the smugglers cove out of which I had to climb again, out and over into Ventnor full of late seasonal visitors and vigorous reconstruction. The latter caused a problem on the waterfront so I clung, spider like, to the chain link barrier for several metres before reaching solid ground again. Afterwards a muddy path went past a land slip, where notices from the land slip committee were still in place. The Luccombe tea gardens, surprisingly, were still open and served beans on toast before my progression through Shanklin and Sandown. On the headland of Bembridge Down, with splendid panoramic sea views, I came to a large striking memorial to :-

Charles Anderson, Earl of Yarborough
Died on the Kestrel near Vigo, Spain
in 1846 (aged 65)

But of his recorded contribution to the local community I could find no account - perhaps it's all in the local Library.

   Scrambling down to Bembridge to buy supplies at Alldays, I asked the young girl assistant about accommodation and on leaving she seemed genuinely concerned for my welfare. At the church, the service had just finished, and they gave permission for sleeping in the porch but also suggested a houseboat B&B along the shore. On arrival this was £25 a night, too much for me, and I walked to St Helens. The shop there knew of no local accommodation so I decided to walk to Ryde in the dark! After only 200 yards I met a lady who had seen me on Dunnose Head. She said she hadn't room but by the grace of God we found another lady, Rosy Hickman, who did do B&B though not normally in the winter. She told me to wait in the nearby pub, where it was all football talk, and then an hour later I found myself ensconced in a warm self-contained flat with all the amenities for only £10.
20m

Day 475
Monday 6th December
A miserable, drizzly day on which an assortment of paths took me to the strangely old fashioned village of Seaview. One building advertised 'E.J.Caws - Sand Shoe Maker' while Little Douglas, Osteopath, invited people to 'walk right in'. I arrived in Ryde at noon and took the 12.20 ferry, from the rail pier to Portsmouth where in docks stood the impressive HMS Warrior, a reminder of past naval dominance and power. Launched in 1860, constructed of wrought iron and powered by steam and sail she was a formidable warship. I had tea in a nearby cafe before it closed for the day and then ventured into the town, sleeping, that evening, on the waterfront.
6m

Interlude twenty
Days 476-478
Tuesday - Thursday
I explored the NFA delights of Portsmouth and rested my body. The sights included Henry VIII's Mary Rose, Nelson's Victory, the Royal Navy Museum and all the sights of a naval port.

- Chapter 9 -
The Southern Seashore Suburbia

Twenty first Stage
Portsmouth to Gillingham via Hastings
Day 479 Friday
With the wind gone, the sun out, returning its warmth, and the grey sea subdued I left my night's shelter on the wide sea frontage and headed east, setting out along the Marine Parade to get a free passage on the ferry from Eastney to Hayling Island and then walking up through this holiday spit of land to Emsworth with its splendid combination of 'Bridge, Chess and Snooker Club'. In the town I shopped, banked and had tea in the Methodist Community Cafe (with biscuits - 25p) before continuing along the Sussex Border Path around Thorney Island, through Southborne and Chidham to Bosham where I arrived in the dark and spoke to the local vicar. He was happy for me to sleep in the church porch after that evening's choir practice but then suggested walking to Chichester and trying the night stop there. Consequently two hours later after negotiating the ring road I found myself at St Joseph's opposite the old convent on the B2145 south of the City. The vicar had thoughtfully phoned ahead, so that a bed was available and a welcoming hot meal awaited. This hostel had been re-opened in 1996 by the Duchess of Portland after being closed for three years. There was one 'resident' who had been coming for nearly ten years apart from the gap and said it was a real home, the only problem was the day time hours which he spent in Chichester at the day centre and library before wasting a couple of hours until the hostel re-opened at seven.
26m

Day 480
Saturday
It was a force 7 day and starting in the cold and wet from the comfort of St Joseph's I took the B2145 through Hunston, turned right on a minor road to the A286 in order to reach Birdham. The 14th century church has a striking stained glass window of Jesus and his fishermen disciples, designed by Michael Farrar-Bell, while outside stands a sentinel gnarled Macrocarpus tree, which is about 200 years old. Continuation was west along tracks and footpath to West Itchenor lying in a rather dull flat landscape and was my destination of the previous night had the ferry from Bosham Hoe been running. Following the coastal path around the marshes to East Head on the eastern mouth of Chichester Harbour, I gratefully turned east away from the wind, wondering who had upset the sea today as it was very angry - a real sight if you enjoy tempests. Moving away from my last views of IoW, into and through East Wittering I found, beside the beach, a track, which was not marked on the map,

to Selsey where there is a plaque to Eric Coates composer of the 'Blue Lagoon', signature tune for Desert Island Discs. Around the corner of the Bill, distracted by the sight of the lifeboat being launched on a practice run I lost the path and had to find another way to Greenlease Farm where a man out shooting directed me to Church Norton and through its church yard with its graves in neatly numbered and labelled rows. A slippery path beside Pagham Harbour took me to Ferry House and in the dark I found a Ferry Reserve hide for a needed break. By good luck I soon found the Visitors Centre which was open and spoke to the bird warden, saw the exhibits and got directions for a bus. And after walking to Sidlesham, the 5.45 took me to St Josephs where the gathering inmates waited outside for the witching hour. Roger and Doug were the wardens with Dr Brian and his good wife Joan as volunteer helpers - making the place homely. After supper we watched the film 'Local Hero', relaxation at the end of a tiring day.
21m

Day 481
Sunday
The warden Doug gave me a lift back to Sidlesham, which has the remains of a tidal mill, and I walked around the 1400 acre Nature Reserve of Pagham Harbour, where up to 200 bird species may be seen during the year together with thirteen types of woodlice (!). The St Thomas a Becket Church at Pagham is one of the earliest dedicated to that saint when it was rebuilt in the late 12th century. The area was drained for farming in mid 19th century but in 1910 the sea took revenge and came back. After an arduous hike to Bognor Regis the route simply followed the coast eastwards all day except for a small detour inland to cross the River Arun into Littlehampton. In Worthing I visited the police station but as the only presence was a phone on the wall the idea of giving myself up dissolved. Since the beginning of the walk I had been plagued by a speeding offence fine which I'd refused to pay and still haven't.

As evening approached I continued towards Sompting and it was dark on starting across the Downs to see my mother in Steyning but half way across a motorist stopped and took me there. Unfortunately on arriving at the Swallowfield residential home, mother had been moved to a nursing home in Sompting! Since I had spoken to her on the IoW she'd had a fall and needed nursing care. I could do little that night so sought out my car which had been moved from Southampton to Steyning. It was parked at my cousin's house and as Peter was away I slept in the car, not able to move it as the keys were in Sompting, although at that stage their whereabouts were unknown.
23m

Day 482
Monday 13th December
As it seemed a round about route by bus, I hitched to Sompting and was lucky to get picked up almost immediately by a 4 x 4 to cross the downs. Over the main A27 road I walked into the village and Rectory Road where I found my mother in the nursing home. But she was not at all well. She hardly recognised me. This was very sad, realising that when I had spoken to her on the phone a few days before she had been so bright and positive. She was due for an assessment later in the day so I said goodbye as best I could, collected my car keys from the matron and walked along the sea front to Shoreham. A hot pasty from a bakery softened a lengthy wait for a bus back to Steyning before stopping at Shoreham Lagoon for the night.
5m

Day 483
Tuesday
Walking eastwards I passed Shoreham's roadside lighthouse, built in 1844, the busy docks and miles of hard pavement. On Brighton's front, watching the sun set over the west pier, I waited for two hours for a bus that never came. Strangely many went eastward but never returned and in the end an Indian contract driver of a bob-about-town bus, who had passed several times, took pity on me, stopped and took me to a proper bus stop, a mile away. From there I soon caught a bus back to Shoreham and returned to the Lagoon.
6m

Day 484
Wednesday
My mother had been transferred to Worthing Hospital. She was still poorly and had problems communicating in a coherent manner. I stayed for couple of hours but couldn't do much more except believe that she would recover, thinking that hospital techniques would pull her round even at the age of 95.

Back in Brighton I walked to Newhaven along the road dispensing with the possible route beneath the cliffs. On the other side of the road another hiker, a well laden continental, trudged his way to Dover and we exchanged greetings as I pressed on past the schools of Roedean and St Dunstan's which stood on the side of the downs in their spreads of private ground, looking out to sea. At the WWI repatriation port of Peacehaven, the Meridian Zero raced through me and out to sea, escaping from Greenwich I thought!. Then I sauntered down into Newhaven to catch the bus back to Brighton before returning again to Newhaven and parking by the Bridge. To amuse myself at midnight I walked across the silent bridge over the Ouse to the bus stop, where I had been earlier and then retraced my steps before falling into a deep slumber.
8m

Day 485
Thursday
After speaking to the receptionist in the adjacent factory and getting permission to park for the day in their forecourt, I found a footpath by the railway and river into Seaford, beyond which a coastal path took me to Cuckmere Haven, where the 63 mile Vanguard Way leaves on route to East Croydon — a short cut back to Bromley? Although a lady said I couldn't do it, I paddled across the pebbly river of Cuckmere in order to walk up to the downland roller-coaster path over the swell Seven Sisters, though a count of the number of crests was lost. It was a glorious afternoon with clear views of white coastal cliffs set against a beautiful blue sea. At Birling Gap, in the Hotel for coffee, John a landscape gardener, with his Finnish friend Tina, persuaded the bar girl Christine that I should be 'treated' - which she did. Half an hour later, as it was starting to darken, the NT warden who had just jumped out of her Land rover said that she wouldn't do it but the path just carried, alongside the cliffs, to Eastbourne. So that was what I did, passing the red and white lighthouse of Beachy Head and the hidden stunning views, that were supposed to abound. After reaching Eastbourne, phoning Owen to tell him the situation about our mother and my current position, I caught the bus to Newhaven for the drive to Eastbourne, supplies and a quiet sea front recess.
15m

Day 486
Friday
From here to Rye was 1066 country and all its historical connections with the Norman invasion, settlement and occupation of Britain that was to last for at least three centuries, not unlike the length of the Roman conquest, that would leave a wealth of castles and laws in its wake. It was a wet, windy, overcast and miserable day as I set out past the pier and my left shoulder and neck still ached despite the recent walking with a light pack. However it wasn't far to Hastings. The promenade eastward was practically deserted while below me the gravel beach continued from way back along the coast. Around the new marina harbour stood new lamp posts and the gravel was being shifted by tractors to form new ground - more 'improvements' were on the way.

I went over locked gates and crossed the waste ground to Pevensey Bay with its private gravel roads, then continued to Norman's Bay, where William landed nine hundred years before and where Harold, after racing down from a skirmish in Yorkshire, lost. Pondering the centuries of Norman Occupation I continued on to Bexhill, birth place of British Motor Racing (1902) with its modern housing fronting on the beach approaches and at the first promenade cafe, which was almost deserted, had tea and a soggy warmed pie. After passing the innovative, but now passé, De La Warr Pavilion, it was a trudge to Hastings, where the 'I' was helpful, directing me to the bus stop for my journey back to

Eastbourne. It had not been an attractive day's walking and that night I drove up to Tonbridge for a meal, a bath and a bed in order to leave the car at my brother's place.
16m

Walking on the edge towards Perranporth:day 448

- Chapter 10 -
Around the Heel of England
- The Last Leg -

Day 487
Saturday
Owen gave me a lift to Tonbridge Station and I took the train to the south coast. It nearly broke my heart to spend so much on one fare but it was relaxing to be whisked along through Kent. Having reached Hastings in mid-morning of a dull damp day I walked with a certain amount of lethargy, my main memory of the town being the wooden fishermen's net huts on the shore, tall dark relics of another era. A variety of roads and paths took me through Fairlight to Cliff End where Romney Marsh spreads out as a flat plain. A coastal road led me to Winchelsea Beach, and beyond to the uninhabited coast around the Nature Reserve (which has a similar Habitat to that in Baie De Somme, Picardy), the deep tidal cut of the River Rother and the undistinguished Rye Harbour. The settlement itself sits on a small hill and is a quaint mediaeval town looking down on the changing state of the country round about. It is from Rye that the Saxon Shore Way begins and runs to its end in Gravesend and I would find myself following this route when it came close to the coast but for now it went inland following the old coast line when the Cinque Ports were of importance after being stranded by the departing sea. At the top of the hill I stopped in the churchyard of the 12th century St Mary's for a food break while a wedding went on about me and they must have thought that the chimney sweep come to give the bride a blessing. By the time I reached the golf course near the mouth of the river it was getting dark and scouting for a night shelter struck out across Camber Sands feeling as though I'd entered a scene of The Longest Day which had been filmed here. In Camber were an open shop and a closed church. But Vicar Joe, after a few words, allowed me use of the community hall for the night.
17m

Day 488
Sunday
It turned out to be a long day's walk from Camber Parish Church. After using the facilities and having a civilised breakfast of beans on toast seated at a table I said my goodbyes to Joe and set off into a frosty clear morning along the shore road beside the Broomhill Sands and continuing due east on a good dyked track across the military Lydd Ranges, with no red flag flying, beside a long shingle beach. At the far end of the ranges the path had been demolished

Day 487 Fishing Stories in Hastings!

by bulldozer operations and this had made a potentially difficult walking surface but, in the early morning, the embankment cast a shadow that kept the gravel frozen and this made my task a great deal easier. At the Dungeness power station was an unlocked gate, with a notice 'You are now entering a nuclear site'. I went through only to find the way blocked further on but fortunately was able to crawl under the wire barricade and escape onto an external concrete path, while the power station hummed peacefully as I went past to the two lighthouses of the Ness. It is certainly an exposed spot and I would not like to be there on a windy day. However for me it was a sunny day with only a light breeze. The scattered shack housing, fishing sheds and boats made a brave picture under the wide sky and a local gallery had a collection of water colours depicting the quiet beauty of the area. A number of folk had made their ramshackle homes here - people in tune with the sea, the silence and the solitude.

Further along the road I stopped in a cafe at Greatstone for coffee and a chat with the only two other clients before moving on to Dymchurch and beyond. The range of Palmarsh was open and this allowed me to stay close to the sea past the Martello Towers and into Hythe. It had been a good day for a walk and although the scenery had not been overwhelming it had its own pleasures. In the evening I walked to Folkestone and with darkness upon me started seeking accommodation. The police at the harbour had told me that there was a Salvation Army Hostel here but it was only the Citadel. The RC priest, in his church hall, told me about B&Bs, filled my flasks but otherwise was not too helpful. As it happened the guest houses were £20+ and so I walked out and up on the Dover road. At the top I found the Sailors Rest with a Wendy House at the side and the publican said it was mine. During these negotiations at the bar I met Brian, Tim and Mike having a few beers. They plied me with drinks and a much needed meal. Two hours in the warmth of a pub was enjoyable but it was time to make tracks for sleep. Brian showed me an aerial photo of the local WW2 airfields, defences and the nearby cliffs and he also pointed out a stable with the suggestion to try it, which I did, finding it was perfect for such a cold night.
29m

Day 489
Monday 20th December
I had slept well amongst the clean hay with a pony for company although in the night she had somehow managed to extract my loaf and large grapefruit out of my strapped down rucksack and must have had an extraordinarily nubile tongue. Six miles of walking on the cliff tops took me to Dover, the last active Cinque Port of Kent. It was a fine but icy morning and far out at sea, across the busy ship lanes of the Dover Straits, the coastline of France was visible, while below me lay the active port, a cacophony of sound growing as the arma-

da of bustling ferries plied their trade with their pennant flags displaying two fingers to the channel tunnel and a steady stream of thundering lorries and swift vans hauled the endless loads of continental goods and 'contraband' into England's hinterland. After descending from the quiet of the downs into the buzzing town, there appeared to be no YMCA, Sally or Day Centre and it was therefore fortunate I hadn't walked here last night. Nor were there any signs of the big influx of refugees who were supposed to be swamping this area. I spent some time at the council offices inquiring about accommodation but the officer for the homeless was situated and isolated on the other end of a telephone so cutting my losses I retired to the Youth Hostel, on the London Road, settled in and ate early. At 6 o'clock I found the soup kitchen in a central car park, had another snack and was given food to take away. There was the usual assortment of NFAs there and one lad did suggest a nearby squat with electricity but already having a bed for the night I made no further investigation of this facility.
7m

Day 490
Tuesday
It was a dull day with a wind from the south as I climbed out of Dover on the Guston road below the castle and past a spread of cemeteries. Up on the downs, once more, I walked through the unguarded, red brick, Duke of York's Royal military School to the main A258. At West Cliffe in the 11th century St Peter's church three old ladies were busy doing seasonal things - arranging the Christmas flowers. In St Margaret's-at-Cliffe, in a bus stop, a lady waiting for a bus told me of the Dover Patrol Memorial on the cliff tops and of the beach where cross-channel swimmers slip into the water for France. Both Noel Coward and Ian Fleming had spent some time here and one can only contemplate the inspirations it might have created. But I fancied staying higher than the beach and so walked past the local with its huge log table, out along the upper bridleway to Kingsdown and along the shore to the gun shrouded castle of Walmer, built by Henry VIII in 1540. In the Cafe on the Green the owner gracefully treated me to shepherds pie before the promenade brought me to the historic Cinque Port of Deal where all was quiet.

At 2.30, as the sun came out, I reached the expensive houses of Sandwich Bay Estate and the beach road where two smart ladies, keen walkers, saw my pack and inquired about my travels. The tarred track continued past exclusive golf courses, devoid of players and then a series of signs directed me on the grassy pathway across the Royal St George's to Sandwich, a town full of pubs. Over the river I took the main road past the giant new Pfizer research laboratories and stopped in a Little Chef, but as tea was 89p a cup had a Mars bar instead! Unwittingly I passed Ebbsfleet where the Saxons had landed in 449 AD and St Augustine with a bunch of monks arrived in 597 AD going from

successes here, including establishing a power base at Canterbury, to meet the leaders of the Celtic Church in Aust on the Severn in AD 602 and achieved alienation through his pompous behaviour. A small diversion to the seasonally relevant Bethlehem took me past the holy well of St Augustine which Roger had marked on his old map but which remained invisible to me in the dark, though there was just enough light to guide me, on the coast path, to Pegwell and Ramsgate. The police station was closed; cheap accommodation was not available so eventually I spent the night in a beach shelter high on the cliffs to weather out the wet and windy night.
23m

Day 491
Wednesday
I remember little of the walk from Ramsgate to Herne Bay. At Broadstair's Age Concern I was given sustenance before following the paths around North Foreland and a promenade to Margate and Westgate on sea. In late afternoon I battled against a strong head wind towards the striking landmark towers, silhouetted in the evening sky, and the lonely remains of St Mary's Church at Reculver, which has had a chequered history since Roman times. After exploring the adjacent caravan park for possible off-chance resting places I had to shelter in the space below the towers for an hour before venturing into Herne Bay for a convenient Promenade shelter.
19m

Day 492
Thursday
The moon sat full on the quiet calm sea as I started my day. In Whitstable, famous for its oyster beds, I tried but failed to find the Over 60's club for tea and instead walked out on the A290, turned off for Seasalter and sat on a wayside seat for a meal of bread, jam and cold coffee. The road took me to and beyond the suburban village as the sun came out and the light breeze died away. The continuing coast road brought me to the Inn on Graveney Marshes - the isolated Ye Olde Sportsman; it looked closed but needing hot water I knocked on the door summoning the publican who asked me what was wanted. On explaining he gallantly opened the bar and gave me tea and soup. Phil Harris had only been there two months after returning from the Middle East after setting up dealerships for Harley Davidson. On my departure he kindly made a payment for a copy of my journal, my first sale, and this kept me solvent a little longer!

I took the sea wall towards Faversham and met up with Lt. Lee, a walker and Lynx helicopter pilot who on retirement hoped to up-grade to airliners. His worst experience had been a near miss by a Harrier hurtling past just above his head. We parted after the path had meandered around to Faversham. The

Umbrella Club had just closed for coffee and they gave me the 'makings' but then I found the local Age Concern behind the main street and they provided tea and toast for only 29p. After shopping at the Co-op I walked past the local duck pond full of frenetic water fowl being fed by a bevy of boys. At Oare the pub was closing and they told me that there was no longer a Harty Ferry to Sheppey - it finished 35 years ago! That took that Island off my agenda and after some lunch on the seat outside the pub I went on to Uplees where there was now no sign of a gunpowder explosion eighty years before which had killed a ton of people. At Luddenham Court the church was in disuse - the porch open, dirty and not at all inviting. On the adjacent farm, farmer Robin was killing, cutting and selling meat and he told me there were no barns to use here. So, using local assistance for night time directions, I pushed on through gloomy orchards to Teynham Street, passing one raw, empty barn, darkly invitational, but instead went on to Teynham Church only to discover that it was locked and without a porch. In the adjacent mixed apple farm I found a sheep transporter, gathered some pallets for protection against the wind and settled down for the night.
18m

Day 493
Friday... Christmas Eve
It was a rough night and the wind howled, buffeting my trailer hideaway, safe I thought from the rain that fell, but in the morning I awoke in a pool of water. Luckily I and my sleeping bag were almost dry - the wet weather gear had saved me. But my other clothing used as my mattress were sodden. The clock of the church told me the time as it struck the hour and half hour. By 8.30 the rain had stopped, the wind abated and after eating some porridge I put on wet clothes before walking SW along the road to Teynham and then west to Sittingbourne. As I moved my trousers started to dry out while my optimism was supported by a wedge of northern blue sky. The StC shop pointed me to the Methodist Church Hall tea rooms - closed! Then a Rotary man sent me back down town to an English Church Housing hostel but the staff, busy with a bedlam of residents, had no real time for a drifter like me. So I made my escape from Sittingbourne and by a labyrinth of streets and roads, unclarified by my map, went on to Bobbing. A dedicated follower of the coast and the Saxon Way would have gone to the bridge at Swale (which leads to Sheppey) and around the Chetney Marshes, circumnavigating Iwade and hence onto Halstow. But tiredness, dismal weather, my old one inch map and the thought of refuge at the Sally in Chatham led me onto this short cut. Bobbing church was over a new embankment beyond the new A249 and the porch was open for my lunch break. I left on the old A249 and went NW to Little Norwood where a young mother filled my flask and gave me sugar for my emergency container.

Up to this point there had been many orchards, the trees looking forlorn as they stood stripped bare, but now the track went across fields of grass and young rape, then over Callum Hill. Down below lay Lower Halstow with its new housing in the midst of this much-farmed area. At the 11th century church on the Saxon Shore Way I met Anthony and Jenny who had lived in the house opposite for 45 years. They took me in for a magnificent ploughman's lunch and naturally we talked of farming, sailing, sculpture and potting, Jenny having had an exhibition of her work in Ledbury. Anthony told me the story of Coleridge, returning from Italy, landing at Sheerness, being rowed to Halstow, gaining entrance to the church and then giving thanks to God as he hadn't liked Italy or the sea. No wonder he had written such a dismal epic of a forlorn mariner. But I couldn't get in! Otherwise they had a fabulous view of the church, weeping willows and a river barge under renovation by the quay.

Back on the SSW winding along beside the twisting shoreline, I continued towards Gillingham through Hawgreen Farm and rested in a barn. The farmer, Philip and his good wife took me in and cooked my belated hot porridge. He reckoned he had made a loss for the past two years and was very despondent about continuing to farm. In the church at Upchurch they were just locking up, but they left it open for me after I had quoted my ideas about churches and their relevance to travellers. On leaving, fascinated by the carved gates, I nearly walked into the path of a passing car - which could have been disastrous. The wood shaped motto on the gate read:-

<blockquote>
Community is a forest,
a river,
a sea
</blockquote>

I trudged the coastal path as it twisted closely beside the convoluted shore into Gillingham. It started to rain and I soaked it up, getting wetter and wetter and on falling into a pub on the Strand, had a drink while asking for the Sally. One mile further on in the middle of Gillingham I was told that the hostel was in Chatham and that a train was leaving for Strood, Paddock Wood and Tonbridge. Tossing a coin over the choices and chickening out in my wet state, I took the easy option and boarded the train to Tonbridge. Walking out of the station and up Tonbridge High Street, aglow with its seasonal lights, I suddenly realised that it was Christmas and stopping for some last minute shopping, my brother Owen arrived in his ancient Rover and took me to their home for a bath, dry clothes and relaxation.
20m

Interlude twenty one
Days 494 - 495
Christmas
Thanks to Helen's hard work, we three brothers Roger, Owen and myself sat down to Christmas dinner - the first meal together for fifteen years. On Boxing Day I drove down to Worthing to see mother but she was still very unwell and did not recognise me, all she wanted to do was to doze.

Twenty second Stage
Gillingham to Greenwich
Day 496
Monday 27th December
Along the Hadlow Road I tried to hitch to Rochester but after some fifteen minutes a bus came instead and took me on the scenic ride which was almost worth the money (£3.40) to visit all the Kent villages on route - Hadlow, Kings Mill Village and its mirror globe sculpture, Malling, Snodland and Halling. We arrived in Rochester at 12.30 and as no bus passed me I walked back to Gillingham Railway Station, before wandering north-west through Gillingham and Brompton to the old docks. At Chatham Marine where there is a wall decorated with all the bus stops that had been used by the 10,000 dock workers who used to be employed there. The place is now a museum and the industry has gone. While stopping at the Heritage Centre of St Mary's opposite Fort Amherst, Britain's premier Napoleonic fort, I mused about the naval history that has paraded through here including the building of HMS Victory. Down below by the river at the Command Post a drunk reeled out, saying that as a fellow traveller I was welcome inside. The barmaid gave me a whisky for listening to the inebriate's alcohol-hazed ideas. Pulling myself away as soon as it was politely possible I went into Rochester High Street and, in a newsagent, found Baker Street on a street map. It was off the Maidstone road past the old alms houses but on arriving, No 10 was empty, so adopting plan two, to find the Sally, I went to the pub across the road for directions. There sitting on a stool was Michael and he was as surprised as me. Being in no hurry we had drinks before he took me for a night-time guided tour of Rochester and all the Dickens connections, the fortress castle with its 100ft high keep, the cathedral and the French Hospital followed by a meal in a busy Weatherspoons pub which was clean but had no music and you could actually talk comfortably - a contrast to most taverns these days. I should explain that I had met Michael, my niece's ex; a few days ago at my brother's and his parting shot to the company had been 'if you're ever in Rochester look......' Later back at his house we watched TV, chatted about his management of a bunch of train drivers and his golfing trips, the next being to South Africa.
5m

Day 497
Tuesday
After coffee and toast I said cheerio to Michael and walked back into Rochester, over the bridge and on to the SSW. My path finding was eased by the appearance of another walker, John, a retired road sweeper, ex-Chatham Dock ship-wright and a Baptist, who had problems at school due to his autism. He was doing the path in bits and could see his house on the other side of the river as we walked together towards the Kingsnorth Power Station. It was a lovely sunny day with a cool breeze and it was good to have a companion to point out the local sights - the ship figureheads at Upnor, the grey legged geese, Hoo spire and the salt marshes. We parted near Hoo, he to return home and myself to circle round the power station to North Street. Then to Stoke, Lower Stoke and Allhallows with a brief stop by the church surrounded by yews, before going down to the marshes. Having decided against the Isle of Grain and its oil refineries, though the tiny hamlet of isolated Grain looked tempting in its possibilities for the fortunes of unexpected succour, I found the *British Pilot* where the landlord wished me God-speed for my pleasant if long walk along the coastal sea wall into Cliffe, with views towards Southend, Canvey Island and the adjacent oil refineries. Unfortunately it became dark near the end and I missed the road into the village and instead stumbled around the lagoons before getting directions from a hard of hearing security guard, having to throw a stone at his hut to wake him up. The road he indicated between two quarries took me to West Street and maybe for the best I went north to Cliffe rather than south.

After finding the church locked I went into the Six Bells, had a chat with the landlord to find the vicarage. Alas the vicar was out. My next try was the Vic, because it was rumoured the landlord would be helpful but alas this was not so, although the barmaid gave me a drink for my troubles. Back in the Six Bells I had a funny time talking to the locals - farmers, clerks and gophers, Lords and plebs, old and young. At closing time I decided on the bus shelter. It was a cold frosty night as I opened my sleeping bag on the bench but the barmaid, Liz Diamond, took pity on me and invited me to her place if I behaved - what a wonderful surprise. We drove to Cliffe Wood and settled in for coffee and stories of her experiences of back-packing in Australia and other places. 24m

Day 498
Wednesday
Up and out into a beautiful, frosty, sunny morning. There had been no sign of my benefactrix, Liz, and I walked back to the quarries before following the conveyer way to the sailing club and Cliffe Fort, another symbol in the long line of gestures to the defence of this area. It was all a bit grubby around here as I simply followed the sea wall towards Gravesend stopping at the ruined

Shornemead fort, also built by Gordon in 1868, complete with thick steel gun embrasures and at the Ship and Lobster where Teresa the barmaid gave me a whisky. This is the pub in Great Expectations and a haunt of Dickens which was and still is a point of smuggling against the ever spiralling taxes on tobacco and alcohol - or so hinted the clientele. The Saxon Way stumbled to an end and in Gravesend I visited the ferry, the Great Expectations, which was running on a reduced schedule, and spoke to the crew, before going up to the town. At the police station, I had hoped to see Liz again but she was backstage. The other constabulary assistant sent me to the Salvation Army and Day Centre but neither was open. Further directions were given and I found the Home of Mercy in Edwin Street to meet the Irish Brother, Roy. There were no beds available but he fed me on ravioli. On a wall a pertinent slogan read:-

'Nothing Happens Unless First a Dream'........ Carl Sandburg

This was apt as I approached the final miles of my journey to London. After stumbling around the back Streets of Northfleet, at Swanscombe Marshes I found a little hut with half a roof and in the evening darkness, collected firewood on the shore before settling in for the cold night ahead.
11m

Day 499
Thursday
I found paths and roads that took me into Dartford where the librarian signed my form and sent me to the YMCA that was hopeless for my purposes. Passing the central Holy Trinity Church I popped in to see the stained glass windows and an ancient board listing the religious benefits to the secular poor. On speaking to the Vicar, he benevolently took me to the adjacent church cafe and issued instructions for a big breakfast which I ate with relish.

While trying to escape from Dartford, I walked a big loop and an hour later, hardly able to believe my eyes, was <u>back in the same place</u>. On the second attempt with proper instructions I made it down the west side of the Darenth, round to Erith and Erith Marshes and the sea wall. Around three o'clock, as rain began, I found an unfenced scrap yard with possible shelter and in the adjacent lorry breaker's yard found a group of hard men having a tea break, obtained their okay together with a cup of tea and slept that last night in the back of the dry, warm and comfortable cab of a broken down Eddie Stobart lorry.

In my dreams not only did I realise the truth behind my father's great belief in the extensive utility of a penknife and a piece of string but that the centre of Britain lies far away from the Midlands. If the circumference is 5000miles, making the radius 800 and allowing for the fact that we walk twice as far as

necessary then we have diameters of 800 miles. Drawing the two longest diagonals of this size on the map they intersect at Carn Ban Mor (a Monroe at 1049m) some 10 miles south of Aviemore and this is then Mainland Britain's centre.
14 m

Day 500
Friday 31st December.
This final day was dull but dry, and there was no need to hurry. I dawdled, in the comfort of my cab, eating a little breakfast and packing up my bag for the last time, then swung out into the morning, climbed the embankment and began the short walk into London. On my right the languid river, lined with piers, wharves and purposeful boats, propelled by a dull throb of diesel power. On my left the struggling patches of green grass, grazed by dark-brown totters' ponies, the survival of a less hurried life style contrasting strongly with the motorised megalith pressing around, engulfing me from each bank. Before my gaze, the skyline of London developed - the finger of Canary Wharf prominent and then, at long last and despite all the controversy around it, at Canary's foot, I had my second sighting of the 'Dome', its gantry supports mocking the now idle dock side cranes. The path continued into London along the stone dyke and then on the complex concrete sea defences threading through the industrial decrepitude of a once beautiful river. As I neared the Woolwich Arsenal a fusillade of gunfire was released, the air rich with cordite - I thought how appropriate for my arrival and lost count of the number of rounds, but it must have been a twenty one gun salute at least! Alas it was not for me, they were practising for next year, the millennium celebration which lay just around the corner. Here I was forced back to reality and the London streets, which were not lined with gold but with chewing gum and a veneer of grime and litter. Once past the free Woolwich ferry the Green Chain Link Way led down to the Thames Barrier and the Thames Side Walk with a sign pointing seductively west 180 miles up river but the construction associated with the Dome contorted the path on its way to Greenwich. The euphoria ended when a police truck stopped me and I really knew of my return to civilisation, as yellow and black, bullet proofed agile officers sprang to work. They wanted to know my intentions with a rucksack.

"What had I inside?",they asked.

"A bomb" I replied, but was able to persuade them of my authenticity and my desire to cross the meridian. They wanted to see the contents of my sleeping bag, but relented and sped off to bother somebody else. I walked toward Greenwich Park and Village, jangling my last £1 coin and its 10p mate. It was three o'clock as I reached the Park which was closed - tight shut, my disappointment tempered by a £2 gift from a young couple passing by. At the main gate, with a crowd of people and a posse of security guards crowding round, I casually walked past two police officers and headed left towards the park.

"Excuse me are you with the band".

"Yes" I said, nearly past their defences and should have whipped out my piccolo to play a tune!

The security officer was a tad too astute and she persuaded me to leave. There was no way in, to cross the line at the Observatory - a ring of steel was in place. So I had my StC form authenticated by a bobby and a photo taken by a freelance snapper before swinging my bag onto my back and setting off around the park and crossing Blackheath to Lewisham and Bromley. I found the front door key, threw myself into a bowl of porridge and then surfaced for a scalding pot of tea. A short while later the sky broke into a pyrotechnic kaleidoscope celebrating a new year, a new century, the next millennium and sadly the finish of my walk.
9m

Or was it?

Uncle Doug's right to roam was never questioned

Courtesy of the Pipe Smoker's Handbook

Appendix

On my journey I met a wide and interesting range of people. Mostly they were warm, generous and helpful, though not overly inquisitive. The foremost question asked was - 'How far do you walk in a day?' Then - 'Are you enjoying it?', and possibly - 'Where are you staying tonight?' My normal reply to mileage was 20m/day and this was about my walking-days average although overall, including stops, it was only 9 or 10 miles as by my reckoning the total mileage was less than 5000 - nowhere near the 7000 that JM walked. But then I took short cuts on ferries and missed headlands where I was unaware of a suitable passage. In reckoning my distances I simply plotted the course with string on the map - not a very accurate method. In addition more miles were added (but not to the tour mileage) when I walked back to the car or during hitching. But to be pragmatic and honest I had no real great concern over the statistic, except that it applies to that most frequent question and the fact that we are always making comparisons - who won? - By what margin? etc as though a split decision by one goal or a hundredth of a second matters that much. Nor does the adage - it's the taking part that counts - hold too much water in the bucket of success. A happy blend of these two ideologies of living is inevitably the more balanced view on achievement. I do know that I used up three pairs of footwear but only wore out one pair of socks of a selection of some ten pairs.

To the question of enjoyment, my usual reply was that there were times when I was not enjoying myself, when I was soaked, tired or battered by the wind. But these were infrequent although I was often tired and it took quite a while to find my walking legs suitable to the journey. Although I always say every day is a holiday, the trip would not have been finished unless I had enjoyed the freedom of the road and the wealth of generosity and good fortune that descended on me. I have no great spiritual inclinations but after a while did realise that there was a little fellow sitting on my shoulder looking after me. I would like to have thought that it was Jack Sprat my companion woolly penguin. But, though he jumped off and left me at some stage - probably caught in some brambles!, many happy strokes of luck and fortune were meted, almost daily, along the way.

Where I was going to stay each night was my burning question - often answered by my protector. After a location target was picked out at the start of the day I allowed fate to intervene. Of the YHs selected there was seldom a problem - except if full - but I was not in a real position to book ahead, which is not my scene. B&Bs were used when wet, dogged tired or for a change - especially if darkness fell or rain threatened. I guessed to having used some twenty - but the real number on reckoning up was twenty two of which two were free. They were generally not much more expensive than YHs considering the breakfast. That was until I discovered the NFA dodge for cost cutting in hostels. I also slept in the car at times and ostensibly this cut costs, but considering motoring expenses this did not really reduce my budget and I would not recommend this method in any future outings of a similar nature as the restrictions outweigh the benefits.

My equipment was very basic and after the learning curve my load was reduced to a minimum. My father used to say that with some string, a knife and a shilling you could go far, but I carried a little more than that. The first essential a sleeping bag and a ground sheet that was eventually an orange survival bag that lasted most of the way. A good warm sleeping bag is essential and a better bivouac would have helped, though a tent was not required. A few spare clothes and socks were carried, the main necessity being a good coat. I started with a Barbour but in the colder weather found a padded yellow (100% waterproof) Regatta more satisfactory although not entirely the best - it did tend to sweat up and to rip on barbed wire - a more expensive rip resistant breathing jacket would be recommended. The good thing about my coat was it was free and it doubled as a mattress. I carried candles, map case, compass and maps as well as a stock of food. My main essentials were oats, biscuits, sugar and a flask for hot water. My cooking equipment was one solitary saucepan after a found the use of tin cans for cooking meals troublesome. I topped up my food supplies each day with bread and a tin of something - corn beef, beans or fish, plus soup, milk and fruit, frequently tinned, and chocolate bars, of which I found Snickers the best and sometimes Wagon wheels which at 99p for 12 were excellent value. Sometimes I bought cheese and jam. Condensed milk was a good substitute for the real thing but it had its own problems with sealing after opening - a self dispensing bottle would be useful.

In total and in real terms I disposed of some £4000 over the whole 500 days an average of £8 a day a little below my estimate of a necessary £10/day. My cost would have increased if I had bought all the maps, each of which lasted for about 3 or 4 days - at £5.25 they were an expensive item on my budget (£ 200). Luckily about half the maps required were sent to me by my brother - Post Restante. At times I had to use a road map for my guidance and this is not the best plan. A major expense for me was tobacco or cigarettes at £1 to £2 a day (total £750) and the car, some £700. Repayment of a debt at £20 a month (£340). For photography I used, for a short time during the second stage, my father's old heavy Pentax, and then took no photographs until reaching Inverness where I reverted to using disposable cameras which give a surprisingly good picture. But this was expensive at £5+ for a 27 exposure film so on the west coast I bought a cheap Boots camera for £6 and thereafter the cheapest film I could find, usually about £2 a roll, though Woolworths did sometimes do £1 films. The camera lasted to the end except for a dodgy trigger and a spool catch breaking (cheap plastic!). The amount spent on the walk was therefore about £2000 of which some £600 was spent on accommodation (YH and B&B) and taking my walking days at about 300 the average spent on food and a few essentials comes to about £7 somewhat below that estimated average of £10 a day.

In reply to another question would I do it again? In hind sight knowing what I learnt I would do it slightly differently with the knowledge of the money required and the purchase of better equipment. With more reading of previous travellers and maps for the entire route. Both JM's Turn Right at Land's End and Andrew McCloy's Coastwalk are to be recommended. Before I left I had skimmed the first but not found the second. Notes from them would have been useful with the maps. For instance JM walked much closer to the Scottish coast than I did as he realised there was right of access to all Scottish land, had previous experience of those parts and was properly mapped out. In addition notes from the Blue Guides are a valuable source of information However it is still a challenge and to me the main thing to realise is that each day will take care of itself, that time is always required to make the best use of fate and it is the people you meet that make the best of time and chance!! In transcribing my journals I hope I have conveyed something of the tedium of the slow trudging miles relieved by the spasmodic but bounteous gifts of beauty and generosity combined with the happiness of the open road.

And what had I learned from my fifteen months on the road? Simply, I had rediscovered the profound truth of my father's philosophy on travel, that in reality life is not a big problem and little is required in its pursuance, although in future I should get a proper knife.

******

During the walk £500 was raised for Save the Children Fund by displaying a printed form in my map case. Hopefully this amount can be increased by those people I wrote to about sponsorship, before the walk started. Any profits from the sale of this book will also be donated to the Charity.

Crozzle Solution
Across Thumb::Raver::Alala::Malic::Place
Down   Tramp::Halal::Uvala::Melic::Brace

Some Useful Dates

251-356 St Anthony of Egypt 1st Christian hermit
400 St Ninian in Whithorn , Galloway
449 Saxons land @ Ebbsfleet, Kent
597 St Augustine lands @ Ebbsfleet
602 St Augustine met Celtic Church in Aust (on the Severn)
654 St Peter's :Anglia
      St Aiden started Abbey on Holy Island
800 Monastery of Tyne sacked by Danes; rebuilt 1095
1000-1100 Hadleigh Castle
1031-1093 Malcolm III :m. English Margaret (d.1093)
1066 The Normans land and beat Harold
1093 Pembroke Castle started in wood
1100- 1200 Cockersand Abbey
1142 Dundrennan Abbey founded by Cistercian Order
1146 Gerald the Welshman born
1244 Braggers Church : Dalgerty Bay
1155 Flemish Attack on Wales - repulsed
1264-1288 Kirkcudbright Castle: Alexander III & St John Comyn
      Weobley Manor House, Gower :D
1270-1305 Wallace
1272-1307 King Edward I reigns
1274-1306-1329 Robert Bruce
1277 Ed I beats Llywelyn & Welsh and starts castle building
1283 David brother of Llywelyn pulled apart
1290 Margaret, Maid of Norway (14) dies on way to marry Ed(II)
1290 Devorguilla Balliol dies (20y after John) : Sweet heart Abbey
  Caerlaverock Castle by Maxwells
1295 Ed I beats Scots at Dunbar
1300-1310 MacSweens retreated to Ireland
1300 Ed I stayed Kirkcudbright: transfer it to vassal King Balliol
1301 Caerlaverock castle taken by Ed I
1306 Kirkcudbright castle stone used to builds town houses
      Bruce murdered Comyn
1307 Ed I dies near Carlisle
1308 Castle Seen taken by Bruce: boats across the isthmus
1312 Caerlaverock castle fell to Bruce.
1313 Dunstanburg Castle started by Earl of Lancaster
1314 Ed II fled Banockburn via Dunbar
1485 to be Hen VII landed Dale : Killed Rich III @ Bosworth
1487 Lambert Simnel landed Piel Island prior to losing at Stoke
1501 Queen slept at Charmouth, Dorset
1509-1547 Henry VIII
1540 Hen VIII built Walmer castle, Kent
1547-1553 Edward VI
1553-1558 Mary
1558-1603 Elizabeth
1560 Mary Q. of Scots uses Dunbar castle
1563 Mary Q of Scots stayed at Dunure Castle on royal progress
1565 Carnassarie Castle : John Carswell, Bishop of Isles
1566 Elizabeth visits Harwich
1568 Mary leaves Dundrennan Abbey for England
1570 Earl of Cassius roasted abbot of Crosraguel in soap
1582 McLellan's Castle :Kirkkudbright
1607 Pilgrim Fathers begin escape to America
      Tidal wave devastates Burnham-on-Sea area, Somerset
1620 Winton House mentioned as an old manor :near Dalkeith
1640 Caerlaverock Castle: 13 week seige by Covenanters
1642- 1727 Isaac Newton
1644 Batle at Acton nr Crewe?
1647 Royalists destroy Castle Sween
      General Leslie massacres 299 catholic Macdonalds:Kintyre
1648 Cromwell demolished priory at Coldingham: Scotland
1650 Cromwell tosses Dunbar castle into sea
1688-1732 William(III) of Orange lands @ Brixham then rules
1700 last Wolf killed in Sutherland
1705-1780 William Cookworthy found china clay in Devon
1715 Moidartcastle burnt down to stop Campbells
1715-21 Donald Murchison; Factor for Earl of Seaforth
1719 Castle of Dornie beaten up by man of war:restored 1912
1722 Bernera Barracks
1723 Alex Selkirk (Robinson Crusoe) dies @ 47 on HMS Wemouth
1730 Anstruther Bridge ; nr St Andrews; rebuilt 1795
1742 John Wesley preaches in Newcastle
1746 Bonnie Prince Charles escape to France after (Culloden
1747-1807 RevJohn Snell : Kintyre
1750 Kings Pit opened: @ 160f in 1793
1752 James Stewart hanged : Appin Murder
1757-1834 Telford
1766 Old Pretender dies

1770 Bridge over the Esk; public subscription
1770-1836 Capt Sir Christopher Cole
1772-1834 Samuel Coleridge
1776-1837 John Constable
1780 Nothing happened
1786 First rebuild of Sunderland Bridge: then also 1857 & 1927
1786 -96 AllSaints church Newcastle
1788 Young Pretender (Bonnie P. Charles) dies & Stuarts finished
1789 Vicious storm Happisburg
1795 -1805 Aqueduct at Trevor on Dee   :Telford
1795 Turner paints Llansteffanon Castle
1796 Burns dies at Dumfries
1797 French invasion captured at Carregwastad Point, Pembroke
1801 HMS Incincible sinks @ Happisburg
1802-1856 Hugh Miller: geologist - ORS 1841
1804-1875 Robert Stephen Hawker
1806-1859 Isambard Kingdom Brunel
1809-1882 Charles Darwin
1810 First saving Bank of Scotland
1812-1870 Charles Dickens
1815 Metal Bridge (R. Esk): Telford
1824 Dean Buckland discovers the Red Lady @ Paviland
1826-1873 Rent Office working at Ryehope:Sunderland
1826-1908 Cuthbert Collingwood Surgeon & Botanist (China)
1828 Jacksman McColl completes clearances in Ardamurchan
      First life boat in Anglesey launched
1829 Davy died abroad
1830 Railway Age begins
1831 Opening of R. Nene Outfall : the Wash
1834- 1845 Plague still a problem
1837 Daymark at Gribbin Head for Fowey harbour
1837-1843-1858 Brunel's ships
1837-1901 Q. Victoria
1838-1914 John Muir, b. Dunbar
1840 Ballast Bank, Troon: Duke of Portland
      Potato famine
1844 Shoreham Lighthouse
1847-1929 Millicent Fawcett: female emancipation fought for
1849 Anne Bronte dies in Scarborough
1852 P Albert opens Grimsby docks
1859 Royal Charter Steam Ship + 400 lost off Lligwy Bay, Anglesey
1859 -64 Forts to defend Milford Haven: £85,000 each of 19
1860 Mock Penrhyn Castle
      HMS Warrior launched
1866 The Elbe swept away to Rascarrel Bay
1868 Lulworth Church received £50 for some rebuilding

Shornemead Fort: General Gordon
1869   Coal House Fort : General Gordon
1874-1938   F C Hirst founder of Zennor museum
1880(?)-1954 Henry Blogg Lifeboat Coxswain: Cromer
1880-1958 Alfred Noyes Poet & Author
1881 dramatic rescue of Visitor at Robin Hood Bay Great East Coast Fishing Disaster
1881-1846 Charles Anderson, Earl of Yarborough died nr Vigo,Sp.
1882-1958 John Anderson Waverley
1883-90 Forth Rail Bridge
1896 Granite cross(navigation aid) Dodman Point
1896-8 St Mary's Island Lighthouse
1896- 1944 Capt F J Walker killed in Atlantic
1897 Sutton Swing Bridge
1899 Lynmouth Life boat hauled to Porlock Weir (cf 1881)
1900 first wireless transmission across Atlantic
1901-1910 Ed VII
1902 British motor racing starts in Bexhill
1903-1997 A L Rowsech: Poet & Historian
1904 Mr Mannering and his Southend protective pillars.   my mother born
1908 Dove Marine Laboratories
1909 Start of Youth Hostelling: in Germany
1910 sea reflooded Pagham farm drainage scheme
1912 SS Titanic sank
1914-69 Gavin Maxwell (Edad - 1958-69)
1914 Laurence Binyon writes the Fa Yllen
1921 Henry Williamson moved to Baggy Point, Woolacombe
1925 Clough William-Ellis starts Porthmeirion
1927 ME Donaldson built a scottish granite house
1927- 1997 John Saul? : Boston area
1930-1993 Robert Innes :Scotland's Grand Prix champion
1933 Dylan Thomas visits Worms Head
1936 Clarendon wrecked off Chale, IoW
1943 6th Brig Paras lost at Taranto, Italy
1944-94 Paul Heard BoscAstle's faithful Council servant
1952Queen Mothere acquires Castle of Mey
1953 Floods of Canvey Island
1960 Snowdrifts close Buchanan Line:
              finally closed 1979
1970 Pembrokeshire Coastal Path opened
1981 Humber Bridge opened
1984 Kylesku Bridge: the Queen : replacing ferry
1991 Dornoch Firth Bridge: the Queen :cast & push method
1993 Whym Farm produced 100m barrels of oil
1996 Sea Empress drops load of crude @ St Ann's Head
1999 sinking of the fishing vessel Katy

INDEX

(numbers given are Days, not pages)

Aage V. Jensen Foundation 321
Ab Cnocgorm 290
Abbey Town 353
Abbotsbury 466
Aberaeron 397
Aberdaron 391
Aberavon Sands 413
Aberdovey 394
Aberdeen 111,131,254,302
Abereiddy 402
Aberdour Abbey Island 101
Aberffraw 386
Abermenai Pt. 387
Aberporth 398
Abersoch 391
Aberystwyth 396
AÕBhainir 281
Achahoish 315
Achateny 295
Acheninver 273
Achiltibuie 273
Achintraid 285
Achmelvich 272
Achmore 286
Achnamara 315
Acle 52
Acnamara 314
Ailsa Craig 335
Ailtanabradhan 272
Ainsdale 370
Airds Bay 310
Airds Point 346
Airor 290
the Alde 15
Aldeburgh 15
Alderton 14
Aldingham 358
All ʾhallows 497
Alligin 280
Allonby 353
Allt aÕBhuc 321
Almornee Ho. 344
Almouth 95
Alnwick 135
Alresford 12
Altan Dearg 266
Altandhu 273
Alt-Gleann-ant-Strathain 287
Altnaharrie Ho. 275
Amble 94
Amlwch 384
Amroth Castle 408
Anchorage 110
Anchor Footpath 332
An Cruin 282
Anelog 390
the Angel of Gateshead 139
Angerton 353
Angle Bay 406
Annan 347
Annaside 355
Anstey's Cove 457
Anstruther Br. 103

Aodan 268
Appledore 431
Arbigail Ho. 345
Arbigland 345
Arbroath 109
Ardaneaskan 285
Ardanstur 312
Ardcastle Forest 326
Ardelve 287
Ardfern 313
Ardgour 301
Ardintoul 288
Ardlamont Pt. 322
Ardlignish 296
Ardmaddy Cast. 312
Ardmair 274
Ardmolich 294
Ardnackaig 314
Ardnacross Br. 320
Ardnaff 286
Ardnamurchan 296
Ardnoe point 314
Ardrishaig 315
Ardroe 273
Ardrossan 332
Ardsheal Ho. 309
Ardtur farm 310
Ardwell 339
Ardwell Point 338
Ardyne point 325
Arinacrinachd 281
Ariogan 311
Arisaig house 293
Arisaig sound 294
Arivegaig 294
the Ark 107
Arneil Bay 332
glen Arnisdale 288
Arnside 360
Arran 321
Arsenal 500
river Arun 481
Ashburton 378
Ashfield 315
Ashford Lime Kiln 431
Askam Green Road Stn 356
Askam-in-Furness 356
Aspatria 353
At Drumshang 335
Atlantic College 415
Attadale 286
Auchencairn 344
Auchenmalg 339
Auchmithie 109
Auchnasaul 311
Auchneight 338
Auckengill 262
Auds 122
Avernish 287
Aviemore 30 Ẽ9
Avoch 128
Avon 418,422,453
Avonmouth 417
river Axe 425,461
Ayr 334,350
Badachre 279
Badbea 259

Badcall 270
Baddidarach 273
Badluarrach 276
Badnabay 270
Badenscallie 273
Badnagyle 273
Badrallach 275
Baggy Point 430
Baglan Moors 413
Balcary Point 344
Balig Hill 343
Balintore 256
Ballant Hotel 452
Ballantrae 336
Ballast bank 334
Balmae 343
Balnakeil 268
Balvica 312
Balyett Farm 336
Bamburgh 95
Banff 122
Bangor 383
Bankend 346
Banks Marsh 369
Baracundle Bay 407
Baravullin 310
Barcaldine Cast. 310
Bardsea 358
Bardsey Island 391
Barking Creek 1
Barling Marsh 4
Barmouth 393
Barnashaig 314
Barnkirk Point 347
Barnluasgan 315
Barnstable 431
Barrisdale 289
Barr-Mor 314
Barrow 357
Barry 415
Barstoisnoch 313
Barton 59,63,472
the Bastard 319
Battisborough Cross 452
Bawdsey 14
Baycliff 358
Beachy Head 485
Beadnell 95
Beagle Point 442
Beal 95
Bealach-Sloc-an-Eich 297
Beauchamp 461
Beaumaris 383
Beaumont Quay 13
Beer 461
Bees sands 454
Bellanoch 313
Bellochantuy 317
Bembridge Down 474
Benacre Broad 16
Benderlochand 310
Ben Hiant 296
Benllech 384
Ben Nevis 309
Bernera Barracks 288
Berriedale Br. 259
Berwick 96
Bessy's Cove 441
Bethlehem 490

Bettyhill 265
Bexhill 486
Bhaile 273
Bideford 431
Bidston 373
Biggar 357
Big Sand 278
Bingley 63,149
Birdham 480
Birling Gap 485
Bispham 365
Blackgang x 474
Blackhall Rock 90
Black Head 442,447
Blackheath 1,500
Black Lion Inn 82
Blackpool 362,364
Black Rock 392
Black Rocks 414
Blackwater 6,11
Bladnoch 341
Blain 294
Blairmore 270
Blair,s Ferry 322
Blakney 39
Bleadon Levels 424
Blue Anchor 427
Blue Dial 353
Blyth 93
river Blyth 16
Boarhills 103
Bobbing 493
Bodfari 380
Bodmin 378
Bognor Regis 481
Bolt Head 453
Boor 277
Bootle Station 355
Borth 395
Borth-y-gest 392
Boscastle 434
Bosham 479
Bosham Hoe 480
Bosherton 406
Bossington 428
Boston 53
Boulby 82
Boulmer 95
Bournemouth 471
Bracora 293
Bracorina 292
Bradford 63,141,149,363
Bradwell River 6
Braggers Ch. 101
Braingortan 324
river Braint 387
Brancaster 40
Branscombe 461
Branyn 410
Braunton Marsh 430
Braystone 355
Brean 425
Brick Ho. Farm 6
Bridgend 320
Bridge St Hostel 82
Bridgewater 425
Bridleway 92, 460
Bridlington 63,78,83
Bridport 465
the Brigg 80
Brighouse 343

Brightlingsea 12
Brighton 483
Brine Moor Pool 89
Bristol 417,422,462
the British Pilot 497
Brixham 455
BroadHaven 4 ý03,407
the Broads 49
Broadstairs 491
Broad Water 394
Bromley 7,19,500
Brompton 496
Brookgreen 473
Broomhill Sands 488
Broom Way 4
Brora 258
Brough 263
Broughton Burrows 411
Browhouses 347
Brown Slate Farm 405
Brow Well 347
Bruan 260
Brunnel Quay 405
Bryn Mawr 390
Bryn Penrhyn 391
Bubbleton 407
Buchanan Way 120
Buckhaven 102
Buckie 123
Bucks Cross 432
Bude 433
Budleigh Salterton 460
Bugle cove 452
Bull Bay 384
Bull Point 430
Bulwarks fort 415
Bunlarie 320
Burnham 40
Burnham- on -Crouch 5
Burnham-on-Sea 425
Burnmouth 96
Burnt Ash Lane 101
the Burrow 407
Burry Holme Head 411
Burton Beach 467
Burton Bradstock 466
Burton Ranges 373
Bury Port 410
Bush Inn 432
island of Bute 323
Butley Hard 14
Bwch i393
Caddleton 312
Cadgwith 442
Cadlan 391
Caegybi Mountain (Holyhead) 386
Cae Mawr 1
Caerlaverock 346
Caernarfon 387
Cafe on the Green 490
Cairngaan 338
Caister 38
Calder Hall 355
Caley & Leake 60
California 38
Callum Hill 493
Cama an Eilean 281
Camas Domhain 290
Camas nan Gealll 296
Camber 487

N F A

Cambo Farm 103
Cambusavie Farm 257
Camp Cottage 322
Campbeltown 319,321
Cam Rock 434
Cannington Brook 426
Canon Winder Farm 358
Canisbay 262
Canvey 3
Cardiff 415
Cardigan 398
Carew 89
Cargo 348
Carnassarie Cast 313
Carn Dearg 278
Carnewas Is. 436
Carnliath 297
Cark 358
Carl Crag 355
Carlisle 348,352
Carmathen 409
Carmel Head 385
Carnforth 361
Carnoustie 109
Carnu Beach 277
Carradale Pen. 320
Carregwastad Point 400
Carsaig 314
Carsenaw 341
Carskiey 319
Carsluith 342
Castell 384
Castlecraig 256
Castle Girnigoes 261
Castle Hill 259
Castlehill Point 345
Castle Martin 406
Cast. Sinclair 261
Castleton 416
Castletown 263
Castock 450
Caswell Bay 412
Catterline 111
Caulkerbush 345
Caulston 452
Cawsand 449
Ceddan Br. 405
Cefni 387
Cemaes 384
Cemlyn 385
Chale 473
Changue Farm 340
Chapel Bay 406
Chapel Finian 340
Chapel Porth 437
Chapelton 343
Chapman's Pool 470
Charlestown 124,447
Chard 461
Charmouth 465
Charnach 269
Chatham 493,496
Chatham Marine 496
Chepstow 419
Cheriton 411
Chesil Bank 467
Chesil Beach 466
Chester 374
Chichester 479
Chichester Harbour 480
Chideock 465

Chidham 479
Chickerill 466
Chirk castle 379
Chivenor 431
Chop Gate (York. Nat. Park) 139
Christchurch 472
Church Bay 385
Church Cove 441
Churchend 4
Church Norton 480
Clachan 318
Clachan Br. 311
Clachanmore 338
Clachtoll 272
Clacton 13
Clais 269
Clanyard Cast. 338
Claonaig Estates 321
the Clarendon 473
Clashaddy 266
Clashnessie 272
Cleave Ho. Farm 433
river Cleddau 405
Cleethorpes 57
Clevedon Pier & Town 423
Cleveland salt mines 82
Clevleys 365
Cliffe 497
Cliff End 487
Cliffe Wood 497
Cloch Point 325
Cloughton 80,84,139
Clynnog Fawqr 389
Clyn-yr-ynys 398
Coalhouse Fort 2
Coaltown 102
Coatbridge 350
Cocken tunnel 357
Cockersand Abbey 362
Cockington Farm 431
Cockpool 346
Coed 410
Colchester 12
Coldbackie 266
Coldingham 9
Coldstream 253
Coleton 455
Colinraine 324
the Colours 452
Colwell Bay Inn 472
Combwich 426
*the Comand Post 496
Commercial Inn 337,425
Commodore Hotel 471
Compton Down 473
Conishead Priory 358
Connage Farm 123
Connel 310
the Convent (St Cath.) 100,107,112
Conway Castle & River 382
Conway Centre 388
Coombe Martin 429
Corbiegoe 260
Corm Farm 391
Cornokey Farm 432
Corra 322

Corran 289,317
Corran narrows & ferry 301,309
Corringham 2
Corse 419
Corwall Port 340
Cotes Stones 361
Countisbury 428
County Gate 428
Cour 320
Courthill Ho. 285
Coverack 443
Cow & Calf Bay 429
Cowgate 99,106
Cox's Farm 426
Crackington Haven 434
Craig 279,286,332
Craig cottage 323
Craighead 128
Craiglin 314
Craig lodge 322
Craignant 379
Craignish 313
Crail 103
Craobh Haven 313
Craster 95
Creagan 310
river Cree 341
Creekmouth 1
Creetown 342
Cremyll 449
Cresswell 94
Crewe 375
Crewkerne 465
Cragfoot 361
Criblaw 253
Criccieth 392
Crinan canal & town 314
Croesyceiliog 409
Crofty 411
Cromarty 128,255,301
Cromer 39
Crook of Baldon 341
Crosby 370
Crossburn 265
Crossflatts 64,142
Crosskirk 264
Croulin 290
Crowlin Islands 282
Crown Inn 379
Croy (electric) Brae 335
Crug Farm 398
Cruggleton Cast. 341
Crusoe Hotel 102
Cuaig 282
Cuckmere Haven 485
Cudden Point 441
Cuil 309
Culbone 428
Cullen 122
Cullercoats 93
Culloden 125
Culzean Country Park 335
Cumbrian Hero 350
Cummingstown 124
Cumnock 350
Cunning Park 335
Cwm 381
Cwm Nash 414

Cwmtydu 397
Cwm-yr-Eglwys 400
Cwrthir 409
Daill 268
Dalbeattie 344
Dale 404
Dale Hotel 40
Dalgerty Bay 101
Dalkeith 99
Dancing Ledge 471
Darrent 499
the Dart 455
Dartford 499
Dartmouth 455
Island of Davaar 319
Dawlish 459
Deal 490
river Deben 14
river Dee 373
Dee Estuary 343
Deepdale 40
Degnish 312
Delacorse River 408
De La Warr Pav. 486
Demesne 348
Derbyshire Miner's Conval. Home 55
Devils Finger 442
Devonport 450
Dinas Fach 403
Dinas Head 400
Dinllaen Pen. 390
Distington 354
Dodman Point 446
Doirlinn 294,298
Donald MurchisonÕs Monument 287
Donna Nook 57
Dornoch 257
Dornock 347
Dornockbrow 347
Doplin 298
Dornie 287
Douganhill 344
river Douglas 369
Dounreay 264
Dournie 314
Dove cove 336
Dover 489
Dovey Junct. & Marshes 395
Dowderry 448
Dowdon,s Farm 426
Down End 426
Drigg 355
Drimnin 299
Druim an Aoinidh 290
Drumantrae Bay 339
Drumbeg 272
Drumbreddan 338
Drumbuie 286
Drumchork 277
Drummore 338
Drumnel Ho. 310
Druridge bay 94
Drws-y-Coed 389
Duartmore Forest 271
Duddon: Sands & Villa 356
Duffryn 416
Dugan 444

315

Duirinish 286
Dulas Bay 384
Dumfries 346,350
Dunashry Cast. 317
Dunaverty 317
Duncraig Abbey 286
Dunbar 97
Dunbeath 259
Duncasby Head 262
Dundee 104,107,132
Dundrennan 343
Dungeness 488
Dunkirk Ferry 60
Dunlaw 253
Dunmor 312
Dunmor Farm 311
Dunmore Farm Woodland 316
Dunnet Head 263
Dunnose Head 474
Dunnottar Cast. 111
Dunollie castle 311
Dunoon 323,325
Dunraven Park 414
Dunrobin Cast. 248
Dunster 427
Diunskeig Bay 317
Dunskey Cast. 337
Dunstanburg Cast. 95
Dunure 335
Dunwich 16
Durness 268
Duror 309
afon Dwyfor]392
Dydack 122
Dyke 125,432
Dymchurch 488
afon Dysynni 394
Earlsferry 102
Eastend 5
Easington 61,90,95
East Barns Quarry 97
Eastbourne 485
East Cleave 429
East Dereham 41
East Fleet 467
East Haven 109
East head 480
East Howcreek 347
Eastney 479
Easton 36
East Runton 39
East Salton 99
East Seaton Nature Reserve 109
E. Wemyss 102
East Wittering 480
Eastwood 422
Ebbsfleet 490
Ebdon 424
Eddrachilles Hotel 271
Edenmore 474
Edgcumbe Country Park 449
Edinburgh 99,106,134,253
Ehen River 355
Eilean-a-Ghambhna272
cast Eilean Donnan287
Eilean Dubh 323
Eilean-Nan-Ron 266

N F A   316

Eileanreach 288
Elgin 123,131
Elie 102
Ellary 315
Elliot Ho. 93
Ellon 120,288
Embo 257
Emsworth 479
End of the World 361
Erbusaig 286
afon Erch 392
Erith 499
Erith Marshes 499
river Erme 452
Erradale 278
Esk 355
river Esk 110,348
isle of Ewe 277
river Exe 459
Exeter Ship Canal459
Exmouth 459
Eyemouth 96
Eype Mouth 465
Fairbourne Rly 394
Fairlie 332
Fairlight 487
Fairy Glen 128
Falls of Cora 311
Falmouth 445
Fammau 380
Fanagmore Farm 270
Fangytavit 317
Farm Cross 432
Fascadale 295
Fast Cast. 97
Fast Geo 262
Faversham 492
Fearnmore 282
Felixstowe 14
Fenning Island bird res 426
Fernaig 286
Ferry Bird Res 480
Ferry Bridge 467
Ferry Ho. 480
Ferry Lane 12,41
Ferry Port 472
Ferryside 410
Festiniog Rly 392
Fife Ness 103
Filey 80
Findhorn 124
Findochty 123
Finnart's: Bay & Hill 336
Firth 104
Fisham Ho. 455
Fishguaerd 400
Fishtoft 53,55
Flamborough Head 79
Fleet 4 67
Fleetwood 365
Flimby 354
Flimston Ch. 406
Flint 373
Fobbing 2
Fochabers 123,131
Foindle 270
Folkestone 488
Foreland 471
Foreland Pt. 428

Forss Br. 264
Fort Amherst 496
Forth Road Br 101
Fort Popton 406
Fortrose 128-9
Fort William 301,309
Foulness 4
Fowey 447
Foxcliffe 81
Foxfield 356
Freckleton 366
Freshwater
406,466,472
Freshwater Bay 473
Freswick 262
Frinton 13
Froward Point 455
Fullarton 333
Gabriel 265
Gairloch 279
Gallow Hill 120
Galoway Ho. 341
Galton 433
Ganavan Bay 311
Garlieston 341
Garnheathwood
Country Park 350
river Garnock 333
Garreeg Fawr 390
Garth 379
Garth Farm 388
Gartnacopaig 319
Garvald 97
Gazick 440
Gemmel River 436
George IV Br. St w. 135
Gewni 403
Gibraltar Pt. 54
Gifford 99
Gileston 415
Gilfach 409
Gillfoot 346
Gillingham 493,496
Giltar point 407
Girder Br. 83,89
Girvan 336
Glac nan Sgadan 290
Gladyfi 395
Glaick 287
Glaisgeo 265
Glasgow 326,350
Gleanna Bhearradl Loch 311
Gleann Meadailand 291
Glenahanty 318
Glenbarr 317
Glen Caladh Farm 323
Glencaple 346
Glen Cottage 29 À3
Glencripesdale 297
Glendra Point 447
Glenelg 288
Glenluce 339
Glenmorven 299
Glenstriven 325
Goat's Hole 411
Godrevy Point 437
Gold Cliff Valley 417
Golden Cap 365

Golspie 257
Gorleston 17,37,49
Gortenachullish 293
Gorteneon 294
Gortenfern 295
Gosforth 360
Gourden 110
Gourock 325
Goerton 411
Goran Head 446
(Gowran) 410
Grainthorpe 57
Grange 111, 359
Grange Chine 473
Graplin 343
Graveney Marshes 492
Gravesend 498
Gray's 2
Great Broughton 139
Great Oaksey 13
Gt Ormes Head 381
Great Ouse 41
Greatstone 488
Great Tar 412
Great Yarmouth
17,38,42,49
Green Chain Walk 1
Greenlease Farm 480
Greenwich 1,500
Grennan: Point &
Plantation 338
Gretna 347
Greyfriars Hostel 99
Gribbin Head 447
Grimsaby 58
Grogport 320
Gruinard 276
Gunners Park 4
Guston 490
Gutterby 355
Gweek 444
Gybi 386
Gyda Chym Moult 406
Hackney 7
Hadleigh Cast. 3
Hadlow 496
Haggerton 96
Halling 496
Halls Cross 432
Haltown 348
Hamble-le-Rice 468
Handa Is. 271
Hapisburg 38
Harbour Quay (Wick) 260
Harcombe 460
Harold's Tower 263
Harrington 354
Harris 271
Harty Ferry 492
Harry Point 471
Hartland Point & Quay 432
Hartlepool 89
Hartley 93
Harwich 13
Hastings 486
Hatch 461
Hauxley 94
the Haven 405
Haverigg 356

Hawgreen Farm 493
Hawking 332
Hayburn Wyke NT 84
river Hayle 438
Hayling Is. 479
Haywain 14
Hazlewood Common 15
Headen Barrows 473
Hean 407
Helford 443
Heligoland 61
Hell's Mouth 391,437
Helmsdale 258
Helmsley 139
Hendy Farm 409
Herbrandston 405
Herne Bay 491
Hesketh marsh 369
Hest Bank 361
Highdown Cottage 432
High Glenadale 319
Hightown 370
the Hoe 450
Hogslaw 253
Holbeach 53
Holberton 452
Holkam Hall 40
Hollesley Bay Colony 14
Holme 359
Holme Br. 355
Holyhead 385
Holy Is. 95
Hoo 497
Hope 267
Hope cove 453
Hopeman 124
Hopesay 410
Hornsea 62
Horse Isles 344
Houps Inn 432
Hull 60
Humber Br. 60,63
Humber Mouth 57
Humphrey Head 359
Hungry Horse 103
Hunstanton 39,40
Hunston 480
Hunter's Quay 325
Hunterston 332
Hurst Cast. 472
Hydro Ho. 294
Hythe 488
Ilfracombe 429
Illingham 58
Ilsey Nat. Res. 431
Immingham DockÊ58
Inshanks 338
Inveary 319
Inverbrevie 110
Inverdale 277
Inverewe 277
Inverguseran Farm 290
Inverie 291
Inverinate 287
Inverkeithing 101
Inverkip 326
Inverness 125,255
Iona 332
Ireland 319
river Irt 355

Irvine d333
Islandadd Br. 314
Isle Martin 274
Isle of Dogs 1,7
Ivor's Cottage 277
Jacobs Ladder 460
Jenny Brown's Pt. 361
Jenny cliffe 452
Johnshaven 110
Jon o'Groats 262
Jura 314
Kames 323
river Kanaird 274
Kearvaig 269
Keiss 261
Kemyel 440
Kenfig: Cast. & Sands 414
Kenmore 281
Kennedy Pass 336
Kentallen 309
Kent bank 359
Keppoch Í 293
Kerrera Ferry 311
river Kerry 279
Kessingland Beach 16
Kettle Ness 81
Kidwelly 410
Kilberry 316
Kilbride Farm 322
Kilby 43,48
Kilchoan 296
Kilchoan Ho. 312
Kilcolnkil 319
Kildavaig 322
Kilkenny Bay 422
Killean 317
Killwinning 333
Killypole 318
Kilmartin 313
Kilmore 311
Kilmory 315
Kilmuir 128
Kilninver 312
Kilnsea 61
Kimmeridge 470
Kincaple Farm 103
Kingairloch 300
Kingholm Quay 346
Kinghorn 101
Kingsand 449
Kingsdown 490
Kings Hotel 101
Kingsmill Village 496
Kingsnorth Pow. Stat.497
the Kingsway 414
Kinlochbervie 270
Kinloch Hourn 289
Kinloss 124
Kintail 287
Kintessack 124
Kintradwell 258
Kintraw Farm 313
Kipperhorn 345
Kippford ¼ 345
Kirby Cross 13
Kirby-le-Soken 13
Kirkaldy 101,106
Kirkandrews 343
Kirkbean 346

N F A

Kirkbride 353
Kirkby-in-Furness 356
Kirkcolm 337
Kirkconnell Ho. 346
Kirkcudbright 343
Kirkpatrick Durham 343
Kirktomy 265
Kirton 287
river Kishorn 285
the Knap 415
Knapsdale Forest Ê314
Knockbrex Ho. 342
Knockencule 338
Knockinaam Lodge 338
Knoydart 290
Knot End-on-Sea 62,65
Knowe 338
Knowle Ho. 461
Kylasmorar 292
Kyle of Durness 268
Kyle (of Lochalsh) 286
Kyleachin 8
Kylesku 271
Kylestrome 271
Ladnagullin 265
Laide 276
Laigh 339
Lamigo bay 266
Lammermuir Hills 253
Lancaster 61
Langton Herring 466
Ho. of Largan 317
Largs 326,332
point of Lag 340
Lagiebaan r319
the Lake 343
Lamorna 440
LandÕs End 440
Largo Bay 102
Latheron 260
Laudale Ho. 297
Latheronwheel 260
Laugharne 408
Laxford 270
Leac an Aiseig 289
Leason 411
Ledbury 376, 419
Lee Abbey 429
Lee Bay 430
Lee-over-sands 12
Leigh 3
Lenaig Farm 317
Lendalfoot 336
Leominster 378
Letterfearn 288
Leuchars 104
Leven Viaduct 358
Lewisham 500
Lift Br }. 83
Lilstock 427
Lingdale 83
Lion Wharf 5
Lismore 310
Littleham 460
Littlehampton 481
Little Haven 403
Little Loch Broom 275
Little Lossit 318
Little Norwood 493
Liverpool 370,372
Lizard 442

Llanbadrig 384
Llanberis 388
Llandegla 379
Llanddwyn Is. 387
Llandudno 381
Llanfairfechan 382
Llanfihangel-y-
........Traethau 393
Llangai 409
Llangranog 397
Llanllyfni 389
LlanMadoc 411
Llan-non 397
Llanreath 405
Llanrhystud 396
Llanridian 411
Llansallos Cove 448
Llanstephan 409
Llanybri 409
Llanymynech 378
Lligwy Bay 384
Llithfaen 389
Llwyngiuril 391
Llwynngwril 394
Llwnysgaw 398
Llyncwellyn 389
Llynpadarn 389
Lochailort 294
Lochaline 299
Loch Alsh 287
L. Assynt 272
L. Borralie 268
L. Buine Moire 273
L. Caolisport 315
Lochcarron 285
Loch Coille-Bharr 314
L. Creran 310
L. Croispol 268
L. Diabaig 280
L. Duich 287
L. Eil 301
L. Eriboll 267
L. Feochan 311
L. Fleet 257
L. Fynne 326
Lochgilphead 315
Loch Hourn 289
L. Inshore 268
Lochinvar 273
Loch Laich 310
L. Leven 309
L. Linnhe 300,309
L. Long 287
L. Melfort 312
L. Morar 292
L. na Cille 312
Lochnacreive burn 318
Loch Nevis 292
L. Osgaig 273
L. Ryan 337
L. Seil 311
L. Striven 324
L. Sunart 297
L. Sween 315
L. Teacuis 298
L. Tearnalt 297
L. Torridon 281
Lochtyn Farm 397
Loch Walsh 288
Locwa 354
Logan Bay 338

Longlands Head 353
Longsands 93
Long Sutton 54
Looe: Island & Town 448
Lossiemouth 124
Loughton 411
Loup Ho. 317
Louth 56
Lower Diabaig 280
Lo. Badcall 271
Lo. Halstead 493
Lo. Largo 102
Lo. Stillaig 322
Lo. Stoke 497
Lowestoft 16
Luccombe 474
Luddenham Courtt 492
Lunan 109
Lundy Is. 434
river Lune 362
Lunga 313
Lybster 260
Lydd Ranges 488
Lydstep 407
Lyme Regis 461,465
Lymington 472
Lynbridge 428
Lynemouth 93
Lynmouth 428
Lynton 428
Mabie Forest 346
Macduff 122
Macharioch 319
Machrihanish Bay 318
Macringan's Pt 320
Maesbrook 378
Maesfron Farm 396
Maesgeirchen 382
Maidens 335
Main Drain 366
Mainsriddle 345
Malcolm Miller 467
Maldon 7,11,17
Mallaig 293
Mallaig Bheag ½ 293
Malling 496
Malltraeth 387
the Maltings 15
Malvern Hills 375,420
Manorbier 407
Maplethorpe 56
Mapp's: Camp 408
Marconi Mem. 442
Margate 491
Margram Sands 414
Marloes YH 403
Marsden 91
Martin's Haven 404
Maryland 6
Maryport 353
MatildaÕs Cottage 443
Maud 121
Mawbray 353
Mawddach Estuary 394
Mawgan Porth 436
isle of May 103
May beach 295
Mayo 452
McLellan's Cast. 343
Mead 432

Melfort 312
Mellon Charles 276
Melvaig 278
Melvich 264
Menai Straits 383
Merrion 406
Mersey Tunnel 371
Merthyr Mawr Cast. 414
Mersea Is. 12
Metal Br. 348
Methlem 390
Mevagissey 446
Mey 263
Mhorand 268
Middle Hope 424
Middlesborough 82,89
Midtown 277
Might Br Ä. 16
Milford Cast. Hall 405
Milford-on-Sea 472
Mill House 49
Millom 356
Milnthorpe sands 360
Milton of Mathers 110
Milton Ness 110
Minehead 427
Minnsmere 15
Moel 380
Moelfre 384
Moel-y-don 387
Moine Mohr 313
Monastery of Tyne 93
Monkash 414
Monk's Haven 404
Monkton 405
Monreith 340
Montrose 109
Moor Lodge 87
Morangie distillery 257
Moray Firth 124
Morecambe 358,361
Moreton 470
Morfa Bychan 396
Morfa Common 403
Morpeth 253
Morrich-More 256
Morston 39
Morte Pt. 430
Morven 297
Morwenstow 432
Mothecombe 452
Motte Hill 354
the Mound 257
Mount pleasant 389
Mousehole 440
Mucking Marsh 2
Mudhall 105
Mullberry Harbour 341
Mullion Cove 442
Mull of Gallowa 'y 338
the Mumbles 412
Muncraig 343
Mundsley 39
Munlochy bay 128
Musdale 317
Musselwick 404
Mutehill 343
Mwnt 398
Naast 277
Nairn 124
Narborough 41

Nare Head 446
Navax Pt. 437
river Naver 265
river Neath 413
Nedd 272
the Needles 473
Nefyn 389
river Nene 52
Neston 373
Neston Carsdale 359
Netherdale 359
Nettleton 355
New Abbey 346
New Aberdour 121
New Barn 466
Newbie 347
Newbiggin 93,358
Newborough Forest 387
New Brighton 371
Newcastle 91,135,251
New Downs 437
Newgale Sands 403
New Fleet 466
Newhaven 484
New Inn 56
Nelands 465
Newlyn 440
Newmachar 120
New Mills 109
Newport 38,399
Newquay 397,436
Newton 128
Newton Arlosh 353
Newton Pond 95
Newton Stewart 341
Next Ness 358
Neyland 405
Nigg 256
river Nith 346,350
Nolton Haven 403
Norman's bay 486
Northam Burrows 431
North Ballachulish 309
N. Dallens 310
Northfleet 498
N. Foreland 491
N.Keanchulish 274
N. Sea Camp 54
N. Shian 310
N. Shields 91,93
N. Street 497
Noss 452
Noss Head 261
Nostie 287
Nunraw Abbey 97,253
Nybster 262
the Oasis 111
Oban 311
Ob-Gorm-Mor 281
Ockle 295
Ogmore-by-Sea 414
river Ogmore 414
Old Castle Head 407
Old Graitney 347
Old Inn 432
Old Man of Wick 260
Old Poltalloch 313
Oldshoremore 270
Orchardton Mains 344
Orford 15
Ormaig 313

N F A
318

Ormilie Hostel 263	Petty 125	Port Talbot 413	Rochville Cross 348	St Michael's Mount 441
Ormiscraig 277	Pevensey Bay j486	Portuairk 295	Rockcliffe 345,348	St Mellons 416
Osea Island 11	Philadelphia 96	Port William 340,434	Rockfield 256	St Morwenna 433
Osmington 467	Phoebe Pt. 447	Portwrinkle 448	Rocks Inn 460	St Ninian's Cave 340
Osmington Mills 467	Piel Is. 357	Portyerrock Bay 340	Rock Vale 343	St Ninian's Well 341
river Otter 460	Pilcalniel 256	Powderham Cast. 459	isle of Rona 282	St Non's: Bay & Ch 402
Oubas Hill 358	Pilgrim's Mem. 54	Powfoot 347	Ronachan Pt. 317	St Peter's Way 6
river Ouse 52	Pill 422	Powillimount 345	Rosemarkie 129	Sail Gharb 272
Overstrand 39	Piltanton Burn 339	Praa sands 441	Rosemullion Pt. 444	Sail Gorm 272
Overton 361	Pirlene Pt. 471	Prawle Pt. 454	Roshven 294	Salcombe 453
Owl's Foot 389	Pitsea 2	Predannack Head 442	Rossal 365	Salcott 11
Oxwich: Bay & Pt. 412	Pittenweem 103	Prestatyn 374,381	Ross Bay 343	Salen 296
Paddockwood 493	Place 445	Preston 362	Rothesay 326	Sally's Ho. 336
Padstow Estuary 435	Plashett 408	Priestside 347	Rough Is. 345	Saltburn 82
Pagham 481	Plas Porthamel 387	Prince Inn 386	Rowhedge Ì 12	Salt Coates 353
Pagham Harbour 480	Pleasant Harbour 415	Prince's Cairn 294	Royal Docks 1	Saltcoats 333
Paignton 455	Plockton 286	Proudfoots 59	Royal Inn 422	Saltfleet 57
Palmallet Farm 341	Plumpton Hall 358	Prussia Cove 441	Rubha an Daraich 290	Salthouse 323
Palmarsh 488	river Plym 450	Pulpit hill 311		Salthouse Bay 423
Park Farm 398	Plymouth 449	Purbeck Quarry 471	Rubha Mor 273	Sand 276
Park Head 436	Polbain 273	Purfleet 2	Rubha Reidh 278	Sanda Is. 319
Park Ho. 343	Polglass 273	Pwllcrochan 406	Rumps Pt. 435	Sandaig 288
Parkmill 412	Polkerris 447	Pwllderi 400	Runswick 82	Sandbanks 471
river Parrett 426	Polperro 448	Pwlldu Head 412	Runswick Bay 81	Sand Bay 424,460
Pawlett 426	Polruan Ï447	Pwllheli 391	Ruthin 379	Sandell Bay 320
Paul 60	Poltalloch 313	Quay Lane 13	Ruthwell 347	Sandgate Farm 358
Paviland 411	Polymore 273	Queen's Arms 465	Ryde 475	Sandhead 339
Pebble Ridge Ä 431	Polzeath 435	isle of Raasay 282	Rye 487	Sandown 474
Pegwell 490	Poole 471	Rabbit Islands 266	Ryehope 90	Sand Pt. 424
Pembrey Cntry Park 410	Poolewe 277	Ragged Stone Hill 420	the Sailors Rest 488	Sandscales Haws 356
Pembroke: Br., Dock & Town 405	Poppit Sands 398	Ragwen Pt. 408	St Abbs 97	Sandwich 490
	Porlock 428	Rainham 1	St Agnes 437	Sandwood Bay 270
Penan 122	Portachoillan 317	Rame Head 449	St Andrews 103	Sandy Haven 405
Penarth 415	Portavadie 322	Ramsey Is. 6,402	St Ann's Head 404	Sandyhills Bay 345
Penberth 440	Portbury Wharf 422	Ramsgate 490	St Ann's Well 348	Sandy Mouth 433
Penbryn 398	Port Clarence 89	Rapehaw 357	St Anthony's Chapel & Pt. 445	Sanna 295
Pencaitland Walk 99	Portencross Cast 332	Rashleigh Inn 447		Saundersfoot 407
Pencarrow Head 448	Port Eynon 411	Ratagan 287	St Anthony's Well 409	Saunton 430
Pen Dal-Aderyn 402	Port.Gill 338	Rat Island Head 406		Scailpaidh 287
Pendeen Watch 439	Porthallow 443	Ravenglass 355	St Augustine 490	Scalby 140
Pendennis Cast. 444	Porthcawl 414	Ravenscar 81	St Austell 447	Scarba 314
Pendine 408	Porth Diullaen 390	Re Òay 264	St Bees 354,360	Scarborough 80,83,139
Pendower Beach 446	Port Gaverne 435	Rectory Farm 61	St Catherine's Pt. 474	Scarth Bight 357
Peninver 320	Porthcothan 436	Reculver 491	St Clears 408	Scoraig 275
Pen-lon 387	Porthcurno 440	Redcar 82	St Columba's Cave 315	Scotties 109
Penmaenmawr 382	Port Henderson 279	Redkirk 347		Scourie 271
Penmon 383	Porthgain 402	Redpoint 279	St Clolumba's Chap.319	Scratby 38
Pennar 405	Porthkerry Country Park 415	Red Wharf Bay 383		Seafield Estates 122
Pennyhole Fleet 11		Reighton 79	St Cyrus Nat. Res. 110	Seafield Farm 314
Penrhyn 384,392	Porthleven 441	Reith Tower 345		Seaford 485
Penrhyndevdraeth 393	Porthllisky 402	Resipole 296	St David's 402	Seaforth 370
Penrhyn-Isaf 392	Porth Madog 392	Rhiconich River 270	St Dogmaels 398	Seahouses 95
Penrhyn Cast. 382	Po. Meirion 393	Rhinns of Galloway337	St Donats 414	Sea Palling 38
Pensarn 381	Po. Naven 439	Rhiw 391	St Gennys 433	Seasalter 492
Pentewan 446	Portholland 446	Rhoose 415	St Govan's Head 406	Seascale Ú 355
Pentir 383	Porthoustock 443	Rhosneigr 386	St Helens 474	Seaton 89,93,448,461
Pentire 436	Porth Tocyn 391	Rhossili 411	St Ishmael 410	Seaton Sluice Br. 93
Pentlepoir 407	Porthtowan 437	Rhuallt 381	St Ishmael's 404	Seatown 465
Pentowyn 409	Portishead 422	Rhuddgaer 387	St Ives 438	Seaview 475
Pentrellwyn 383	Portknockie 123	Rhunahaorine 317	St Joseph's 479	Sea-view-cafe 326
Peny Bont Sewage Works 414	Port Laire 280	Rhyll 374,381	St Just 439	Sea Zoo 387
	Portland Bill 466	river Ribble 369	St Keverne 443	Sefton 370
Penygroes 389	Portmellon 446	Rienachait 272	St Lawrence 474	Sellafield 355
Penzance 441	Port Mulgrove 82	Rigfoot 347	St Levan 440	Selsey 480
	P. nan Cuil 311	Rigg Bay 341	St Lythams 366	Sennen Cove 440
	Portobello 384	Ringstead 467	St Margaret's-at-Cliffe 490	Seven Men of Moidart 294
Percuil 445	Portpatrick 337	Riverside (Newcastle) 136		
Perranporth 436	Port Quin 435		St Mary's Island 93	Seven Sisters 485
Perranuthnoe 441	Portreath 437	Roa Island 358	St Mary's Isle 343	Severn Beach 418
Perth 107	Portscatho 445	Robins Hood Bay 81	St Mawes 445	Severn Br. 417
Peterburn 278	Portsmouth 475	Rochester 496	St Michael's Inn 104	Sewerby 79,83
Peter Scott Walk 52	Portsoy 122	Rochford 4		Shaldon 457

N F A

Shanklin 474
Sheephouse Farm 422
Sheep Way 422
Sherringham 39
Shepherds Port 41
river Shiel 294
Shiel Br. 287,294
Shieldaig 281
Shiel Estates 294
Shiel Is. 312
Shielings 282
Shingle Street 14
the Ship & Lobster 498
Ship Inn 357
Shipley 149
Shirehampton 418,422
Shoesbury 4
Shoreham 482
Shoreham Lagoon 483
Shotton 373
Shropshire Canal 379
Sidestrand 39
Sidbury 460
Sidlesham 480
Sidmouth 460
Silecroft 356
Silloth 353
Silverdale 361
Sinniness 339
Sir John's Hill 408
Sittingbourne 493
the Six Bells 497
Sizewell 15
Skegness 55
Skerray 265
Skerryback Farm 404
Skinburness 353
Skipness 321
Skipton 362
Skir House 414
Skirza 262
Skulomie 266
Skyreburn 342
Slaggan 276
Sletell 266
Smedmore 470
Snape 15
Snap Pt. 357
Snodland 496
Snowdon 388
Soldiers Pt . 385
Solva 403
Solway Estuary 346
Solway firth 340
Somercotes 57
Somerset Flats 425
Sompting 481
Sourlie 291
Souter 91
Southampton 468
South Bay 333
South Beach 78
South Benfleet 3
Southbourne 471,479
Southend 3,7,17,35,291
Southerndown 414
Southerness Pt. 345
Southern Upland Way 97
South Hook Pt. 405
Southport 369
Southwold 16
South Shields 91

Sowerty Lodge 357
river Spey 123
Splott 416
Spurn Pt. 60
Square & Compass 470
Stachpole Warren 407
Stac Poly 273
Stairhaven 339
Staithes 82,89
castle Stalker 310
Stanhope 347
Stanley Embankment 385
Starcross 459
Star gate 365
Star Inn 109
Star Rock 406
Start Pt. 454
Staxigoe 261
Steamer Point Nat. Res. 472
St Devenston 333
Steyning 481
Stiffkey 40
Stockton 82
Stoer 272
Stoke 467,497
Stoke Fleming 455
Stoke Gregory 425
Stokesley 139
Stonehaven 111
Stone Pt. 12
Stonfield 316
Stow 39
Stowmarket 17
Staithkirkcraig 273
Stranraer 337
Strathan 266
Strathchailleach 269
Strathy 264
Strete 454
Stroma 262
Strone 314
Strone Pt. 324
Stronefield Estate 315
Strontian 297
Strood 493
Strood Br. 12
Stanford-le-Hope 2
Strichen 121
Strome: Is. & Cast. 285
Strome Ferry 286
Stubbs Place 355
Sudbourne Marshes 15
Summer Isles 273
Summer St Day Centre 112
Sunderland 90
Sunderland Pt. 361
Sutton Br. 52,54
Sutton Br. Farm 4
Sutton-on-sea 55
Swanage 471
Swanbridge 415
Swanscombe 498
Swansea 410
Castle Sween 315
Sweet Charity Forest Walk 315
Sweetheart Abbbey 346
Swing Br. 4
river Taf 408

Tain 256
Talyllyn Rly 94
Tarbat Ness 256
Tarbet 271,292
Tarkaline Trail 431
Tarrs Park 430
Tavintoan 317
the Taw 431
river Tawe 413
the Tay 104,106
Tayport 104
Tayvallich 314
river Tees 83
Teignmouth 457
Telpyn Farm 408
Tenby 407
Tennyson Downs 473
Texas Coal Terminal 332
Teynham 493
Teynham Street 492
the Thames 1
Thames Barrier 1,500
Thameside Path 1
Thatcher's Rock 457
Thorney Is. 479
Thornham 40
Thurso 263
Tignabruaich 323
Tilbury 2
Tinner's Pub 438
Tintagel 434
Titchwell 40
Tollesbury Wick Msh 11
Tollgate 414
Tollsbury 11
Tonbridge 486,493
Tongue 266
Topsham 459
Tor Bay 455
Tore 129
Toremore 259
Torinturk 316
Torquay 456
Torres 124
river Torridge 431
Torridon 280
Torrisdale 320
Toscaig 282
Totaig 288
Tournaig Farm 277
Toward Pt. 325
Towie Farm 121
Townhead 343
Towy Cast. 410
Towyn 381,394
Traeth-yr-ynys 397
Traguaina 312
Traigh nam Musgan 312
Travers Haven 470
Trearddur 386
Trefin 401
Tref `onen 378
Treheli 391
Trenance 436
Tresaith 398
Trevone 435
Trevor 379,389
Trevorrick 436
Trevose Head 435
Treyarnon 435
Trimmington 39

Trohne 402
Troon 333
Troustan 324
Trumpet 378
Trwyn-Llanbedrog 391
Tubeg 266
Tumore 272
Turf Pub 459
Turnberry 335
Two Tree Is. 3
river Tyne 91
afon Tywi 410
Tywyn 394
Uags 282
Udny 120
Ulbster 260
Ullapool 274
Ulverston 358
Unapool 272
Upchurch 493
Uphill 425
Uplees 492
Upnor 497
Upper Badcall 271
Upper borth 396
Urdd Centre 397
river Usk 417
Uskmouth 417
Valle Crucis Abbey 379
Vange Marshes 2
the Vic 497
Vickerstown 357
Victoria Ho. 112 ?
Victoria Inn 466
Vineye Middle 41
Wain Hill 424
Wakering Sands 4
Walberswick 16
Wallasea Island 5
Wall End 356
Wallog 396
Walmer 490
Walney Is. 357
Walton-on-Naze 13
Warren Mill 95
Warren Pt. 452
Warton 361,366
Watchet 427
Waterfront 347
Waterloo 370
Waulkmill 323
Wave Crest Cafe 442
river Waver 353
Waverley 322,423
Waverley Br. 99
Waxham 38
river Wear walk 91
Welcombe 432
Weldon Br. 253
river Welland 53
Wellington St. 82
Wells marsh 40
Wembury 452
Wemyss 102
Wemyss Bay 326
afon Wen 392
Wennington 2
Weobley Cast. 411
West Angle Bay 406
West Bay 465
W. Bexington 466

Westcliffe 35,490
Westerlock 261
West Freugh 339
W. Galloway .Sanc 337
Westgate-on-Sea 491
West Itchenor 480
W. Kilbride 332
W. Kirby 372
Westhay 465
West ELulworth 470
W. Lynn 52
W. Mains Inn 95
W. Murkle 263
Weston 424,461
West Plain Farm 359
W. Street 497
W. Tarbet 316
Westward Hoe 431
Weymouth 467
Wheale Coates 437
Whitby 81,83,89
Whiteash Hill Wood 123
White Cairns 120
Whitehaven 354
Whitehills 122
White Sands Cafe 402
Whithorn 340
Whitstable 492
Whym Farm 471
Wick 260
Wick St Lawrence 424
Wife Geo 262
Wigton 353
Wigtown 341
Winchelsea Beach 487
Winnianton 441
Winter iton 38
Winton Ho. 99
Withernsea 62
Wivenhoe 12
Woodbridge 36
Woodspring Priory 424
Woody Ho. 285
Woolacombe 430
Woole 253
Wooltack Pt. 404
Woolwich 500
Workington 354
Worm's Head 411
Worthing 481
Worth Matravers 470
Wrafton 431
cape Wrath 269
Wreath 449
Wyke farm 359
river Wyre 365
Yarmouth 472
Yatton 424
Yealm River 452
the Yeo 253
Ye Olde Sportsman 492
Ynys Dulas 384
Ynys-Hir Nat. Res. 395
Ynyslas 395
York 77
Yspitty 410
Zennor 438
Zone Point ...445

Save the Children

Fund

Sponsored Walk

Round mainland Britain

By Douglas Legg

19th August '98 to 31st December '99

****

Please give generously

1 SANDHEAD, STRANRAER 23/7/99 10.29 AM
GLENLUCE NEWTON STEWART 23.7.99 3.20 PM.
STAIR HAVEN, GLENLUCE 23/7/99 5.50 pm
Auchenmalg near Glenluce 23/7/99 7.45 PM
"MONREITH" Dumfries & Galloway - Mill & Garden 24/7/99 12.30 pm
Isle of Whithorn D&G AF Johnston Commodore WBSC 24/07/99 1952
Crugglton Farm Yorkieto am 25/7/99.
2 WILLIAMS WHITHORN 25-7-99
J. Turner Legg Day Sorbie 25-7-99
3 GARDINER WOODPARK K.P.D. 25-7-99 12.40 -
Ailean Cowan Newton Stewart 26-7-99

One Example of the 'Forms' carried and displayed in my pack's mapcase